Beyond Prejudice

Edited by John Dixon and Mark Levine

D1409634

The concept of prejudice has profoundly influenced how we have investigated, explained and tried to change intergroup relations of discrimination and inequality. But what has this concept contributed to our knowledge of relations between groups and what has it obscured or misrepresented? How has it expanded or narrowed the horizons of psychological inquiry? How effective or ineffective has it been in guiding our attempts to transform social relations and institutions? In this book, a team of internationally renowned psychologists re-evaluate the concept of prejudice, in an attempt to move beyond conventional approaches to the subject and to help the reader gain a clearer understanding of relations within and between groups. This fresh look at prejudice will appeal to scholars and students of social psychology, sociology, political science and peace studies.

DR JOHN DIXON is a professor of social psychology at the Open University, having lectured previously at Lancaster University, the University of Worcester and the University of Cape Town. He has published widely on the topics of prejudice, intergroup conflict and prejudice reduction and is the coauthor, with Kevin Durrheim, of *Racial Encounter: the Social Psychology of Contact and Desegregation* (2005). He is currently a coeditor, with Jolanda Jetten, of the *British Journal of Social Psychology*.

DR MARK LEVINE is a professor of social psychology at the University of Exeter. His research, which focuses on the relationship between social identity and pro-social behaviour, has appeared in a range of international journals, including the *Journal of Personality and Social Psychology*, *American Psychologist* and *Psychological Science*.

Beyond Prejudice

Extending the Social Psychology of Conflict, Inequality and Social Change

Edited by

John Dixon

and

Mark Levine

Property of
Baker College
of Allen Park

CAMBRIDGE
UNIVERSITY PRESS

CAMBRIDGE UNIVERSITY PRESS
Cambridge, New York, Melbourne, Madrid, Cape Town,
Singapore, São Paulo, Delhi, Tokyo, Mexico City

Cambridge University Press
The Edinburgh Building, Cambridge CB2 8RU, UK

Published in the United States of America by Cambridge University Press,
New York

www.cambridge.org
Information on this title: www.cambridge.org/9780521139625

© Cambridge University Press 2012

First published 2012

Printed in the United Kingdom at the University Press, Cambridge

A catalogue record for this publication is available from the British Library

ISBN 978-0-521-19816-5 Hardback
ISBN 978-0-521-13962-5 Paperback

Contents

List of figures　　　　　　　　　　　　　　*page* vii
List of tables　　　　　　　　　　　　　　　viii
List of contributors　　　　　　　　　　　　ix
Acknowledgements　　　　　　　　　　　　　xi

Introduction
JOHN DIXON AND MARK LEVINE　　　　　　　1

Part I　Beyond prejudice　　　　　　　　　25

1　From perception to mobilization: the shifting
　paradigm of prejudice
　STEPHEN REICHER　　　　　　　　　　　　　27

2　Prejudice, social identity and social change: resolving
　the Allportian problematic
　KATHERINE J. REYNOLDS, S. ALEXANDER
　HASLAM AND JOHN C. TURNER　　　　　　　48

3　An ambivalent alliance: hostile and benevolent sexism
　as complementary justifications for gender inequality
　PETER GLICK AND SUSAN T. FISKE　　　　　70

4　Prejudice and dehumanization
　NICK HASLAM AND STEPHEN LOUGHNAN　　89

5　Stereotyping, prejudice and discrimination revisited:
　from William James to W. E. B. Du Bois
　STANLEY O. GAINES, JR　　　　　　　　　105

6　Beyond 'old' and 'new': for a social psychology of
　racism
　SAMUEL PEHRSON AND COLIN WAYNE LEACH　120

7   The notion of 'prejudice': some rhetorical
    and ideological aspects
    MICHAEL BILLIG   139

8   The prejudice problematic
    MARGARET WETHERELL   158

9   Implicit prejudice in mind and interaction
    KEVIN DURRHEIM   179

10 Rethinking the prejudice problematic: a collaborative
    cognition approach
    SUSAN CONDOR AND LIA FIGGOU   200

Part II Prejudice and social change revisited   223

11 Models of social change in social psychology:
    collective action or prejudice reduction? Conflict or
    harmony?
    STEPHEN C. WRIGHT AND GAMZE BARAY   225

12 From attitudes to (in)action: the darker side of 'we'
    JOHN F. DOVIDIO, TAMAR SAGUY, SAMUEL
    L. GAERTNER AND ERIN L. THOMAS   248

13 Contact and social change in an ongoing
    asymmetrical conflict: four social-psychological
    models of reconciliation-aimed planned encounters
    between Israeli Jews and Palestinians
    IFAT MAOZ   269

14 From prejudice to collective action
    CLIFFORD STOTT, JOHN DRURY AND STEPHEN
    REICHER   286

    Conclusions and future directions: the nature,
    significance and inherent limitations of the concept of
    prejudice in social psychology
    JOHN DIXON AND MARK LEVINE   304

    Index   332

Figures

3.1	Factor structure of the ambivalent sexism inventory	*page* 75
3.2	Hostile sexism across countries	81
3.3	Benevolent sexism across countries	82
11.1	Two models of social change	229
12.1	Confederate social identity and support for race-targeted policies	260
12.2	Intergroup contact, perceptions of fairness and support for social change	262
C.1	Indirect effects of contact on perceptions of group discrimination	319

Tables

3.1 Correlations between ambivalent sexism inventory
      (ASI) averages and national indexes of gender equality   *page* 80

Contributors

GAMZE BARAY is an instructor in the Psychology Department at Bilkert University.

MICHAEL BILLIG is Professor of Social Sciences at Loughborough University.

SUSAN CONDOR is a professor of social psychology and Director of the Social Conflict and Solidarity Research Unit at Lancaster University.

JOHN DIXON is a professor of social psychology at the Open University.

JOHN F. DOVIDIO is a professor of psychology at Yale University.

JOHN DRURY is a senior lecturer in social psychology at the University of Sussex.

KEVIN DURRHEIM is a professor of psychology at the University of KwaZulu-Natal.

LIA FIGGOU is a lecturer in social psychology at the Aristotle University of Thessaloniki.

SUSAN T. FISKE is the Eugene Higgins Professor of Psychology at Princeton University.

SAMUEL L. GAERTNER is a professor of psychology and Director of the Social Psychology Graduate Program at the University of Delaware.

STANLEY O. GAINES, JR is a senior lecturer in psychology at Brunel University.

PETER GLICK is the Henry Merritt Wriston Professor in the social sciences and a professor of psychology at Lawrence University.

NICK HASLAM is a senior lecturer in the School of Psychology at the University of Melbourne.

S. ALEXANDER HASLAM is Professor of Social and Organizational Psychology at the University of Exeter.

COLIN WAYNE LEACH is a professor of psychology at the University of Connecticut.

MARK LEVINE is a senior lecturer in social psychology at Lancaster University.

STEPHEN LOUGHNAN is a research associate in the School of Psychology at the University of Kent.

IFAT MAOZ is a professor in the Department of Communication and the Swiss Center for Conflict Studies at the Hebrew University of Jerusalem.

SAMUEL PEHRSON is a lecturer in the School of Psychology at Queen's University, Belfast.

STEPHEN REICHER is a professor of social psychology at the University of St Andrews.

KATHERINE J. REYNOLDS is a research fellow and an associate professor in the Department of Psychology at the Australian National University.

TAMAR SAGUY is an assistant professor of psychology at the Interdisciplinary Center (IDC), Herzliya.

CLIFFORD STOTT is a senior lecturer in the School of Psychology at the University of Liverpool.

ERIN L. THOMAS is a third-year graduate student in the Social Psychology Program at Yale University.

JOHN C. TURNER is a professor of psychology and Australian Professorial Fellow at the Australian National University.

MARGARET WETHERELL is a professor of social psychology at the Open University.

STEPHEN C. WRIGHT is a professor of psychology at Simon Fraser University and the Canada Research Chair in Social Psychology.

Acknowledgements

This book has had a long gestation, during which we have benefited from the support, commentary and criticism of numerous people. First and foremost, we would like to thank our contributors. They facilitated the project not only by writing a series of scholarly, thought-provoking chapters on the theme 'beyond prejudice', but also by producing the work that originally inspired us to create this edited book. Sadly, this chapter's third author, John Turner, died on the 24th of July, 2011. The ideas presented here form part of John's *strategic reconceptualization of the whole field of prejudice* in which all intergroup attitudes are considered to be a product of a complex interaction between people's collective psychology as group members and the reality of intergroup relationships as historically and collectively defined. Without John's passion and brilliance this chapter would have been far less interesting to read and far less interesting to write. He was a towering, peerless figure whose leadership, intellect and friendship are greatly missed. We would also like to thank Hetty Marx, Josephine Lane and the rest of the production team at Cambridge University Press, who worked hard behind the scenes to ensure that the book came to a successful fruition, despite the inevitable delays that accompany the process of academic writing. Finally, we are grateful to the Economic and Social Research Council (ESRC), whose financial backing both indirectly and directly enabled this joint venture.

Introduction

John Dixon and Mark Levine

Gehart Saenger's book, *The Social Psychology of Prejudice*, was one of the first systematic attempts by a social psychologist to consolidate the early literature on prejudice. Its publication in 1953 was heralded by no less a figure than Gordon Allport as setting 'forth truths that if applied would certainly diminish the ravages of bigotry in our society'. The book opens on a parable. An anonymous narrator deliberates upon the potential admission of a Jewish man, Sidney Levy, to an exclusive social club. Mr Levy seems to be 'a nice person', the narrator notes, and 'Personally I would not mind if he joined the club'. However, he is 'definitely Jewish', and 'you never know with them. Sooner or later their true nature will show through. Moreover, once we take him, he may invite his Jewish friends and before long the whole club will be overrun by these kikes' (Saenger, 1953, p. 3).

Published the following year, the introduction to Allport's own canonical text, *The Nature of Prejudice* (1954, pp. 13–14), featured a similarly vivid example. In this case, the reader is invited to overhear an imaginary conversation between a Mr X and a Mr Y, who are debating 'the trouble with Jews'.

MR X: The trouble with Jews is that they only take care of their own group.
MR Y: But the record of the Community Chest campaign shows that they give more generously, in proportion to their numbers, to the general charities of the community than do non-Jews.
MR X: That shows they are always trying to buy favour and intrude into Christian affairs. They think of nothing but money; that is why there are so many Jewish bankers.
MR Y: But a recent study shows that the percentage of Jews in the banking business is negligible, far smaller than the percentage of non-Jews.
MR X: That's just it; they don't go for respectable businesses; they are only in the movie business or run nightclubs.

In both books, then, stark parables of anti-Semitism introduced a concept that was to dominate the social psychology of intergroup relations in ensuing decades. In the readiness of Saenger's and Allport's protagonists

1

to make hostile generalizations about members of another group and in the detachment of their attitudes from the facts of social reality, we find personified the elementary features of the concept of *prejudice*. Saenger (1953, p. 3) went on to define prejudice formally as a process whereby we 'judge a specific person on the basis of preconceived notions, without bothering to verify our beliefs or examine the merits of our judgements'. Allport's definition was more succinct. Prejudice, he famously observed, is 'an antipathy based upon a faulty and inflexible generalization' (1954, p. 9): it involves 'thinking ill of others without sufficient warrant' (1954, p. 6).

More than fifty years later, it is not an exaggeration to claim that the concept of prejudice is fundamental to the social psychology of intergroup relations. In fact, a strong case could be made that it is *the* defining concept of the field. In the period following the end of the Second World War, impelled by the work of scholars such as Allport (1954) and Adorno *et al.* (1950), as well as that of earlier researchers such as Bogardus (1925), Katz and Braly (1933) and Dollard *et al.* (1939), the project of understanding prejudice became viewed by many social psychologists as central to solving a host of social problems, including problems of racial discrimination, ideological extremism and genocide. The concept subsequently came to underpin an astonishing profusion of theoretical, empirical and applied work in the discipline. Nowadays the term 'prejudice' is ubiquitous in our journals, monographs and conference proceedings, and rarely is it far from the lips of those of us who teach courses on intergroup relations. As Reynolds, Haslam and Turner (Chapter 2, this volume) observe, the concept of prejudice has consumed 'many minds and research budgets'.

Given its historical significance in social psychology, we believe that a broad reappraisal of what the concept of prejudice can and cannot tell us is both timely and important. This edited collection of essays provides such a reappraisal. The book's overall aim is not primarily to review specific traditions of research on prejudice (e.g. Brown, 1995) or to explore how competing theories might be integrated (e.g. Duckitt, 1992). Rather, we wish to trace the deeper implications of what Margaret Wetherell (Chapter 8) has called the 'problematic' of prejudice for how social psychologists have framed the entire problem of investigating, under-standing and changing intergroup relations. What has this problematic contributed to our knowledge of relations between groups and what has it obscured or traduced? How has it expanded or narrowed the horizons of psychological inquiry? How effective or ineffective has it been in guiding our attempts to transform social relations and institutions? We also wish to discuss some emerging perspectives that have attempted, in various and sometimes contradictory ways, to move beyond the Allportian framework of prejudice research that has loomed so large over the social psychology of intergroup relations for over fifty years.

This introduction sets the scene. The first section describes the emergence of prejudice research in social psychology and situates its contribution in historical context. The second section outlines some foundational assumptions of the prejudice problematic, notably its individualistic orientation and its assumptions about the role played by cognitive irrationality and affective negativity within intergroup relations. We argue that these assumptions inform the model of social change espoused by prejudice researchers, which is based around the cognitive and emotional rehabilitation of majority group bigots. The third section presents a chapter by chapter outline.

The origins and historical significance of prejudice research in social psychology

In order to appreciate the historical significance of the prejudice problematic, we must consider the scientific paradigms it challenged and ultimately supplanted in social psychology. During the eighteenth, nineteenth and early twentieth centuries, scientific thinking about racial relations was informed by beliefs about racial difference and hierarchy (e.g. see Haller, 1971; Goldberg, 1993). Often employing conceptual frameworks based on the concept of biological inheritance, such thinking portrayed some groups as innately inferior and backward, rooting the causes of racial hostility in the supposed characteristics of its targets.

When the fledgling discipline of social psychology was consolidated in the early years of the twentieth century, it was mired in this way of framing the 'problem' of race relations (see Richards, 1997; Samuelson, 1978). During this period – aptly labelled 'the nadir' by Pettigrew (2008) – psychologists were preoccupied with the study of racial differences, particularly differences in intellectual abilities. Journal articles published at the time indicate that empirical research did not focus exclusively on comparisons between blacks and whites. As prominent were investigations of the so-called Nordic thesis, which proposed that Northern Europeans are genetically and culturally advantaged relative to other groups (including 'Mediterranean' and 'Alpine' Europeans).

Both implicitly and explicitly, this research refracted wider political arguments about the nature, course and governance of race relations, and formed part of the ideological project that is now known as scientific racism (see Pehrson and Leach, Chapter 6, this volume, for further discussion). On the one hand, it quietly perpetuated the traditional doctrine of the 'well-deserved reputation' (Zadwadzki, 1948), treating racial conflict as an inevitable outcome when a biologically superior group encounters the deficiencies of less developed groups. On the other hand, some social psychologists attempted to use psychological research as a platform from which to influence social policy. William McDougall, for example, openly supported eugenic policies of immigration control as a means of limiting contact between certain groups, proclaiming that 'some blends of human sub-races are eugenically admirable and others disastrous' (McDougall, 1918, cited in Richards, 1997, p. 197). It is important to acknowledge, too, that many commentators were sceptical about the concept of innate racial differences and questioned both its underlying assumptions and its evidence base. Some also recognized its political consequences – one of which was to confer legitimacy on institutions such as colonialism, slavery and segregation – and thus sought to 'puncture the biological myths' of race (Fairchild and Gurin, 1978).

According to Samelson (1978), between the 1920s and 1940s an 'abrupt reversal' occurred within psychological research on ethnic and racial relations. Emphasis shifted away from the project of measuring, explaining and debating the nature of group differences, and psychologists became increasingly concerned with the problem of intergroup prejudice. Thus, by 1950, Allport could assert that research on prejudice had 'spread like a flood both in social psychology and in adjacent social sciences. Publications are cascading from the presses. The outpouring within the past decade surely exceeds the output in all previous human history' (p. 4). Samelson (1978) astutely cautions against interpreting this shift as a simple victory of empirical science over politics. To the contrary, the rise of the problematic of prejudice was itself the complex outcome of a range of political processes unfolding both globally and within the US. For one thing, fascism acquired a decidedly bad name in the post-war era, giving global impetus to a search for the causes of irrational hatred towards minorities. In addition, the passing of the Immigration Restriction Law of 1924 in the US reduced political momentum for finding scientific justifications for excluding 'undesirable' immigrant groups, while the problem of maintaining peaceful coexistence among different groups of Americans grew on the national agenda. Moreover, psychology itself became somewhat less 'lily white' after the 1920s (Samelson, 1978, p. 271) and the discipline's increased social diversity probably heightened psychologists' awareness of problems of racial discrimination.

Whatever its causes, the shift in focus from race differences to race prejudice had a profound impact on social psychology. Perhaps most important, it reversed the social target of psychological research. No longer were the causes of social disharmony attributed mainly to the psychological and cultural deficiencies of minorities; instead, they were attributed to the racial prejudices of majority group members. As Montagu (1949) emphasized, 'It is the discriminators, not the discriminated, the prejudiced, not those against whom prejudice is exhibited, who are the problem' (p. 176).

Early work quickly established the scale and severity of this problem of dominant group prejudice. For example, in their classic study – later replicated by Rosenblith (1949) – Allport and Kramer (1946) reported that racial prejudice and anti-Semitism were widespread among white Americans and associated with factors such as childhood experiences, acceptance of parental authority and segregation. Their study also painted an unflattering early picture of the prejudiced person, highlighting their lack of insight, conventionality and suspiciousness, as well as the 'dull', 'unaware' and 'stencilled' quality of their thinking (p. 35). At the same time, Allport and Kramer (1946, p. 9) proclaimed the existence of 'almost unanimous agreement' among their contemporaries that prejudice should be regarded not as an inborn, fixed state, but as amenable to reduction. They predicted that research on prejudice would ultimately yield interventions to promote social change and proposed intergroup contact as one such intervention, anticipating a rich tradition of later research (see Pettigrew and Tropp, 2006; Brown and Hewstone, 2005). Although the relationship between theories of prejudice and processes of social change would turn out to be complex and, at times, fraught, early work successfully established the field's *applied emphasis* as another defining feature. Relaxing their customary posture of scientific detachment, many prejudice researchers became passionate advocates of a more tolerant society and sought to understand how scientific knowledge might promote social transformation. The challenge was clear. 'Prejudice,' as Adorno *et al.* (1950) wrote in the preface to *The Authoritarian Personality*, 'is one of the problems of our times for which everyone has a theory but no one has an answer.'

The conceptual and methodological foundations of the 'prejudice problematic'

Overviews of the subsequent development of prejudice research have rightly highlighted the field's diversity (e.g. Brown, 1995; Dovidio, 2001; Dovidio *et al.*, 2005; Duckitt, 1992; Nelson, 2009). In his useful periodization, Dovidio (2001) has identified three distinct phases in its evolution. Early work treated prejudice primarily as the product of abnormal personality development; in an intermediate phase, prejudice was viewed mainly as the outcome of ordinary, if imperfect, forms of information processing; and nowadays researchers increasingly emphasize unconscious, automatic and 'aversive' prejudices. Each of these phases has been marked not only by the development of new theoretical perspectives, but also by the emergence of new methodological techniques for measuring intergroup attitudes and stereotypes. The concept of prejudice has been decomposed into an array of forms, captured by emerging distinctions between old-fashioned and symbolic prejudice (Kinder and Sears, 1981), implicit and explicit prejudice (Greenwald and Banaji, 1995), subtle and blatant prejudice (Pettigrew and Meertens, 1995), and Jim Crow and laissez faire prejudice (Bobo et al., 1997), among others.

While respecting its historical diversity, the contributors to this book hold that prejudice research is also unified by a number of deep-seated assumptions about the nature of the social psychological processes that underlie intergroup relations. These assumptions have become institutionalized within the conceptual frameworks and research practices of social psychologists, lending coherence to an otherwise disparate array of perspectives on the nature of intergroup relations. In this section, we outline some foundations of the *prejudice problematic* and trace their implications for how psychologists have framed questions of social change. As the book unfolds, several of its other core features will become apparent.

Individualism   With some notable exceptions (e.g. Sherif, 1967), prejudice researchers have given causal priority to processes of cognition, emotion and personality lying within the individual, while acknowledging – with varying degrees of enthusiasm and theoretical sophistication – that such processes are also shaped by the contexts in which they unfold. The individualism of psychological research is evidenced most clearly in work focused on individual differences in prejudice, which stretches from early research on personality characteristics such as authoritarianism and dogmatism through to more recent work on topics such as social dominance and aversive racism (e.g. Pratto et al., 1994). The overarching goal of such work has been to explain how and why people vary in their propensity to express prejudice towards others, based on the assumption that 'the cognitive processes of prejudiced people are in general different from the cognitive processes of tolerant people' (Allport, 1954, p. 170). Other work has proceeded from the opposite assumption, viewing prejudice as the result of psychological processes that are universal and part of ordinary cognition (see Fiske, 2005). Again, however, the individual has served as the primary locus of causality. Prejudice has been conceived as a process that arises – unaided and sometimes contrary to our conscious intentions – from the inner workings of our minds, even if its precise form and expression is modulated by environmental factors.

The theoretical individualism of psychological research on prejudice is complemented by its methodological individualism. Indeed, as Reicher (2007, p. 825) observes, the design of psychological research often fabricates 'a monadic world of isolates and a world of silence, which we might try to create within our experimental studies but which exists in few places outside'. In such a world, the isolated individual is the main methodological and analytic unit of analysis, a fact that has profound, if often unacknowledged, consequences for the kinds of 'data' prejudice researchers collect and the forms of knowledge they generate. Durrheim (Chapter 9) and Condor and Figgou (Chapter 10) explore this point in some depth.

Of course, the argument that prejudice research prioritizes the role of individual psychology has a long pedigree and complex historical roots that need not be elaborated here (e.g. see Gordon, 2010). Suffice to say that the theme of individualism has been the subject of considerable discussion within social psychology (and without); and the problem of understanding the so-called 'interaction' between individual and contextual determinants of prejudice remains a live debate. Historically, sociologists and other social scientists have lined up to criticize psychologists for individualizing the historical, structural and political roots of intergroup conflict (e.g. Blumer, 1958; Rose, 1956). Psychologists, in their turn, have defended the value of research focused on the 'intrapsychic' level of analysis. We suspect that most social psychologists (ourselves included) would nowadays accept the ecumenical view expressed by Allport (1962, p. 134) in his paper titled: 'Prejudice: is it societal or personal?', who argued that 'There are no good reasons for professional rivalry and back-biting among social scientists preferring one approach or the other. They can and should be blended in our outlook.'

We also believe, however, that the history of psychological work on prejudice shows that such general statements hide as much as they reveal. What do we mean by 'societal' and 'personal' factors? How can or should they be 'blended'? What kinds of methodological and analytic frameworks might allow us to clarify best their complex interrelations? Although acknowledging that there are a variety of positions within this debate, and that valuable attempts to forge integrative models have been made (e.g. Duckitt, 1992), several contributors to the present volume argue that the conceptual frameworks and methodological practices that inform psychological research on prejudice continue to perpetuate an individualistic perspective on intergroup relations (e.g. see Chapters 1, 3, 8, 9 and 10). One reason for this, we would argue, is psychologists' abiding emphasis on the role of individual irrationality and error as the main source of prejudice.

Irrationality and error   The modern roots of the term 'prejudice' lie in the Enlightenment liberalism of the eighteenth century, which distinguished opinions based on religious authority and tradition from opinions based on reason and scientific rationality. As Billig notes in Chapter 7, the Enlightenment injunction to live one's life in the 'light of reason' found its antithesis in the concept of prejudice, which became synonymous with unreasoning faith. As its usage became established in the social sciences during the early years of the twentieth century, the term acquired a more restrictive set of meanings. Prejudice came to designate *negative* opinions about members of certain *categories of person*, particularly the categories of ethnicity, race and nation. The semantic links to irrationality remained foundational, however (Newman, 1979). Whereas Enlightenment philosophers had berated the blind faith of the clerics, early psychologists berated the blind hatred of Jews, blacks, immigrants and other historically disadvantaged groups.

Subsequent generations of prejudice researchers have faced the challenge of designing research that clarifies how, when and why such irrationality infects our reactions to other people. This challenge has inspired numerous, often highly innovative, methodological paradigms, which demonstrate that prejudice produces judgements whose outcomes seem biased, distorted, misdirected, error prone and sometimes plain wrong. Some of the most famous studies in the history of prejudice research fall into this category (e.g. Allport and Postman, 1946; Duncan, 1976; Hamilton and Gifford, 1976). On a more general level, researchers have employed methods that demonstrate how the prejudiced mind departs from ideal models of *rational thought processes*. Individuals who score high in prejudice are more likely, for example, to persevere with inefficient problem-solving strategies (Rokeach, 1948), to produce simplistic memories of physical objects (Fisher, 1951) and to display a variety of other forms of cognitive rigidity, including inflexibility, concretization, overgeneralization and intolerance of ambiguity (Kutner and Gordon, 1964). In the 'third wave' of prejudice research (Dovidio, 2001), the irrationality of the prejudiced mind has been further exposed by new techniques for measuring implicit associations (see Durrheim, Chapter 9 of this volume, for a detailed review). A disturbing implication of this research is that prejudice operates not only beneath the threshold of conscious awareness, but also in ways that may run contrary to what individuals experience as their conscious rationality (e.g. see Devine, 1989; Dovidio and Gaertner, 2004). If earlier studies suggested that the prejudiced are poor judges of the extent to which others share their social attitudes (e.g. Koenig and King, 1964), this emerging work suggests that they are also often poor judges of their own implicit attitudes.

At a theoretical level too, work on prejudice has been dominated by assumptions about its irrational nature. Early work focused on the general psychodynamic mechanisms through which prejudiced individuals may project unacceptable aspects of themselves onto others or displace environmentally induced aggression onto 'scapegoat' groups (e.g. Dollard *et al.*, 1939). Subsequent waves of research on the 'prejudiced personality' conceived prejudice primarily as the result of aberrant personality development, which creates a maladjusted view of social reality. In research on the authoritarian personality, for instance, the irrationality of prejudice was viewed as distorting not only individuals' relationships with others, but also their relationships to broader social and political structures, rendering them susceptible to ideological extremism (Adorno *et al.*, 1950). Anticipated in social psychology by the work of Allport (1954; see also Chapter 2) and Tajfel (1969), the cognitive revolution entrenched the notion that negative reactions towards others are grounded in *misperceptions* of social reality (Fiske and Taylor, 1984). Broader streams of theoretical work on the fallibility of human judgement (e.g. Tversky and Kahneman, 1973) entered the discipline primarily via research on stereotyping and also via research on related phenomena such as illusory correlations, errors of attribution, confirmation biases and false consensus effects. In contrast with earlier theories, such work emphasized the all too human nature of prejudiced cognitions, which were treated as a regrettable byproduct of otherwise adaptive mechanisms for processing information (see Fiske, 2005; McCrae and Bodenhausen, 2000 for reviews of work in this tradition). This remains overwhelmingly the dominant perspective on the relationship between cognition and prejudice. It is a perspective, however, that is critically interrogated by several contributors to the present volume (e.g. see Chapters 1, 2, 7, 8, 9, 10, 14 and the Conclusion).

Affective negativity Yet prejudice has seldom been treated purely as a matter of cold cognition. Allport (1954, p. 22) argued that our emotional responses to others sometimes take precedence over cognitive judgements. Emotions, he noted, operate 'like sponges. Ideas, engulfed by an overpowering emotion, are more likely to conform to the emotion than to objective evidence.' He argued further that emotions help to explain why prejudice is sometimes impervious to rational counterarguments and disconfirming evidence, memorably noting that even when it is 'defeated intellectually' prejudice often 'lingers emotionally' (p. 328).

Theories of the nature of such emotional reactions have varied extensively. In instinctive accounts of human aggression – delightfully labelled 'blood and guts' theories by Tajfel (1969) – the human propensity for intergroup fear and hatred has long been construed as part of our biological and evolutionary inheritance, an idea that is witnessing a revival (e.g. see Schaller *et al.*, 2003; Neuberg and Cottrell, 2006). Classic motivational theories (e.g. the frustration–aggression hypothesis) have used psycho-analytic concepts such as ambivalence, catharsis and displacement to explain the intensity of aggressive feelings that minorities receive under certain social conditions. Such work has cashed out Freud's (1930/1975, p. 51) bleak dictum that: 'It is always possible ... to bind together a considerable number of people in love, so long as there are other people left over to receive the manifestations of their aggressiveness.' Until fairly recently, social cognition research somewhat neglected the affective dimension of prejudice. Certainly, it disregarded the more extreme man-ifestations of intergroup emotions that engaged social psychologists in the post-war period. However, even in this tradition, the affective dimensions of prejudice have always been tacit (e.g. within motivational concepts such as 'ingroup bias'), and they have become increasingly overt, with work on stereotypic beliefs about others being integrated with work on feelings towards them (Bodenhausen *et al.*, 2001; Mackie and Hamilton, 1993).

Yet what exactly is the nature of the emotional responses that define prejudice? Some early researchers argued that they should be treated as differentiated rather than unitary in character. Notably, Kramer (1949) advocated disaggregating prejudiced emotions into sub-categories such as fear, disgust, contempt, envy and anger. He insisted that both the cogni-tive and emotional components of prejudice vary markedly depending on the nature of outgroup being appraised and are associated with quite different predispositions to act (e.g. to engage in inclusion/exclusion, withdrawal/non-withdrawal). His essay prefigured the kind of work that has enriched the study of intergroup emotions in recent years (e.g. see Mackie and Smith, 2002; Mackie *et al.*, 2008). For much of the history of prejudice research, however, the emotional specificity and complexity of prejudice has not been a central concern. To the contrary, prejudice has been defined as a kind of *generic* affective response towards members of other groups, which varies in intensity from low to high and is in practice defined by its negative valence (even if textbook discussions dutifully remind readers that prejudice can, in principle, involve warm as well as hostile feelings). Theories of its antecedents have varied widely, sometimes achieving considerable sophistication, but prejudiced emotion itself has been conceived in remarkably simple terms in most research. In a nut-shell, prejudice occurs when 'we' dislike 'them' and don't have a sensible reason for doing so. As we shall see, however, several chapters in the present volume complicate this seemingly self-evident claim, revealing how prejudice typically involves a complex blend of positive and negative feelings (see especially Chapters 1, 3, 4, 11, 12 and the Conclusion). They also indicate that the relationship between getting people to like one another and changing intergroup relations may be more complex than the prejudice problematic suggests.

The prejudice reduction model of social change   The model of social change proposed by prejudice researchers has generally aimed to transform the kind of cognitive and emotional reactions discussed above in order to improve intergroup relations. The model has installed a particular conception of: (a) the main targets of change; (b) the psychological processes involved; (c) the behavioural outcomes desired; and (d) the kinds of interventions required (Wright and Lubensky, 2008; Dixon *et al.*, 2010).

Prejudice reduction interventions have been implemented in many societies, focusing on many kinds of intergroup relations, including relations of race, ethnicity, culture, nationality and sexual orientation. They have also been grounded in varying theoretical perspectives on how, when and why social psychological change can be accomplished. Perspectives treating prejudice as the outcome of deep-seated personality dynamics or universal cognitive biases, for example, have conceived the problem of change rather differently than perspectives treating prejudice as the outcome of more tractable forces such as social norms (e.g. see Long, 1951). From the outset, however, work on prejudice reduction has also shared a number of common features. It has tended to focus on social groups who are *historically advantaged*, either in terms of access to power and resources or by virtue of sheer demographic numbers. This pattern was established in the earliest work in the field, which focused on the problems of racism and anti-Semitism in the US, and sought to understand how to change the attitudes of white Americans towards blacks and Jews. Psychologically, such models have attempted to explain how to correct inaccurate stereotypes about disadvantaged groups and to promote positive emotional responses towards them, such as liking and empathy. Behaviourally, they have sought to decrease incidences of aggression or discrimination.

Examples of interventions designed to achieve these goals include work on cooperative learning, common identification, re-education, empathy arousal and, perhaps most important, intergroup contact (e.g. Aronson and Patnoe, 1997; Lilienfeld *et al.*, 2009; Pettigrew and Tropp, 2006; Stephan and Finlay, 1999; Dovidio *et al.*, 2009). Although some have voiced scepticism about the overall strength of their supporting evidence (Paluck and Green, 2009), such interventions rank among the most important applied contributions of social psychology: a powerful example of how the discipline can work in the public interest and promote a better society. Certainly, the contributors to the present volume do not dispute that interventions to promote prejudice reduction have had many beneficial impacts. However, they do raise several searching questions about the limitations of prejudice reduction models of social change (e.g. see Chapters 1, 2, 11, 12, 13, 14 and the Conclusion).

Book structure and chapter outline

The book is organized loosely into two parts, which inevitably overlap and interpenetrate. Part I, 'Beyond prejudice', presents a wide range of critical alternatives to, or substantive elaborations of, conventional treatments of prejudice in social psychology. This section draws on developments in research, for example, on social identity and self-categorization, dehumanization, power relations that operate via 'benevolence' as well as 'hostility', the distinction between 'old' and 'new' forms of prejudice and discursive and rhetorical psychology. Each chapter addresses key features of the prejudice problematic and, crucially, suggests alternative (or sometimes complementary) perspectives for understanding and studying intergroup processes.

Part II, 'Prejudice and social change revisited', explores the book's more specific implications for understanding the question of how to 'improve' intergroup relations, a problem that has impelled prejudice research for over half a decade. Each of the authors acknowledges the profound historical and applied significance of the prejudice reduction interventions. By the same token, each also points to the limitations of the prejudice problematic as a framework for 'improving' intergroup relations. The authors also highlight some of the unexpected tensions that characterize the relationship between so-called collective action and prejudice reduction models of social change and flag some of the unintended, and indeed paradoxical, consequences of models of change based on the psychological rehabilitation of the majority group bigot.

Part I: Beyond prejudice

Chapter 1: From perception to mobilization: the shifting paradigm of prejudice   In Chapter 1, Steve Reicher seeks to provoke discussion about the general framework within which psychologists have addressed social inequality and discrimination – the so-called 'prejudice problematic'. He begins by challenging four underlying assumptions of this problematic, notably that: (1) prejudice is about *the outgroup*; (2) prejudice is about *perceptions* of the outgroup; (3) prejudice is about the *negative qualities* that are perceived in the outgroup; and (4) prejudice is about *ordinary group members* perceiving negative qualities in the outgroup. He holds that, far from being rooted in faulty cognitions about an outgroup, prejudice is a practice relating to ingroup authority and ingroup power. As a consequence, we need to redirect our analytic gaze from perceptions of the outgroup to the contestation of ingroup definitions. We also need to re-direct our practical attention from changing the views of dominant group members to sustaining the collective actions of subordinate group members.

Chapter 2: Prejudice, social identity and social change: resolving the Allportian problematic Prejudice has traditionally been defined as a negative attitude towards members of a given group based exclusively on their membership of that group. On that basis, it is typically seen to be problematic by definition: after all, the truth about people is presumed to lie in their individuality. From a social identity perspective, however, there are several problems associated with this traditional approach, and some of these problems are discussed by Kate Reynolds, Alex Haslam and John Turner in Chapter 2. First, since in a range of social situations people's behaviour *is* determined by their group member-ship (i.e. by social identity), the process of perceiving and judging people in terms of group membership is not necessarily faulty. Second, and more generally, prejudice can be conceptualized as a process that is bound up with perceivers' social identities and with the dynamics of ongoing inter-group relations. Indeed, it can be seen to *veridically* represent aspects of those intergroup relations as perceived from a particular social vantage point. In this way, as Sherif (1967) argued, there is a 'psycho-logic' to prejudice that is derived from important social realities. Elaborating on this idea, a third point is that the identification of a particular set of beliefs as 'prejudicial' is itself a process that is grounded in group-based status relations and consensus. Thus, stereotypes held by one's own group are rarely seen as prejudicial, and the labelling of others' views as prejudicial can be seen as an aspect of the *political process* through which insecure status relations are negotiated and contested. In these terms, the problem of prejudice is a problem of politics and ideology (to do with different groups' disagreement about how group interests should be advanced) rather than of group psychology and social perception per se.

Chapter 3: An ambivalent alliance: hostile and benevolent sexism as complementary justifications for gender inequality Chapter 3 reproduces Peter Glick and Susan Fiske's classic account – published originally in 2001 – of the challenge posed by research on ambivalent sexism to the orthodox concept of prejudice as 'unalloyed antipathy'. Initially employed in research using US samples, the ambivalent sexism inventory has now been administered to thousands of men and women living in a wide range of cultural contexts. The majority of evidence suggests that hostile and benevolent sexism are fundamentally complementary, cross-culturally prevalent ideologies, both of which predict and sustain gender inequality. Women tend to reject hostile sexism more readily than men, but they often endorse benevolent sexism. By rewarding women for conforming to a patriarchal status quo, benevolent sexism inhibits gender equality. On a more general level, this tradition of research illustrates a core limitation of the traditional concept of prejudice that is explored in other parts of this book (e.g. see Chapters 4, 11, 12 and the Conclusion). Namely, it shows that the domination of one group by another is not necessarily founded on emotional hostility: all too frequently it involves an insidious combination of antipathy and paternalistic regard.

Chapter 4: Prejudice and dehumanization   Nick Haslam and Steve Loughnan's chapter examines the role of dehumanization in group perception. It reviews a growing body of work that addresses the nature, causes and consequences of dehumanization and presents a model of dehumanization that explains how humanness can be denied to people in two distinct ways, which involve people being likened to animals (denied uniquely human attributes) or machines and objects (denied 'human nature'). This work challenges and supplements the psychology of prejudice in a number of ways. First, it suggests that prejudice cannot be understood only in terms of negativity, as groups are commonly denied humanity independently of being evaluated negatively. Second, it suggests that prejudice is not monolithic in character. It assumes different forms when different kinds of humanness are denied to groups or when group members are metaphorically assimilated to different kinds of nonhuman.

Chapter 5: Stereotyping, prejudice and discrimination revisited: from William James to W. E. B. Du Bois   For most of its history, research on prejudice has focused squarely on the perceptions and feelings of members of historically advantaged groups. More recently, however, psychologists have been paying increasing attention to the reactions of the historically disadvantaged, and the chapter by Stanley Gaines is in this tradition. Gaines's starting point is that the literature on intergroup relations could benefit greatly from the perspective provided by W. E. B. Du Bois's classic, *The Souls of Black Folk* (1903), especially with regard to mainstream social psychologists' attempts to understand the impact of racism on African Americans' identity development and associated patterns of behaviour (e.g. responses to so-called 'stereotype threat'). He argues that the concept of racial identity advocated by Du Bois offers insights into the nature of American race relations and racism that are as important as those advocated by Allport's work, *The Nature of Prejudice*.

Chapter 6: Advancing the social psychology of racism and anti-racism: moving beyond 'old' and 'new' prejudice Sam Pehrson and Colin Leach challenge the consensus that old forms of racism, based on biological hierarchies and blatant derogation, have been largely replaced by new, subtle versions that criticize cultural difference and deny discrimination. They argue that the notions of 'symbolic' and 'modern' racism are strongly rooted in the prejudice problematic, in that they conceive of racism as the intrusion of a stubborn antipathy towards black people into contemporary life. As such, these approaches define racism as prejudice in order to offer a particular characterization of its development. The authors set out an alternative way for social psychology to grasp both the continuity and the change in expressions of racism over time, centred on racialization (as a particular kind of social categorization) and devaluation (implying inferior regard or treatment).

Chapter 7: The notion of 'prejudice': some rhetorical and ideological aspects Originally published in 1988, Michael Billig's seminal essay explores the ideological meaning of the denial of prejudice, which is ubiquitous in contemporary discourse on race. He argues that even fascists deny and disclaim their own prejudice. Why? The general norm against being perceived as prejudiced has not received nearly as much direct investigation as, for example, the expression of negative attitudes towards outgroups, even if social psychologists have widely acknowledged the powerful norm against appearing prejudiced. According to Billig, we need to interrogate more carefully what is meant by 'prejudice' within common-sense understandings (see also Chapters 8, 9 and 10) and to trace its wider historical and ideological significance. He holds that every-day conceptions of 'prejudice' reveal the heritage of Enlightenment liberalism. In everyday life, as in Enlightenment philosophy, 'prejudice' refers to psychologically irrational beliefs. Speakers attempt to justify, and particularly to self-justify, their own rationality, portraying their views as 'reasonable' by finding external reasons for discrimination. The ideological implications of this liberal, but discriminatory, form of discourse are discussed and illustrated.

Chapter 8: The prejudice problematic   Originally published in 1992, Margaret Wetherell's chapter coined the phrase 'prejudice problematic'. It also laid some foundations for a constructionist and critical psychological alternative to mainstream prejudice research, two more recent incarnations of which are illustrated by the work of Durrheim (Chapter 9) and Condor and Figgou (Chapter 10). The chapter begins by clarifying some core features and tensions of the prejudice problematic, notably its emphasis upon generic failings of the individual, cognitive irrationality and prejudgement and the rehabilitation of the prejudiced mind. The next section explores the ideological implications of the prejudice problematic, examining how, for example, it has functioned to individualize social problems that are better understood as the product of modes of political and social organization. The interpenetration of social psychological and lay accounts of prejudice is also explored within the chapter, which analyses Pakeha New Zealanders' talk about racism, discrimination and disadvantage as an extended illustration. In conclusion, moving beyond the 'prejudice problematic', some implications for anti-racist practice are discussed.

Chapter 9: Implicit prejudice in mind and interaction   Kevin Durrheim discusses work on implicit attitudes and stereotypes, a field of inquiry that has burgeoned in the last decade and is now a core area of the social psychology of prejudice. The first section of his chapter reviews some central findings, methods and suppositions of work in the field. The second section assesses some emerging criticisms of the concept of implicit prejudice, exploring, for example, its definition of racism and its underlying assumptions about the nature of the psychological subject. The rest of the chapter develops an alternative framework for studying 'implicit' forms of prejudice. Rather than seeking to uncover stereotypes in the hidden recesses of the mind, this framework treats them as interactional resources that are used rhetorically to characterize social life and account for social action. Stereotypes are formulated in (and demanded by) social interaction. To serve these functions, they typically take a probabilistic, noncategorical form and rely on local, contextually circumscribed, understandings of group life in order to accomplish stereotyping 'by implication'. Crucially, in this form of interaction, listeners share with speakers the labour of doing stereotyping. The stereotypes that underlie common sense serve as the unspoken backcloth to banal forms of interaction, invoking pejorative images of others without articulating them explicitly.

Chapter 10: Rethinking the prejudice problematic: a collaborative cognition approach   Susan Condor and Lia Figgou similarly argue that researchers have generally adopted a *monistic* approach to conceptualizing and investigating prejudice, an approach in which the analytic focus is on the responses of the isolated individual bigot. By contrast, drawing on developments in research on 'collaborative cognition', they argue that social psychologists need to appreciate more fully the dynamic and interactional nature of prejudice construction, as expressed within everyday conversations about others. They explore how concepts such as scaffolding, joint construction and distributed inhibition allow us to rethink the prejudice problematic. By studying how prejudice is oriented to, and accomplished within, social encounters 'in the wild', we can appreciate more fully how its everyday expression and suppression is irreducible to the actions of any single individual.

Part II: Prejudice and social change revisited

Chapter 11: Models of social change in social psychology: collective action or prejudice reduction? Conflict or harmony?   Social psychology's main approach to improving intergroup relations has involved reducing prejudice. This chapter compares and contrasts this approach with another that treats collective action and social protest as the catalysts for increasing social justice. Steve Wright and Gamze Baray examine the lack of integration between these two approaches and trace a number of critical divergences in their underlying assumptions and objectives. Many prejudice reduction strategies are thought to be effective because they reduce: (a) differentiation between groups; (b) ingroup identification; (c) perceived impermeability of group boundaries; and (d) negative characterizations of the outgroup. By contrast, endorsement of collective action is associated with: (a) clear group differentiation; (b) strong ingroup identification; (c) perceptions of boundary impermeability; and (d) characterization of the outgroup as perpetrator of injustice. Collective action and prejudice reduction thus appear to require disadvantaged group members to hold opposing perceptions of the ingroup, the intergroup context and the outgroup. In addition, at its heart the prejudice reduction approach is about creating harmony, whereas the collective action approach is about producing intergroup conflict. Developing this argument, Wright and Baray discuss a number of studies showing that, among disadvantaged group members, positive intergroup contact is associated with less prejudice towards the advantaged outgroup, but also with less endorsement of social protest and collective action.

Chapter 12: From attitudes to (in)action: the darker side of 'we'   The common ingroup identity model hypothesizes that prejudice is reduced when members of different groups are induced to conceive of themselves within a single, more inclusive collective identity. This chapter extends the model by examining the different preferences, functions and consequences of different forms of shared identity, as one group or as a dual identity, for members of advantaged and disadvantaged groups. Specifically, Jack Dovidio, Tamar Saguy, Samuel Gaertner and Erin Thomas propose that intergroup contact focusing on commonality can reinforce the status quo, which benefits the advantaged group, and undermine collective action for equality by disadvantaged group members. They explore the different motivations and preferences of members of advantaged and disadvantaged groups and how they operate to shape intergroup interactions and influence intergroup relations in the short and long term. They conclude by discussing practical implications and directions for future research.

Chapter 13: Contact and social change in an ongoing asymmetrical conflict: four social-psychological models of reconciliation-aimed planned encounters between Israeli Jews and Palestinians   In the past few decades, planned contact interventions between groups in conflict have played an important role in efforts to improve intergroup relations and achieve peace and reconciliation. Ifat Maoz's chapter focuses on interventions designed to improve relations between Israeli Jews and Palestinians. Like other contact interventions conducted in settings of intergroup conflict, encounters between Israeli Jews and Palestinians represent a paradoxical project aiming to produce equality and cooperation between groups that are embedded in a protracted, asymmetrical conflict. Though existing research teaches us valuable lessons on the effectiveness of contact conducted under optimal conditions, relatively little is said about contact between groups entangled in violent and seemingly 'intractable' disputes. This chapter appraises the historical evolution of these reconciliation-aimed contact interventions between Israeli Jews and Palestinians over the past twenty-five years. It discusses the development of four major social-psychological models: the coexistence model, the joint projects model, the confrontational model and the narrative-story-telling model. The strengths and limitations of each model as well as its effectiveness in inducing social change are discussed, as are some broader implications for evaluating prejudice reduction as a model of social change. The chapter is particularly effective in tracing such implications within a concrete, historically specific context of intergroup conflict.

Chapter 14: From prejudice to collective action   In this chapter, Clifford Stott, John Drury and Steve Reicher contend that 'prejudice' should be understood as dynamic, intergroup processes that emerge as social categories and relations between them are defined and redefined. Rather than being 'irrational', (negative) intergroup perceptions often make sense in the context of antagonistic relations. Moreover, definitions of the nature of social groups and intergroup relations are the object of intense intragroup and intergroup struggle, with the dominance of any particular version being determined by historical dynamics of power, social action and legitimacy.

This perspective on prejudice has important implications for how we conceptualize and investigate social change. Rather than exploring shifts enacted within the heads of irrational individuals, we need to explore how broader patterns of collective action and struggles over the meaning of social categories may transform intergroup relations. Stott and colleagues argue that research on crowd behaviour provides a particularly instructive context in which to observe the dynamics of this process. By way of illustration, they present data from their own research on crowd events, focusing particularly on case studies of protest and football crowds. Using this case material, they trace the emergence, development and transformation of particular sets of 'prejudices' between groups and show how the social psychology underpinning intergroup hostility during these events was both produced by, and productive of, intergroup dynamics.

Conclusions and future directions: the nature, significance and inherent limitations of the concept of prejudice in social psychology The book's Conclusion reviews some central themes and appraises, in light of previous chapters' contributions, the opportunities and challenges of going 'beyond prejudice'. We give particular emphasis to the problem of reconciling prejudice reduction with alternative models of social change and thereby anticipate a debate that, we hope, the social psychological community will revisit and take forward.

Beyond prejudice?

The title of our book is *Beyond Prejudice*. The term 'beyond' can be read in various ways. For some of our authors, for example, the prejudice problematic remains the foundation of social psychological work on intergroup relations, even if they recommend important revisions, extensions and elaborations. Others propose a more revolutionary shift. They hold that the traditional concept of prejudice may have outlived its usefulness or at least that it may require a radical overhaul if it is to continue to undergird the social psychology of intergroup processes. Our own reservations, as we elaborate in the book's Conclusion, focus on the value of prejudice research in the arena of social change. The book, then, does not ultimately offer a single, overall message, but instead accommodates a diversity of perspectives.

The danger of the term 'beyond', however, is that it may be misread as wholesale rejection. This is not the purpose of our book or of any of the chapters written by our contributors. Indeed, as it nears publication, we have come to realize that the book records our love affair with the social psychology of prejudice as much as an indictment of its supposed limitations. As such, we conclude by reminding readers that the 'abrupt reversal' (Samuelson, 1978) produced by the prejudice problematic issued a profound challenge to social psychologists, whose moral and political force remains urgent. Lippitt and Radke (1946, p. 167) stated this challenge as follows: 'The need for an understanding of the dynamics of prejudice has no equivalent importance in the social sciences. In no other aspects of interpersonal and intergroup relations is there a more urgent need for social scientists to *get out and do something*' (our emphasis).

References

Adorno, T. W., Frenkel-Brunswik, E., Levinson, D. J. and Sanford, R. N. (1950). *The Authoritarian Personality*. New York: Harper.

Allport, G. W. (1954). *The Nature of Prejudice*. Garden City, NY: Doubleday.

(1962). Prejudice: is it societal or personal? *Journal of Social Issues*, **18**, 120–34.

Allport, G. W. and Kramer, B. M. (1946). Some roots of prejudice. *Journal of Psychology*, **22**, 9–39.

Allport, G. W. and Postman, L. (1946). An analysis of rumor. *Public Opinion Quarterly*, **10**, 501–18.

Aronson, E. and Patnoe, S. (1997). *The Jigsaw Classroom: Building Cooperation in the Classroom* (2nd edn). New York: Longman.

Blumer, H. (1958). Race prejudice as a sense of group position. *Pacific Sociological Review*, **1**, 3–7.

Bobo, L., Kleugel, J. R. and Smith, R. A. (1997). Laissez-faire racism: the crystallization of a kinder, gentler, antiblack ideology. In S. A. Tuch and J. K. Martin (eds.), *Racial Attitudes in the 1990s: Continuity and Change* (pp.15–42). Westport, CT: Praeger Publishers.

Bodenhausen, G., Mussweiler, T., Gabriel, S. and Moreno, K. (2001). Affective influences of stereotyping and intergroup relations. In J. P. Forgas (ed.), *Handbook of Affect and Social Cognition*. Mahwah, NJ: Lawrence Erlbaum Associates.

Bogardus, E. (1925). Measuring social distance. *Journal of Applied Sociology*, **9**, 299–308.

Brown, R. (1995). *Prejudice: Its Social Psychology*. Oxford, UK: Basil Blackwell.

Brown, R. and Hewstone, M. (2005). An integrative theory of intergroup contact. In M. P. Zanna (ed.), *Advances in Experimental Social Psychology* (pp.255–343). San Diego, CA: Academic Press.

Devine, P. G. (1989). Stereotypes and prejudice: their automatic and controlled components. *Journal of Personality and Social Psychology*, **56**, 5–18.

Dixon, J., Tropp, L. R., Durrheim, K. and Tredoux, C. G. (2010). 'Let them eat harmony': prejudice reduction and the political attitudes of historically disadvantaged groups. *Current Directions in Psychological Science*, **19**, 76–80.

Dollard, J., Doob, L., Miller, N. E., Mowrer, O. and Sears, R. (1939). *Frustration and Aggression*. New Haven, CT: Yale University Press.

Dovidio, J. F. (2001). On the nature of contemporary prejudice: the third wave. *Journal of Social Issues*, **57**, 829–49.

Dovidio, J. F. and Gaertner, S. L. (2004). Aversive racism. In M. P. Zanna (ed.), *Advances in Experimental Social Psychology* (Vol. 36, pp. 1–52). San Diego, CA: Academic Press.

Dovidio, J. F., Gaertner, S. L. and Saguy, T. (2009). Commonalty and the complexity of 'we': social attitudes and social change. *Personality and Social Psychology Review*, **13**, 3–20.

Dovidio, J. F., Glick, P. and Rudman, L. A. (eds.) (2005). *On the Nature of Prejudice: Fifty Years after Allport*. Malden, MA: Blackwell.

Duckitt, J. (1992). Psychology and prejudice: an historical analysis and integrative framework. *American Psychologist*, **47**, 1,182–93.

Duncan, B. L. (1976). Differential social perception and attribution of intergroup violence: testing the lower limits of stereotyping of blacks. *Journal of Personality and Social Psychology*, **34**, 590–8.

Fairchild, H. H. and Gurin, P. (1978). Traditions in the social psychological analysis of race relations. *American Behavioral Scientist*, **21**, 757–78.

Fisher, J. (1951). The memory process and certain psychosocial attitudes, with special reference to the law of Praganz. *Journal of Personality*, **19**, 406–20.

Fiske, S. T. (2005). Social cognition and the normality of prejudgment. In J. F. Dovidio, P. Glick and L. A. Rudman (eds.), *On the Nature of Prejudice: Fifty Years after Allport*. Malden, MA: Blackwell.

Fiske, S. T. and Taylor, S. E. (1984). *Social Cognition*. Reading, MA: Addison-Wesley.

Freud, S. (1930/1975). *Civilization and its Discontents*. London: Hogarth Press.

Goldberg, D. T. (1993). *Racist Culture*. Oxford, UK: Blackwell.

Gordon, L. N. (2010). The individual and the 'general situation': the tension barometer and the race problem at the University of Chicago, 1947–1954. *Journal of the History of the Behavioral Sciences*, **46**, 27–51.

Greenwald, A. G. and Banaji, M. R. (1995). Implicit social cognition: attitudes, self-esteem, and stereotypes. *Psychological Review*, **102**, 4–27.

Haller, J. (1971). *Outcasts from Evolution: Scientific Attitudes of Racial Inferiority*. Urbana, IL: University of Illinois Press.

Hamilton, D. L. and Gifford, R. K. (1976). Illusory correlation in interpersonal perception: a cognitive basis of stereotypic judgments. *Journal of Experimental Social Psychology*, **12**, 392–407.

Katz, D. and Braly, K. (1933). Racial stereotypes in 100 college students. *Journal of Abnormal and Social Psychology*, **28**, 280–90.

Kinder, D. R. and Sears, D. O. (1981). Prejudice and politics: symbolic racism versus racial threats to the good life. *Journal of Personality and Social Psychology*, **40**, 414–31.

Koenig, F. W. and King, M. B. (1964). Cognitive simplicity and outgroup stereo-typing. *Social Forces*, **42**, 324–7.

Kramer, B. M. (1949). Dimensions of prejudice. *Journal of Psychology*, **27**, 389–451.

Kutner, B. and Gordon, N. B. (1964). Cognitive functioning and prejudice: a nine year follow up study. *Sociometry*, **27**, 66–74.

Lilienfeld, S. O., Ammirati, R. and Landfield, K. (2009). Giving debiasing away. Can psychological research on correcting cognitive errors promote human welfare? *Perspectives on Psychological Science*, **4**, 390–8.

Lippitt, R. and Radke, M. J. (1946). New trends in the investigation of prejudice. *Annals of the American Academy of Political and Social Science*, **244**, 167–76.

Long, H. H. (1951). Race prejudice and social change. *American Journal of Sociology*, **57**, 15–19.

Mackie, D. M. and Hamilton, D. L. (eds.) (1993). *Affect, Cognition, and Stereotyping: Interactive Processes in Group Perception* (pp.297–315). San Diego, CA: Academic Press.

Mackie, D. M. and Smith, E. R. (eds.) (2002). *From Prejudice to Intergroup Emotions: Differentiated Reactions to Social Groups*. Philadelphia, PA: Psychology Press.

Mackie, D. M., Smith, E. R. and Ray, D. G. (2008). Intergroup emotions and intergroup relations. *Personality and Social Psychology Compass*, **2**, 1,866–80.

McCrae, C. N. and Bodenhausen, G. V. (2000). Social cognition: thinking cate-gorically about others. *Annual Review of Psychology*, **51**, 93–120.

Montagu, M. F. (1949). Some psychodynamic factors in race prejudice. *Journal of Social Psychology*, **30**, 175–87.

Nelson, T. D. (ed.) (2009). *Handbook of Prejudice, Stereotyping and Discrimination*. New York: Psychology Press.

Neuberg, S. L. and Cottrell, C. A. (2006). Evolutionary bases of prejudices. In M. Schaller, J. A. Simpson and D. T. Kenrick (eds.), *Evolution and Social Psychology* (pp.163–87). New York: Psychology Press.

Newman, J. (1979). Prejudice as prejudgment. *Ethics*, **90**, 47–57.

Paluck, E. L. and Green, D. P. (2009). Prejudice reduction: what works? A review and assessment of research and practice. *Annual Review of Psychology*, **60**, 339–67.

Pettigrew, T. F. (2008). The social scientific study of American race attitudes in the twentieth century. *Personality and Social Psychology Compass*, **2**, 318–45.

Pettigrew, T. F. and Meertens, R. W. (1995). Subtle and blatant prejudice in Western Europe. *European Journal of Social Psychology*, **25**, 57–75.

Pettigrew, T. F. and Tropp, L. R. (2006). A meta-analytic test of intergroup contact theory. *Journal of Personality and Social Psychology*, **90**, 751–83.

Pratto, F., Sidanius, J., Stallworth, L. M. and Malle, B. F. (1994). Social domi-nance orientation: a personality variable predicting social and political atti-tudes. *Journal of Personality and Social Psychology*, **67**, 741–63.

Reicher, S. (2007). Rethinking the paradigm of prejudice. *South African Journal of Psychology*, **37**, 820–34.

Richards, G. (1997). *'Race', Racism and Psychology: Towards a Reflexive History*. London: Routledge.

Rokeach, M. (1948). Generalized mental rigidity as a factor in ethnocentrism. *Journal of Abnormal and Social Psychology*, **43**, 259–78.

Rose, A. M. (1956). Intergroup relations vs prejudice: pertinent theory for the study of social change. *Social Problems*, **4**, 173–6.

Rosenblith, J. F. (1949). A replication of 'Some roots of prejudice'. *Journal of Abnormal and Social Psychology*, **34**, 470–89.

Saenger, G. (1953). *The Social Psychology of Prejudice*. New York: Harper.

Samelson, F. (1978). From 'race psychology' to 'studies in prejudice': some observations on the thematic reversal in social psychology. *Journal of the History of the Behavioral Sciences*, **14**, 265–78.

Schaller, M., Park, J. H. and Faulkner, J. (2003). Prehistoric dangers and contemporary prejudices. *European Review of Social Psychology*, **14**, 105–37.

Sherif, M. (1967). *Group Conflict and Cooperation: their Social Psychology*. London: Routledge and Kegan Paul.

Stephan, W. G. and Finlay, K. (1999). The role of empathy in improving intergroup relations. *Journal of Social Issues*, **55**, 729–43.

Tajfel, H. (1969). Cognitive aspects of prejudice. *Journal of Social Issues*, **25**, 79–97.

Tversky, A. and Kahneman, D. (1973). Availability: a heuristic for judging frequency and probability. *Cognitive Psychology*, **5**, 207–32.

Wright, S. C. and Lubensky, M. (2008). The struggle for social equality: collective action vs prejudice reduction. In S. Demoulin, J. P. Leyens and J. F. Dovidio (eds.), *Intergroup Misunderstandings: Impact of Divergent Social Realities* (pp.291–310). New York: Psychology Press.

Zadwadzki, B. (1948). Limitations of a scapegoat theory of prejudice. *Journal of Abnormal and Social Psychology*, **33**, 127–41.

Part I

Beyond prejudice

1   From perception to mobilization: the shifting paradigm of prejudice

Stephen Reicher

Introduction: defining the problem

On 18 July 1950, the United Nations Educational, Scientific and Cultural Organization (UNESCO) issued its first statement on 'the race question'. Shortly afterwards, this was published in a document entitled 'UNESCO and its programme'.[1] The introduction to this document starts by asserting that '[t]he importance which the problem of race has acquired in the modern world scarcely needs to be pointed out'. It goes on to cite a resolution passed at the sixth session of UNESCO in 1948 which called for 'the general adoption of a programme of dissemination of scientific facts designed to bring about the disappearance of that which is commonly called race prejudice'.

The resolution reflects a somewhat optimistic belief that prejudice is the product of a misunderstanding of the facts concerning racial categorization and racial difference and that, once these misunderstandings are resolved in the glare of scientific truth, so the problem of prejudice will likewise be resolved. In time, this optimism has faded; for all the best efforts of science over the ensuing sixty years, 'the race question' has not gone away. Accordingly, the 'Outcome document' from the latest United Nations conference on racism – the Durban Review Conference held in Geneva in 2009 – 'emphasizes the need to address with greater resolve and political will all forms and manifestations of racism, racial discrimination, xenophobia and related intolerance, in all spheres of life and in all parts of the world'.[2] Or, to cite Ban Ki-moon, Secretary General of the United Nations, speaking amid the controversies that blighted this Conference, the priority continues to be 'to build constructive solutions to the very real problem of racism'.[3]

The focus, then, is entirely on solutions. What solutions work? How should they be implemented? How can they be prioritized? By contrast, little attention is paid to the nature of the problem. It is as if that is self-evident. We don't have to question it. We simply have to deal with it. And yet the way a problem is framed and the nature of its solutions are interdependent. If you misconceptualize the former, you will never arrive at the latter. My argument in this chapter, then, is that we need to devote somewhat more attention to what we understand by what was once known as 'the race question' and is now probably better known as the problem of racism.

There is an irony in all this. After all, the most important thing about the early UNESCO initiatives – not only the 1950 statement, but also subsequent publications such as *The Roots of Prejudice* (Rose, 1951), *Race and History* (Lévi-Strauss, 1952) and *Race, Prejudice and Education* (Bibby, 1959) – was that they fundamentally *reconceptualized* the question itself.

Prior to the Second World War, 'the race question' primarily referred to a problem *for* white people *caused by* black people. The analytic gaze was therefore focused on the oppressed group, upon their various problematic, pathological or deviant characteristics which led them to make life difficult for the dominant group. One can find many examples of this. Sometimes the 'others' were deemed a problem because of what they supposedly lacked – intelligence, restraint or manners, for instance (see Gould, 1997; Kamin, 1974). Sometimes the other was both envied and feared for what they had in excess – enthusiasm, energy and potency. This is encapsulated in frequent fantasies about the sexual potency of certain groups and their danger to 'our' genteel womenfolk, an argument which Kamin (1993) forensically dismembers in a chapter that is worth citing if only for its coruscating title: 'On the length of black penises and the depth of white racism'. It is reflected, for instance, in the experience of the over one million three hundred thousand Indian troops who came to fight for Britain in the First World War (see Visram, 1986). Far from being thanked or feted, they were treated as a menace. Often, as with the Pavilion and Dome grounds in Brighton, their quarters were surrounded with high fences, not to protect them but to keep them in. To cite but one Indian voice: 'convicts in India are sent to the Andaman Islands; but we have found our convict station here in England' (Visram, 1986, p. 133).

As can be seen from this example, this way of looking at the 'race question' as a problem rooted in the nature of the oppressed group was very much bound up with the concerns of colonial masters and the issues of colonial rule. This is particularly well illustrated in a chapter on 'The crowd in primitive societies', written in 1934 by Georges Hardy. Hardy, Rector of the University of Algiers and an important French colonial administrator, sought to gain insight into his 'primitive' charges in order to understand better how to control and influence them. His insights are summarized in the following passage: 'the mentality of primitive people is above all a crowd mentality. That better explains such marked characteristics as a general weakness of judgement and of reasoning, conceptual incapacity, the absence of coherent inventions ... the permanent recourse to supernatural explanation, instability etc' (Hardy, 1934, p. 46, translation by the author).

After the Second World War, however, everything changed. The experience of Nazism during the war and the wave of decolonization that followed it led politicians and academics alike to reframe 'the race question' as a problem *for* the oppressed *caused by* the oppressor. The analytic gaze was shifted towards the dominant group – or at least certain members of it – in order to ask not 'what is wrong with the oppressed?' but rather 'what is wrong with those who justify oppression?' Why do they see black people (and others) as a problem? Why do they subscribe to the notion that certain groups are inferior? Why are they so prejudiced? This perspective is exemplified in the first words of the introduction to a UNESCO book, *Racism, Science and Pseudo-science*: 'any man, whether he be learned or no, who deems himself great enough to despise his fellows, is like a blind man holding a candle: he sees nothing himself, but he gives light to those around him' (Boisson, 1983, p. 11). Prejudice, that is, reveals to us something about its author, but not about its target.

Psychology played a fundamental part in this shift, and one text above all served to underpin it: Gordon Allport's *The Nature of Prejudice*, first published in 1954. As Pettigrew observed in his tribute to Allport twenty years after his death, '[the book] has organized the study of prejudice over the past 50 years' (1999, p. 415). The book is immensely readable (and should be read in the original). It is full of sparkling insights with which contemporary research, even half a century later, has still not caught up. To take just one example, there is a section on 'sensory aversion' in Chapter 8 where Allport discusses the embodied nature of prejudice – the fact that when people express distaste for others (the metaphor is not incidental) they frequently start by referring to the smell or sight or touch of others. Group theorists are only now returning to the role of emotion in intergroup relations (e.g. Tiedens and Leach, 2004; Parkinson *et al.*, 2004). Yet even here, emotion is generally linked to cognitive appraisals. The sensual dimension is not yet even on the agenda.

But, as I have already intimated, the real importance of Allport's book is far greater than the sum of its individual insights. It is about establishing prejudice as the problem and the origins of prejudiced perception as the subject of enquiry. The importance of this shift, both conceptually and socially, is hard to overestimate. Conceptually, it lies at the root of the perceptual and cognitive perspectives which so dominate our discipline, especially in its American heartland (although it should be acknowledged that non-cognitivist approaches have a somewhat larger hearing elsewhere, including South Africa – see, for instance, Levett *et al.*, 1996).

Socially, it challenges the perpetrator, not the victim of discrimination. In a world where migrant workers, asylum seekers and ethnic minorities are constantly blamed for the informal violence, the institutional procedures and the laws which afflict them, this remains an achievement of the greatest significance. What is more, Allport's own work, and the tradition he inspired, brings these conceptual and social commitments together in the form of contact research. To paraphrase Marx, the priority is not simply to understand prejudice but to change it. Work on contact has done precisely that, and its role in the desegregation of schools and other institutions in the US is probably the best example of 'action research' that psychology can muster (see Dovidio *et al.*, 2005; Pettigrew, 1979).

Any criticism of the Allportian 'prejudice problematic' must bear these achievements in mind. And yet my purpose in this chapter is precisely to criticize the premises upon which it is founded and thereby question 'contact' as the primary means of challenging prejudice. The spirit in which I do so is well expressed by Billig (1987). That is, any powerful argument alters the context in which it is expressed and therefore creates the terms of its own transcendence. The position I shall advance would not have been possible without the tradition that Allport initiated. My criticism should therefore be seen as much a recognition of (and tribute to) that work as an argument against it.

In essence my argument is that the current 'paradigm of prejudice' views the problem as resulting from the distorted and negative perceptions that ordinary members of a dominant group hold about ordinary members of subordinate groups. Prejudice reflects a fatal flaw in the human psyche – either that of particular individuals or that of human beings in general. The hatred of others is something done in error and from which no-one gains. Strategies to reduce prejudice must thereby concentrate on ways to correct the mistakes of the prejudiced mind. By contrast, I suggest that, wherever we find prejudice, it has been mobilized, it has been mobilized deliberately and it has been mobilized for gain. Strategies to reduce prejudice must therefore be based on counter-mobilization against prejudice. They are about collective action, not individual cognition, and they primarily involve those who are the targets of prejudice rather than the prejudiced themselves. In the next section, I will spell out my criticisms of the dominant 'perceptual' paradigm in more detail.

Four assumptions of the 'perceptual paradigm' of prejudice

The above-mentioned view that prejudice has to do with the 'distorted and negative perceptions that ordinary members of a dominant group hold about ordinary members of subordinate groups' carries four key assumptions. These are:

(1) prejudice is about *the outgroup*;
(2) prejudice is about *perceptions* of the outgroup;
(3) prejudice is about the *negative qualities* that are perceived in the outgroup;
(4) prejudice is about *ordinary group members* perceiving negative qualities in the outgroup.

All these assumptions lead to the conclusion that the solution to prejudice lies in *altering the views of dominant group members*. I shall examine this fifth tenet of the perceptual paradigm in the next section. For now let us look at each of the first four assumptions in turn.

(1) Prejudice is about the outgroup

It might seem so obvious as to be hardly worth saying but prejudice research is about looking at how prejudiced people see members of other groups. The explanatory focus may have shifted from the targets of prejudice to the prejudiced themselves. But what we are trying to explain is how the prejudiced look out on others in the world. It is about how the prejudiced see 'them'. After all, a statement like 'black people are stupid' is a statement about what 'they' are like. It raises questions about why 'they' are seen this way. It demands that we expend all our analytic efforts on understanding how people view others.

But are things really that straightforward? Consider again the statement 'black people are stupid'. To position someone as a member of a specific category (like black) is to presuppose the relevance of a particular category system ('race') and is therefore to categorize oneself ('I am white'). What is more, as social identity theorists stress (e.g. Tajfel, 1978; Tajfel and Turner, 1979), it is also to relate the other to the self. A statement about any group is comparative. To say 'they are stupid' is shorthand for saying 'they are more stupid than us', and is therefore not only to define who we are ('white') but also what we are like ('intelligent').

To take this one step further, if we move away from the rather abstracted statements which are typically used in psychological research, when people say something like 'black people are stupid' it is usually in the context of discussing some issue such as immigration or employment. The statement is part of a claim that 'they' constitute a problem for 'us' – i.e. 'let them in and they will drag us down' (cf. Miles, 1989). Hence it serves to specify not only how blacks compare to whites but also to appraise what blacks signify for whites.

So, we see that even the simplest statement of prejudice actually involves a rather rich view of how the world is organized, of how 'they' relate to 'us' and of what 'they' mean for 'us'. It requires us to consider the definition of both the ingroup and the outgroup. And, just as 'we' are implicitly defined through statements that are ostensibly just about 'them', so 'they' can be defined through statements that are ostensibly just about 'us' (thus to define oneself as 'white' is implicitly to position anyone 'black' as being outside 'our' group).

Indeed, we have argued that, even though ingroup and outgroup definitions are necessarily yoked together, it is often the definition of the ingroup that takes precedence in producing exclusion, inequality and oppression (Reicher *et al.*, 2008). Thus, even without mention of an outgroup, the way we define ourselves – what are the boundaries of the ingroup, who belongs and who doesn't belong – determines who reaps the various benefits of group membership. There is, by now, a substantial literature that documents how we tend to relate more positively to those we regard as fellow group members. We feel closer to them, trust and respect them more, cooperate with them, help them, support them (see Reicher and Haslam, 2009 for a review). This means that all those placed outside the group boundary are denied these positives: they are trusted, respected and helped less. To take but one example, when we define Scottish identity in inclusive terms as including all those living in the country and committed to the country we find more help given to a Chinese woman than when we define Scottishness exclusively, as reliant on being of Scottish descent (see Reicher *et al.*, 2010).

To appreciate the significance of these self definitions, consider the contrasting fate of Jewish people in Bulgaria and Germany during the Second World War. In the lands of old Bulgaria the Nazis twice pressured the regime to deport Jews to the death camps. Twice, the population mobilized to prevent the deportation. When we look to the basis of this mobilization (see Todorov, 2001) we find that there is little reference to Jews as Jews. Rather the emphasis is on an attack upon a national minority – on fellow Bulgarians. The cry is that 'we' are under threat of death, not 'they', and it thereby becomes self evident that 'we' – the national community – should stand up in solidarity against this attack (see Reicher *et al.*, 2006).

In Nazi Germany, too, there was much talk of national solidarity, of people standing together and of looking after others. In this respect there was no difference with Bulgaria. Indeed, Goebbels went so far as to insist that the first commandment for every national socialist was: 'love Germany above all else and your ethnic comrade as yourself!' (Koonz, 2003, p. 7). But, of course, the sting is in the tail. For the definition of the national community (among which such mutual love should thrive) is *ethnic*. Jews, gypsies and others stand outside these ethnic boundaries. They are excluded from the loving embrace of fellow Germans. So even if ingroup solidarity features equally in the two countries, the different definitions of ingroup boundaries lead to very different outcomes.

But, of course, the fate of the Jews under the Nazis went far beyond the mere denial of positive ingroup benefits. It involved the imposition of the most severe negative sanctions. But in this respect as well, the definition of the ingroup played a critical part. Koonz (2003) relates how, between 1933 and 1939, Hitler hardly ever spoke in public about the Jews. Rather, he constantly emphasized the virtue of the German people – exemplified not least by their selfless devotion to others. But this did not indicate any diminution of his anti-Semitism. To the contrary, it laid the ground for extreme anti-Semitic measures. For, once the Germans were established as a supremely virtuous people, then any threat to the nation could be constituted as an assault on virtue, and the elimination of that threat could be constituted as the defence of virtue. It was exactly this logic which allowed Himmler to address an audience of death camp officers as 'men with human kindness, with human hearts, and absolute kindness' (Koonz, 2003, p. 228).

In sum, then, the psychological path to genocide derives from two pairs of ingroup and outgroup definitions, in each of which the ingroup is the dominant term:

(1) ingroup boundaries – outgroup exclusion;
(2) ingroup virtue – outgroup threat.

My point, more generally, is that if we are to understand the nature of prejudice, we need once again to alter the way we look at the phenomenon. We need to broaden our gaze from looking at how the prejudiced see the other to looking at how the prejudiced see both self and other – and, moreover, we often have to privilege ingroup definitions over outgroup definitions. It is this, perhaps, which makes it so difficult to challenge prejudiced views. For it may be much easier to change what we think of 'them' than to alter what we think of ourselves.

(2) Prejudice is about (mis)perception

Prejudice is generally viewed as a result of flaws in the way people process information (especially the perception of groups) leading to errors in the way we see the nature of the world in front of us. Allport saw such distortions largely – though not exclusively – as a matter of individual differences. He states: 'prejudice is basically a *trait of personality*' (1958, p. 71; emphasis in the original). Or again: 'we come now to what is perhaps the most momentous discovery of psychological research in the field of prejudice. To state it broadly: the cognitive processes of prejudiced people are *in general* different from the cognitive processes of tolerant people' (1958, p. 170; emphasis again in the original).

Allport did, however, concede that perhaps there is a general tendency for all people to view members of other groups negatively. He himself viewed this as a factor of minor importance compared to the scale of differences between individuals – although it is intriguing to note that a visit to South Africa – where the racism of white people was the norm rather than the exception – may have led Allport to reappraise the relative importance of individual differences and generic group-level processes in prejudice. In the foreword to the 1958 edition of *The Nature of Prejudice*, Allport writes: 'I would, on the basis of my experience in South Africa, give extra weight to the portions of this book dealing with conformity and with socio-cultural factors in prejudice' (1958, p. vii).

Over time, the scales have tipped still further and (perhaps ironically) Allport is now generally invoked to support the notion that the ways that all human beings are wired to handle information leads to distorted and prejudiced perceptions. There are many variants of this argument. But perhaps the best known (the 'cognitive miser' viewpoint – see Fiske and Taylor, 1984) is that the human mind is not equipped to deal with the full complexity of the social world. We therefore simplify and distort information about other groups in order to be able to cope.

This view has its critics, but on the whole these tend to dispute the specifics of the perceptual processes underpinning the 'cognitive miser' approach. They do not dispute the focus on prejudice as a perceptual process. One exception lies in the work of Henri Tajfel and the tradition that he inspired of work on social identity processes (see Tajfel, 1981 for a collection of his seminal papers). But, as with Allport, what Tajfel actually said and how his work has been used are not one and the same thing. Tajfel did not deny the importance of perceptual processes. Indeed, he conducted some of the early seminal studies which show how we tend to overestimate differences between groups and underestimate differences within groups (Tajfel and Wilkes, 1963). Yet he also insisted that prejudice and discrimination were bound up with issues of power and ideology and politics. In a chapter written just before he died (Tajfel, 1981) he expressed his dismay that his studies of difference estimation had been taken in isolation and shaped a dominant perceptualist approach to stereotyping and prejudice that ignores their social dynamics. So, there are voices which tell us that prejudice is not simply about how we see the world. But even when they speak loud and clear, they tend not to be heard.

Nonetheless, let us try again, and, in order to do so, let us again consider the statement 'black people are stupid'. Certainly it is an observation about black people, and it is based on observations about the world: the levels of educational attainment of black people, the jobs that they occupy, and so on. But it is equally an explanation of that reality (black people fail at school because of their inherent inability and not the nature of the system) and a plan of how to deal with that reality (there is no point trying to promote black people into better jobs because they are doomed to fail). Indeed, in this last sense, a racist statement is a declaration of intent to keep black people in their place. It is about doing as much as saying. It is about shaping the future as much as about describing the present.

This is true at an interpersonal level. Someone who describes another as 'yid' or 'nigger' is acting to keep Jewish people or black people in their place. It is also true at a societal level. When slave traders declared Africans to lack a human soul it was to sustain an inhuman trade (see Fryer, 1984). Or else, when – just after the discovery of gold and diamonds – British colonialists declared black South African pastoralists to be 'lazy' it was to justify depriving them of their land and to force them to work underground in the mines (Harsch, 1979).

It follows from this that, if it is limiting to think of prejudice as perception, it is equally problematic to judge prejudice in terms of its accuracy. For if prejudice is about creating social reality as much as describing reality, the relevant question is not so much 'are such views right or wrong?' as 'are they effective?'. By the same token, it is of little benefit to judge the prejudiced in terms of their cognitive ability to tell right from wrong. A number of years ago, for instance, the British Commission for Racial Equality produced a poster showing four brains labelled 'Asian', 'African', 'European' and 'Racist', the first three being identical and the fourth being considerably smaller, the implication being racists are mentally limited and deficient. However, racists are not fools. They are people who are seeking to maintain and extend their privilege – and past and present histories of inequality show that they are all too skilful in doing so. The problem with racists, then, is not that they are wrong but that they are successful. And the problem of prejudice is less that it is false than that it all too often becomes true.

So, building on our first point, we can now see that prejudice is not just part of a rich model of how the world is. It is more a model of how the world should be and a part of the process of producing that world.

(3) Prejudice is about the negative qualities of the other

Although there is some controversy concerning exactly what sort of mental state is involved in prejudice – is it an affect, an attitude, how does it relate to cognitions (stereotypes)? – it is still true to say that, overall, prejudice is generally viewed as feeling and thinking bad things about others. It is certainly true that various oppressed groups such as black people, women, the disabled and so on are routinely described in highly negative terms – as irrational, emotional, stupid, lazy and so on (see Kidder and Stewart, 1975 for a general psychological analysis and Dower, 1986 for a situated historical example). At the same time, it is possible to think of seemingly positive attributes that are central to the stereotypes of certain disadvantaged categories – Jews as 'clever', Asians as 'hard-working' and so on. Indeed, sociological and historical studies suggest that even the most negative outgroup representations involve a degree of ambivalence. Moreover, as Glick and Fiske emphasize in Chapter 3, the justification of inequality may be accomplished via a 'complementary' blend of hostile and benevolent images of others.

Allport himself notes this phenomenon. Drawing on an example of Merton's, he notes that Abraham Lincoln was admired for being 'thrifty, hardworking, eager for knowledge, ambitious, devoted to the rights of the average man and eminently successful in climbing the ladder of opportunity' (1958, p. 184) – and that Jews are disliked for exactly the same characteristics. The lesson he draws from this is that stereotypes are not a full explanation for rejection. However, our analysis suggests a different explanation. That is, prejudice and stereotyping are about more than 'what we think of them' and hence the significance of any given quality cannot be determined simply from what it says about 'them'. Rather, prejudice and stereotyping are about our representation of the social world – of how they relate to us and what they signify for us. Hence the significance of any given quality is determined by what it says about how they impinge upon us. Does it indicate that the other is a problem for us or a boon to us? It is this which will determine if we are ill- or well-disposed to members of that other group (Miles, 1989).

Another way of saying this is that the meaning of characteristics cannot be understood if we abstract them from the way we see the broader relations between groups. And, when we do take this broader perspective, it not only becomes easily explicable why apparently positive characteristics might be a source of negative attitudes, it becomes almost inevitable that we attribute positive characteristics to those we dislike, hate and fear.

The clue lies in the word 'fear'. For why should we fear another – why should we see them as a problem to us – if they have no ability to challenge us in any way? In the nineteenth century, for instance, there was a profound and widespread fear of the newly formed masses of the industrial age. For the social elite, the ever-present concern was that these masses would rise up and tear apart the existing social fabric. This was translated into a stereotype of the mass and the crowd as mindless, emotional, fickle and barbaric (views which still persist both in society and in psychology; see Reicher and Potter, 1985). However, as Barrows (1981) points out, this is only to look at one side of the story. Crowds were also seen as vibrant, energetic and, as a consequence, powerful. In a word, crowds were *potent*.

What is more, as Nye (1995) points out, this ambivalent representation of the crowd was matched by an ambivalent evaluation. Crowds were certainly fearful things, yes, but they were also admirable things. The social elite saw the turbulent masses as simultaneously the nemesis and the saviour of an increasingly dissolute and decadent society. Moreover, the one crowd psychologist whose ideas ultimately took root, Gustave Le Bon, succeeded less because of his theoretical originality than his eminently practical emphasis on harnessing the energies of the mass for the interests of the bourgeoisie (Le Bon, 1895).

This notion of potency has more general application. Anti-Semites do not hate Jews because of their industry and intelligence. They hate Jews because their industry and intelligence make them a potent threat. For different groups, the attribution of potency may take different forms: racists view Asian people as hard working; they see black people as physically and sexually powerful. However, in every case we find that it is far too simple to suggest that the more hostile people are to a given group, the more their view of the group will comprise a bundle of negative characteristics.

There are a number of points here that are worth commenting upon. One concerns the importance of *ambivalence*. Academic psychology often seems to view human thought as very compartmentalized: we either see things one way or the other, as right or wrong, good or bad, or whatever. We organize our studies and our analyses accordingly. But when we look at how people think in the world, we generally find things to be much more nuanced (Billig, 1987). We see right and wrong in the same thing, we see good and bad in the same group. Our views of others are generally highly ambivalent.

The next point is to stress, again, that we will never grasp what people think of others by treating their views as an abstract list of characteristics. We need to put the elements together in two ways: first, how the characteristics fit together to give an overall picture of the other; and second, how the nature of the other has consequences for us. The meaning of any given element is entirely dependent upon how it fits into this overall picture and hence carries no particular meaning and has no particular implications on its own.

Last, then, we come back to the point that prejudice needs to be understood as something much wider than just our perception of others. It needs to be seen as an element within our overall orientation to the social relations that constitute our social world. What is a problem from the narrow perspective (that we may look negatively at others for having ostensibly positive qualities) becomes easily and instantly explicable from the broader perspective (those qualities are precisely what makes them a problem for us). In short, this specific issue of 'qualities' is highly diagnostic of the general difference between paradigms.

(4) Prejudice is about the views of ordinary people

In all that has been written thus far, the suggestion has been that prejudice is something that people come to on their own. The assumption is that we come to our views of others unaided, through solitary contemplation and as a function of the inner workings of our minds. The more one thinks about it, the more bizarre this perspective comes to seem. It is a sad, strange and very lonely view of the world (cf. Condor, 1996) – a solitary world of silence in which people never talk to each other and never hear what others have to say. It may be the type of world that we might try to create within our experimental studies (for fear of compromising the independence of different participants) but, apart from the occasional hermit, it is not the type of world we would recognize outside.

In practice, it would be hard to avoid the views of others even if we wanted to. When it comes to how we should view and treat others – what should we do about immigration? Do we need tougher laws to outlaw racism? and so on – our experience is not of silence but of a fearful cacophony. Politicians, activists and the media are all blaring at us, telling us what the issues are and how we should respond. To analyse prejudice without taking this into account is not only bizarre, it is dangerous. It exonerates those activists and politicians who actively peddle a world view in which 'we' are endangered by the presence of others – though, once again, in criticizing the tradition generated by Allport, we must exonerate Allport himself who devoted a whole chapter to racist leadership (Chapter 26: Demagogy): an issue almost totally neglected in subsequent research. Indeed, neither leadership nor demagogy are even mentioned in Dovidio *et al.*'s (2005) fiftieth anniversary retrospective on *The Nature of Prejudice*.

The critical point, then, is that our views of how others relate to us in the world (and of what should be done about it) do not arise spontaneously. They are *mobilized*. And leaders do not mobilize prejudice by accident or by chance. There are very good reasons to invoke hostility towards out-groups and these have to do with the psychological dynamics of influence and power. In order to understand this, we need to recognize two things about leadership (Haslam *et al.*, 2010; Reicher *et al.*, 2007). First, leadership is essentially a group process. Leaders are never just leaders. They are always leaders of a nation, a political party, an organization, a religious denomination or whatever. Second, leaders are able to gain the support of group members to the extent that they are seen as supporting the group interest and representing group values. Or, to put it the other way around, those leaders who are successful in portraying themselves and their proposals as representing a group position will be able to mobilize the power of the collective to achieve their ends.

There are at least four ways in which denigration of the outgroup can help establish the leader's authority and influence over the ingroup. First, as Thomas Hobbes (1651/1998) recognized in his *Leviathan* long ago, outside threat is the fundamental justification for any sort of authority. 'Why should anyone accede to a sovereign?' he asked. And he answered his own question: 'out of fear of death'. What is more, a particular leader can claim their credentials by identifying an outgroup threat and being seen to stand up against it. Ludden (2005) provides a contemporary example of this. He argues that the rise of communalism in India can be related to a change in the traditional bases of authority for the Congress Party. Previously, votes had been delivered by a system of clientelism whereby 'head men' in villages and towns could deliver blocks of voters. As this declined, so Congress sought to appeal directly to voters, and they did this by claiming to defend them against Muslim encroachments.

Second, one can identify an outgroup threat in order to accuse one's rivals of a failure to defend the ingroup and hence of forfeiting their right to represent the group interest. Thus, to pursue the Indian example, contemporary Hindu nationalists in India invoke a variety of outgroup threats, not only Muslims but also Christians, Arabs and foreign corporations. The one constant in their accusations is the claim that government has failed to respond to these threats – either out of complacency, out of lack of concern or even out of direct collusion with the enemy (see Reicher *et al.*, 2006). Whatever the reason, the conclusion is that the government no longer has the ability of the right to represent Indians.

Third, those in power can use the notion that 'we are under threat' to demand unity and loyalty from rivals and to suggest that attacks which undermine existing authority are attacks on the group as a whole. Such techniques were clearly used by Stalin to eliminate his internal enemies in the 1930s. These purges are generally referred to as 'the terror'. But, as Overy (2004) points out, according to the discourse of the time, the purges were a necessary response to those who weakened the nation in the face of the Nazi terror. More recently, Slobodan Milosevic in Serbia generated hostility and war against Croatia and Bosnia in order to marginalize dissent against his own regime (Gagnon, 2004). In this regard, the mobilization of hostility can be seen as the demobilization of potential movements against authority.

The fourth use of outgroup hostility also has to do with subduing dissent and ensuring compliance – though, this time, more with regard to ordinary group members than rivals for power and more in relation to policing particular forms of behaviour than outlawing disagreement in general. As illustration, Peukert (1987) argues that Nazi anti-Semitism served a crucial function in policing the German population. Anyone who behaved in ways associated with Jews came under suspicion of being an 'alien' and was at least potentially liable to the terrible fate that awaited the Jews (the more so because the definition of Jewishness was profoundly ambiguous). To the extent that these behaviours were the antithesis of those which constituted the Nazi representation of German identity, this meant that – on pain of death – there was no room for departing from Nazi norms. More generally, dominant views of how group members should act can be effectively policed by associating alternative versions with a demonized outgroup.

This four-part listing is not meant to be exhaustive. Rather, it is meant to show, on the one hand, that leadership is critical to an understanding of prejudice, and, on the other, that prejudice may serve as a particularly potent tool of leadership. Keeping outsiders in their place is a good way for leaders to consolidate their own place (and also, although I have had less time to deal with this explicitly, of allowing ordinary group members to maintain their place in the world). Leaders mobilize prejudice, and followers are mobilized to be prejudiced, because important social functions are thereby served. We simply cannot understand why outgroup antipathies emerge, when they emerge or the forms they take without taking mobilization and its functions into account. Nor can we devise effective strategies to challenge prejudice.

Challenging prejudice: the limits of contact

Problems and solutions are inextricably interlinked. If prejudice and discrimination derive from dominant group misperceptions of the subordinate group then the solution is to try and correct those misperceptions and the obvious way to do so is to bring people into contact so they can see what the other is really like.

There is a huge literature (and a huge industry) devoted to contact (see Pettigrew, 1986, 1998) and – while the findings are complex and the effects of contact are heavily dependent upon the conditions under which it occurs – the headline story seems to be that, overall, contact leads dominant group members to think more positively and to be more friendly towards subordinate group members (Pettigrew and Tropp, 2006). But the question that we need to ask is not so much whether contact leads us to like outgroup members, but whether liking outgroup members is the way to get rid of prejudice. In other words, does contact theory have an adequate model of social change? This is a question addressed in more detail by other chapters of this book, especially the chapters by Wright and Baray (Chapter 11), Dovidio *et al.* (Chapter 12) and Dixon and Levine (Conclusion).

To start with, we need to ask whether a positive attitude to outgroup members necessarily indicates a lack of prejudice. Now, of course, if prejudice is defined in terms of this attitude, the answer has to be yes. But, as we begin to challenge this definition, the answer becomes less clear cut. Changing one's view of others does not change the view that they are other. That is, it leaves untouched how we see the ingroup and hence the fact that the people in question belong to an outgroup. To be more concrete, liking black people does not, in and of itself, change whether we see them as fully British (or French or American or whatever) and hence whether they are fully deserving of the rights and privileges of British people.

What is more, liking others does not necessarily change the way we view their relationship, as a group, to our group. Others may be seen as charming and delightful people, but still their presence may be a problem for 'us' (and perhaps even their delightful and charming nature may exacerbate the problem if, for instance, it helps them gain power and position in our midst). In this regard, I am reminded of the experience of Charlie Husband, author of a very influential text on '"Race" in Britain' (Husband, 1982), while interviewing people about immigration. Charlie first talked to a young man who was full of racist bile, who spoke of black people in hateful terms and who insisted that they be kept out of the country. Next, a very different young man came through the door. He expressed horror at racist prejudice. He spoke of black people with care and respect. But then he sadly concluded that we must have immigration controls to protect race relations. So, for all their difference in the traditional terms of prejudice, both saw the presence of black people in Britain as a problem and both supported the same measures to keep black people out. Indeed, as Essed (1991) suggests, it might even be that the latter type of individual is ultimately more problematic for black people than the former. For if, as a minority group member, you are treated badly and shut out, there is at least a clear target against which to fight back. However, if you are treated kindly but still shut out, it is harder to identify your experience as racism and you are more reluctant to treat the agent of your exclusion as your foe. This is a crucial point to which I shall return shortly.

For now, though, I want to add just one more caution to the limits of 'niceness' as the antidote to prejudice. It leaves the power of racist mobilization entirely untouched. Above, I referred to the use of hate by Milosevic in Serbia. The tragedy was that, at first, many Serbs completely rejected the notion of ancient antipathies between themselves and their Balkan neighbours. They had highly harmonious relations with Croats and Bosnians. Many were friends or were even married. But once Milosevic was able to mobilize some Serbs to attack these groups, and once these groups in turn became distrustful and hostile to Serbs, so it became difficult to avoid the spiral of conflict and friendships, even partnerships, were torn apart (Gagnon, 2004). Niceness does not stop the process of mobilization. It does not innoculate people against being drawn into the process of mobilization. It is necessary to understand the dynamics of mobilization and intervene in them directly to challenge and undermine the authority of those who propagate hate.

But, having raised the issue of mobilizing the dominant group, let us now return to the mobilization of the subordinate group. And here we confront what is perhaps the most profound problem with the contact approach. That is, its focus is almost entirely upon changing the views of the dominant group and the underlying assumption is that the way to stop oppression is to stop the oppressors being oppressive. But, not for the first time, we find a way of looking at the phenomenon which is completely at odds with reality.

The lesson of history is that dominant groups hardly ever just give away their power. It is taken from them by the collective action of subordinate group members. It may be that we continue (quite literally) to be told tales in school that make those in power seem magnanimous, but it takes little excavation to discover the limits of these accounts. Thus, British children have long been taught that William Wilberforce abolished slavery. Clearly Wilberforce is a figure of considerable importance, but ultimately, he was giving legal expression to the reality that – through the resistance and revolt of the slaves themselves – slavery was no longer politically feasible or economically viable (Fryer, 1984; James, 1980).

Or else, to take a contemporary example, one will find the following statement if one looks up the Wikipedia entry for the former white president of South Africa, F.W. De Klerk: 'De Klerk is best known for engineering the end of apartheid' (http://en.wikipedia.org/wiki/Frederik_Willem_de_Klerk). Certainly de Klerk played an important role, but it was principally to recognize that the old system had been fought to a standstill by the black struggle and that change had to come. In South Africa, as elsewhere, no one hands over freedom on a plate. It has to be claimed through a long and arduous black struggle – a struggle that was certainly helped by solidarity among the privileged both in South Africa itself and in the international

Anti-Apartheid Movement (Fielding, 2004), but nonetheless a struggle which ultimately played the determining role in producing change.

Now, at best the emphasis on contact underplays the importance of the mobilizations of the oppressed. It privileges the privileged over the oppressed in the abolition of privilege. It also distracts our attention from understanding (and supporting) anti-racist mobilization. But, at worst, the emphasis on contact and its beneficial effects upon the attitudes of the privileged actually undermines anti-racist mobilization. This is the point to which I promised to return. There are a variety of processes through which demobilization may occur. The one I alluded to above concerned the difficulty of seeing 'nice people' as the enemy and hence of conducting a struggle against them. Another, also referred to by Essed (1991), is the way in which 'friendly exclusion' leads people to doubt an understanding of their experience as racism: 'how could such a nice person be a racist, perhaps I was not denied resource because of my group membership but because of something I myself did'. A third, for which there is more systematic evidence, is that friendliness from dominant group members encourages the sense that the social system is permeable (that is, subordinate group members can achieve full success in society), which in turn makes collective action redundant (Saguy *et al.*, 2009; Tausch *et al.*, 2008; Wright, 2001). In short, contact might make for a more civil society, but it maintains an unequal society.

But perhaps I have overstated the case. And perhaps there is more to learn than I have indicated from the lessons of history. For, while it is true that social change is the success of the oppressed, it is nonetheless true that the chances of success are much enhanced by divisions which limit the ability of dominant groups to maintain their privilege. The Anti-Apartheid Movement certainly made it harder for Western governments and Western corporations to continue supporting the Apartheid State, and this in turn made it harder for the Apartheid State to continue suppressing their own population. So there is nothing wrong in exploring ways (such as contact) to make dominant group members question inequality, as long as it is acknowledged that these must be ancillary to (rather than predominate over) the core question of facilitating the mobilization of subordinate group members.

Conclusion

In this chapter, I have sought to make three broad points. The first is that 'prejudice' should be understood as a rich representational practice. It is bound up with 'our' understanding of what 'they' mean for 'us' – and, more specifically, in constituting 'them' as a problem for 'us'. It is bound up with managing this threat by putting and keeping them 'in their place'.

I made various points about the implications of this view, not least that our understanding of prejudice – and hence both our analytic and practical focus – should lie as much with how we define the ingroup as with how we define the outgroup.

My second point is that these understandings and practices do not arise spontaneously in the individual, but rather that they are mobilized. Leaders, activists, journalists and others constantly tell us about what the presence of others means and what should be done about it. We therefore need to incorporate leadership as a critical element in the understanding of prejudice and racism and, equally, racism and prejudice give us insight into the ways that leadership works and how people are able to get authority over a group.

Third, then, I equally argue that we need to understand the way of challenging racism and prejudice in terms of mobilization. These are not the result of ignorance and error but of motivated social action. They will therefore be eliminated not by clarification but by struggle. Therefore, the key questions are, how can we fracture racist mobilizations and build anti-racist mobilizations? Initiatives such as contact may play a role in the former but they must not continue to dominate over an understanding of when and how the oppressed will act together to challenge their shared position.

By now, then, the meaning of my title 'from perception to mobilization' should be clear. I am advocating a mobilization analysis of prejudice. Like any such shift, this serves as much to define new questions as to provide new answers (see Elcheroth *et al.*, 2011). Thus, to view prejudice as mobilization impels us to address the following questions:

- First, how is prejudice mobilized? What sorts of constructions of 'them' and 'us' lead 'us' to exclude and even hate 'them'?
- Second, why is hate mobilized? What leads people to highlight the existence of a threatening other?
- Third, when is hate mobilization successful? What leads people to take on board the idea that others threaten them and to respond with hostility?
- Fourth, how can we weaken racist mobilization and strengthen mobilizations against racism?

In these pages, I have begun to provide some embryonic answers to these questions, and I have provided some lengthier answers elsewhere (e.g. Haslam *et al.*, 2010; Reicher *et al.*, 2008). But there is far more to be done. This chapter has been an agenda setting exercise. Its success will be measured in my ability to persuade others that these questions are worth pursuing and to fill in the many gaps that remain in our knowledge of prejudice and racism in society.

Notes

1. This can be accessed at http://unesdoc.unesco.org/images/0012/001282/128291eo.pdf.
2. See www.un.org/durbanreview2009/pdf/Durban_Review_outcome_document_En.pdf, point 5.
3. See www.un.org/News/Press/docs/2009/sgsm12193.doc.htm.

References

Allport, G. W. (1954). *The Nature of Prejudice*. Boston, MA: Addison-Wesley. (1958). *The Nature of Prejudice*. New York: Doubleday Anchor.
Barrows, S. (1981). *Distorting Mirrors*. New Haven, CT: Yale University Press.
Bibby, C. (1959). *Race, Prejudice and Education*. Paris: UNESCO.
Billig, M. (1987). *Arguing and Thinking*. Cambridge, UK: Cambridge University Press.
Boisson, J. (1983). Introduction. In UNESCO, *Racism, Science and Pseudo-science*. Paris: UNESCO.
Condor, S. (1996). Unimagined community: social psychological issues concerning English national identity. In G. Breakwell and E. Lyons (eds.), *Changing European Identities: Social Psychological Analyses of Social Change* (pp. 285–316). Oxford, UK: Butterworth-Heinemann.
Dovidio, J. F., Glick, P. and Rudman, L. A. (2005). *On the Nature of Prejudice*. Oxford, UK: Blackwell.
Dower, J. W. (1986). *War Without Mercy*. New York: Pantheon Books.
Elcheroth, G., Doise, W. and Reicher, S. D. (2011). On the knowledge of politics and the politics of knowledge: how a social representations approach helps us rethink the subject of political psychology, *Political Psychology*, **32**, 729–58.
Essed, P. (1991). *Understanding Everyday Racism*. London: Sage.
Fielding, R. (2004). *Anti-Apartheid: a History of the Movement in Britain 1959–1994*. London: Merlin Press.
Fiske, S. T. and Taylor, S. E. (1984). *Social Cognition*. New York: McGraw-Hill.
Fryer, D. (1984). *Staying Power*. London: Pluto.
Gagnon, V. P. (2004). *The Myth of Ethnic War*. Ithaca, NY: Cornell University Press.
Gould, S. J. (1997). *The Mismeasure of Man*. New York: Allen Lane.
Hardy, G. (1934). La foule dans les sociétés dites primitives. In Centre International de Synthèse, *La Foule*. Paris: Félix Alcan.
Harsch, E. (1979). *South Africa: White Rule, Black Revolt*. New York: Monad.
Haslam, S. A., Reicher, S. D. and Platow, M. (2010). *The New Psychology of Leadership*. London: Psychology Press.
Hobbes, T. (1651/1998). *Leviathan*. Oxford, UK: Oxford Paperbacks.
Husband, C. (1982). *Race in Britain: Continuity and Change*. London: Hutchinson University Library.
James, C. L. R. (1980). *The Black Jacobins*. London: Allison and Busby.
Kamin, L. J. (1974). *The Science and Politics of IQ*. London: Routledge. (1993). On the length of black penises and the depths of white racism. In L. J. Nicholas (ed.), *Psychology and Oppression*. Johannesburg: Skotaville.

Kidder, L. H. and Stewart, V. M. (1975). *Psychology of Intergroup Relations.* New York: McGraw-Hill.

Koonz, C. (2003). *The Nazi Conscience.* Cambridge, MA: Harvard University Press.

Le Bon, G. (1895, trans. 1947). *The Crowd: a Study of the Popular Mind.* London: Ernest Benn.

Levett, A., Kottler, A., Burman, E. and Parker, I. (1996). *Culture, Power and Discourse: Discourse Analysis in South Africa.* London: Zed Books.

Lévi-Strauss, C. (1952). *Race and History.* Paris: UNESCO.

Ludden, D. (2005). *Making India Hindu.* Delhi: Oxford University Press.

Miles, R. (1989). *Racism.* London: Routledge.

Nye, R. (1995). Savage crowds, modernism and modern politics. In E. Barkan and R. Bush (eds.), *Prehistories of the Future: the Primitivist Project and the Culture of Modernism.* Stanford, CA: Stanford University Press.

Overy, R. (2004). *The Dictators.* London: Allen Lane.

Parkinson, B., Fischer, A. and Manstead, A. (2004). *Emotion in Social Relations.* Hove, UK: Psychology Press.

Pettigrew, T. F. (1979). Foreword. In G. W. Allport, *The Nature of Prejudice.* Cambridge, MA: Perseus Books.

(1986). The intergroup contact hypothesis reconsidered. In M. Hewstone and R. Brown (eds.), *Contact and Conflict in Intergroup Encounters.* Oxford, UK: Blackwell.

(1998). Intergroup contact theory. *Annual Review of Psychology,* **49,** 65–85.

Pettigrew, T. F. and Tropp, L. R. (2006). A meta-analytic test of inter-group contact theory. *Journal of Personality and Social Psychology,* **90,** 751–83.

Peukert, D. J. K. (1987). *Inside Nazi Germany: Conformity, Opposition and Racism in Everyday Life.* New Haven, CT: Yale University Press.

Reicher, S. D. and Haslam, S. A. (2009). Beyond help: a social psychology of collective solidarity and social cohesion. In S. Sturmer and M. Snyder (eds.), *The Psychology of Prosocial Behaviour* (pp.289–310). Oxford, UK: Wiley-Blackwell.

Reicher, S. D. and Potter, J. (1985). Psychological theory as intergroup perspective: a comparative analysis of 'scientific' and 'lay' accounts of crowd events. *Human Relations,* **38,** 167–89.

Reicher, S. D., Cassidy, C., Hopkins, N., Levine, M. and Wolpert, I. (2006). Saving Bulgaria's Jews: an analysis of social identity and the mobilisation of social solidarity. *European Journal of Social Psychology,* **36,** 49–72.

Reicher, S. D., Haslam, S. A. and Platow, M. (2007). The new psychology of leadership. *Scientific American Mind,* Aug/Sep, 22–9.

Reicher, S. D., Haslam, S. A. and Rath, R. (2008). Making a virtue of evil: a five step model of the development of collective hate. *Social and Personality Psychology Compass,* **2,** 1,313–44.

Reicher, S. D., Hopkins, N. P. and Harrison, K. (2010). Identity matters: on the importance of Scottish identity for Scottish society. In F. Bechhofer and D. McCrone (eds.), *National Identity, Nationalism and Constitutional Change* (pp.17–40). London: Palgrave Macmillan.

Reicher, S. D., Hopkins, N., Levine, M. and Rath, R. (2006). Entrepreneurs of hate and entrepreneurs of solidarity: social identity as a basis for mass communication. *International Review of the Red Cross,* **87,** 621–37.

Rose, A. (1951). *The Roots of Prejudice*. Paris: UNESCO.

Saguy, T., Tausch, N., Dovidio, J. F. and Pratto, F. (2009). The irony of harmony: positive intergroup contact produces false expectations for equality. *Psychological Science*, **20**, 114–21.

Tajfel, H. (1978). *Differentiation Between Social Groups*. London: Academic Press. (1981). *Human Groups and Social Categories*. Cambridge, UK: Cambridge University Press.

Tajfel, H. and Turner, J. C. (1979). An integrative theory of intergroup conflict. In W. G. Austin and S. Worchel (eds.), *The Social Psychology of Intergroup Relations* (pp.33–47). Monterey, CA: Brooks/Cole.

Tajfel, H. and Wilkes, A. L. (1963). Classification and quantitative judgement. *British Journal of Psychology*, **54**, 101–14.

Tausch, N., Saguy, T., Dovidio, J. F. and Pratto, F. (2008). *The Irony of Harmony: Examining the Effects of Intergroup Contact on Social Change*. Paper presented at EAESP-SPSS Joint Small Group Meeting 'Intergroup contact: recent advancements in basic and applied research', Marburg, Germany.

Tiedens, L. A. and Leach, C. W. (2004). *The Social Life of Emotions*. Cambridge, UK: Cambridge University Press.

Todorov, T. (2001). *The Fragility of Goodness*. London: Weidenfeld and Nicolson.

Visram, R. (1986). *Ayahs, Lascars and Princes: Asians in Britain 1700–1947*. London: Pluto Press.

Wright, S. (2001). Strategic collective action: social psychology and social change. In R. Brown and S. Gaertner (eds.), *Blackwell Handbook of Social Psychology: Intergroup Processes* (pp. 409–30). London: Blackwell Press.

2   Prejudice, social identity and social change: resolving the Allportian problematic

Katherine J. Reynolds, S. Alexander Haslam and John C. Turner

> The world as a whole suffers from panic induced by rival ideologies of east and west, each corner of the earth has its own special burdens of animosity. Moslems distrust non-moslems. Jews who escaped extermination in Central Europe find themselves in the new State of Israel surrounded by anti-Semitism. Refugees roam inhospitable lands. Many of the colored people of the world suffer indignities at the hands of whites who invent a fanciful racist doctrine to justify their condescension. Allport (1954, p. xiii)

It requires little imagination to identify the similarities between current events and this description offered by Gordon Allport in the preface to his seminal 1954 text, *The Nature of Prejudice*. In the same opening pages, Allport also expresses his optimism that psychological science will ultimately be able to shed light not only on matters of 'material progress' but also on issues of human nature and social relationships that might help understand the factors that are responsible for both hatred and tolerance (p. xiv). Yet at the same time as arguing that this scientific study of social relations should be possible, he states that it 'required years of labor and billions of dollars to gain the secret of the atom. It will take a still greater investment to gain the secrets of man's irrational nature' (p. xv). And, as a final reflection, he notes that it 'is easier, someone has said, to smash an atom than a prejudice' (p. xv).

There is no doubt that the issue of prejudice has consumed many minds and research budgets in the intervening five decades since Allport expressed these views. But what progress has been made? What are the obstacles to progress? And are we yet at a point of knowing how to 'smash a prejudice'? More significantly, perhaps, we might ask whether Allport's goal was realistic and whether it ever will be.

Sadly, one of those contributors, Professor John Turner, passed away during the production of this book. He will be remembered as an immense social psychologist who contributed profoundly to the development of our discipline. We are proud that something of the nature of his theoretical imagination and contribution is captured in Chapter 2 of our book.

In this chapter we explore the state of the science of prejudice from a social psychological perspective. Through this analysis it becomes clear that, although much has been achieved, a fundamental obstacle to progress lies in the theory of prejudice that underpins the very definition of the topic and, more specifically, the meta-theory that informs usage of the term 'prejudice' as it is widely understood both by researchers and in society at large (e.g. Oakes *et al.*, 1994; Turner, 1996, 2001; Turner and Reynolds, 2001).

Famously, Allport himself defined prejudice as 'thinking ill of others without sufficient warrant' (a definition that was itself derived from the moral philosophy of Thomas Aquinas and his followers; see Stangor, 2000, p. 22). Influenced strongly by this definition, prejudice is typically defined as a negative attitude towards members of a given group based exclusively on their membership of that group (e.g. see Brown, 1995, p. 6). It is also assumed, either implicitly or explicitly, that these attitudes are, in some deep sense, both unfounded and unreasonable. As a defining topic both in social psychology as a whole and in the study of intergroup relations, prejudice is thus widely regarded as irrational and unjustifiable. There is already an explanation for prejudice in its definition – 'faulty and flawed' psychology.

Each of us can point to negative outgroup attitudes which we are more than willing to condemn as irrational, objectionable and problematic for all kinds of reasons: political, moral, religious or scientific. A critical question, though, is whether, in whole or in part, any of these kinds of attitudes – or even the positive attitudes which we may hold towards certain groups – are in any sense a product of irrationality, limitation, error, flaw or failing in the functioning of human psychology. It needs to be emphasized that to question the prejudice meta-theory of 'faulty and flawed' psychology is not to question whether prejudice exists, or the negative, harmful affairs that flow from its expression.

A trajectory of work has emerged over many years that, while recognizing the harm and negativity of prejudice as a phenomenon, offers a new scientific theory of prejudice. In this chapter our review charts the emergence of this rethinking of the nature of prejudice, and argues that it is only made possible by questioning the assumptions embodied in the definition of prejudice itself (Turner, 2001; Turner and Reynolds, 2001). Based on work on the nature of the self-process, stereotyping and social change, it is clear that a reappraisal was required, and is gaining momentum (of which this book as a whole is testament). Moreover, this reappraisal relies heavily on work by Allport himself, but also that of Sherif, Asch, Lewin and Tajfel (and many others). It is clear that in a range of social situations people's behaviour is determined by their group memberships and by the sense of social identity with which they are associated. Going further, we see that prejudice is bound up with the dynamics of ongoing intergroup relations, and the way that people make sense of these relations and form a shared collective view of their social world (e.g. Tajfel, 1969; Tajfel and Turner, 1979).

Appreciation of these points takes us towards a position from which we see that the process of perceiving and judging people in terms of group membership need not necessarily be faulty. More strongly still, we assert that prejudice can veridically represent aspects of intergroup relations as they are apprehended from a particular social vantage point (Oakes *et al.*, 1994; Turner and Oakes, 1997). In this way, as Sherif (1967) argued, there is a 'psycho-logic' to prejudice that is derived from, and which serves to reflect, important social realities. Ultimately, too, it is this recognition that prejudice flows from social realities, through group identities and associated political and social ideologies, to shape the psychology of the individual, that defines the new theory of prejudice. This not only exposes our prejudices about prejudice, but also shows that the key to 'smashing prejudice' is not psychological readjustment but *social change* within which the narrative of prejudice plays an integral part.

The prevailing meta-theory of prejudice: the Allportian problematic

Prejudice is always with us. It is a fact of life and is born of fear and ignorance. It will continue to flourish, like a virus, wherever fear and ignorance have a stranglehold. (Bell (2006))

One might well assume not only that prejudice is 'always with us', but that it always has been. Yet, as both an area of scientific enquiry and as a topic of public discourse, prejudice only emerged in the 1920s and 1930s (Richards, 1997). Prior to that, as Dixon and Levine discuss in this book's Introduction, for most of the second half of the nineteenth century, psychology embraced a doctrine of scientific racism. This meant that psychologists believed that race was a critical scientific construct. Indeed, reflecting this, there was a domain of study called 'race psychology', within which researchers sought to explore the psychological differences between supposedly biological entities called 'races'. From this perspective the construct of race was rarely questioned, and the quest to describe and explain 'racial differences' was taken as self-evidently valid and justifiable. It was only in the 1920s, when psychologists and social scientists in the US and elsewhere started to abandon these doctrines of scientific racism, that prejudice as a field got under way. The term was not needed before this time because these attitudes were not previously considered irrational or prob-lematic. They were assumed to be a reasonable response to real differences between groups that had a clear scientific basis.

For the purposes of our analysis, the process whereby scientists and society moved away from this position is highly instructive. On the one hand, it arose partly from the failure of the scientific project that defined race psychology, which produced only weak evidence for the essential notion that there were fundamental psychological differences between 'races'. At the same time, though, the emergence of 'prejudice' as a concept and field was also a function of significant political, social, historical and ideological changes in the US and elsewhere. As a result, social scientists began to feel uncomfortable with the agenda of race psychology, and ultimately came to understand it as fundamentally racist. Associated with this shift, the legitimacy of 'race'-based attitudes was also fundamentally re-evaluated. Indeed, in the space of just a few generations these moved from being seen as rational, justified and unproblematic to being seen as irrational, unjustifiable and unacceptable. In short, attitudes that were once seen as a reflection of social reality came to be seen as a social problem. Moreover, psychologists and other social scientists now found that they had something called 'prejudice' to describe, to measure, to explain and to seek to eradicate (see Brown, 1995; Duckitt, 1992; Richards, 1997, for detailed reviews).

From the very outset the definition of the prejudice field and of the prejudice problematic implied a definite approach to explanation. Because the social judgement that these attitudes were irrational and unjustifiable was highly political, the trend in theory was to focus on psychological irrationality and psychological flaws in the people who held such views. Clear examples of this point can be found in early approaches to prejudice that were couched in terms of *scapegoating* and the *prejudiced personality*.

Initial work on scapegoating saw prejudice as a manifestation of unconscious and irrational defence mechanisms, such as repression and projection. The influential work of John Dollard and his Yale colleagues led to the publication of the seminal text *Frustration and Aggression* (Dollard *et al.*, 1939). Heavily influenced by Freudian theory, this publication outlined the 'scapegoating' theory of prejudice. This analysis asserted that in their daily lives people experience a range of frustrations for all kinds of reasons. These frustrations are assumed to lead to aggressive tendencies and needs that are often hard to channel appropriately. For example, if your (male) boss keeps overloading you with work while at the same time refusing to give you a pay rise, it may be hard to confront him directly in order to improve your situation. Accordingly, aggressive energy may continue to build up – so that a reservoir of instinctual aggression is accumulated – that has to be released. And in the absence of being able to direct this towards the target of that aggression, it may be 'displaced' onto safer and more vulnerable targets. If you can't take it out on your boss, you may take it out on your (female) secretary instead. Rather than being legitimate targets of aggression, these targets are therefore psychological scapegoats.

In this way, Dollard and colleagues suggested that victims of scapegoating tend to be members of minority groups who are in the scapegoater's field of view but who are weaker and of lower social status. But by definition, the motivational dynamics that underpin this process were understood to be irrational. This was because, once triggered by some stimulus, state or event, scapegoating produced hostility automatically – through a sequence that was defined purely psychologically and which was affected neither by the social context nor by any meaningful social relationship between aggressor and victim.

The second example of prejudice being seen as the product of psychological flaws emerged in the aftermath of the Second World War, as prejudice researchers focused on the challenging task of explaining the psychological underpinnings of Nazism, Fascism and anti-Semitism. At this time the American Jewish Committee commissioned a series of books, the most famous of which was *The Authoritarian Personality*, coauthored by Theodor Adorno, Else Frenkel-Brunswik and colleagues at Berkeley (Adorno *et al.*, 1950). This centred on the idea that, as a result of their upbringing, certain individuals develop conflicted and maladjusted personalities that dispose them towards expressions of prejudice. As the researchers put it:

A basically hierarchical, authoritarian, exploitive parent–child relationship ... culminate[s] in a political philosophy and social outlook which has no room for anything but a desperate clinging to what appears to be strong and a disdainful rejection of whatever is relegated to the bottom. The inherent dramatization likewise extends from the parent–child dichotomy to the dichotomous conception of sex roles and moral values as well as the dichotomous handling of social relations as manifested especially in the formation of stereotypes and of ingroup–outgroup cleavages. (Adorno *et al.* (1950, p. 971))

In these terms, specific family practices are understood to create individuals whose personality structure leads them to become slavish followers of those who have power and cruel abusers of those who do not. As with Dollard *et al.*'s (1939) frustration–aggression hypothesis, there is thus no sense in which authoritarians have any particular relationship with the targets of their prejudice. Instead, this is understood simply as a generalized orientation to outgroups that arises from unresolved inner conflicts.

In the wake of research into the nature of authoritarianism, further research identified a catalogue of related personality dimensions that could give rise to prejudice. These included 'dogmatism' or 'closed-mindedness' (Rokeach, 1954) as well as intolerance of ambiguity, rigidity and concreteness (see Oakes *et al.*, 1994, for a discussion). As this work developed, it began to assert that prejudice was less a matter of personality and more one of 'cognitive style' (see Kruglanski, 2004, for a review). Again, though, cognitive style is primarily a psychological construct and, as such, it is empty of political content. Here researchers have sought to demonstrate that authoritarians (and other prejudiced individuals) have some such style, and have taken this as evidence for an underlying psychology that predisposes them towards particular political orientations. It is the personality of the fascist that is seen to draw them naturally towards Fascism, and the broader social context within which Fascism (or other social movements) arises and is promulgated is largely ignored.

Alongside these various notions, the analysis of prejudice also came to be closely associated with the concept of stereotyping. Introduced by the journalist Walter Lippmann in his 1922 book, *Public Opinion*, stereotypes, like prejudice, were understood from the outset to constitute an inherently flawed way of representing the social world. And as with prejudice, this conclusion follows from the very definition of stereotypes as simplified generalizations about members of social groups. Because the truth about people is seen to lie in their status *as individuals* who are unique, idiosyncratic and individually different, stereotyping must pervert that truth – so that, in Lippmann's words, it constitutes 'a very partial and inadequate way of representing the world' (1922, p. 72). To stereotype people is to see them as group members; to see them as group members is to blur and deny their individuality; to deny individuality is to distort people's true character.

At the same time, though, Lippmann argued that stereotyping was a necessary process because the task of perceiving everyone as individuals was simply too overwhelming. In the interests of cognitive economy, people therefore stereotype inevitably and automatically with a view to making the task of social judgement manageable. Yet once more, the implication of this analysis is that group-based perceptions owe their structure and content more to the drive for simplicity than to any rational social or political meaning.

Allport (1954) captures many of these elements in his book *The Nature of Prejudice*. There is thus (a) sympathy with Freudian ideas of primitive, instinctual impulses that drive certain motivational processes, (b) a strong emphasis on personality, and (c) a recognition of categorization as a universal but biasing quality of human cognition. Yet Allport also brings together work on social norms and cultural socialization – recognizing (a) that prejudice could be a social norm in a given group, culture or society, (b) that there are 'community patterns' in prejudice, and (c) that socialization and leadership both have important roles to play in the development of prejudice.

Moreover, weaved into Allport's treatment of prejudice is work on ethnocentrism, which speaks to the idea that human groups have a general tendency to view aspects of their own groups as better than those of other groups. There is also recognition that one's group memberships and associated loyalties can change, and that the conception or nature of the ingroup can itself shift (e.g. so that over time, a nation's members will develop more positive attitudes towards immigrants).

All of these arguments relating to prejudice sit together rather uncomfortably and are never fully integrated. In the end, Allport's work provides a strong statement of the prejudice meta-theory where the emphasis is placed on (a) the pathology of the prejudiced personality, (b) the invalidity of social stereotypes and (c) the inevitability of general psychological processes (motivational and cognitive) that produce those stereotypes (including ethnocentrism and socialization). Together, these ideas serve to consolidate the thesis that stereotypes and prejudice are both *necessary evils* – false and unjustified, but a reflection of the inherent limitations of human cognition.

All of these areas also characterize themes in more recent work. On the personality front, for example, there has been renewed interest in right-wing authoritarianism (Altemeyer, 1996), and there has been a revival of research into various cognitive style variables that might explain simplistic thinking and associated negative intergroup attitudes (e.g. cognitive closure, personal need for structure, intolerance of ambiguity). In the 1970s and 1980s there was also a resurgence of empirical interest in the idea that human cognition is inherently limited and flawed, and that stereotypes and prejudice are the unfortunate manifestation of this fact. In particular, individuals' reliance on group-based categorizations was ultimately explained as a product of their having too few cognitive resources to apprehend the complexities of the social environments with which they have to interact (e.g. Fiske and Neuberg, 1990; Macrae *et al.*, 1994).

For their proponents, these various streams of research have followed Allport in consolidating the view that prejudice is a product of childhood socialization, of rigid aspects of personality, or an inevitable consequence of human motivation and cognition. Yet in striving to explain why people come to hold prejudicial views towards others, one question that they routinely overlook is how it is that these views frequently *change*. If personality or universal cognitive processes are ineluctable forces that lead people to perceive and treat others unreasonably, then where is the potential for social change and for more progressive social relations? Of course, one depressing answer is that there is no prospect for any such improvement. Yet the course of history (and longitudinal analysis of stereotype and prejudice content; see Oakes *et al.*, 1994) suggests that this answer is wrong. For just as some groups have come to be seen and treated more unfavourably over time, so others have come to be seen and treated more positively. For example, there are plenty of contexts within which sexism, racism and homophobia have been both identified as social problems and then tackled directly – with considerable success.

In this regard, a key problem with the prevailing meta-theory of prejudice is that the causal sequence of explanation starts with a decontextualized understanding of individual psychology and then maps this psychology on to an appreciation of social problems in the world at large. This sequence is generally treated as unmediated by the social meaning of intergroup relationships, and neglects the potential for such boundaries of inclusion and exclusion to be renegotiated so that they become more (or for that matter, less) inclusive, tolerant and progressive. Not only, then, is the prejudice meta-theory very pessimistic, but also it is at risk of becoming an apology for the problems of stereotyping and prejudice as intractable – by suggesting that they are impossible to overcome.

The new 'social identity' view of prejudice in social psychology

The new view of prejudice that has emerged over the last thirty or so years in social psychology offers a very different view to that which is presented by the Allportian problematic (e.g. Oakes et al., 1994; Oakes and Turner, 1990; Spears and Haslam, 1997; Turner, 1996; Turner and Oakes, 1997; Turner and Reynolds, 2001). In particular, work that has explored processes of self, stereotyping and social change has helped to slowly unravel the assumptions that underpin the prejudice meta-theory. The result is an alternative explanation for prejudice that does not centre on the notion of 'faulty and flawed' psychology.

Over the last three decades the alternative view has become much more powerful theoretically and empirically and, recently, much more explicit in its themes (e.g. Turner, 1996, 2001; Turner and Reynolds, 2001). The key insight of this view – the insight from which all else flows – is that psychologically, and not merely socially, human beings are group members as well as individual persons (e.g. Oakes and Turner, 1990; Turner, 1982; Turner et al., 1994). That is, it is recognized that as well as being individual persons (with unique personal identities; Turner, 1982), people also have social identities that are grounded in their group memberships. Social identities reflect the cognitive and emotional significance of such groupings, and they are implicated in processes that are critical in shaping and changing people's minds, motivations and behaviours.

There are three distinctive contributions of social identity research that together define the alternative view of prejudice. The first concerns the nature of the self-process: the argument that people are both individuals and group members and have social identities that represent the group-based aspect of the self. The second is that stereotyping and prejudice can be an outcome of one's position as a group member in the context of a particular set of intergroup relations. The third is that it is by understanding the dynamic nature of social identity processes that one gains insight both into the dynamics of social change and into the capacity for this change to be a driver for the 'smashing' of prejudice.

The nature of the self-process: human beings as both individuals and group members

First and foremost, the social identity perspective argues that human beings are group members as well as individuals; that there is a collective psychology as well as individual psychology. Human beings act as group members and they define themselves as group members. As Sherif (1967) notes, where people form group memberships they come together to create collective products such as shared identities, slogans, symbols, rituals, stereotypes, norms, values and goals (see also Asch, 1952). These collective cultural products are in turn internalized by individual members and transform their psychology. To the degree that people act in terms of this transformed psychology, they are no longer strictly individuals. Instead, they are now group beings whose behaviour *and psychology* is socially structured by virtue of their belonging to a shared reference group (Turner, 1991; Turner and Oakes, 1997).

As an extension of these ideas, in the social identity view (incorporating insights from both social identity theory and self-categorization theory; Tajfel and Turner, 1979; Turner *et al.*, 1987) a basic distinction exists between personal identity and social identity, reflecting the fact that people can categorize themselves at differing levels of inclusiveness. At one level people can categorize themselves as individuals in contrast to other individuals – as 'me' versus 'you'. At other times, they can categorize themselves as members of a social category defined in contrast to other categories – as 'us' versus 'them'. As importantly, group behaviour is only made possible by this human capacity to shift from the personal to the social level of identity and to act in terms of that shared, social level of identity (Turner, 1982). It is only because people are capable of 'rising above' a self that is defined in exclusive terms, and instead defining the self in a way that is inclusive of other ingroup members, that they are able to join together with those others to engage in collective action that is coherent, coordinated and consequential.

In contemporary work this idea has been developed systematically in self-categorization theory. The key hypothesis relating to group behaviour is that as self-categorizing shifts from the level of personal identity to the level of social identity, there is a transformation of how the self is perceived and this has consequences for cognitions, attitudes, likes and dislikes, processes of social influence and actions (e.g. Turner and Oakes, 1997; Turner and Onorato, 1999). More specifically, there is a transformation in the content of the self that goes hand-in-hand with the transformation in the level of the self, referred to as depersonalization (e.g. Turner, 1982).

Within self-categorization theory the importance of depersonalization is that it explains the psychological difference between being and acting as an individual, and being and acting as a group member. It argues that people act in terms of their self-definitions or self-categories which are flexible, and reflexive social judgements are generated on the spot as a function of the psychological resources that individuals bring to the situation (their motives, values, expectations, higher-order theories, the knowledge they have about the world, themselves and others) and the social reality they confront (see Haslam *et al.*, 2010; Turner and Reynolds, 2010, for recent reviews).

As already noted, under certain conditions, the self can be categorized at more inclusive levels of self-representation and depersonalized, but, under other conditions – and theoretically it is the same set of processes at work – the self is categorized at lower, less inclusive levels and personalized (e.g. Oakes *et al.*, 1994; Reynolds and Oakes, 2000). In the same way that group identities are created at varying levels with varying kinds of meanings on varying kinds of dimensions, the same occurs with respect to individuality and personality processes (e.g. Reynolds and Turner, 2006; Reynolds *et al.*, 2010; Turner *et al.*, 2006). In one case we categorize in terms of between-group differences and enhance within-group similarities; in the other case we categorize in terms of within-group differences and enhance our personal identity and differences from other individuals. It follows from this analysis that individuality is as much a dynamic product of psychology and the situation as is group-based self-categorization. It is not, as psychologists typically assume, that the personal self (e.g. personality) is fixed and fundamental, and the social self is then superimposed on top of this layer of individuality. The fact that we can behave both as individuals *and* group members is a highly adaptive feature of the human mind and one that makes the broad range of human social behaviour possible.

Along these lines, experimental research by Hogg and Turner (1987) showed that as changes to judgemental context made it appropriate for perceivers to define themselves as an 'us' opposed to a 'them', those perceivers' self-perception was transformed so that they defined themselves more in terms of collective similarities than individual differences. Specifically, female and male undergraduates were assigned randomly to experimental conditions of 'intragroup comparison' or 'intergroup comparison'. In the intragroup condition one male argued about a number of issues with one other male, or one female argued about a set of issues with one other female. It was found, in line with predictions, that relative to the intragroup comparison condition, in the intergroup condition both the males and the females tended to stereotype themselves more as men and women respectively, and to report that they perceived themselves to be more typical of their own gender group. These changes in level of identity also had an impact on the language the participants used, their self-esteem and discriminatory behaviour.

These findings accord with those from a large number of other studies in the social identity literature which demonstrate that social identity tends to become more salient, and that this has a range of distinct consequences for social behaviour (e.g. increasing levels of liking for fellow group members and levels of within-group consensus), as perceivers move from social contexts in which they make social comparisons within groups to ones in which comparisons are made between groups (e.g. Haslam *et al.*, 1995; Onorato and Turner, 2004; see Onorato and Turner, 2002, for a review). In this way, the salience of social identity leads not only to the *perceptual* homogenization of groups as their members come to *see* themselves as members of a common ingroup, but also to *behavioural* alignment as they come to *act* in terms of that shared group membership. As we have already intimated, this is important because the social behaviour that derives from shared social identity is the basis for a range of other important group processes – including cohesion and cooperation, communication and influence, and coordination and organization (e.g. Haslam, 2004; Turner, 1987a, 1987b, 1991).

It follows from this argument that when one seeks to understand these various processes, it is not possible to make sense of what one group feels about another group – or the way it behaves towards it – simply by pointing to individual differences, asocial motivational drives, or cognitive limitations. Individual differences on one dimension (call it individuality) may be quite good at predicting individual differences on other related dimensions, such as prejudice, when individuals are acting (and are tested) alone and in psychological isolation. But the critical point is that they become much less relevant and much less predictive of intergroup attitudes the more that psychological conditions are actually dictated by social identity concerns and intergroup relations.

None of this means that personality–prejudice correlations at the individual level are not informative. What it does imply, though, is that personality is likely to become least useful at the very point where prejudice becomes most socially and politically potent – that is, at the point of conflictual intergroup interaction. At this point social identity concerns come to the fore, and in order to understand prejudice (and much else besides) an appreciation of these concerns now becomes absolutely essential.

Stereotyping and prejudice as an outcome of one's vantage point as a group member

The previous section gives some insight into the ways in which social identity can have a profound bearing on the perceptions and behaviour of individuals. Yet, contrary to the picture that emerges from much of the psychological research on this topic, prejudice is not simply a problem of individual perception. Indeed, as Tajfel (1981) argued, stereotypes and prejudice are not primarily individual-level issues at all – and to the extent that they are problems, this is largely because they are products of social interaction that is *shared* by group members and ultimately serve group purposes (see Haslam, Turner, Oakes, McGarty and Reynolds, 1998). Prejudices are thus products of social processes of influence, communication and leadership and always have an ideological dimension. Beliefs about women, immigrants, criminals, the unemployed, religious groups and people of different ethnicities are part of specific political and cultural currents and traditions that relate to the nature of the intergroup relationships in particular societies. The social identity approach, therefore, argues that in order to understand prejudice it is crucial to examine the nature of these intergroup relations – with a view to appreciating both the kind of relationships that exist between groups and the collective theories that are located within particular groups (e.g. Billig, 1976; Tajfel, 1969, 1981; Tajfel and Turner, 1979).

People hold the attitudes they do towards members of particular groups because of the social norms, values and beliefs shared among members of their own group, that in turn are influenced by the social-structural realities of intergroup relationships and understandings of 'them'. For example, the kinds of theories that groups develop, both about their own group and others, depend in no small part on the status of their ingroup in relation to others and the extent to which that status is seen as legitimate and stable (Tajfel and Turner, 1979). Among other things, this means that if relations between high- and low-status groups are seen as legitimate and stable then groups are likely to endorse views about each other that are more positive and 'accommodating' than would be the case if they were seen as illegitimate and unstable (Ellemers, 1993; Reicher and Haslam, 2006). As social identity theory predicts, this is because the former views reflect strategies of social creativity while the latter reflect strategies of social competition.

The nature of intergroup relationships also encompasses other features of the social system within which they are embedded – for example, whether there is a conflict of interests between the groups, or a super-ordinate, joint goal that they share. As a function of whether there is conflict, stress and tension in the real relationships between groups there will be a display of quite different kinds of attitudes to the outgroup, ranging from the positive and harmonious to the negative and hostile.

Consistent with this point, Sherif and his colleagues showed in their naturalistic 'boys camp' studies that within a very short period of time (several weeks) they could either create or eliminate hostility simply – although in fact these things are not quite that simple (e.g. see Reicher and Haslam, 2006) – by manipulating the nature of the relationship between groups (i.e. whether they had competitive or interdependent group goals; Sherif, 1956; Sherif *et al.*, 1961). As is well known, these researchers investigated the idea that groups will tend to develop competitive relations that give rise to antagonistic stereotypes and behaviour to the degree that they perceive their interests as in conflict. However, as a corollary, if groups perceive their interests as compatible and complementary (e.g. because they are framed by shared superordinate goals) then perceptions and actions are likely to be more positive. Along similar lines, the exper-imental and historical literature is replete with examples of stereotypes becoming very negative or very positive over a very short time span as the relationships between groups become the basis for either enmity or friend-ship (see Oakes *et al.*, 1994, for a review). Clearly, then, a scientific approach to prejudice needs to be able to account just as readily for evidence of continuity and consistency in prejudice as the alternative.

In all this, it is necessary to recognize that human beings assess what is appropriate, right, just and valid about the world around them through processes of social comparison, social influence and consensual validation that motivate them to reach agreement with other ingroup members (e.g. Turner, 1991). Illustrative of this point, a series of studies by Haslam, Turner and colleagues showed that if individuals were asked to articulate stereotypes in intragroup contexts then there was far less con-sensus in those stereotypes than there was when they were elicited in intergroup contexts (e.g. Haslam, Turner, Oakes, Reynolds, Eggins *et al.*, 1998). The researchers also showed that these patterns reflected the fact that in intergroup contexts perceivers were far more likely to define themselves in terms of shared social identity (Haslam *et al.*, 1999). Qualitative and quantitative analysis also confirmed the point that here it was a shared sense of 'us-ness' that motivated participants to work hard to align their views – through exchange of information, negotiation and argument – so that they came to embrace a consensual view about the nature of both their ingroup and comparison outgroups. Importantly too, this process of social identity-based consensus is also central to the trans-formation of such views from personal opinion into social *fact*. Again, this transformation is critical to the ultimate force of prejudices in the world at large – since it helps to explain not only the conviction with which they are held, but also the vigour with which they are translated into social action.

In their attempts to understand the social world and to interact mean-ingfully within it, people's reactions to social reality are therefore always mediated by their shared beliefs and knowledge about themselves and others, and by collective ideologies that inform their understanding of the ingroup, its relationship with outgroups and the wider society within which they are located. These elements allow group members to develop a collective theory of their relationship to others (e.g. who we are, what our values are, what our goals are, what is preventing progress, who shares our views, who is opposed to our views, what we can do about it). As Tajfel (e.g. 1969) argued, this means that if one wants to know why groups dislike each other or why they feel positively about each other, the simplest and easiest thing to do is to ask their members how they understand their relationship to each other. For it is in the context of intergroup relation-ships (whose structure is typically nuanced, complex and negotiable) that groups develop belief systems that give those relations their sense of coherence, meaning and stability.

From these various observations we can abstract three core points. First, the social and value judgements that shape intergroup behaviour always reflect the particular perspective of the perceiver. Rather than 'standing above' the world we always perceive it from a particular vantage point. Yet, second, while this vantage point will never be shared with all perceivers (and hence is often a basis for disagreement and conflict), to the extent that the perceivers' sense of self is shaped by a shared social identity (as it is in most of the situations in which prejudice is a concern), they will be motivated to coordinate their views with ingroup members. Third, this means that people's perspective on the social world is typically a collective one (again, especially when it comes to matters of prejudice), galvanized through processes of social interaction and influence.

One implication of these three points is that we rarely see the views of our ingroups, in the here and now, as expressions of prejudice – especially if we identify strongly with them (Reicher *et al.*, 2008). On the contrary, we work hard to do what we can with fellow ingroup members to ensure – and assure ourselves – that our beliefs are understood as factual and accurate. In precisely this way, the race psychologists of old saw their work not as institutionalized racism but as rational science (Richards, 1997). From our perspective, of course, their 'science' seems irrational and unfathomable. But the point here is precisely that this is *our perspective*. Accordingly, when we condemn particular attitudes as prejudiced or biased this is a basic reflection of the fact that there are a range of groups in the world (both presently and in the past) whose vantage point and whose social identity we do not share, and whose consensual understandings we find not only hard to comprehend but also sometimes extremely objectionable. Very definitely, this does not mean that we are wrong to do so. But what it does mean – again – is that we need to look beyond notions of pathological personality or faulty cognition in order to explain what is going on here.

Prejudice, group action and social change

It is through an acceptance of the group-based properties of prejudice that it becomes possible to identify why and how such views can change – so that they become more negative, extreme and widespread in the face of intergroup conflict, but are minimized and sometimes eradicated as new social relations come to re-define both 'what we are' and 'what we are not'. As we have already noted, psychological processes do not operate in a social vacuum. Societies and cultures create, and can and do change, their norms, values and beliefs (e.g. Turner, 2006; Turner and Reynolds, 2001, 2003). The boundaries between groups, and processes of social exclusion from 'us', can be renegotiated and changed as people come to embrace new understandings of 'who they are' and what they value and believe. In this way, categorization and group process are not only the basis of stereotypes and prejudice, they also are part of the solution.

Again the history of prejudice research provides a good illustration of this point. For it was precisely at the point that academic researchers started to question the legitimacy of relations between other 'races' and the elite white upper classes of which they were part that they started to question the legitimacy of the scientific assumptions and beliefs which underpinned the race psychology project in which they were participants. Thus, hand-in-hand with the development of the new field of prejudice research there was a rejection of what had gone before. This meant that the 'science' of race psychology – and all its many trappings – was ultimately consigned to the dustbin of scientific history.

By affecting the way people think about their group memberships it is therefore possible to shape their prejudice (and their reflexive awareness of this). From Sherif's work, we know, for example, that under certain conditions, the creation of a superordinate identity can precipitate a shift from intergroup ('us' versus 'them') to intragroup ('we') categorizations, and can thereby lead to increased cooperation and a reduction in prejudice. The same point is also clearly illustrated in research by Gaertner *et al.* (1989). In the spirit of the minimal group studies (Tajfel *et al.*, 1971), these researchers allocated six participants to one of two three-person groups and showed that this subsequently led to intergroup discrimination (e.g. so that members of the ingroup were much more liked than those in the outgroup). However, these researchers then changed the experimental situation to create either a 'one-group' condition (in which participants interacted as members of the same six-person group) or a 'separate individuals' condition (in which participants acted as six separate individuals). In both conditions, there was a reduction in intergroup discrimination and prejudice. In the 'one-group' condition the attractiveness of hitherto outgroup members increased, but in the 'six-individuals' condition there was a reduction in the perceived attractiveness of former ingroup members.

Such findings are consistent with work on intergroup contact where, under certain conditions, the softening of the boundaries between ingroups and outgroups has been shown to lead to prejudice reduction. Often the conditions of contact initially outlined by Allport (1954) result in the emergence of a different *subjective* understanding of the intergroup relations in question (e.g. Pettigrew and Tropp, 2006). When groups have equal status, common goals, a cooperative stance and such contact is sanctioned or encouraged by relevant authorities, we often talk about a change in the nature of intergroup relations. A redefinition of the ingroup is necessary where norms and customs become more inclusive and representative of both groups. Under such conditions, there are likely to be stronger affective ties and less anxiety associated with future contact, a correction of false beliefs held by the two groups and an alignment of positive behavioural experiences with underlying attitudes (e.g. Dovidio *et al.*, 2003; Mummendey and Wenzel, 1999). Contact and the associated creation of a new inclusive superordinate social identity ('we') thus represents one very clear way in which it may be possible to reduce prejudice.

Going further than this, though, just as group life is a basis for prejudice, so too is it the basis for collective and political action that can challenge and eliminate prejudice. It is in the theories and ideas that groups develop to make sense of the social structure and their position in it that identity (re)formation and social change originates (e.g. Subasic *et al.*, 2008). In short, as much as groups can be used to bolster the status quo, so too can they become vehicles for resistance and *social change*.

For example, in the BBC Prison Study (Reicher and Haslam, 2006), where individuals were assigned to the role of 'prisoners' or 'guards', it is clear that the formation of a shared social identity was critical to collective action on the part of the low-status prisoners that allowed them to undermine and ultimately overthrow the high-status guards' regime. In this context, social identity also had an important protective function (reducing stress and depression; Haslam and Reicher, 2006), that allowed individuals to deal effectively with the range of challenges that they faced in the process of collectively engineering social change. At the same time, the guards' inability to develop a sense of shared social identity led to disorganization and a host of negative personal and social outcomes.

For our present purposes, it is also interesting to note that over the course of the study there was a substantial increase in all participants' right-wing authoritarianism (a perceived 'cause' of prejudice). In particular, this arose from the failure not only of the guards' regime but that of the 'commune' that was set up to replace it. Yet, rather than being the manifestation of a generalized sense of aggression (following frustration; as Dollard *et al.*'s frustration–aggression hypothesis might assert) it is clear that this was a response to a particular set of circumstances in which a particular set of leaders made the collective case for the return to the more tyrannical prisoner–guard regime. When leadership was exercised by a trade unionist who espoused democratic beliefs (that would bring prisoners and guards together behind a common cause), the participants thus moved in a very different direction. Participants' readiness to endorse authoritarian ideals was thus predicted neither by their inherent personality nor by inherent features of the situation (see Haslam and Reicher, 2007). Instead, it was a product of the collective understandings of that situation that served to make sense of social relations for participants, and which appeared to provide them with the prospect of a positive collective future. And, again, rather than being in any sense 'given', this orientation towards the world was a product of context-specific processes of negotiation, influence and leadership that all centred on questions of social identity. Such is the nature of all prejudice.

Looking at contemporary social psychology in this much more social and political sense, there is not any (psychological) reason to suppose that prejudice cannot be changed by historical events in the very same way that authoritarianism was in the BBC Prison Study (Reynolds *et al.*, 2010; Turner *et al.*, 2006). The person, then, does not have an abstract fixed psychological structure that produces particular politics and prejudices. Rather, prejudice is an *outcome* of social and political dynamics. It is constructed dynamically – in the long term and contemporaneously – as an aspect of theories, ideologies and knowledge that shapes the needs and realities of the individual person in specific settings (e.g. Reynolds *et al.*, 2010; Turner *et al.*, 2006).

If it was not already apparent, it should be clear by now that the implications of this analysis are quite different from those of the classical theory of prejudice. For what we see is that social and political change is not prevented by individual mindsets, by the existence of certain personalities, or by ineluctable cognitive biases. On the contrary, social change is not only possible, but it is made possible by group identities and associated beliefs, values and norms that provide a basis for people to question the sets of social relationships that impinge upon them and, where it is perceived necessary, to try to change them. Such an analysis of the dynamic interaction between society, the group and the individual opens up the possibility that, along with genuine social change and new understandings of 'who we are' (the sense of 'we'), prejudice can first be identified as a problem, and then through concerted effort be eradicated.

As the history of race psychology shows, this is no straightforward process. Change is the product of a complex interplay of factors – and a great deal more work is needed to understand these properly. Nevertheless, the central point is that by taking on board new social, political and human identities, progressive social realities are possible.

Conclusion

In this chapter we have presented an analysis of prejudice that moves beyond the prejudice meta-theory of 'faulty and flawed' psychology to one where prejudice is understood to be shaped by the nature of social relations and associated social identity processes. Through a systematic exploration of the self-process, social identity and the role of the group in stereotyping, prejudice and social change, it is argued that the nature of intergroup relations and collective explanations of these relations both shape prejudiced attitudes and make change possible.

On this basis, we reject any suggestion that prejudice is rendered inevitable by the workings of human psychology – whether understood in terms of personality or general cognitive processes. Even at the very darkest moments of human history there has always been, and there will always be, the prospect of positive social and political change. It is this that offers hope for further scientific advance in understanding prejudice and its elimination. On this firm theoretical and empirical basis there is hope that through coordinated scientific efforts all the secrets to 'smashing' prejudice will be revealed.

References

Adorno, T. W., Frenkel-Brunswik, E., Levinson, D. J. and Sanford, R. N. (1950). *The Authoritarian Personality*. New York: Harper.

Allport, G. W. (1954). *The Nature of Prejudice*. Reading, MA: Addison-Wesley.

Altemeyer, B. (1996). *The Authoritarian Specter*. Cambridge, MA: Harvard University Press.

Asch, S. E. (1952). *Social Psychology*. Englewood Cliffs, NJ: Prentice Hall.

Bell, J. (2006). Australia: state of fear. *The Age*. Retrieved 6 May 2010 from: www. theage.com.au/news/opinion/australia-state-of-fear/2006/01/26/1138066918372. html.

Billig, M. (1976). *Social Psychology and Intergroup Relations*. London: Academic Press.

Brown, R. J. (1995). *Prejudice: its Social Psychology*. Oxford, UK: Blackwell.

Dollard, J., Doob, L. W., Miller, N. E., Mowrer, O. H. and Sears, R. R. (1939). *Frustration and Aggression*. New Haven, CT: Yale University Press.

Dovidio, J., Gaertner, S. L. and Kawakami, K. (2003). Intergroup contact: the past, present, and the future. *Group Processes and Intergroup Relations*, **6**, 5–21.

Duckitt, J. (1992). *The Social Psychology of Prejudice*. New York: Praeger.

Ellemers, N. (1993). The influence of socio-structural variables on identity enhancement strategies. *European Review of Social Psychology*, **4**, 27–57.

Fiske, S. T. and Neuberg, S. L. (1990). A continuum of impression formation, from category-based to individuating processes: influences of information and motivation on attention and interpretation. In M. P. Zanna (ed.), *Advances in Experimental Social Psychology* (Vol. 3, pp.1–73). New York: Random House.

Gaertner, S. L., Mann, J., Murrell, A. and Davidio, J. F. (1989). Reducing intergroup bias: the benefits of recategorization. *Journal of Personality and Social Psychology*, **57**, 239–49.

Haslam, S. A. (2004). *Psychology in Organizations: the Social Identity Approach* (2nd edn). London: Sage.

Haslam, S. A. and Reicher, S. D. (2006). Stressing the group: social identity and the unfolding dynamics of stress. *Journal of Applied Psychology*, **91**, 1,037–52.

   (2007). Beyond the banality of evil: three dynamics of an interactionist social psychology of tyranny. *Personality and Social Psychology Bulletin*, **33**, 615–22.

Haslam, S. A., Ellemers, N., Reicher, S., Reynolds, K. J. and Schmitt, M. (2010). Social identity today: the impact of its defining ideas. In T. Postmes and N. Branscombe (eds.), *Rediscovering Social Identity: Core Sources* (pp.341–56). New York: Psychology Press.

Haslam, S. A., Oakes, P. J., Reynolds, K. J. and Turner, J. C. (1999). Social identity salience and the emergence of stereotype consensus. *Personality and Social Psychology Bulletin*, **25**, 809–18.

Haslam, S. A., Oakes, P. J., Turner, J. C. and McGarty, C. (1995). Social categorization and group homogeneity: changes in the perceived applicability of stereotype content as a function of comparative context and trait favourableness. *British Journal of Social Psychology*, **34**, 139–60.

Haslam, S. A., Turner, J. C., Oakes, P. J., McGarty, C. and Reynolds, K. J. (1998). The group as a basis for emergent stereotype consensus. *European Review of Social Psychology*, **8**, 203–39.

Haslam, S. A., Turner, J. C., Oakes, P. J., Reynolds, K. J., Eggins, R. A., Nolan, M. and Tweedie, J. (1998). When do stereotypes become really consensual? Investigating the group-based dynamics of the consensualization process. *European Journal of Social Psychology*, **28**, 755–76.

Hogg, M. A. and Turner, J. C. (1987). Intergroup behaviour, self-stereotyping and the salience of social categories. *British Journal of Social Psychology*, **26**, 325–40.

Kruglanski, A. W. (2004). *The Psychology of Closed Mindedness*. New York: Psychology Press.

Lippmann, W. (1922). *Public Opinion*. New York: Harcourt Brace.

Macrae, C. N., Milne, A. B. and Bodenhausen, G. V. (1994). Stereotypes as energy-saving devices: a peek inside the cognitive toolbox. *Journal of Personality and Social Psychology*, **66**, 37–47.

Mummendey, A. and Wenzel, M. (1999). Social discrimination and tolerance in intergroup relations: reactions to intergroup difference. *Personality and Social Psychology Review*, **3**, 158–74.

Oakes, P. J. and Turner, J. C. (1990). Is limited information processing capacity the cause of social stereotyping? *European Review of Social Psychology*, **1**, 111–35.

Oakes, P. J., Haslam, S. A. and Turner, J. C. (1994). *Stereotyping and Social Reality*. Oxford, UK: Blackwell.

Onorato, R. and Turner, J. C. (2002). Challenging the primacy of the personal self: the case for depersonalized self-conception. In Y. Kashima, M. Foddy and M. J. Platow (eds.), *Self and Identity: Personal, Social, and Symbolic* (pp.145–78). London: Erlbaum.

   (2004). Fluidity in the self-concept: the shift from personal to social identity. *European Journal of Social Psychology*, **34**, 257–78.

Pettigrew, T. and Tropp, L. (2006). A meta-analytic test of intergroup contact theory. *Journal of Personality and Social Psychology*, **90**, 751–83.

Reicher, S. D. and Haslam, S. A. (2006). Rethinking the psychology of tyranny: the BBC prison experiment. *British Journal of Social Psychology*, **45**, 1–40.

Reicher, S. D., Haslam, S. A. and Rath, R. (2008). Making a virtue of evil: a five-step social identity model of the development of collective hate. *Social and Personality Psychology Compass*, **2**, 1,313–44.

Reynolds, K. J. and Oakes, P. J. (2000). Variability in impression formation: investigating the role of motivation, capacity and the categorization process. *Personality and Social Psychology Bulletin*, **26**, 355–73.

Reynolds, K. J. and Turner, J. C. (2006). Individuality and the prejudiced personality. *European Review of Social Psychology*, **17**, 233–70.

Reynolds, K. J., Turner, J. C., Branscombe, N. R., Mavor, K. I., Bizumic, B. and Subasic, E. (2010). Interactionism in personality and social psychology: an integrated approach to understanding the mind and behaviour. *European Journal of Personality*, **24**, 458–82.

Richards, G. (1997). *'Race', Racism and Psychology: Towards a Reflexive History*. London: Routledge.

Rokeach, M. (1954). The nature and meaning of dogmatism. *Psychological Review*, **61**, 194–204.

Sherif, M. (1956). Experiments in group conflict. *Scientific American*, **195**, 54–8.
    (1967). *Group Conflict and Co-operation: their Social Psychology*. London: Routledge and Kegan Paul.

Sherif, M., Harvey, O. J., White, B. J., Hood, W. R. and Sherif, C. W. (1961). *Intergroup Conflict and Co-operation: the Robbers Cave Experiment*. Norman, OK: University of Oklahoma.

Spears, R. and Haslam, S. A. (1997). Stereotyping and the burden of cognitive load. In R. Spears, P. J. Oakes, N. Ellemers and S. A. Haslam (eds.), *The Social Psychology of Stereotyping and Group Life* (pp.144–70). Oxford, UK: Blackwell.

Stangor, C. (ed.) (2000). *Stereotypes and Prejudice: Essential Readings*. New York: Psychology Press.

Subasic, E., Reynolds, K. J. and Turner, J. C. (2008). The political solidarity model of social change: dynamics of self-categorization in intergroup power relations. *Personality and Social Psychology Review*, **12**, 330–52.

Tajfel, H. (1969). Cognitive aspects of prejudice. *Journal of Social Issues*, **25**, 79–97.
    (1981). *Human Groups and Social Categories*. Cambridge, UK: Cambridge University Press.

Tajfel, H. and Turner, J. C. (1979). An integrative theory of intergroup conflict. In W. G. Austin and S. Worchel (eds.), *The Social Psychology of Intergroup Relations* (pp.33–47). Monterey, CA: Brooks/Cole.

Tajfel, H., Flament, C., Billig, M. and Bundy, R. F. (1971). Social categorization and intergroup behaviour. *European Journal of Social Psychology*, **1**, 149–78.

Turner, J. C. (1982). Towards a cognitive redefinition of the social group. In H. Tajfel (ed.), *Social Identity and Intergroup Relations* (pp.15–40). Cambridge, UK/Paris: Cambridge University Press/Editions de la Maison des Sciences de l'Homme.
    (1987a). Introducing the problem: individual and group. In J. C. Turner, M. A. Hogg, P. J. Oakes, S. D. Reicher and M. S. Wetherell (eds.), *Rediscovering the Social Group: a Self-categorization Theory* (pp.1–18). Oxford, UK: Blackwell.
    (1987b). The analysis of social influence. In J. C. Turner, M. A. Hogg, P. J. Oakes, S. D. Reicher and M. S. Wetherell (eds.), *Rediscovering the Social Group: a Self-categorization Theory* (pp.68–88). Oxford, UK: Blackwell.
    (1991). *Social Influence*. Pacific Grove, CA: Brooks-Cole.
    (1996). Henri Tajfel: an introduction. In W. P. Robinson (ed.), *Social Groups and Identity: Developing the Legacy of Henri Tajfel* (pp.1–21). Oxford, UK: Butterworth Heinemann.
    (2001). Rethinking the nature of prejudice from psychological distortion to socially structured meaning. The Second Freilich Foundation Eminent Lecture Series, Australian National University, October, 2001.
    (2006). Tyranny, freedom and social structure: escaping our theoretical prisons. *British Journal of Social Psychology*, **45**, 41–6.

Turner, J. C. and Oakes, P. J. (1997). The socially structured mind. In C. McGarty and S. A. Haslam (eds.), *The Message of Social Psychology* (pp.355–73). Oxford, UK: Blackwell.

Turner, J. C. and Onorato, R. (1999). Social identity, personality and the self-concept: a self categorization perspective. In T. R. Tyler, R. Kramer and O. John (eds.), *The Psychology of the Social Self* (pp.11–46). Mahwah, NJ: Lawrence Erlbaum Associates.

Turner, J. C. and Reynolds, K. J. (2001). The social identity perspective in intergroup relations: theories, themes and controversies. In R. Brown and S. Gaertner (eds.), *Handbook of Social Psychology: Vol 4: Intergroup Processes* (pp.259–77). Oxford, UK: Blackwell.

(2003). Why social dominance theory has been falsified. *British Journal of Social Psychology*, **42**, 199–206.

(2010). The story of social identity. In T. Postmes and N. Branscombe (eds.), *Rediscovering Social Identity: Core Sources*. New York: Psychology Press.

Turner, J. C., Hogg, M. A., Oakes, P. J., Reicher, S. D. and Wetherell, M. S. (1987). *Rediscovering the Social Group: a Self-categorization Theory*. Oxford, UK: Blackwell.

Turner, J. C., Oakes, P. J., Haslam, S. A. and McGarty, C. (1994). Self and collective: cognition and social context. *Personality and Social Psychology Bulletin*, **20**, 454–63.

Turner, J. C., Reynolds, K. J., Haslam, S. A. and Veenstra, K. E. (2006). Reconceptualizing personality: producing individuality by defining the personal self. In T. Postmes and J. Jetten (eds.), *Individuality and the Group* (pp.11–36). London: Sage Publications.

3 An ambivalent alliance: hostile and benevolent sexism as complementary justifications for gender inequality

Peter Glick and Susan T. Fiske

> If woman had no existence save in the fiction written by men, one would imagine her a person ... very various; heroic and mean; splendid and sordid; infinitely beautiful and hideous in the extreme.
>
> Virginia Woolf, *A Room of One's Own* (1929/1981)

What Woolf saw as 'astonishing extremes' in men's images of women date back to ancient texts. Pomeroy (1975), a social historian, suggested that classical representations of women fit into the polarized categories of goddesses, whores, wives and slaves. Feminists who analyse contemporary society (e.g. Faludi, 1992) argue that similarly extreme characterizations of women are alive and well in popular culture, such as film depictions that divide women into faithful wives and murderous seductresses. Although what Tavris and Wade (1984) termed the pedestal–gutter syndrome (or the Madonna–whore dichotomy) has long been recognized by psychologists, historians and feminists, most empirical researchers have identified sexism only with regard to hostility towards women, ignoring the corresponding tendency to place (at least some) women on a pedestal.

This chapter reviews recent theory and empirical research on hostile and benevolent sexism. Hostile sexism is an adversarial view of gender relations in which women are perceived as seeking to control men, whether through sexuality or feminist ideology. Although *benevolent sexism* may sound oxymoronic, this term recognizes that some forms of sexism are, for the perpetrator, subjectively benevolent, characterizing women as pure creatures who ought to be protected, supported and adored and whose love is necessary to make a man complete. This idealization of women simultaneously implies that they are weak and best suited for conventional gender roles; being put on a pedestal is confining, yet the man who places a woman there is likely to interpret this as cherishing, rather than restricting, her (and many women may agree). Despite the greater social acceptability of benevolent sexism, our research suggests that it serves as a crucial complement to hostile sexism that helps to pacify women's resistance to societal gender inequality.

In nineteen nations, more than 15,000 participants have completed the ambivalent sexism inventory (ASI; Glick and Fiske, 1996; Glick *et al.*, 2000), a twenty-two-item self-report measure of sexist attitudes with separate eleven-item hostile and benevolent sexism scales. Hostile and benevolent sexism are prevalent across cultures, and cross-cultural differences in ambivalent sexism are predictable and systematic, with both ideologies relating to national measures of gender inequality. Moreover, underlying the differences between cultures are important consistencies in the structure and consequences of sexist beliefs. What ASI research reveals about the nature of sexism challenges current definitions of prejudice as an unalloyed antipathy and draws attention to the manner in which subjectively benevolent, paternalistic prejudices (e.g. benevolent sexism) may reinforce inequality between groups.

The nature of sexism

Allport (1954), in his foundational book, *The Nature of Prejudice*, defined prejudice as 'an antipathy based upon a faulty and inflexible generalization' (p. 9). Although some (e.g. Brown, 1995) have questioned the latter part of this definition, virtually all psychological theorists have likewise equated prejudice with antipathy. From antipathy, it is assumed, flow the discriminatory acts that disadvantage targets of prejudice. In addition, because people seek to justify social systems by believing that groups deserve their place in the social hierarchy (Jost and Banaji, 1994; Tajfel, 1981), a group's disadvantaged status reinforces prejudice, presumably creating a vicious positive feedback loop between antipathy and social inequality. Even members of low-status groups may endorse such system-justifying ideologies, despite the fact that these beliefs bolster their group disadvantage (Jost and Banaji, 1994).

On the basis of cross-cultural indicators of status and power, women are clearly a disadvantaged group. Although some cultures are more egalitarian than others, patriarchy is widespread (Eagly and Wood, 1999; Harris, 1991; Pratto, 1996), though not necessarily universal (Salzman, 1999). Hunter–gatherer societies (common to an earlier era of human history), in which wealth could not be accumulated, may have been relatively egalitarian, but the idea that matriarchy was once common has been thoroughly debunked (Harris, 1991). Simply put, men typically rule, dominating the highest status roles in government and business across the globe (United Nations Development Programme (UNDP), 1998).

The standard model of prejudice would suggest, then, that attitudes towards women must be overwhelmingly hostile and contemptuous. Recent research, however, shows that overall attitudes towards women are quite favourable. Eagly and Mladinic (1993) found that both men and women have more favourable attitudes towards women than towards men, attributing an extremely positive set of traits to women. Known as the 'women are wonderful' effect, this finding is extremely robust and has been replicated (though more strongly for women than for men) even with implicit (i.e. nonconscious) attitudes (Carpenter, 2000). The preference for women creates a conundrum for prejudice theorists: how can a group be almost universally disadvantaged yet loved?

Answers to this riddle come from several quarters. Eagly and Mladinic (1993) pointed out that the favourable, communal traits ascribed to women (e.g. nurturing, helpful and warm) suit them for domestic roles, whereas men are presumed to possess the traits associated with competence at high-status roles (e.g. independent, ambitious and competitive). Furthermore, women's stereotypically communal attributes are also the traits of deference that, when enacted in daily interaction, place a person in a subordinate, less powerful position (Ridgeway, 1992). Thus, the favourable traits attributed to women may reinforce women's lower status. Indeed, Jackman (1994), in her persuasive analysis of race, class and gender relations, argued that subordination and affection, far from being mutually exclusive, often go hand-in-hand. Dominant groups prefer to act warmly towards subordinates, offering them patronizing affection as a reward for 'knowing their place' rather than rebelling. Open antagonism is reserved for subordinates who fail to defer or who question existing social inequalities.

But can subjectively benevolent attitudes be a form of prejudice? By Allport's (1954) definition of prejudice as an antipathy, the answer is no. Yet, Allport immediately followed his definition by stating that 'the net effect of prejudice ... is to place the object of prejudice at some disadvantage' (p. 9). Allport's afterthought suggests that the crux of prejudice may not be antipathy but social inequality; if so, a patronizing but subjectively positive orientation towards women that reinforces gender inequality is a form of prejudice.

Why benevolent prejudices matter

Benevolent sexism is a subtle form of prejudice, yet the ideology it represents may be far from trivial in promoting gender inequality. Both hostile and benevolent sexism are presumed to be 'legitimizing ideologies', beliefs that help to justify and maintain inequality between groups (Sidanius *et al.*,

1994). Ideologies of benevolent paternalism allow members of dominant groups to characterize their privileges as well deserved, even as a heavy responsibility that they must bear. Consider, for example, the ideology of the 'White Man's burden' articulated by Rudyard Kipling, the poet–apologist of British imperialism:

> Take up the White Man's burden –
> Send forth the best ye breed –
> Go, bind your sons to exile
> To serve your captives' need;
> To wait in heavy harness,
> On fluttered folk and wild –
> Your sullen, new-caught peoples,
> Half devil and half child.   Kipling (1899, p. 290)

The widespread belief that Europeans were redeeming the primitive masses was essential to maintaining colonialism (Hochschild, 1998). The resources (including cheap labour) of occupied territories were viewed as fair payment for European enlightenment. Indigenous peoples who rebelled were perceived as ungrateful children or savages who must be severely disciplined. In the US, even outright slavery was legitimated through paternalistic ideologies (Jackman, 1994).

Benevolent sexism may serve functions similar to belief in the White Man's burden, allowing men to maintain a positive self-image as protectors and providers who are willing to sacrifice their own needs to care for the women in their lives. On its own, this ideology may seem unobjectionable, even laudable, but what if (similar to the case of the White Man's burden) it is a crucial complement to hostile sexism, helping to justify men's greater privilege and power? If men's power is popularly viewed as a burden gallantly assumed, as legitimated by their greater responsibility and self-sacrifice, then their privileged role seems justified. Furthermore, women who seek power may consequently be perceived as ungrateful shrews or harpies deserving of harsh treatment, consistent with Kipling's (1899) lament that the White Man could expect only to 'reap his old reward/The blame of those ye better/The hate of those ye guard' (p. 290).

Equally important is the way in which benevolent paternalism may reduce women's resistance to patriarchy (cf. Jackman, 1994). Benevolent sexism is disarming. Not only is it subjectively favourable in its characterization of women, but it promises that men's power will be used to women's advantage, if only they can secure a high-status male protector. To the extent that women depend on men to be their protectors and providers, they are less likely to protest men's power or to seek their own independent status. For instance, Rudman and Heppen (2000)

found that college women who implicitly associated male romantic partners with chivalrous images (e.g. Prince Charming) had less ambitious
career goals, presumably because they were counting on a future husband
for economic support. In a related study, Moya *et al.* (1999) found, in a
community sample of Spanish women, that those who did not have paid
employment scored higher in benevolent sexism. These researchers also
explored the women's reactions to discriminatory scenarios (e.g. losing a
promotion to a less qualified man or having their husband forbid them to
go out at night). The same acts of discrimination were perceived as less
serious when the perpetrators expressed a benevolent, protective justification as opposed to a hostile one. Furthermore, women who scored
higher in benevolent sexism were more likely to excuse not only benev-
olently justified discrimination by nonintimate men (e.g. a boss) but also
overtly hostile discrimination by a husband. The latter effect occurred
only for women without paid employment, suggesting that women who
are highly dependent on male partners are prone to forgive even hostile
acts, perhaps reinterpreting them as a sign of the husband's passionate
attachment. Thus, women who endorse benevolent sexism are more likely
to tolerate, rather than challenge, sexist behaviour when the sexist's
motivation can be interpreted as being protective.

Hostile and benevolent sexism: universal prejudices?

We hypothesized that hostile and benevolent sexism are predictable products of structural relations between men and women that are common to
human societies: (a) men are typically accorded more status and power
than women (Harris, 1991); (b) men and women are often differentiated
in terms of social roles (Eagly and Wood, 1999) and trait ascriptions
(Williams and Best, 1982); and (c) male–female relations are conditioned
by sexual reproduction, a biological constant that creates dependencies
and intimacy between the sexes. These three factors – patriarchy, gender
differentiation and sexual reproduction – together create both hostile and
benevolent attitudes towards the other sex (Glick and Fiske, 1996; Glick
et al., 2000).[1]

Patriarchy and gender differentiation create and reinforce hostile sexism because dominant groups seek to justify their privileges through
ideologies of their superiority (Jost and Banaji, 1994; Sidanius *et al.*,
1994) and through exaggeration of perceived differences with other
groups (Tajfel, 1981). In addition, we suggest that sexual reproduction
promotes hostile sexism because men often resent women's perceived
ability to use sexual attractiveness to gain power over them. At the same
time, men's dependence on women (due to sexual reproduction and role

differentiation) fosters benevolent sexism, an ideology that counterbalances sexist hostility with a paternalistic protectiveness towards women as a 'weaker' but essential group. Men's recognition of their reliance on women to bear and nurture children, to provide domestic labour and to fulfil sexual and intimacy needs makes women a valuable resource (cf. Guttentag, 1983). Thus, even though benevolent sexism presumes women's inferiority, it is subjectively positive (from the perspective of the sexist perceiver), characterizing (at least some) women as wonderful, pure creatures whose love is required to make a man whole.

Does sexism encompass separable but related hostile and benevolent components that appear as coherent belief systems in a variety of cultures? Factor analyses of the ASI suggest that it does. The ASI was predicted to have a complex structure with separate hostile and benevolent sexism factors, each of which incorporates attitudes related to the structural factors that affect male–female relations: power (patriarchy), gender differentiation and heterosexuality. Subfactors emerge empirically only for benevolent sexism (see Glick and Fiske, 1996, 2001a, for speculations as to why this is the case). Confirmatory factor analysis (Jöreskog and Sörbom, 1993) for samples from nineteen nations (Australia, Belgium, Botswana, Brazil, Chile, Colombia, Cuba, England, Germany, Italy, Japan, the Netherlands, Nigeria, Portugal, South Africa, South Korea, Spain, Turkey and the US), ranging in size from 250 to 1,600 men and women, has replicated the factor structure illustrated in Figure 3.1, which outperforms a variety of alternative factor models (see Glick *et al.*, 2000).

Hostile and benevolent sexism consistently emerge as separate but positively correlated factors. Furthermore, three benevolent sexism subfactors typically appear: protective paternalism (e.g. women ought to be rescued first in emergencies), complementary gender differentiation (e.g. women are purer than men) and heterosexual intimacy (e.g. every man ought to have a woman whom he adores). Hostile sexism items also

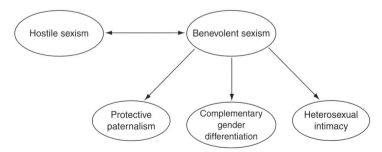

Figure 3.1: Factor structure of the ambivalent sexism inventory

address power relations (e.g. women seek to gain power by getting control over men), gender differentiation (e.g. women are easily offended) and sexuality (e.g. many women get a kick out of teasing men by seeming sexually available and then refusing male advances), even though the factor structure of the hostile sexism scale has proved to be unidimensional in both the US and elsewhere (Glick and Fiske, 1996; Glick *et al.*, 2000).

The factor analyses indicate that hostile and benevolent sexism are meaningful, coherent ideologies not only in the US but also in a number of other countries. If the ideologies tapped by the ASI were not recognizably similar in other nations, the same factors would not emerge. Although the set of nations in which the ASI has been administered is not random and, in many cases, participants are mostly undergraduate students, the countries sampled are culturally, geographically and economically diverse. That the structure of the ASI held up well in such diverse nations provides support for the pervasiveness of hostile and benevolent sexism across cultures.

Another cross-cultural consistency emerged: both factor analyses and correlations of raw scores on the ASI confirmed that, within samples, hostile and benevolent sexism were moderately positively correlated. This correlation, however, often dropped (sometimes to nonsignificance) for high-scoring respondents – correlations were generally smaller among respondents in the most sexist nations, among those who scored above the median on hostile sexism, and for men (who tend to score higher in sexism) – suggesting that for sexist respondents hostile and benevolent sexism are only modestly related or independent. More striking was the correlation between national averages on the two scales across nations. When we used nations as the unit of analysis (so that N = 19), hostile and benevolent sexism means correlated .89 (p < .01) for both men and women. Thus, nations in which hostile sexism was strongly endorsed were those in which benevolent sexism was also embraced, indicating that at the systemic level these ideologies are complementary, mutually supportive justifications of patriarchy and conventional gender relations.

Polarized images of women

If hostile and benevolent sexism do in fact predict opposing valences in attitudes towards women, then individuals who endorse both ideologies can be viewed as ambivalent about women. Ambivalence is usually conceptualized as either the simultaneous experience of or an oscillation between conflicting feelings or beliefs, such as loving and hating the same individual at the same time (Blueler, 1910, cited in Katz, 1981).

Such conflicting beliefs ought to be negatively correlated, making it surprising that (among individual respondents) hostile and benevolent sexism were typically either moderately positively correlated or independent. Although we believe that ambivalent sexists do often experience conflicting feelings when dealing with individual women, the underlying ideologies that precipitate these conflicts need not be in opposition. The reason for this is evident when one examines how hostile and benevolent sexism relate to stereotypes about women.

A major consequence of ambivalence is polarized responses towards the target of ambivalent feelings (for examples involving race and the stigma of having a physical handicap, see Katz, 1981). In twelve nations in which the ASI has been administered, respondents also indicated their spontaneous stereotypes of women (Glick et al., 2000) by generating up to ten traits that came to mind as characteristics they associated with women. Respondents then evaluated each trait on a −3 (extremely negative) to 3 (extremely positive) scale. The valence ratings were averaged for each respondent to yield a score of the positivity–negativity of his or her stereotypes of women. Examples of traits that participants generated included warm, sweet and sensitive (positively valenced), and sly, touchy and selfish (negatively valenced). Partial correlations, used to control for the typically positive relationship between hostile and benevolent sexism, consistently showed that hostile sexism predicts unfavourable, and benevolent sexism predicts favourable, stereotypes or images of women.

In the US, Glick et al. (1997) conducted two studies that help to solve the puzzle of how hostile and benevolent sexism can be reconciled in the minds of ambivalent sexists without creating cognitive dissonance. In everyday interaction, women are more commonly stereotyped at the level of subtypes, such as 'housewives', 'career women', 'babes' or 'lesbians' (e.g. Six and Eckes, 1991), as opposed to a general, overarching 'woman' category. Glick et al. reasoned that this subtyping is what allows hostile and benevolent sexism to be complementary, rather than conflicting, belief systems, even though they predict attitudes of opposing valences – at the ideological level, they target different types of women. Hostile sexism is elicited by women who are viewed as directly challenging or surreptitiously stealing men's power (e.g. feminists, career women or seductresses), whereas benevolent sexism is directed towards women who reinforce conventional gender relations and serve men as wives, mothers and romantic objects (e.g. homemakers).

In study (1), Glick et al. (1997) asked participants to generate and then evaluate their own categories of women. Overall, men who scored high on both hostile and benevolent sexism had more polarized ratings of the different types of women they generated; that is, they were more likely to evaluate some of these types extremely positively and others extremely negatively. In study (2), Glick *et al.* asked participants to evaluate two specific female types, one nontraditional (career women) and the other traditional (homemakers). Men's hostile sexism scores uniquely predicted negative attitudes towards career women, whereas their benevolent sexism scores predicted positive attitudes towards homemakers.

These results suggest that hostile and benevolent sexism can be simultaneously endorsed because they are directed at different female subtypes. The complementarity of these ideologies (and their sexist tone) stems from how women are split into 'good' and 'bad' types; women who fulfil conventional gender roles that serve men are placed on a pedestal and rewarded with benevolent solicitude, whereas women who reject conventional gender roles or attempt to usurp male power are rejected and punished with hostile sexism.

The subtyping explanation solves one problem (how the two forms of sexism can be reconciled in the sexist's mind), but it introduces another: if hostile and benevolent sexism are directed at different targets, is this really a form of ambivalence (i.e. conflicted feelings)? We believe that men who endorse both hostile and benevolent beliefs about women are likely to experience ambivalence towards individual women. At the level of ideology, it may be easy for sexists to classify women into distinct groups that are viewed either favourably or unfavourably, but individual women (e.g. a younger sister who becomes a feminist) may often defy easy categorization. Consider, for instance, the well-known pattern that occurs in domestic abuse with a husband reacting with violence when his authority is challenged but later expressing remorse and affection (the subsequent 'honeymoon' period) – a pattern that suggests considerable sexist ambivalence. Furthermore, we strongly suspect that another oscillating form of ambivalence is likely when men who score high on both hostile and benevolent sexism find that an initial categorization of a woman does not hold. For example, a sexist man might initially place a woman in whom he is romantically interested on a pedestal but abruptly change his views when she rejects him, reclassifying her from 'babe' to 'bitch'. Demonstrating that the ASI predicts such conflicted or oscillating feelings and behaviour towards individual women is an important task for future research.

Gender inequality

The evidence on evaluations of female subtypes is consistent with the notion that benevolent sexism is used to reward women who embrace conventional gender roles and power relations, whereas hostile sexism punishes women who challenge the status quo. This combination of reward and punishment may be particularly effective in maintaining gender inequality. Psychologists well know that punishment, by itself, is not the most effective means of shaping behaviour. Being subjected to hostility alone would be likely to elicit a hostile counter-reaction among women, even among those who do not consider themselves to be feminists (see Glick and Fiske, 1999). Combining punishment for nonconformity with rewards for conformity creates a much more effective system for reinforcing 'correct' behaviour (cf. Jackman, 1994).

Does benevolent as well as hostile sexism serve to justify gender inequality in society? Although it is impossible to conduct an experiment that would demonstrate a causal relationship between sexist ideologies and gender inequality at the societal level, cross-cultural comparisons offer a correlational test of this relationship. The UNDP (1998) publishes two indices of cross-national gender inequality. The gender empowerment measure (GEM) assesses women's (relative to men's) participation in a country's economy (percentage of administrators and managers, professional and technical workers who are women, and women's share of earned income) and political system (percentage of seats in parliament held by women). The gender development index (GDI) is a form of the UN's human development index (HDI), which focuses on longevity (life expectancy), knowledge (adult literacy rates and years of schooling) and standard of living (purchasing power). The GDI uses the same measures as the HDI, but a country's score is decreased for gender inequality (e.g. women having a lower literacy rate than men). The greater the gender disparity, the lower the GDI relative to the HDI. Glick et al. (2000) examined the correlation of national averages on hostile and benevolent sexism with the two UN indices.

In addition to the standard warning that causation cannot be inferred, several cautions must be kept in mind when one is interpreting these correlations. First, the high degree of correlation between hostile and benevolent sexism averages across nations (close to .90) makes it impossible to pull apart their relative contributions to predicting inequality (however, that hostile and benevolent sexism are so strongly correlated is central to our point that these ideologies are complementary justifications of inequality). Second, most samples within each country could not be presumed to be representative, and the number of countries in our set is relatively small for computing correlations (both of these facts, however, would be likely to depress correlations with the UN measures, rather than privilege our hypothesis). The correlations of men's and women's average hostile and benevolent sexism scores with the two UN gender equality measures across nineteen nations are reported in Table 3.1. Not

Table 3.1 *Correlations between ambivalent sexism inventory (ASI) averages and national indexes of gender equality*

ASI scale	Gender development index (GDI)	Gender empowerment measure (GEM)
Men's averages		
Hostile sexism	$-.47^{**}$	$-.53^{**}$
Benevolent sexism	$-.40$	$-.43$
Women's averages		
Hostile sexism	$.03$	$-.38^{*}$
Benevolent sexism	$-.32$	$-.42^{*}$

Note. All correlations with GDI are partial correlations controlling for overall level of human development (human development index; HDI) in each country. Sample sizes were nineteen countries for GDI correlations and eighteen countries for GEM correlations (because GEM was not available for Nigeria). From Glick *et al.* (2000). Copyright by the American Psychological Association. Reprinted with permission.
* $p < .10$.
** $p < .05$.

surprisingly, given that men are the dominant group, men's sexism scores tended to be more strongly related to gender inequality. Men's average scores on hostile sexism significantly predicted greater inequality as assessed by the UN measures, and both genders' scores on benevolent sexism tended to do so. Even though the benevolent sexism correlations did not quite reach statistical significance, they were consistently negative and close in magnitude to the hostile sexism correlations. Although causality cannot be inferred and the relative roles of hostile and benevolent sexism cannot be disentangled, these results are consistent with the notion that both forms of sexism serve as justifications for gender inequality.

Women's acceptance of sexist ideologies

Jost and Banaji's (1994) system-justification perspective emphasizes how subordinate groups tend to accept system-justifying ideologies of their own inferiority (at least on status-relevant dimensions) that are propagated by dominant groups. Cross-cultural comparisons of men's and women's sexism averages (see Figures 3.2 and 3.3) allowed us to test the system-justification hypothesis by seeing whether women expressed greater endorsement of sexist ideologies in countries where men more strongly expressed these views. Using national means as the unit of

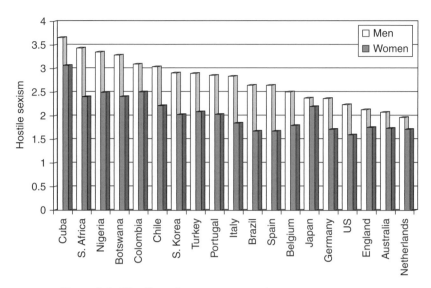

Figure 3.2: Hostile sexism across countries

analysis, Glick *et al.* (2000) found that men's averages on both hostile and benevolent sexism strongly predicted women's averages on these scales. Men's hostile sexism means correlated .84 and .92, respectively, with women's mean scores on hostile and benevolent sexism. Men's benevolent sexism mean scores correlated .84 and .97, respectively, with women's hostile and benevolent sexism mean scores. Thus, when men in a nation more strongly endorsed sexist ideologies, women followed suit, providing strong correlational evidence of system justification.

These correlations, however, are not the whole story. Initial results in the US (Glick and Fiske, 1996) had shown that women (relative to men) were more likely to reject hostile than benevolent sexism (see also Kilianski and Rudman, 1998). A central part of our argument is that benevolent sexism is a particularly insidious form of prejudice for two reasons: (a) it does not seem like a prejudice to male perpetrators (because it is not experienced as an antipathy); and (b) women may find its sweet allure difficult to resist. Benevolent sexism, after all, has its rewards; chivalrous men are willing to sacrifice their own well-being to provide for and to protect women. In the nineteen countries studied (Glick and Fiske, 1996; Glick *et al.*, 2000), without exception, men's average hostile sexism scores are considerably (and significantly) higher than women's (see Figure 3.2). In contrast, in about half of the countries we have studied, women endorse benevolent sexism about as much as men do (see

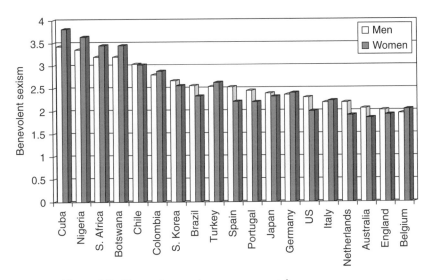

Figure 3.3: Benevolent sexism across countries

Figure 3.3). In the six countries in which women scored significantly lower on benevolent sexism than men, this difference was typically significantly less than the sex difference in hostile sexism (with two exceptions, Australia and the Netherlands). Most intriguing is the finding that in the four nations with the highest sexism scores (Cuba, Nigeria, South Africa and Botswana), the gender gap in benevolent sexism was reversed, with women endorsing this form of sexism more strongly than men.

Thus, even though women in more sexist, relative to less sexist, countries are more likely to accept both hostile and benevolent sexism, women everywhere (when compared with men) are more resistant to the former than to the latter. In fact, the gender gap between men's and women's hostile sexism scores increases the more sexist the country is. Glick *et al.* (2000) found that, across nations, the gender gap in hostile sexism scores was positively correlated with men's average hostile sexism ($r = .61$, $p < .01$) and benevolent sexism ($r = .41$, $p < .10$) scores, suggesting that as men's sexism increases, women's acceptance of hostile sexism is increasingly tempered by resistance to men's hostility. In contrast, the gender gap in benevolent sexism scores was negatively correlated with men's hostile ($r = -.75$, $p < .01$) and benevolent ($r = -.65$, $p < .01$) sexism means; the more sexist the men, the more likely women were to embrace benevolent sexism, even to the point of endorsing benevolent sexism more strongly than men.

Virginia Woolf (1929/1981) argued that true gender equality will happen only when 'womanhood has ceased to be a protected occupation'

(p. 40), but women's relatively greater acceptance of benevolent sexism suggests that some women may resist this change. Perhaps many women want what benevolent sexism brings (e.g. protection), without the corresponding costs of sexist hostility. There is a fine line, however, between acknowledging women's responsibility in maintaining benevolent sexism and blaming the victim. Another explanation for women's acceptance of benevolent sexism is that it is a form of self-protection in response to men's sexism. Smuts (1996) argued that pair-bonding among humans is, in part, an evolved female response to the threat of sexual violence (because a pair-bonded male mate offers protection from other men). In a similar manner, endorsing benevolent sexism may be a way in which women cope when many men in a culture tend to be hostile sexists (cf. Jackman, 1994). The irony is that women are forced to seek protection from members of the very group that threatens them, and the greater the threat, the stronger the incentive to accept benevolent sexism's protective ideology. This explains the tendency for women in the most sexist societies to endorse benevolent sexism more strongly than men. Furthermore, the countries in which women (as compared with men) rejected benevolent sexism as strongly as hostile sexism were ones in which men had low hostile sexism scores. As sexist hostility declines, women may feel able to reject benevolent sexism without fear of a hostile backlash.

Implications for theories of prejudice: paternalistic versus envious prejudices

The pervasiveness of benevolent sexism across cultures and its relation to both hostile sexism and women's subordination suggest that it is time to rethink the equation of prejudice with antipathy and to acknowledge that there is more than one type of prejudice. Prejudice can manifest itself not only in unalloyed hostility but also in sweet, yet patronizing, guises that may be insidiously effective at maintaining social inequalities. Although benevolent paternalism is most evident in sexist ideology, it is not unique to this form of prejudice. We have already referred to historical examples of paternalistic prejudices – benevolent justifications of slavery and colonialism – that represent group relations in which (as with gender) the dominant group was dependent on groups they subordinated (for their labour). There are contemporary examples as well. For example, some liberal whites may have paternalistic attitudes towards African Americans, characterized by pity and an implicit belief that African Americans are incapable of helping themselves (Katz and Hass, 1988).

Recent research that we have conducted with our colleagues suggests that paternalistic stereotypes are directed at a number of groups that are perceived to be low in status and capability but not threatening, such as people who are blind, people with handicaps, older individuals and (of course) housewives (Fiske, 1998; Fiske, Glick *et al.*, 1999; Fiske, Xu *et al.*, 1999; Glick and Fiske, 2001b). These paternalistic prejudices can themselves be considered ambivalent in that they combine subjectively benevolent stereotypes (of the group's warmth) and feelings (sympathy, affection and pity) with beliefs in the group's incompetence, need to be helped and unsuitedness for high-status roles – the ambivalence of liking coupled with disrespect.

In contrast, the resentful tone evident in hostile sexism may be similar to prejudice directed towards socioeconomically successful minorities who are perceived as a competitive threat. Just as sexist men resent career women who succeed in traditionally male-dominated areas, minorities who are perceived to be successful (e.g. Jews or Asian Americans) may be envied and viewed as overly ambitious rivals. This can constitute another form of ambivalence – a grudging respect coupled with dislike and fear – that we have called 'envious prejudice'. Hostile sexists' views of career women, feminists and 'temptresses' seem to fit this category, as evidenced by hostile sexism items that characterize both feminism and female sexuality as usurping men's power and by hostile sexists' tendency to attribute competence to career women but also to say they fear, envy, resent and feel competitive towards this type of woman (Glick *et al.*, 1997).

Paternalistic and envious prejudices may be quite distinct in their causes and their consequences. The one-size-fits-all conception of prejudice, rooted in the idea that prejudice is pure hatred and contempt, has obscured these differences (Young-Breuhl, 1996). One commonality between envious and paternalistic stereotypes, however, is that seemingly favourable traits attributed to a group may only add fuel to the fire of prejudice. Paternalistic stereotypes assign the favourable traits of warmth to low-status groups, but this represents an amiable way of helping to ensure these groups' subordination. For example, the positive value placed on warm, communal traits also lends them a more prescriptive tone that sets up powerful norms for women's behaviour. Although progress has been made in combating prescriptions that women ought not to be too competent, prescriptions for women's niceness remain strong (Rudman, 1998; Spence and Buckner, 2000). Praising women's nurturing traits, for some, is part of expressing the belief that women are especially suited to a domestic role (a much more acceptable political position than trumpeting women's lack of suitedness for high-status roles). Furthermore, communal traits are associated with deferent and subordinate behaviour; enacting these traits in interactions with men reinforces women's subordinate status (Ridgeway, 1992).

Likewise, even though envied groups (e.g. Jews or Asian Americans) may be attributed the normally positive traits of competence (e.g. ambitious or smart), these attributions often become part of the justification for discriminating against them; they are perceived to be too clever and manipulative. The statement 'Jews are extraordinarily shrewd' is as likely as not to be diagnostic of an extreme, envious form of anti-Semitism (e.g. the belief in a dangerous international Jewish conspiracy). In a similar manner, perceiving certain types of women as overachievers may only add to sexist men's hostility.

This perspective on prejudice suggests a closer link between affect and cognition than recent theorists have posited. For example, Eagly and Mladinic (1989) noted a lack of correlation between traditional views about women and affect towards women as a group, but as our research shows, this is not because affect and stereotypes are unrelated. Rather, sexists direct positive affect towards subtypes of women who embrace conventional roles and negative affect towards those who do not. Our approach suggests more generally that group stereotypes are strongly related to the affect experienced towards groups. Rather than predicting undifferentiated negative affect towards outgroups, however, our theoretical perspective predicts more specific and often ambivalent emotional reactions (Cuddy, 2000). The negative emotions directed at members of high-status groups who are viewed as a competitive threat are likely to revolve around feelings of resentment, fear and envy, but also may be accompanied by feelings of grudging admiration. Low-status, cooperative groups, the targets of paternalistic prejudice, may predominantly evoke positive feelings, but these feelings would be confined to patronizing affection and pity rather than respect. In short, it is possible to understand the relationship between affect and stereotypes only by abandoning the notion that prejudice is a generalized antipathy, and examining more specific emotional reactions towards groups (cf. Smith, 1993). Our approach suggests that these relationships are systematic and predictable, even though the emotions may be more differentiated and complex than the antipathy model of prejudice implies.

Conclusion

Although sexist antipathy is the most obvious form of prejudice against women, our evidence suggests that sexist benevolence may also play a significant role in justifying gender inequality. Together, these ideologies represent a system of rewards and punishments that provide incentive for women to remain in conventional gender roles. Benevolent sexism, though a kinder and gentler form of prejudice, is pernicious in that it is more likely to be accepted by women, as well as men, especially in cultures in which women experience a high degree of threat from men. Both hostile and benevolent sexism appear to be cross-culturally prevalent, supporting the argument that these ideologies arise from structural aspects of male–female relations that are common across human groups. More generally, we suggest parallels between the two forms of sexism and prejudice against other groups. Hostile sexism is similar to other forms of envious prejudice, directed at groups who are seen as threats to the ingroup's status and power, whereas benevolent sexism corresponds to other paternalistic prejudices, directed at groups that are lower in status and viewed as cooperative or nonthreatening. These notions challenge the assumption that prejudice is an antipathy and suggest that emotions towards outgroups, though complex and ambivalent, can be predicted and understood.

Note

1. Ambivalence towards the other sex does not flow in only one direction. Glick and Fiske (1999) explored women's ambivalence towards men (as assessed by the ambivalence toward men inventory).

References

Allport, G. W. (1954). *The Nature of Prejudice*. Cambridge, MA: Addison-Wesley.

Brown, R. A. (1995). *Prejudice: its Social Psychology*. Oxford, UK: Blackwell.

Carpenter, S. (2000). Implicit gender attitudes: group membership, cultural construal, valence-consistency, and stability. Unpublished doctoral dissertation. Yale University.

Cuddy, A. C. (2000). Prejudice and emotion. Unpublished raw data.

Eagly, A. H. and Mladinic, A. (1989). Gender stereotypes and attitudes toward women and men. *Personality and Social Psychology Bulletin*, **15**(4), 543–58.

(1993). Are people prejudiced against women? Some answers from research on attitudes, gender stereotypes and judgments of competence. In W. Stroebe and M. Hewstone (eds.), *European Review of Social Psychology* (Vol. 5, pp. 1–35). New York: Wiley.

Eagly, A. H. and Wood, W. (1999). The origins of sex differences in human behavior – evolved dispositions versus social roles. *American Psychologist*, **54**(6), 408–23.

Faludi, S. (1992). *Backlash: the Undeclared War against Women*. New York: Doubleday.

Fiske, S. T. (1998). Prejudice, stereotyping, and discrimination. In S. T. Fiske and G. Lindzey (eds.), *The Handbook of Social Psychology* (4th edn, pp. 357–411). New York: McGraw-Hill.

Fiske, S. T., Glick, P., Cuddy, A. C. and Xy, J. (1999). *Ambivalent Content of Stereotypes, Predicted by Social Structure: Status and Competition Predict Competence and Warmth*. Paper presented at the 22nd General Meeting of the European Association of Experimental Social Psychology (July).

Fiske, S. T., Xu, J., Cuddy, A. C. and Glick, P. (1999). Respect versus liking: status and interdependence underlie ambivalent stereotypes. *Journal of Social Issues*, 55, 473–89.

Glick, P. and Fiske, S. T. (1996). The ambivalent sexism inventory: differentiating hostile and benevolent sexism. *Journal of Personality and Social Psychology*, 70(3), 491–512.

(1999). The ambivalence toward men inventory – differentiating hostile and benevolent beliefs about men. *Psychology of Women Quarterly*, 23(3), 519–36.

(2001a). Ambivalent sexism. In M. P. Zanna (ed.), *Advances in Experimental Social Psychology* (pp.115–88). San Diego, CA: Academic Press.

(2001b). Ambivalent stereotypes as legitimizing ideologies: differentiating paternalistic and resentful prejudice. In J. T. Jost and B. Majore (eds.), *The Psychology of Legitimacy: Emerging Perspectives on Ideology, Justice and Intergroup Relations* (pp.278–306). Cambridge, UK: Cambridge University Press.

Glick, P., Diebold, J., BaileyWerner, B. and Zhu, L. (1997). The two faces of Adam: ambivalent sexism and polarized attitudes toward women. *Personality and Social Psychology Bulletin*, 23(12), 1,323–34.

Glick, P., Fiske, S. T., Mladinic, A., Saiz, J., Abrams, D., Masser, B. *et al.* (2000). Beyond prejudice as simple antipathy: hostile and benevolent sexism across cultures. *Journal of Personality and Social Psychology*, 79, 763–75.

Guttentag, M. (1983). *Too Many Women: the Sex Ratio Question*. Beverly Hills, CA: Sage.

Harris, M. J. (1991). *Cultural Anthropology* (3rd edn). New York: HarperCollins.

Hochschild, A. (1998). *King Leopold's Ghost: a Story of Greed, Terror, and Heroism in Colonial Africa*. Boston, MA: Houghton Mifflin.

Jackman, M. R. (1994). *The Velvet Glove: Paternalism and Conflict in Gender, Class, and Race Relations*. Berkeley, CA/London: University of California Press.

Jöreskog, K. G. and Sörbom, D. (1993). *Lisrel 8: Structural Equation Modeling with the SIMPLIS Command Language*. Hove, UK/Chicago, IL: Lawrence Erlbaum Associates/Scientific Software International.

Jost, J. T. and Banaji, M. R. (1994). The role of stereotyping in system-justification and the production of false consciousness. *British Journal of Social Psychology*, 33, 1–27.

Katz, I. (1981). *Stigma: a Social Psychological Analysis*. Hillsdale, NJ: Erlbaum.

Katz, I. and Hass, R. G. (1988). Racial ambivalence and value conflict: correlational and priming studies of dual cognitive structures. *Journal of Personality and Social Psychology*, 55, 893–905.

Kilianski, S. and Rudman, L. A. (1998). Wanting it both ways: do women approve of benevolent sexism? *Sex Roles*, 39, 332–52.

Kipling, R. (1899). The White Man's burden: a poem. *McClure's Magazine*, 20, 290.

Moya, M., Exposito, F. and Casado, P. (1999). *Women's Reactions to Hostile and Benevolent Sexist Situations*. Paper presented at the 22nd General Meeting of the European Association of Experimental Social Psychology (July).

Pomeroy, S. B. (1975). *Goddesses, Whores, Wives, and Slaves: Women in Classical Antiquity*. New York: Schocken.

Pratto, F. (1996). Sexual politics: the gender gap in the bedroom, the cupboard, and the cabinet. In D. M. Buss and N. M. Malamuth (eds.), *Sex, Power, and Conflict* (pp.179–230). New York: Oxford University Press.

Ridgeway, C. (1992). *Gender, Interaction and Inequality.* New York: Springer-Verlag.

Rudman, L. A. (1998). Self-promotion as a risk factor for women: the costs and benefits of counter-stereotypical impression management. *Journal of Personality and Social Psychology*, **74**, 629–45.

Rudman, L. A. and Heppen, J. (2000). Some day my prince will come: implicit romantic fantasies and women's avoidance of power. Unpublished manuscript. Rutgers: The State University of New Jersey.

Salzman, P. C. (1999). Is inequality universal? *Current Anthropology*, **40**(1), 31–61.

Sidanius, J., Pratto, F. and Bobo, L. (1994). Social-dominance orientation and the political psychology of gender – a case of invariance. *Journal of Personality and Social Psychology*, **67**(6), 998–1,011.

Six, I. and Exckes, T. (1991). A closer look at the complex structure of gender stereotypes. *Sex Roles*, **24**, 57–71.

Smith, E. (1993). Social identity and social emotions: toward new conceptualizations of prejudice. In D. M. Mackie and D. L. Hamilton (eds.), *Affect, Cognition, and Stereotyping: Interactive Processes in Group Perception* (pp.297–315). San Diego, CA: Academic Press.

Smuts, B. (1996). Male aggression against women: an evolutionary perspective. In D. M. Buss and N. M. Malamuth (eds.), *Sex, Power, and Conflict* (pp.231–68). New York: Oxford University Press.

Spence, J. T. and Buckner, C. E. (2000). Instrumental and expressive traits, trait stereotypes, and sexist attitudes. *Psychology of Women Quarterly*, **24**, 44–62.

Tajfel, H. (1981). *Social Identity and Intergroup Relations.* London: Cambridge University Press.

Tavris, C. and Wade, C. (1984). *The Longest War: Sex Differences in Perspective* (2nd edn). San Diego, CA: Harcourt Brace Jovanovich.

United Nations Development Programme (UNDP) (1998). *Human Development Report 1998.* New York: Oxford University Press.

Williams, J. E. and Best, D. L. (1982). *Measuring Sex Stereotypes.* Beverly Hills, CA: Sage.

Woolf, V. (1981). *A Room of One's Own.* New York: Harcourt Brace Jovanovich (original work published 1929).

Young-Breuhl, E. (1996). *The Anatomy of Prejudices.* Cambridge, MA: Harvard University Press.

4   Prejudice and dehumanization

Nick Haslam and Stephen Loughnan

Prejudices are demeaning views of others, and what could be more demeaning than to view them as less than human? Instances of dehumanization appear in the historical record when groups are in violent conflict and in toxic contexts of genocide, atrocity and interethnic hatred. Familiar examples include Nazi portrayals of Jews as vermin and colonial images of Africans as simian brutes. Expressions of extreme prejudice often seem to involve metaphorical equations of disdained humans with degraded nonhumans. Of course, dehumanization is not simply a historical relic. There is ample evidence that forms of it continue into the present. A few contemporary examples from recent scholarly work may help to set the scene.

Hagan and Rymond-Richmond (2008) examined the experiences of Darfurian refugees from southern Sudan, who have suffered atrocities at the hands of Janjaweed militia and Sudanese government forces. These atrocities have been motivated in part by a racial agenda of Arabization. Attacking forces have used transparently dehumanizing epithets during their raids: 'They called her Nuba dog, son of dogs'; 'You donkey, you slave, we must get rid of you'; and 'You blacks are like monkeys. You are not human.'

Holtz and Wagner (2009) explored postings about Africans, Turks, Jews, Muslims and other groups on extreme right-wing German Internet discussion boards. In different ways these groups were commonly portrayed as parasites, barbarians, ape-like or as contagious agents.

Harris and Fiske (2006) conducted a neuroimaging study of social perception. When perceiving members of groups stereotyped as lacking warmth and competence (i.e. homeless people and drug users), brain structures that reliably activate during social cognitive tasks failed to activate, and those that subserve disgust were activated instead. By implication these people were perceived as vile objects rather than persons.

Research conducted in Canada by Esses *et al.* (2008) and by Hodson and Costello (2007) indicates that people commonly dehumanize immigrants and refugees, perceiving them as immoral barbarians. These dehumanizing perceptions are associated both with ideological orientations such as a belief in social hierarchy and with basic emotional responses of disgust and contempt.

These four examples of dehumanization differ widely in their targets and in their geographic location. One is directly linked to genocidal violence and others to race-hatred, distancing or social exclusion. What unites them is a denial of full humanity to particular individuals, often but not always accompanied by a metaphorical likening of those individuals to nonhumans. Dehumanization can be a particularly toxic form of prejudice, and a response to extraordinary situations (Castano and Giber-Sorolla, 2006), but it is also diverse in its expressions and not, we will argue, invariably extreme. Indeed, a key finding of recent research is that subtle forms of dehumanization occur and denials of humanness are in some respects banal and commonplace. To understand dehumanization we need to understand the full spectrum of its manifestations, and in the process a more nuanced understanding of prejudice may emerge.

In this chapter we will attempt to clarify how the emerging psychology of dehumanization relates to the established psychology of prejudice. We begin by outlining an abstract framework or model of dehumanization processes that has guided our own research programme. We emphasize how the model encompasses a wide variety of dehumanization-related phenomena, ranging from the subtle, mild and everyday to the explicit and atrocious, and that the milder variants are on a continuum with the more severe. By implication, although traditional understandings of dehumanization portray it as an extreme phenomenon, and the most appalling type of prejudice, these extreme manifestations are grounded in more innocent and everyday processes of social perception. We illustrate how our model illuminates several forms of prejudice, including those involving race, gender and social class, before concluding with a few reflections to what our research on dehumanization says about the prejudice problematic.

Understanding humanization: a new model

Making sense of dehumanization has been a very active concern in recent social psychology after a relatively long hiatus that followed the classic works by Kelman (1976), Opotow (1990) and Staub (1992). The emergence of this 'new look' at dehumanization can be credited to the work of Jacques-Philippe Leyens and colleagues (e.g. Leyens *et al.*, 2000), who documented the 'infrahumanization' effect. Leyens and colleagues found that people tend to reserve uniquely human emotions to their own national group and deny them to outgroups. By implication, the ingroup is more human than the outgroup, and the outgroup is more animal-like than the ingroup. Importantly, this effect was distinct from any simple favouring of the ingroup and occurred even when the relevant intergroup contrast was not marked by conflict or antagonism.

The infrahumanization effect is deeply important for a variety of reasons. First, although we might be reluctant to say that a group that has been denied uniquely human emotions has been 'dehumanized', we would have to admit that it has been denied some of its humanity. By implication, dehumanization-like phenomena can take relatively mild forms that occur, in principle at least, on a severity continuum that extends upwards to the harshest, most degrading denials of humanity. Second, Leyens and colleagues made a crucial theoretical advance by demonstrating that humanness is a fundamental dimension of social perception. In a theoretical field dominated by valence – liking versus disliking, positive versus negative affect, warmth versus coldness and so on – they showed that an orthogonal dimension of human uniqueness was also in play during group perception. Third, the infrahumanization researchers produced a working definition of humanness, in the absence of which the concept of dehumanization is vague and slippery. Indeed, many earlier theoretical treatments of dehumanization lacked a clearly stated understanding of the property of humanness that is denied to the dehumanized. Fourth, by recognizing the banal and subtle nature of some dehumanization-like phenomena, they rendered these phenomena tractable to experimental social psychologists.

Our own work on dehumanization was stimulated by Leyens's research programme, and also by an almost accidental finding about the meaning of humanness. Whereas researchers in the infrahumanization tradition identified humanness as that which distinguishes humans from (other) animals, we found that people distinguish this sense of human uniqueness from an equally accessible sense of humanness as 'human nature'. To our initial surprise (Haslam et al., 2004), ratings of personality traits on the two senses of humanness were unrelated and different conceptual themes arose in each. Uniquely human traits tended to revolve around civility, refinement, higher cognition and morality, whereas human nature traits centred on emotionality, interpersonal warmth and openness. Subsequent research (Haslam et al., 2005) replicated and clarified this distinction. Uniquely human attributes were understood to reflect late-acquired social learnings (i.e. products of enculturation) whereas human nature attributes were seen as innate, essence-like (i.e. deep-seated and fundamental), cross-culturally universal and prevalent within the population. Human uniqueness thus corresponds to encultured humanity and human nature to common or shared humanity.

If humanness has two distinct senses then there should be two distinct ways in which people's humanness can be denied. This simple insight was the basis for our new theoretical framework for understanding dehumanization processes (Haslam, 2006). Individuals or groups that are denied human uniqueness will be perceived as lacking civility, refinement, rationality and morality, and hence seen as coarse, unintelligent, immoral: in a word, bestial. As non-human animals represent the contrast against which this sense of humanness is defined, people who are denied uniquely human attributes will be likened to animals. People who are denied human nature, on the other hand, will be perceived as lacking emotion, warmth and openness, and thus seen as mechanical, cold, rigid and lacking in vitality and animation. The contrastive nonhuman entity is less self-evident than in the case of human uniqueness, but we proposed that when people are denied human nature they are implicitly or explicitly likened to objects, automatons, robots or machines. Two broad types of dehumanization can therefore be posited: animalistic and mechanistic.

An important aspect of this theoretical framework is that it encompasses diverse forms and degrees of dehumanization. People may be denied each kind of humanness to varying extents, from the subtle to the categorical. The associated likening of people to particular kinds of nonhuman entity may be merely implicit, or may be explicitly expressed as verbal metaphor or dehumanizing imagery. The emotional temperature of the denial of human attributes and metaphorical likening to nonhuman entities may be cool or passionately heated. In the spectrum of animalistic dehumanization, for example, infrahumanization represents a mild version: uniquely human attributes are denied to a group in the absence of explicit animal metaphors and of overt conflict, derogation or intentions to inflict harm. Nazi ideology represents a much harsher manifestation of the same basic phenomenon: Jews were not only denied uniquely human attributes but also explicitly likened to degrading animals in a context of organized hatred and genocidal policy. In both cases it is the human–animal distinction that organizes the perception of groups, and it is the extent to which people are positioned towards the bestial pole of that distinction, and the conscious elaboration, hatred and violent intent that attaches to that pole, that determines the severity of the variants.

Similar differences of degree can be observed in denials of human nature. In the mildest cases, akin to infrahumanization, individuals or groups may simply be seen as lacking particular attributes with no strong evaluative charge attached to this denial. Such a phenomenon occurs in the everyday perception of self. Numerous studies have now shown that people tend to believe that they embody human nature to a greater extent than others, an effect that is cross-culturally robust and independent of the self-enhancing tendency to see the self as better than others (Haslam *et al.*, 2005; Haslam and Bain, 2007; Loughnan *et al.*, 2010b). A more severe form of human nature denial involves objectification, where people are perceived primarily as physical objects or attractive surfaces and thereby emptied of such humanizing qualities as warmth and emotion. In this case the person may not be explicitly described by object metaphors but the perceiver adopts an instrumental stance towards the person that is clearly dehumanizing.

Our model offers an abstract, two-dimensional framework for organizing the diverse forms of dehumanization. It recognizes that humanness is not monolithic, and neither is its denial. Moreover, it is elastic enough to encompass phenomena that are mild, everyday and perhaps undeserving of the grave term 'dehumanization' as well as terms that involve clear repudiations of people's humanity. The model aims to encompass dehumanization phenomena as they appear in all forms of social diversity, but in the next section we focus on how it might help to clarify prejudice based on race, gender and social class.

Applying the model to forms of prejudice

Race and ethnicity

Ethnicity or race is the domain in which dehumanization has most often been explored. Many of the prototypical examples of dehumanization involve the perception or treatment of particular ethnic or racial groups. In addition to the familiar example of vermin metaphors during the Holocaust and simian metaphors of Africans in colonial discourse, two of the examples that opened this chapter directly involved ethnicity. The third example, involving dehumanizing perceptions of refugees, almost certainly has an ethnic component as well rather than merely being a response to perceived incursion on national boundaries. Although our model argues that dehumanization phenomena occur in relation to many forms of social diversity – gender, disability, class, mental disorder and so on – race and ethnicity supply many of the clearest instances and attract much of the attention of researchers. Most likely the prominence of racial and ethnic categories reflects the explicit and organized nature of interethnic conflicts and also the ease with which ethnic groups can be essentialized (Haslam *et al.*, 2000), and thus treated as if they were different species.

Most psychological research on the dehumanization of ethnic groups involves our framework's animalistic version, in which uniquely human attributes are denied to group members and they may be likened, implicitly or explicitly, to animals. Most of the early demonstrations of the infrahumanization effect (see Leyens *et al.*, 2003, for a review) involved perceptions across national borders, or at least between ethnically distinct groupings within a single nation (e.g. mainland Spaniards versus Canary Islanders, Flemish versus Walloon Belgians). Thus the denial of uniquely human emotions to ethnic outgroups, in the absence of strong prejudice and without evidence of explicit use of animal metaphors, appears to be a basic and widespread phenomenon in the perception of ethnic groups.

More recent research has explored forms of ethnic group dehumanization that are considerably further along the severity spectrum but still clearly of the animalistic type. Perhaps the most remarkable demonstration is the work of Goff *et al.* (2008). Noting that ape metaphors have been used to describe African peoples from the days of colonial era 'racial science' and since, Goff *et al.* asked whether this metaphor persisted among contemporary white Americans. They showed that African-Americans were implicitly associated with apes, despite almost all of their participants professing no awareness of the historical link. This association was specific to apes and did not extend to big cats, as it might if animality in general (or wild and predatory animality) were seen as characteristic of African-Americans.

Importantly, Goff *et al.* went beyond simply revealing the implicit association, and showed how it may have a variety of implications. For example, priming apes led participants to believe a police beating of a racially ambiguous suspect was more justified if the target was described as black rather than white. In addition, subtle and not-so-subtle ape-related language (e.g. 'barbaric', 'beast', 'brute', 'jungle', 'savage', 'wild') featured much more often in reports of crimes with black defendants than in those with white defendants in one of the US's more esteemed newspapers. Perhaps more worryingly, higher levels of ape-related language in those reports predicted death penalty verdicts for black defendants even after controlling for crime severity and aggravating and extenuating circumstances. This work has a variety of crucial implications. First, it shows that animalistic views of a group can exist and operate unconsciously among people who would likely disavow explicit racial prejudice. Second, it shows that these implicit understandings of race, organized by animal metaphors with a deep history, can be present in half-hidden form within public discourse. Third, the work makes clear that the ape metaphor, when activated in relation to African-Americans, has consequences in the form of harsh and punitive treatment, or belief that such treatment is justified.

One reading of Goff *et al.*'s work is that certain forms of race-based dehumanization involve a perception of primitiveness, such that groups are perceived as phylogenetically backward or 'not yet human'. By this account, being associated with animals amounts to being seen as incompletely evolved, a meaning of animality that is particularly well captured by apes, which stand metaphorically for being prehuman. If it is true that perceived primitiveness underpins racial dehumanization, then we might expect that indigenous people are apt to be dehumanized in the same fashion as African-Americans. People living in traditional societies are often represented as primitives or 'savages' (Jahoda, 1999), so we might expect traditional peoples to be likened to animals. In recent work, Saminaden *et al.* (2010) tested this possibility, and found that traditional people were implicitly associated more with animals than people from modern, industrialized societies, and were also less associated with uniquely human attributes. This occurred despite using multi-ethnic stimuli to represent both traditional and modern peoples. Unpublished work by Loughnan (2009) similarly established an implicit association between one indigenous group (Aboriginal Australians) and one kind of animal (apes). By implication, prejudice towards indigenous and other traditional people may be influenced by an implicit perception of animality.

Interestingly, although 'primitives' were implicitly associated with animals in Saminaden *et al.* (2010), there was no tendency for participants to evaluate them negatively, either implicitly or explicitly. Indeed, our participants tended to report somewhat more positive explicit evaluations of traditional people. In this respect our findings suggest a milder form of dehumanization than the one documented by Goff *et al.* (2008), in which the white participants similarly associated African-Americans with apes, but also held negative implicit attitudes towards them. Dehumanizing associations may accompany neutral or even positive perceptions of groups, perhaps reflecting an unspoiled 'noble savage' view of indigenous people. Once again, it is necessary to decouple dehumanization from extreme dislike, although the two can of course be coupled in appalling ways. In the case of perceptions of indigenous people it is not difficult to imagine how perceived animality might be linked to paternalistic intervention or 'taming' forms of social control, even in the absence of explicit denigration. Arguably the recent Northern Territory intervention, visited on Aboriginal citizens in Australia, exemplifies this linkage.

Although in racial or ethnic contexts dehumanizing perceptions may tend to take the animalistic form, there is some evidence that the mechanistic form also appears. Bain *et al.* (2009) investigated white Australians' perceptions of East Asians and, symmetrically, Chinese immigrants' perceptions of white Australians. Our expectation was that white Australians would be likely to ascribe fewer human nature traits to Asians than to their own group, in accordance with stereotypes of Asians as lacking emotion, openness and warmth. According to our framework, denials of human nature should be accompanied with an implicit or explicit likening of Asians to robots, automatons or machines. Using a similar methodology to Saminaden *et al.* (2010), we found evidence of both patterns of implicit association: East Asian faces were associated with human nature traits less and robot- and machine-related words more than white faces. Interestingly, our Chinese participants demonstrated a more familiar infrahumanization-like effect, implicitly associating white faces with uniquely human traits less than East Asian faces, but not revealing an accompanying association of whites with animals.

Although this is the only demonstration to date of a mechanizing form of subtle dehumanization in an ethnic context, we believe that it is potentially important. Ethnic outgroups that cannot be plausibly demeaned as lacking civility and refinement – such as those that are more materially or culturally developed, or seen as threatening to outdo one's own group in these domains – can still be denied humanity along another dimension. They may not be closer to animals than us, but they have lost their essential humanity and become denatured robots. The behavioural implications of this mechanistic form of dehumanization are unclear, but in theory they might be expected to involve distancing, emotional or moral disengagement and a lack of concern for harm experienced by group members. If the group is denied the capacity for emotion or interpersonal warmth, its members' suffering and their proclivity to desire social connection are likely to be underestimated.

Gender

Gender is another major arena for the psychological study of prejudice, and the dehumanization of women in particular has attracted scholarly interest in several fields. Commonly dehumanization is mentioned in connection with pornography which, it is claimed, represents women as bodies for instrumental use rather than as autonomous experiencing subjects. Our dehumanization framework suggests that there may be two distinct ways in which women are denied humanness, both of which are germane to the study of sexism. There may be ways in which women are perceived as animal-like and denied uniquely human attributes, and there may also be ways in which women are viewed more as inanimate objects and denied human nature.

There is relatively little research addressing the denial of uniquely human attributes to women, but some work suggests that there are symbolic links between women and animals. In unpublished work similar to the research on race-related associations reviewed earlier, Reynolds (2008) has shown that women are implicitly associated with animals more than men. Her more recent work (Reynolds and Haslam, 2011) indicates that this may be a specific case of a more general tendency to associate women with nature. Analysis of media images revealed that women are much more commonly pictured in (and by implication *of*) nature, and analysis of people's conscious associations between gender and nature clearly showed the same pattern. In both of these studies the women–nature association was at least superficially positive. The implicit association between women and nature coexisted with an implicit preference for women over men, and people preferred women when they were associated with nature, and nature when it was characterized as feminine. However, this culturally supported woman–nature association may have mixed consequences, also linking women to the dark and wild side of nature (e.g. women's supposedly tempestuous or volcanic emotionality). Feminist theorists (Ortner, 1972; Plumwood, 1993; Roach, 2003) have argued that the women–nature association is deeply ambivalent, and underlies the subordination of women.

There has been little psychological study of this possibility. However, from a terror management theory perspective, negative reactions to women have been argued to stem in part from their association with animals. Goldenberg and Roberts (2004) theorized that women's distinctive biological functions in reproduction and breastfeeding serve as unwanted reminders of our similarity to other mammals, which is repugnant on existential grounds and therefore disparaged. The possibility that women are associated with animals in a way that has negative consequences for them is therefore plausible on theoretical and empirical grounds. In some respects women may be viewed as wild and bestial, much like animalized ethnic groups. Just as 'primitive' people may be evaluated in superficially positive ways while concurrently being likened to animals, women may be positively evaluated while implicitly linked to the ambivalent symbolic legacy of animal nature.

The other form of dehumanization recognized by our model also operates in the context of gender. Rather than being denied uniquely human attributes or likened to animals, women (and sometimes men) may be denied human nature and treated as inanimate objects. Objectification has rarely been discussed as a form of prejudice, perhaps in part because the focus of objectification research has been on the intrapersonal consequences of self-objectification (Fredrickson and Roberts, 1997), but it undoubtedly constitutes a demeaning perception of one group by another.

Recent research has begun to explore objectification from the standpoint of the perceiver rather than the target. This work acknowledges that objectification involves not only an overemphasis on people's attractive bodily surfaces, the component that has dominated earlier research on objectification, but also a denial of their minds. As Nussbaum (1995) has argued, objectification is problematic because it involves denying mental states and moral status to people and enables purely instrumental treatment of them. Consistent with this claim, Loughnan *et al.* (2010a) found that people who are pictured in objectifying ways (i.e. emphasizing the body or presenting it in a state of undress) were perceived as lacking a wide range of mental states, and were seen as having diminished moral standing and sensitivity to pain. In sum, objectified people were seen as easier to harm, less worthy of moral concern and less capable of suffering than others. Related findings have been obtained by Heflick and Goldenberg (2009), who asked participants to focus on either the appearance or personhood of Angelina Jolie or Sarah Palin. As our dehumanization model would predict, the objectifying condition produced a specific denial of human nature traits relative to the personhood condition.

The evidence that objectification brings about diminished mind attribution, particularly to female targets, is not confined to self-report questionnaire studies. Recent social neuroscience research by Cikara *et al.* (2011) suggests that objectified women simply fail to elicit social processing in (heterosexual) men. When viewing images of objectified and non-objectified women in a magnetic resonance imaging (MRI) scanner, male participants did not activate the brain regions involved in social cognition (i.e. the medial pre-frontal cortex, posterior cingulate and temporal poles) when observing the objectified images. Put simply, the objectified women were not appraised as social agents.

This new work on objectification is noteworthy because it shows how processes that interact with the depictions of women that saturate our visual culture produce subtly dehumanizing results. People who are perceived in ways that emphasize their sexualized bodies are denied mental states and traits that define our humanness. Once again, this subtle dehumanization need not be accompanied by hostility or even mild negative evaluation. Indeed, men who consume objectifying images of women are likely to evaluate them positively, and are motivated by appetite rather than aversion (Cikara *et al.*, in press). Although an objectifying view of women is not an intrinsically derogatory one, it can be considered prejudiced because it degrades and instrumentalizes them.

Class

Prejudice based on social class or economic disadvantage has received much less attention from psychologists than forms of prejudice based on race and gender. Nevertheless, perceptions of people from lower social class backgrounds are often demeaning and derogatory, and voicing class-based prejudice is often uninhibited by the taboos that surround expressions of racism or sexism. Despite its neglected status, class prejudice may be another domain in which prejudice takes a subtly dehumanizing form.

Intuitively, stereotypes of lower-class people tend to have rather similar content to those of Africans or other 'primitives'. Such people are often caricatured as uncivilized, unintelligent, lacking self-control, morally deficient, loud and libidinous or, to adopt a quaint Victorianism, 'just beastly'. As Jahoda (1999) observed:

> During the second half of the 19th century . . . the 'otherness' of the savage came to be extended to a whole series of European 'Others', as viewed from the pedestal of the educated male middle class . . . Savages, in this context, form part of a cluster that includes not only children but also the rural and urban poor, criminals, the mentally ill, and even women.

We might therefore suspect that class prejudice involves a denial of uniquely human qualities, the implicit or explicit likening of lower-class people to animals, and an accompanying attitude of contempt, disgust or disdain. We set out to explore the content of lower-class stereotypes in a recent series of studies conducted in three cultures: the 'white trash' stereotype in the US, the 'chav' stereotype in the UK, and the 'bogan' stereotype in Australia (Haslam *et al.*, 2009). Although some previous work had suggested that stereotypes of the poor were characterized primarily by low warmth and low competence (Fiske *et al.*, 2002), we examined whether, independently of these established dimensions of stereotype content, lower-class individuals were stereotyped as animal-like.

In the first study, participants in each country rated how people belonging to the relevant lower-class group differed from other people on a set of traits, or rated how apes differed from humans on the same traits. Averaged ratings of the two comparisons were then correlated across the traits. In every sample, the extent to which traits were seen as characteristic of the lower-class group was positively correlated ($rs = 0.35$–0.40) with the extent to which they were seen as more characteristic of apes than humans. There was some evidence that this correlation was especially strong for positive traits, indicating that lower-class people are denied the same human virtues that are denied to apes, rather than being ascribed specifically simian vices. By implication, animality, or ape-ishness specifically, was part of the lower-class stereotypes, which were remarkably concordant across the three cultures.

In our second study we focused on the bogan stereotype in Australia. Once again, some participants rated how bogans differed from other

Australians on a new set of traits. Other participants rated the same traits on the extent to which they represented the warmth, competence or morality (Leach *et al.*, 2007) stereotype content dimensions. Still other participants rated the traits on the extent to which they were more characteristic of apes, dogs or rats than humans. Mean ratings of the traits on the bogan stereotype item were regressed on the three stereotype content dimensions and the three animal stereotype items individually. Each animal stereotype was positively associated with the bogan stereotype independent of the stereotype content dimensions, confirming our hypothesis that animality is a distinct component of lower-class stereotypes.

One reason why animality appeared to be linked to the class stereotype beyond the more familiar dimensions is that it was less straightforwardly evaluative. Warmth, competence and morality are all transparently desirable, and to see a group as lacking them is to disparage it. However, lower-class stereotypes were ambivalent rather than simply derogatory, and include several perceived strengths. Animal stereotypes are equally ambivalent, a finding that mirrors Leyens and colleagues' observation that the uniqueness to humans of emotions is independent of their valence. Some aspects of animality that are judged positively appear to attach to lower-class people, picturing them as lovably simple and straightforward, and lacking the psychic burdens of civility. If this is the case then an approach that takes dehumanization seriously can help us to understand the specificity of social class prejudice. People of lower-class backgrounds may be seen as primitive and bestial, and lacking in uniquely human virtues, but they are not thereby intensely disliked. Rather, they are objects of condescension and patronization. This is still a form of prejudice, of course, but it is less likely to manifest itself as intense dislike than to be expressed in relatively gentle disdain and ridicule. Indeed, the stereotypic backwardness, primitiveness and simplicity of lower-class people makes them favoured targets for humour, unimpeded by the taboo that would attach to demeaning humour if it singled out racial or gendered targets.

Dehumanization and the 'prejudice problematic'

So what are the implications of our work on dehumanization for the 'prejudice problematic', the focus of this volume? We do not see our approach as radically incompatible with dominant existing models of prejudice by any means, but some elements of it do complicate, challenge or supplement those approaches. We will address two of these implications.

First, our approach accords with the view that prejudice cannot be equated with the negative evaluation of a group. Although some of the

more extreme forms of prejudice have been accompanied by dehumanizing rhetoric, incandescent hatred and inhumane cruelty, it is important
not to equate dehumanization with demonization (cf. Bar-Tal, 2000).
Subtle forms of dehumanization can occur in which the other's humanity
is attenuated or called into question without any explicit derogation.
Likening someone to an animal may occur in the context of disgust and
disparagement, but it can also occur in the context of loving condescension. Indeed, many animal metaphors are at least superficially positive.
Similarly, people can be objectified in the absence of any disdain for them
as persons: indeed, it may be the absence of affective engagement, positive
or negative, that enables the instrumental treatment of them as mere
means to ends. In short, dehumanization can be observed in the most
extreme forms of bigotry but also in milder forms in which others are
viewed not in straightforwardly negative terms, but with indifference or
even with superficially positive attitudes inflected by patronizing, conde-
scending or even idealizing perceptions. We claim no originality for this
idea – it is clearly expressed in Glick and Fiske's (1996) work on benevolent sexism – but we believe that our model of dehumanization points to
additional ways in which superficially positive or neutral views of others
can be counted as forms of prejudice.

Second, our work on dehumanization emphasizes the diversity of prejudices, and the need to attend to their qualitative differences rather than
reducing them all to negative evaluation. Again, we are far from the first to
make this argument, and again Fiske et al.'s (2002) work on the stereotype
content model has priority. Just as their work shows how different groups
are targets of prejudice that have different emotional colourations
depending on their stereotype content – envious towards cold but competent competitive groups, pitying and patronizing towards friendly but
incompetent groups, disgusted towards cold and incompetent groups –
ours similarly implies different tones of prejudice. Groups that are denied
uniquely human attributes and likened to animals are likely to be patron-
ized, condescended to and treated in paternalistic ways. By contrast,
groups that are denied human nature are likely to be disregarded, dis-
tanced, objectified and treated instrumentally.

In closing, we would argue that our dehumanization perspective shines
a new light on the existing psychology of prejudice. When prejudice is
understood traditionally as antipathy towards a social group, it is frequently accompanied by a denial of humanness to group members and
sometimes by explicit or implicit likening of them to nonhuman entities.
Some phenomena that appear to be prejudices but do not feature obvious
antipathy – viewing indigenous people as noble savages, benevolent sexism, objectifying attractive women, chuckling about the boorishness of the

poor – also appear to involve denials of humanness to members of a group. Could it be that a key ingredient of prejudice is that people are dehumanized, more or less subtly, rather than that they are viewed negatively?

References

Bain, P., Park, J., Kwok, C. and Haslam, N. (2009). Attributing human uniqueness and human nature to cultural groups: distinct forms of subtle dehumanization. *Group Processes and Intergroup Relations*, **12**, 789–805.

Bar-Tal, D. (2000). *Shared Beliefs in a Society: Social Psychological Analysis.* Thousand Oaks, CA: Sage.

Castano, E. and Giner-Sorolla, R. (2006). Not quite human: infrahumanization in response to collective responsibility for intergroup killing. *Journal of Personality and Social Psychology*, **90**, 804–18.

Cikara, M., Eberhardt, J. and Fiske, S. (2011). From agents to objects: sexist attitudes and neural responses to sexualized targets. *Journal of Cognitive Neuroscience*, **23**, 540–51.

Esses, V. M., Veenvliet, S., Hodson, G. and Mihic, L. (2008). Justice, morality, and the dehumanization of refugees. *Social Justice Research*, **21**, 4–25.

Fiske, S. T., Cuddy, A. J. C., Glick, P. and Xu, J. (2002). A model of (often mixed) stereotype content: competence and warmth respectively follow from perceived status and competition. *Journal of Personality and Social Psychology*, **82**, 878–902.

Fredrickson, B. and Roberts, T. (1997). Objectification theory: towards understanding women's lived experiences and mental health risks. *Psychology of Women Quarterly*, **21**, 173–206.

Glick, P. and Fiske, S. (1996). The ambivalent sexism inventory: differentiating hostile and benevolent sexism. *Journal of Personality and Social Psychology*, **70**, 491–512.

Goff, P. A., Eberhardt, J. L., Williams, M. J. and Jackson, M. (2008). Not yet human: implicit knowledge, historical dehumanization, and contemporary consequences. *Journal of Personality and Social Psychology*, **94**, 292–306.

Goldenberg, J. L. and Roberts, T. (2004). The beauty within the beast: an existential perspective on the objectification and condemnation of women. In J. Greenberg, S. L. Koole and T. Pyszczynski (eds.), *Handbook of Experimental Existential Psychology* (pp.71–85). New York: Guilford.

Hagan, J. and Rymond-Richmond, W. (2008). The collective dynamics of racial dehumanization and genocidal victimization in Darfur. *American Sociological Review*, **73**, 875–902.

Harris, L. T. and Fiske, L. T. (2006). Dehumanizing the lowest of the low: neuroimaging responses to extreme outgroups. *Psychological Science*, **17**, 847–53.

Haslam, N. (2006). Dehumanization: an integrative review. *Personality and Social Psychology Review*, **10**, 252–64.

Haslam, N. and Bain, P. (2007). Humanizing the self: moderators of the attribution of lesser humanness to others. *Personality and Social Psychology Bulletin*, **33**, 57–68.

Haslam, N., Bain, P., Douge, L., Lee, M. and Bastian, B. (2005). More human than you: attributing humanness to self and others. *Journal of Personality and Social Psychology*, **89**, 937–50.

Haslam, N., Bastian, B. and Bissett, M. (2004). Essentialist beliefs about personality and their implications. *Personality and Social Psychology Bulletin*, **30**, 1,661–73.

Haslam, N., Loughnan, S., Sutton, R. and Spencer, B. (2009). White trash, chavs, and bogans: animality in lower-class stereotypes. Unpublished manuscript.

Haslam, N., Rothschild, L. and Ernst, D. (2000). Essentialist beliefs about social categories. *British Journal of Social Psychology*, **39**, 113–27.

Heflick, N. and Goldenberg, J. (2009). Objectifying Sarah Palin: evidence that objectification causes women to be perceived as less competent and less fully human. *Journal of Experimental Social Psychology*, **45**, 598–601.

Hodson, G. and Costello, K. (2007). Interpersonal disgust, ideological orientations, and dehumanization as predictors of intergroup attitudes. *Psychological Science*, **18**, 691–8.

Holtz, P. and Wagner, W. (2009). Essentialism and attribution of monstrosity in racist discourse: right-wing internet postings about Africans and Jews. *Journal of Community and Applied Social Psychology*, **19**, 411–25.

Jahoda, G. (1999). *Images of Savages: Ancient Roots of Modern Prejudice in Western Culture*. London: Routledge.

Kelman, H. C. (1976). Violence without restraint: reflections on the dehumanization of victims and victimizers. In G. M. Kren and L. H. Rappoport (eds.), *Varieties of Psychohistory* (pp.282–314). New York: Springer.

Leach, C. W., Ellemers, N. and Barreto, M. (2007). Group virtue: the importance of morality (vs. competence and sociability) in the positive evaluation of ingroups. *Journal of Personality and Social Psychology*, **93**, 234–49.

Leyens, J-P., Cortes, B., Demoulin, S., Dovidio, J. F., Fiske, S. T., Gaunt, R. *et al.* (2003). Emotional prejudice, essentialism, and nationalism: the 2002 Tajfel lecture. *European Journal of Social Psychology*, **33**, 703–17.

Leyens, J.-P., Paladino, P. M., Rodriguez-Torres, R., Vaes, J., Demoulin, S., Rodriguez-Perez, A. *et al.* (2000). The emotional side of prejudice: the attribution of secondary emotions to ingroups and outgroups. *Personality and Social Psychology Review*, **4**, 186–97.

Loughnan, S. (2009). Implicit perceptions of Aboriginal Australians. Unpublished data.

Loughnan, S., Haslam, N., Murnane, T., Vaes, J., Reynolds, C. and Suitner, C. (2010a). Objectification leads to depersonalization: the denial of mind and moral concern to objectified others. *European Journal of Social Psychology*, **40**, 709–17.

Loughnan, S., Leidner, B., Doron, G., Haslam, N., Kashima, Y., Tong, J. *et al.* (2010b). Universal biases in self-perception: better and more human than average. *British Journal of Social Psychology*, **49**, 91–105.

Nussbaum, M. (1995). Objectification. *Philosophy and Public Affairs*, **24**, 249–91.

Opotow, S. (1990). Moral exclusion and injustice: an introduction. *Journal of Social Issues*, **46**, 1–20.

Ortner, S. (1972). Is female to male as nature is to culture? *Feminist Studies*, **1**, 5–31.

Plumwood, V. (1993). *Feminism and the Mastery of Nature.* London: Routledge.

Reynolds, C. (2008). Implicit associations between women and nature. Unpublished data.

Reynolds, C. and Haslam, N. (2011). Evidence for an association between women and nature: an analysis of media images and mental representations. *Ecopsychology,* **3,** 59–64.

Roach, M. (2003). *Mother/Nature.* Bloomington, IN: Indiana University Press.

Saminaden, A., Loughnan, S. and Haslam, N. (2010). Afterimages of savages: implicit associations between 'primitive' peoples, animals, and children. *British Journal of Social Psychology,* **49,** 91–105.

Staub, E. (1992). *The Roots of Evil: the Origins of Genocide and other Group Violence.* New York: Cambridge University Press.

5 Stereotyping, prejudice and discrimination revisited: from William James to W. E. B. Du Bois

Stanley O. Gaines, Jr

During the mid-to-late 1990s, Edward Reed and I (Gaines and Reed, 1994, 1995; Reed and Gaines, 1997) published a series of articles on prejudice. We consistently contrasted Gordon Allport's (1954) mainstream, white-oriented perspective on prejudice with W. E. B. Du Bois's (1903/2004) non-mainstream, black-oriented perspective on prejudice. We argued that in order to understand the causes and consequences of prejudice in all their complexity, mainstream social psychologists would need to acquaint themselves with Du Bois's (1903/2004) *The Souls of Black Folk* as well as with Allport's (1954) *The Nature of Prejudice*. Although our perspective was criticized in some quarters (e.g. Lee, 1996; see also Collins and Gleaves, 1998), the overwhelmingly positive responses that we received (e.g. Jones, 1997; Markus, 2008; Phinney, 1996; Sellers *et al.*, 1998) suggested to us that we had identified a genuine gap in the mainstream literature on stereotyping, prejudice and discrimination (for a discussion of the links among these concepts, see Fiske, 1998).

At the time of Ed Reed's death (see Mace, 1997), Ed and I were beginning to move away from our original Allport–Du Bois comparisons and towards a deeper understanding of Du Bois's (1903/2004) self-theory in its own right. Indeed, Sellers *et al.* (1998) pointed out that although Ed and I (Gaines and Reed, 1994, 1995) ostensibly focused on mainstream versus non-mainstream perspectives on prejudice, we actually devoted much of our commentary to mainstream versus non-mainstream perspectives on racial identity. Our brief comparisons between James's (1890) white-oriented self-theory and Du Bois's (1903/2004) black-oriented self-theory hint at our fascination with the implications of Du Bois's self-theory for black racial identity development. In the present chapter, I shall expand on the theme of racial identity as articulated in Du Bois's self-theory.

Intergroup relations from the perspective of stigmatized individuals: an overview

In a review of the literature on intergroup relations, Shelton (2000) noted that one of the most striking changes from the third edition of the

Handbook of Social Psychology (edited by Lindzey and Aronson, 1985) to the fourth edition of the *Handbook of Social Psychology* (edited by Gilbert, Fiske and Lindzey, 1998) was the addition of a chapter on stigmatized persons' perspectives (Crocker *et al.*, 1998) to the requisite chapter on nonstigmatized persons' perspectives (Brewer and Brown, 1998; see also Stephan, 1985). The *Handbook of Social Psychology* chapter on stigmatized persons' perspectives on intergroup relations (Crocker *et al.*, 1998) emphasized the concept of *stereotype threat*, or the anxiety stigmatized persons experience when they are confronted with the possibility that they will behave in a way that reinforces existing societal overgeneralizations about their entire ingroup (Steele, 1997). In turn, stereotype threat has emerged as a major influence on stigmatized individuals' academic performance within Helms's (2006) individual difference model for conceptualizing test score fairness. In Helms's model, stereotype threat would be expected to undermine stigmatized individuals' academic performance.

The concept of stereotype threat (Steele, 1997) is informed largely by Erving Goffman's (1963) interactional role theory, which posits that stigmatized individuals face an uphill climb in attempting to persuade nonstigmatized individuals to view them as they view themselves (for a review, see Stryker and Statham, 1985). Accordingly, the literature on stereotype threat emphasizes the difficulty that stigmatized individuals face in trying to persuade nonstigmatized individuals not to view their potentially suboptimal performance as symptomatic of the entire stigmatized ingroup (Crocker *et al.*, 1998). Most studies treat stereotype threat as a situationally induced variable to which all members of a stigmatized group are vulnerable (Jones, 1997). Exactly what stigmatized individuals can do proactively to prevent nonstigmatized persons from applying societal overgeneralizations to entire stigmatized groups remains somewhat unclear.

I believe that another individual–difference influence on academic test performance in Helms's (2006) model – namely, *racial identity* (i.e. individuals' acknowledgement of, and affective responses towards, those ethnic ingroups that are defined on the basis of presumed biological heritage; Gaines and Reed, 1994) – shows promise as a positive predictor of stigmatized persons' academic performance, but has not received the same attention that stereotype threat has received within the mainstream social-psychological literature on intergroup relations. Unlike stereotype threat, the concept of racial identity is derived largely from Du Bois's (1903/2004) self-theory. For reasons described above, I focus on Du Bois's self-theory, which in turn was derived largely from James's (1890) self-theory but diverges from James's self-theory in certain important respects, as I examine the concept of racial identity. Moreover, drawing upon the second edition of Jones's *Prejudice and Racism* (1997), I consider the extent to which the concept of stereotype threat can be reinterpreted and, thus, can be integrated with the concept of racial identity within Du Bois's self-theory.

Origins of W. E. B. Du Bois's self-theory: William James's self-theory

As Hall and Lindzey (1957) pointed out, every self-theory in psychology ultimately owes its existence to James's (1890) self-theory, either directly or indirectly. James contended that the self (i.e. individuals' awareness that they are simultaneously separate from, yet connected to, all other living entities) is multidimensional in nature. Within James's self-theory, components of the self include the *material self* (i.e. those aspects of the self that can be regarded as physical possessions); the *spiritual self* (i.e. those aspects of the self that can be regarded as psychological attributes); the *social self* (i.e. those aspects of the self that can be regarded as products of interaction with other persons); and *pure ego* (i.e. individuals' ongoing streams of consciousness). The material, spiritual and social selves reflect the self-as-object; whereas the pure ego reflects the self-as-subject (Hall and Lindzey, 1957).

Given the dominance of social-cognitive theories and research in mainstream social psychology since the 1970s (Jones, 1985; Taylor, 1998), it might seem surprising that James's (1890) emphasis on consciousness was ever controversial. However, in developing psychoanalytic theory, Freud (1900) argued that James had overemphasized individuals' conscious experience. Subsequently, in developing operant reinforcement theory, Skinner (1938) argued that both James and Freud had overemphasized the self as a determinant of individuals' behaviour. It was only after the cognitive revolution of the 1960s that social psychologists began to rediscover James's self-theory en masse (Fiske and Taylor, 1984).

In *The Principles of Psychology*, James (1890) distinguished between the concepts of *self* (which presumed that the origins of human beings' awareness were biologically prewired) and *soul* (which presumed that the origins of human beings' awareness were divinely preordained; Hall and Lindzey, 1957). However, James's (1890) use of the term *spiritual self* to describe individuals' psychological attributes was not accidental. In *The Varieties of Religious Experience*, James (1902) blurred the distinction between self and soul even further, invoking the concept of a divided self or divided soul as a primary source of mental illness. Thus, although James's (1890) theory is properly regarded as a theory of the self, James did not entirely rule out the viability of a theory of the soul.

Du Bois's self-theory as distinct from James's self-theory

Merely a concrete test of the underlying principles of the great republic [of the US] is the Negro Problem, and the spiritual striving of the freedmen's sons is the travail of souls whose burden is almost beyond the measure of their strength, but who bear it in the name of an historic race, in the name of this the land of their fathers' fathers, and in the name of human opportunity. (W. E. B. Du Bois, *The Souls of Black Folk* (1903/2004, p. 7))

Shortly before the publication of James's (1890) *The Principles of Psychology*, Du Bois – who is known today as a sociologist and historian (Zuckerman, 2002) – completed an undergraduate course on psychology, taught by James (Kloppenberg, 2004). In his writings, Du Bois did not explicitly comment upon the impact of James's self-theory on Du Bois's (1903/2004) self-theory. Nevertheless, Du Bois's recognition of James's concept of the divided self or divided soul is evident in Du Bois's self-theory (Zuckerman, 2002).

In *The Souls of Black Folk*, Du Bois (1903/2004) introduced the concept of *double consciousness* (i.e. the simultaneous African/interdependent and American/independent aspects of the self) to the psychological literature (Markus, 2008). According to Du Bois, in an ideal world, persons of African descent in the US need not experience conflict between their African and American selves. However, American society imposes a dichotomy between individuals' African and American selves, thus leading some African Americans to conclude that they must embrace one aspect of themselves even as they reject the other aspect of themselves in order to maintain sanity (Gaines and Reed, 1995).

As noted above, Du Bois's (1903/2004) concept of double consciousness calls to mind James's (1890) concept of the divided self or divided soul. However, Du Bois's concept of double consciousness differs from James's concept of the divided self or divided soul in two major respects. First, Du Bois's concept of double consciousness specifically addresses African Americans' social-psychological experiences; whereas James's concept of the divided self or divided soul does not specifically address the social-psychological experiences of any stigmatized group (Reed and Gaines, 1997). Second, Du Bois's concept of double consciousness allows for the possibility that two distinct aspects of the self potentially can coexist in relative harmony; whereas James's concept of the divided self or divided soul does not allow for such a possibility (Gaines and Reed, 1995).

Racial identity as a key construct in Du Bois's self-theory

We feel and know that there are many delicate differences in race psychology, numberless changes that our crude social measurements are not yet able to follow minutely, which explain much of history and social development. At the same time, too, we know that these considerations have never adequately explained or excused the triumph of brute force and cunning over weakness and innocence. (W. E. B. Du Bois, *The Souls of Black Folk* (1903/2004, p. 87))

Much as Karen Horney eventually did in the late 1920s when she advocated a 'feminine psychology' (published several decades later in Horney, 1967) as a complement to Freud's (1900) male-oriented psychoanalytic theory, Du Bois (1903/2004) advocated a 'race psychology' as a complement to James's (1890) white-oriented self-theory. However, unlike Horney and Freud, Du Bois and James never engaged in a public feud; and Du Bois never framed his self-theory in explicit opposition to James's self-theory. Du Bois simply charted a different theoretical course for himself, and for psychology, than James could have charted experientially (Curtis-Tweed, 2003).

The quotation from Du Bois (1903/2004) cited above is noteworthy for two reasons. First, more than seventy years before *The Journal of Black Psychology* was established, Du Bois was advocating a version of psychology that would examine the differential impact of race relations on the social and personality development of blacks versus whites (Cokley *et al.*, 2001). Second, more than a hundred years ago, Du Bois was alerting researchers to potential problems regarding the measurement of racial similarities and differences in social and personality development; such problems continue to plague research on racial identity (Sellers *et al.*, 1998).

In Du Bois's (1903/2004) self-theory, individual African Americans' racial identity ultimately arises as a product of those individuals' particular responses to the historical and cultural conditions into which those individuals were born. Within the US, prominent historical conditions include slavery and emancipation, segregation and integration; prominent cultural conditions include white Christianity's frequent tolerance of injustice and black Christianity's equally frequent insistence upon justice, white minstrel singers' blackface mimickry and black jazz musicians' invention of a uniquely American art form (Jones, 1997). This is not to say that African Americans' racial identity is predetermined, either by genes or by the environment. To the contrary, African Americans' racial identity is acquired rather than inherited, dynamic rather than static (Coviello, 2003).

Racial identity as a unique form of ethnic identity

Phinney (1996) argued that Du Bois's (1903/2004) self-theory primarily addresses links between ethnicity and minority status, rather than links between ethnicity and identity. Furthermore, drawing upon Erik Erikson's (1968) ego psychology, Phinney (1990) contended that the concept of racial identity can be subsumed within the broader concept of *ethnic identity* (i.e. individuals' acknowledgement of, and affective responses towards, those ethnic ingroups that are defined on the basis of presumed biological and/or cultural heritage; Landrine and Klonoff, 1996). However, Sellers *et al.* (1998) countered that (1) Phinney's perspective on ethnic identity was more compatible with mainstream psychology than with black psychology, and (2) Du Bois's self-theory not only deals directly with racial identity (as opposed to other types of ethnic identity) but is more compatible with black psychology than with mainstream psychology.

Racial identity is not the only type of ethnic identity that one encounters in Du Bois's self-theory. Granted, *The Souls of Black Folk* (Du Bois, 1903/2004) primarily addresses racial identity among African Americans. However, later writings by Du Bois, such as the enlarged edition of *The World and Africa* (Du Bois, 1965), also address *national identity* (i.e. individuals' acknowledgement of, and affective responses towards, those ethnic ingroups that are defined on the basis of citizenship or naturalization; Gaines, 2002). During the final years of his life, Du Bois repatriated to Ghana (Taylor, 2004). Du Bois (1965) noted that the national identity of African-descent persons in a predominantly black nation such as Ghana was qualitatively different from the national identity of African-descent persons in a predominantly white nation such as the US.

Nevertheless, a conceptual thread that links *The Souls of Black Folk* (Du Bois, 1903/2004), the expanded edition of *The World and Africa* (Du Bois, 1965) and other expositions of Du Bois's self-theory is a strongly pan-African theme. For Du Bois, a shared racial identity possessed the potential to unify persons of African descent around the globe. Whether responding to slavery in the US or to colonization in Ghana, persons of African descent have battled racism throughout the past several hundred years in numerous historical and cultural contexts (Jones, 1997).

The historical role of the African American church in nurturing black racial identity development

The Preacher is the most unique personality developed by the Negro on American soil. A leader, politician, an orator, a 'boss', an intriguer, an idealist, – all these he is, and ever, too, the centre of a group of men, now twenty, now a thousand in number. The combination of a certain adroitness with deep-seated earnestness, of tact with consummate ability, gave him his preeminence, and helps him maintain it. (W. E. B. Du Bois, *The Souls of Black Folk* (1903/2004, p. 102))

Despite the enduring legacy of anti-black racism in the US, African Americans consistently score as high as (and, if anything, higher than) European Americans on measures of self-esteem (Gray-Little and Hafdahl, 2000; Hafdahl and Gray-Little, 2002). Mainstream theories of intergroup relations, such as social identity theory (Tajfel, 1981), provide a ready explanation: individuals' social and personal identities exert a positive influence on individuals' self-esteem; and black pride can foster high self-esteem as surely as can individual uniqueness (Brown, 1986). How, though, do African Americans develop positive racial identity in the first instance? Du Bois's (1903/2004) self-theory offers a provocative answer: the African American church historically has nurtured black racial identity development.

Du Bois was the first scholar to systematically examine the role that institutionalized religion plays in African Americans' everyday lives (Zuckerman, 2002). Not coincidentally, *The Souls of Black Folk* (Du Bois, 1903/2004) is laced with references to black spirituals, or 'sorrow songs' (Kahn, 2004). More to the point, according to Du Bois, the African American church historically has performed the vital functions of mediating African Americans' individual relationships with their Creator and of mediating African Americans' collective relationships with each other (Zuckerman, 2002). In the process, Du Bois's self-theory suggests, African Americans' African/interdependent and American/independent selves typically have developed with the support and sustenance of the African American church.

From the standpoint of Du Bois's (1903/2004) self-theory, it comes as no surprise that civil rights icon and Nobel Peace Prize winner Martin Luther King, Jr was nurtured by the African American church (Curtis-Tweed, 2003). King embodied the successful coexistence of the African/interdependent and American/independent selves like few other African Americans have done before or since his time (Jones, 1997). Ironically, even Du Bois could not make such a claim about his own two souls (Stikkers, 2008). As *The Autobiography of Martin Luther King, Jr.* (edited by Carson, 1999/2004) makes clear, the African American church served as a political and spiritual bedrock throughout King's life.

Beyond the African American church: the civil rights movement and racial identity in the age of Obama

In the years that have passed since Jones (1997) wrote about Martin Luther King, Jr as an exemplar of the relatively harmonious coexistence of African/interdependent and American/independent selves that can occur within individual African Americans, an epochal political event occurred that few students of intergroup relations foresaw: Barack Obama was elected as the first black President of the US in November 2008. Like King, Obama earned his reputation as a community organizer, eventually won the Nobel Peace Prize, and epitomizes the successful reconciliation of Du Bois's (1903/2004) 'two souls' (Gaines, 2010). However, unlike King, Obama was not nurtured by the African American church during his formative years (e.g. Obama, 1995/2008). How, then, can we explain the nurturance of Obama's two souls – or, indeed, the nurturance of the two souls of any African American who is part of Obama's age cohort?

No less a figure than Martin Luther King, Jr credited the civil rights movement with affirming African Americans' African/interdependent and American/independent souls (Allen and Bagozzi, 2001). In *Dreams from My Father*, Obama (1995/2008a) made it clear that he is a direct beneficiary of the seeds of the civil rights movement that Du Bois helped to plant and that King helped bring to fruition. Further reading of Obama's books suggests that *Dreams from My Father* (1995/2008a) captures Obama's African/interdependent soul; whereas *The Audacity of Hope* (2006/2008b) captures Obama's American/independent soul (Gaines, 2010). Of course, Obama's life story does not parallel that of most African Americans; Obama is the son of a black man from Kenya and a white woman from the US (Williams, 2008). However, Obama's ties to his father's native country may give Obama an even stronger claim to the African part of his heritage than would be the case for most African Americans (Gaines, 2010). In any event, among public figures, Obama may well embody the 'souls of black folk' more overtly than anyone else since King.

The ability to bring together African/interdependent and American/independent selves is not the special province of Martin Luther King, Jr, Barack Obama, or other public figures. Especially in the age of Obama (arguably the culmination of the civil rights era), African Americans increasingly may come to believe that they can lay claim to both of their 'souls'. It remains to be seen whether the candidacy, election and presidency of Obama will have such an effect on everyday African Americans. At a minimum, Obama's successful resolution of his 'two souls' not only mirrors the experiences of many African Americans but also offers hope for many other African Americans who are struggling with persistent stereotyping, prejudice and discrimination (Gaines, 2010).

Du Bois's concept of double consciousness: an unsustainable argument?

Judging from my review of the literature thus far, one might conclude – falsely, as it turns out – that scholars within black psychology unanimously accept Du Bois's (1903/2004) concept of double consciousness. Few, if any, concepts in black psychology (or, for that matter, in mainstream psychology) enjoy uncritical acceptance; and Du Bois's concept of double consciousness is no exception. Despite the widespread acclaim that scholars have accorded to Du Bois's concept of double consciousness within black psychology (e.g. Allen and Bagozzi, 2001; Jones, 1980; Lyubansky and Eidelson, 2005; Shelton and Sellers, 2000), some scholars within black psychology dispute that concept. For example, Allen (2003) asserted that Du Bois and his followers have fundamentally misconstrued African Americans' self-construals (see Markus and Kitayama, 1991).

Like many mainstream psychologists (see Shelton and Sellers, 2000, for a commentary), Allen (2003) denied that African Americans in the post-civil rights era possess multiple selves. Furthermore, Allen denied that African Americans in Du Bois's post-reconstruction era possessed multiple selves. Finally, in perhaps the most damning critique of double consciousness, Allen accused Du Bois (1903/2004) of engaging in 'sl[e]ight of hand' (2003, p. 25) by proposing such a concept.

Allen's (2003) critique of Du Bois's (1903/2004) concept of double consciousness serves as a useful reminder that no concept should escape critical evaluation. However, the weight of theoretical insight and empirical evidence simply does not lend credence to Allen's claim. In a content analysis of the *Journal of Black Psychology* from 1985 through to 1999, Cokley *et al.* (2001) found that personality was the dominant topic covered in articles from that journal; in turn, racial identity as conceived by Du Bois was the dominant topic within articles on personality from that journal.

Stereotype threat: a complement to racial identity?

Earlier in the present chapter, I noted that unlike the concept of racial identity (Gaines and Reed, 1995), the concept of stereotype threat (Steele, 1997) was derived from Goffman's (1963) interactional role theory, not from Du Bois's (1903/2004) self-theory. However, James Jones (1997) proposed that the concept of stereotype threat can be readily (re)interpreted from the vantage point of Du Bois's self-theory. As such, the concept of stereotype threat might function effectively as a complement to the concept of racial identity in helping social psychologists understand African Americans' responses to stereotyping, prejudice and discrimination.

According to Jones (1997), stereotype threat promotes conflict between African/interdependent and American/independent selves; whereas racial identity promotes cooperation between African/interdependent and American/independent selves. If Jones was correct, then Du Bois's (1903/2004) self-theory offers a substantive theoretical base for the predictions that Helms (2006) made regarding the impact of stereotype threat and racial identity on academic test performance. That is, stereotype threat undermines African Americans' academic test performance by forcing African Americans to question who they are (e.g. am I the exception to the rule; or am I just like the rest?); whereas racial identity bolsters African Americans' academic test performance by affirming African Americans' sense of who they are (e.g. I am proud of my race and can stand toe-to-toe with any white student).

Armed with knowledge about the pitfalls of stereotype threat, individual African Americans may decide not to succumb to stereotype threat. In testing situations, individual African Americans are not in a position to openly challenge examiners' claims about the diagnostic value of the exams (Steele, 1997). However, before as well as during those situations, individual African Americans can choose to acknowledge the existence of societal overgeneralizations and resolve to prove those overgeneralizations wrong.

Implications for research on racial identity and Du Bois's self-theory

Based on the preceding review of the literature on racial identity and Du Bois's (1903/2004) self-theory, one of the most important implications for research is that Helms's (2006) individual-difference model of academic test performance is fully compatible with Du Bois's (1903/2004) self-theory but is in need of empirical evidence. To my knowledge, no published study has examined individual differences in racial identity and stereotype threat together as predictors of individual differences in academic test performance. Such research would provide invaluable insight into the psychological tools that African Americans have at their disposal for responding effectively to stereotyping, prejudice and discrimination.

Another important implication for research on racial identity and Du Bois's (1903/2004) self-theory is that the causes, as distinct from the consequences, of racial identity are poorly understood and need empirical verification. In her individual-difference model of academic test perform-ance, Helms (2006) drew upon James Jones's (1972) first edition of *Prejudice and Racism* in identifying African Americans' experiences as targets of individual, institutional and cultural racism as predictors of African Americans' racial identity. Specifically, following Du Bois (1903/2004), one might expect African Americans' racial identity to develop as a positive response to various aspects of racism (although stereotype threat might develop as a negative response to those same aspects of racism). However, to my knowledge, no published study has verified such links at an empirical level.

Yet another important implication for research on racial identity and Du Bois's (1903/2004) self-theory is that, going beyond Helms's (2006) individual-difference model of academic test performance, immersion into Du Bois's self-theory might yield a multidimensional perspective on racial identity. For example, drawing upon Du Bois (1903/2004), Sellers *et al.* (1998) identified salience, centrality, regard and ideology as inter-related yet separate aspects of racial identity. However, Sellers *et al.*'s multidimensional model of racial identity has been largely ignored empir-ically, amid conceptual and empirical debates over the relative merits of racial identity (e.g. Helms, 2007) versus ethnic identity (e.g. Phinney and Ong, 2007) within the literature on ethnic and race psychology (for a discussion of the opposing positions, see Cokley, 2007).

Conclusion

Earlier in the present chapter, I observed that the fourth edition of the *Handbook of Social Psychology* included a chapter on stigmatized individ-uals (Crocke *et al.*, 1998) for the first time in the series (Shelton, 2000). However, in one respect, the more things change, the more they remain the same: Du Bois's (1903/2004) self-theory is nowhere to be found either in the chapter on intergroup relations from the third edition of the *Handbook of Social Psychology* (Stephan, 1985) or in the chapter on inter-group relations from the fourth edition of the *Handbook of Social Psychology* (Brewer and Brown, 1998). Although both chapters on inter-group relations cited Tajfel's (1981) social identity theory (which at least provides the conceptual space necessary to begin examining racial iden-tity; Gaines and Reed, 1994), and although both chapters on intergroup relations draw upon Allport's (1954) *The Nature of Prejudice*, neither chapter cited Du Bois's (1903/2004) *The Souls of Black Folk*. It is little wonder that neither chapter dealt specifically with racial identity, or that neither chapter had much to say about African Americans' perspectives on intergroup relations. Such perspectives, as several later contributors to this volume elaborate, are of vital significance, for no theory of prejudice or prejudice re-education can afford to overlook the responses of historically disadvantaged groups.

In conclusion, I return to the series of articles by Ed Reed and myself regarding social-psychological perspectives on prejudice and racial identity (Gaines and Reed, 1994, 1995; Reed and Gaines, 1997) that inspired the present chapter. Collins and Gleaves (1998, p. 531) referred to our advocacy of black psychology as 'controversial'. To the extent that we held out the possibility of Du Bois's (1903/2004) *The Souls of Black Folk* as supplanting Allport's (1954) *The Nature of Prejudice* within the literature on intergroup relations, I agree that our advocacy was controversial. However, to the extent that we ultimately recommended supplementing *The Nature of Prejudice* with *The Souls of Black Folk*, I do not view our advocacy as controversial at all. Rather, I believe (as I did during the mid-to-late 1990s when Ed and I were publishing articles on prejudice and racial identity) that *The Souls of Black Folk* is an undervalued yet rich source of insight into African Americans' social-psychological experiences. Hopefully, the present chapter reinforces that basic premise.

References

Allen, E., Jr (2003). Du Boisian double consciousness: the unsustainable argument. *Black Scholar*, **33**, 19–24.

Allen, R. L. and Bagozzi, R. P. (2001). Cohort differences in the structure and outcomes of an African American belief system. *Journal of Black Psychology*, **27**, 367–400.

Allport, G. W. (1954). *The Nature of Prejudice*. Reading, MA: Addison-Wesley.

Brewer, M. B. and Brown, R. J. (1998). Intergroup relations. In D. T. Gilbert, S. T. Fiske and G. Lindzey (eds.), *Handbook of Social Psychology* (4th edn, pp. 554–94). New York: McGraw-Hill.

Brown, R. (1986). *Social Psychology* (2nd edn). New York: Free Press.

Carson, C. (2004). *The Autobiography of Martin Luther King, Jr*. London: Abacus (original work published 1999).

Cokley, K. (2007). Critical issues in the measurement of ethnic and racial identity: a referendum on the state of the field. *Journal of Counseling Psychology*, **54**, 224–34.

Cokley, K., Caldwell, L., Miller, K. and Muhammad, G. (2001). Content analysis of the *Journal of Black Psychology* (1985–1999). *Journal of Black Psychology*, **27**, 424–38.

Collins, J. M. and Gleaves, D. H. (1998). Race, job applicants, and the five-factor model of personality: implications for black psychology, industrial/organizational psychology, and the five-factor theory. *Journal of Applied Psychology*, **83**, 531–44.

Coviello, P. (2003). Intimacy and affliction. *Modern Language Quarterly*, **64**, 1–32.

Crocker, J., Major, B. and Steele, C. (1998). Social stigma. In D. T. Gilbert, S. T. Fiske and G. Lindzey (eds.), *Handbook of Social Psychology* (Vol. 2, pp.504–53). Boston, MA: McGraw-Hill.

Curtis-Tweed, P. (2003). Experiences of African American empowerment: a Jamesian perspective on agency. *Journal of Moral Education*, **32**, 397–409.

Du Bois, W. E. B. (1965). *The World and Africa: an Inquiry into the Part which Africa has Played in World History* (enlarged edn). New York: Viking Press.

   (2004). *The Souls of Black Folk*. New York: Signet (original work published 1903).

Erikson, E. H. (1968). *Identity: Youth and Crisis*. New York: Norton.

Fiske, S. T. (1998). Prejudice, stereotyping, and discrimination. In D. T. Gilbert, S. T. Fiske and G. Lindzey (eds.), *Handbook of Social Psychology* (4th edn, pp.357–411). New York: McGraw-Hill.

Fiske, S. T. and Taylor, S. E. (1984). *Social Cognition*. Reading, MA: Addison-Wesley.

Freud, S. (1900). *The Interpretation of Dreams* (Joyce Crick, trans.). London: Oxford University Press.

Gaines, S. O., Jr (2002). Discredited and discreditable identities: one black American's experiences in the United States, Jamaica, and England. *Western Journal of Black Studies*, **26**, 159–64.

   (2010). The 'two souls' of Barack Obama. *The Western Journal of Black Studies*, **34**, 316–24.

Gaines, S. O., Jr and Reed, E. S. (1994). Two social psychologies of prejudice: Gordon W. Allport, W. E. B. Du Bois, and the legacy of Booker T. Washington. *Journal of Black Psychology*, **20**, 8–28.

   (1995). Prejudice: from Allport to Du Bois. *American Psychologist*, **50**, 96–103.

Gilbert, D. T., Fiske, S. T. and Lindzey, G. (eds.) (1998). *Handbook of Social Psychology* (4th edn, Vols. 1 and 2). New York: McGraw-Hill.

Goffman, E. (1963). *Stigma: Notes on the Management of Spoiled Identity*. Englewood Cliffs, NJ: Prentice-Hall.

Gray-Little, B. and Hafdahl, A. R. (2000). Factors influencing racial comparisons of self-esteem: a quantitative synthesis. *Psychological Bulletin*, **126**, 26–54.

Hafdahl, A. R. and Gray-Little, B. (2002). Explicating methods in reviews of race and self-esteem. *Psychological Bulletin*, **128**, 409–16.

Hall, C. S. and Lindzey, G. (1957). *Theories of Personality*. New York: John Wiley and Sons.

Helms, J. E. (2006). Fairness is not validity or cultural bias in racial group assessment: a quantitative perspective. *American Psychologist*, **61**, 845–59.

   (2007). Some better practices for measuring racial and ethnic identity constructs. *Journal of Counseling Psychology*, **54**, 235–46.

Horney, K. (1967). *Feminine Psychology*. New York: Norton.

James, W. (1890). *The Principles of Psychology* (Vols. 1 and 2). New York: Dover.

   (1902). *The Varieties of Religious Experience*. Glasgow, UK: Collins.

Jones, E. E. (1985). Major developments in social psychology during the past five decades. In G. Lindzey and E. Aronson (eds.), *Handbook of Social Psychology* (3rd edn, Vol. 1, pp.47–107). New York: Random House.

Jones, J. M. (1972). *Prejudice and Racism*. Reading, MA: Addison-Wesley.
  (1997). *Prejudice and Racism* (2nd edn). New York: McGraw-Hill.
Jones, R. S. (1980). Finding the black self: a humanistic strategy. *Journal of Black Psychology*, 7, 17–26.
Kahn, J. S. (2004). Religion and the binding of *The Souls of Black Folk*. *Philosophia Africana*, 7, 17–31.
Kloppenberg, J. T. (2004). Pragmatism and the practice of history: from Turner and Du Bois to today. *Metaphilosophy*, 34, 202–25.
Landrine, H. and Klonoff, E. A. (1996). *African American Acculturation*. Thousand Oaks, CA: Sage Publications.
Lee, Y.-T. (1996). Difference, not prejudice, engenders intergroup tension. *American Psychologist*, 52, 267–8.
Lindzey, G. and Aronson, E. (eds.) (1985). *Handbook of Social Psychology* (3rd edn, Vols. 1 and 2). New York: Random House.
Lyubansky, M. and Eidelson, R. J. (2005). Revisiting Du Bois: African American double consciousness and its relationship to beliefs about one's racial and national groups. *Journal of Black Psychology*, 31, 3–26.
Mace, W. M. (1997). In memoriam: Edward S. Reed, 1954–1997. *Ecological Psychology*, 9, 179–88.
Markus, H. R. (2008). Pride, prejudice, and ambivalence: toward a unified theory of race and ethnicity. *American Psychologist*, 63, 651–70.
Markus, H. R. and Kitayama, S. (1991). Culture and the self: implications for cognition, emotion, and motivation. *Psychological Review*, 98, 224–53.
Obama, B. (2008a). *Dreams from my Father: a Story of Race and Inheritance*. Edinburgh, UK: Canongate Books (original work published 1995).
  (2008b). *The Audacity of Hope: Thoughts on Reclaiming the American Dream*. Edinburgh, UK: Canongate Books (original work published 2006).
Phinney, J. S. (1990). Ethnic identity in adolescents and adults: a review of research. *Psychological Bulletin*, 108, 499–514.
  (1996). When we talk about American ethnic groups, what do we mean? *American Psychologist*, 51, 918–27.
Phinney, J. S. and Ong, A. D. (2007). Conceptualization and measurement of ethnic identity: current status and future directions. *Journal of Counseling Psychology*, 54, 271–81.
Reed, E. S. and Gaines, S. O., Jr (1997). Not everyone is 'different-from-me': toward an historico-cultural account of prejudice. *Journal of Black Psychology*, 23, 245–74.
Sellers, R. M., Smith, M. A., Shelton, J. N., Rowley, S. A. J. and Chavous, T. M. (1998). Multidimensional model of racial identity: a reconceptualization of African American racial identity. *Personality and Social Psychology Review*, 2, 18–39.
Shelton, J. N. (2000). A reconceptualization of how we study issues of racial prejudice. *Personality and Social Psychology Review*, 4, 374–90.
Shelton, J. N. and Sellers, R. M. (2000). Situational stability and variability in African American racial identity. *Journal of Black Psychology*, 26, 27–50.
Skinner, B. F. (1938). *The Behavior of Organisms: an Experimental Analysis*. New York: Appleton-Century-Crofts.

Steele, C. M. (1997). A threat in the air: how stereotypes shape the intellectual identities and performance of women and African-Americans. *American Psychologist*, **52**, 613–29.

Stephan, W. G. (1985). Intergroup relations. In G. Lindzey and E. Aronson (eds.), *Handbook of Social Psychology* (3rd edn, Vol. 2, pp.599–658). New York: Random House.

Stikkers, K. W. (2008). An outline of methodological Afrocentrism, with particular application to the thought of W. E. B. Du Bois. *Journal of Speculative Philosophy*, **22**, 40–9.

Stryker, S. and Statham, A. (1985). Symbolic interaction and role theory. In G. Lindzey and E. Aronson (eds.), *Handbook of Social Psychology* (3rd edn, Vol. 1, pp.311–78). New York: Random House.

Tajfel, H. (1981). *Human Groups and Social Categories*. Cambridge, UK: Cambridge University Press.

Taylor, P. C. (2004). What's the use of calling Du Bois a pragmatist? *Metaphilosophy*, **35**, 99–114.

Taylor, S. E. (1998). The social being in social psychology. In D. T. Gilbert, S. T. Fiske and G. Lindzey (eds.), *Handbook of Social Psychology* (4th edn, Vol. 1, pp.58–95). New York: McGraw-Hill.

Williams, R., III (2008). Barack Obama and the complicated boundaries of blackness. *Black Scholar*, **38**, 55–61.

Zuckerman, P. (2002). The sociology of religion of W. E. B. Du Bois. *Sociology of Religion*, **63**, 239–53.

6 Beyond 'old' and 'new': for a social psychology of racism

Samuel Pehrson and Colin Wayne Leach

In 1950, the United Nations Educational, Scientific and Cultural Organization (UNESCO) issued a paper entitled *The Race Concept* that had been drafted by a group of prominent biological and social scientists (reproduced in UNESCO, 1952). The statement used the term 'racism' – then a relatively new term – to refer to a faulty and illegitimate science of human categories. It denounced racism in terms of two related elements: scientifically, it was seen to rest on beliefs about the attributes of social groups that were unsubstantiated by available evidence; morally, it debased human dignity by relating to people in terms of their ascribed 'race', rather than simply as human beings. It was therefore an aberration from the liberal project based on a false pseudoscience of 'race'. *The Race Question* set the agenda for an anti-racist programme consisting of undermining the scientific validity of the notion of 'race' and combating ignorance about such matters through education. This agenda became known as the UNESCO tradition, and has gone on to form the basis for most top-down forms of anti-racism (Lentin, 2005).

In a similar vein, a statement had been issued in 1938 by the American Psychological Association (APA; reproduced in Benedict, 1942/1983), repudiating theories of genetic inequality of races. The APA statement suggests an 'emotional', rather than factual, basis for such theories. This, along with the publication of *The Authoritarian Personality* (Adorno *et al.*, 1950) and *The Nature of Prejudice* (Allport, 1954), marks a shift in focus within psychology away from the study of racial differences towards the question of why beliefs in such differences arise and persist despite being false (Billig, 1985; Duckitt, 1992; Pettigrew, 2007; Reicher, 2007; Reicher and Hopkins, 2001).

Unlike the UNESCO tradition, which deals directly with racial theories and challenges the biological reality of racial categories, the psychology of prejudice leaves the ontological status of racial categories unexamined. The agenda has been to explain when and how certain racially defined groups come to feel a certain way about others. Thus, while psychology (with some exceptions) gave up the notion of race superiority, it has rarely scrutinized the notion of race as other social sciences have done. However, it is instructive to situate the birth of the prejudice paradigm within the intellectual climate set up by the UNESCO statement. Just as racism was understood as a view of human categories that contradicted available evidence, prejudice was defined as a 'faulty and inflexible generalisation' (Allport, 1954, p. 9). The UNESCO tradition and the prejudice paradigm share a view of racism (whether originating in pseudoscience, psychopathology or both) as infecting modern nation states from without and contradicting the liberal values on which they are founded.

Towards the end of the 1970s, it became apparent that Allport's own country, the US, remained deeply structured along racial lines even though *de jure* segregation had been abolished and most white people did not seem to endorse genetic beliefs about the inferiority of black people or to advocate segregation. Far from standing against liberalism, those who opposed initiatives for social justice such as busing and affirmative action appeared to do so on the very basis of egalitarian and individualist commitments. Trying to understand the politics of race in terms of inflexible and genetic racial theories no longer seemed to make sense.[1]

It was in this context that the notions of 'symbolic racism' (Henry and Sears, 2002; Sears and Henry, 2003; Sears et al., 1979, 1997) and 'modern racism' (McConahay, 1981, 1983) were introduced. According to this group of theories, contemporary racists deny that black people are still discriminated against, instead attributing their low status to their personal and cultural (but not necessarily biological) failings: being lazy and expecting special treatment on a group basis rather than striving for personal achievement. Policies designed to overcome disadvantage are opposed ostensibly on the grounds that such policies violate American values of self-reliance and individualism and violate democratic values of freedom and equal treatment. Thus, the notion of modern racism expands the conceptualization of racism beyond theories about biological hierarchies to a broader construct that allows for forms of racism that do not involve such theories. This expansion is justified by drawing on the concept of prejudice. Were racism to be conceptualized as a specific (pseudo)scientific doctrine of 'race', then the notion of a racism devoid of such a doctrine would be nonsensical (Leach, 1998, 2005). However, where racism is conceptualized as prejudice – that is, as antipathy – it becomes possible to claim that racism persists while finding expression in novel claims and beliefs not previously recognized as racist. Indeed, advocates of the symbolic racism construct are explicit that 'the word "*racism*" was chosen because the construct was thought in part to reflect racial *antipathy*' (Henry and Sears, 2002, p. 254, our emphasis). In short, modern racism is seen as both new and old. It is new, because theories of genetic racial hierarchies and segregationism are absent from it. It is also old, because it is an expression of race prejudice, which has continued from the past.

We make two related criticisms of this characterization of contemporary racism. First, we take issue with the assumption that racism in the past (that is, before the civil rights movements of the 1960s and 1970s) always involved claims of biological superiority and inferiority, and argue that there is therefore nothing new about forms of racism in which such claims are absent. Attempts to draw a dichotomy between new and old forms of racism are further complicated by the persistence of supposedly anti-quated racist representations. Second, we suggest that conceptualizing racism as prejudice has led psychologists to neglect the particularity of racism as an ideological phenomenon. We advance an alternative con-ception, based on that developed by Benedict (1942/1983) and Miles (1988; Miles and Brown, 2003), that can serve as a basis for a social psychology of racism that is sensitive to both its continuity and its chang-ing forms.

Racism, old and new

From civilizing missions to racelessness

It is easy to see how the project of European colonial domination would have been bolstered by a representation of the colonized as having an inferior biological endowment. If colonized populations were eternally incapable of anything other than servitude, while their European masters were naturally endowed with the qualities needed to govern, then perhaps such subjugation would have seemed reasonable. Unequal relations of power would follow straightforwardly from unequal aptitude and dispo-sition. Inequality rooted in biology need never change. Indeed, various such theories of immutable hierarchies of human types have been influ-ential over the centuries. Notable examples include Arthur de Gobineau's tripartite hierarchy and Samuel George Morton's craniometry in the nineteenth century, as well as the particular hereditarian arguments articulated by eugenicists such as Charles Davenport and Madison Grant from the early twentieth century (Benedict, 1942/1983; Kevles, 1985; Miles and Brown, 2003; Smedley and Smedley, 2005).

Yet, as straightforward as this might seem, such immutable inferiority was not the sole view of race underpinning colonial projects. Rather, representations of natural and eternal inferiority coexisted with an alter-native conception whereby 'inferior' racial categories were positioned at earlier stages in an overall progression towards civilization, rather than being eternally fixed somehow outside of history in their state of savagery (Goldberg, 2002; Todorov, 1984). Colonialism was legitimated as a mission to civilize, whereby European refinement could be learnt by those currently lacking it. This representation of race, termed 'progressivist' by Goldberg, was even invoked to defend slavery, on the grounds that for Africans to move from a condition of savagery to that of slavery was itself considered a kind of progress (Miles and Brown, 2003). The notion that colonized people could and should be civilized through contact with Europeans became particularly influential from the mid-nineteenth century, even as theories of immutable inferiority were becoming more formalized and more popular in the biological sciences (Goldberg, 2002). Thus, representations of the inferiority of the racial other have long been varied and contradictory in their expression (Leach, 2002a, 2005).

If the goal for Europeans was to extend their civilized virtues even to the 'backward' corners of the world, then the people they ruled over had the task of becoming more civilized, which meant becoming more European. As Fanon (1967/2008) puts it: 'The colonized is elevated above his jungle status in proportion to his adoption of the mother country's standards. He becomes whiter as he renounces his blackness, his jungle' (p. 9). Similarly, Carmichael and Hamilton (1967) explain the notion of the 'assimilado', whereby it was possible for Africans in Portuguese colonies to attain a legal status similar to that of white people, so long as they could demonstrate assimilation to Portuguese norms, including the rejection of African heritage as inferior (see also Stoler, 1995). By introducing a sense of progress, a dynamic towards enlightenment, this understanding of race establishes whiteness as the standard to which the whole of humanity should strive, rather than as pertaining only to a supreme race as hereditarian racists would have it. We shall see shortly how this equation of whiteness with advancement and normality persists and informs contemporary racial systems.

Colonial rule, therefore, need not entail a doctrine of a biologically determined hierarchy of races. Rather, the idea that non-Europeans were *culturally* underdeveloped – as-yet uncivilized – but potentially able to become more like their European masters, informed representations of the colonized other. This stands in sharp contrast to the common identification of 'old fashioned' racism with doctrines of immutable biological hierarchy, and racisms based on cultural attributes characterized in contrast as 'new' or 'modern'. We see instead that racist projects have long invoked historically contingent conditions of inferiority, with racial traits understood in terms of culture rather than genetics. If one seeks a dichotomy between old and new racisms, then it cannot be found in the distinction between biological and cultural interpretations of difference (Leach, 2005; Todorov, 1984).

The constructs of symbolic and modern racism (e.g. Henry and Sears, 2002; McConahay, 1983), developed and applied principally within the US, capture a refusal to see the relations between white and black people in terms of the relative privilege of the former and the longstanding subjugation of the latter. Goldberg (2002) uses the term 'racelessness' to describe this condition. Black people are not seen as *biologically* incapable of success, as would be the case within what has been called 'old fashioned' racism. However, their unwillingness to adopt the appropriate modern virtues of individualism, self-reliance and so forth, which characterize the 'American way of life', is to blame. Black inferiority is understood in terms of inferior work ethic and values rather than inferior DNA. In turn, the relative prosperity and status of white people is not seen by symbolic/modern racists as a case of privilege based in domination, but as the norm, and a standard fully available to black people if only they would adopt the superior values established by the white majority. Thus, whiteness embodies progress and normality, just as it did within the civilizing mission of nineteenth-century colonialism. This comparison is made explicit in Carmichael and Hamilton's (1967) argument that the relationship between white and black Americans is literally one of colonialism: 'As with the black African who had to become a "Frenchman" in order to be accepted, so to be an American, the black man must strive to become "white"' (p. 46).

Kundnani (2007) has remarked similarly on the subtext of contemporary discussions about how best to render migrants to western European states as capable citizens. Deliberations over declining civility and measures to counter this are directed particularly at ethnic minorities, and even more particularly at Muslims, whose democratic commitment is constantly called into question. Under these conditions, naturalization is no longer simply the transition from one nationality to another, but comes to symbolize instead an 'initiation into a higher civilization' (p. 138).

Essentialism and problematization in 'antiquated' forms

We have seen that there is nothing particularly new about forms of racism in which the negatively evaluated attributes of devalued social categories are represented as cultural rather than biological. This should call into question any straightforward view that cultural racism has come into existence recently as a way of evading the egalitarian norms that have gained ground over the past few decades. Rather, they can be seen as a continuation of discourses of civilizing missions that were present throughout the 'golden age' of European imperialism. Not only do 'new' racisms have a long history, but supposedly antiquated elements are still expressed directly and continue to be influential. By looking at survey evidence, it is possible to assess the degree to which supposedly 'old fashioned' racist sentiments are openly endorsed by research participants and therefore get a sense of both their normativity and their explanatory importance. Our intention in this section is to call into question the view that old-fashioned forms of racism are being progressively replaced by modern ones as egalitarianism takes hold. This is not to deny the fluidity of the forms that racism takes, but rather to question the extent to which certain forms have declined in importance.

Survey research carried out in the US since the 1980s finds respondents still willing to ascribe negatively evaluated characteristics explicitly to black people. Even early work on the construct of modern racism in fact revealed higher mean levels of 'old fashioned' than of 'modern' racism among white Americans when the data were collected by a white interviewer (McConahay, 1981). Bobo and Kluegel's (1997) analysis of representative data from 1990 finds 58 per cent of white Americans willing to claim that black people prefer to live on welfare, while 54 per cent claim that they are lazy. Only 4 and 5 per cent respectively make the same claims about white people. In contrast, 'intelligence' is ascribed to blacks by 21 per cent of the white respondents, while 58 per cent make the same claim about white people. These responses indicate a continued willingness of white Americans to explicitly devalue black people in the context of a formal survey interview, branding them lazier and less intelligent than white people.

Similarly, Leach et al. (2000) have examined survey responses indicating a devaluation of a number of ethnic minority groups in France, the Netherlands, Germany and the UK. In the nationally representative Eurobarometer survey conducted in 1988, respondents were asked the extent to which each target group came from 'inferior races' and 'less well developed' cultures. Thus, they indicated their agreement with blatant statements of inferiority. Although responses did tend towards the 'disagree' side of the midpoint, these statements were hardly unanimously rejected: proportions of respondents indicating at least mild agreement were 26 per cent in France, 30 per cent in the Netherlands, 38 per cent in West Germany and 41 per cent in the UK. In western Europe, as well as in the US, then, it seems that while the direct statements of relative inferiority associated with 'old fashioned' racism may not have been the most popular responses in surveys, they were far from being eclipsed by 'new' forms at the end of the 1980s.

Leach et al. (2000) also demonstrate that while mean levels of endorsement of relative inferiority were lower than claims of cultural difference, it was the former that more strongly predicted general attitudes towards the various minority groups in most cases. Similarly, in Bobo and Kluegel's (1997) analysis, white respondents' ascriptions of intelligence, laziness and welfare dependency to African Americans were predictive of outcomes associated with both old-fashioned racism (objection to a close relative marrying a black person) and with modern racism (opposition to government assistance). Thus, ascription of inferiority to historically devalued social categories can still be both explicit and consequential.

Furthermore, social categories are still widely construed in terms of biology, even in contexts in which one might expect 'old fashioned' racism to have been displaced. For example, definitions of English nationality in terms of biological criteria received remarkably high levels of endorsement from samples of adolescents in south-east England, especially given the very direct way in which this was measured, with survey items using the word 'blood' (Pehrson *et al.*, 2009). Although the tendency was to disagree with the items, less than half of the sample indicated more than slight disagreement. More importantly, construing Englishness in a biologically essentialist way was causally related to reported negative intentions towards asylum seekers, such as signing petitions and taking part in demonstrations to prevent them from living in one's locality. Similarly, in the US, survey and experimental research demonstrates that a biological conception of racial categories reduces non-black participants' concern about racial inequalities (Williams and Eberhardt, 2008). Other representative survey evidence also indicates that explicit genetic explanations of 'perceived race differences' in intelligence, ambition, mathematical ability and proclivity for violence are endorsed by a substantial minority in the US (Jayaratne *et al.*, 2006). Again, such explanations appear to be consequential, as they were related to both 'traditional' segregationist sentiments and to 'modern' racist beliefs about black Americans' culpability for their own low status. Thus, while social psychologists often view biological racism as antiquated and largely displaced by cultural racism, this appears to be premature.

A very particular derogatory representation that has historically been involved in racism is a view of black people as being like apes. Originating before scientific racism, but taking momentum from it, this association encapsulates a sense of black people as biologically inferior to, and needing to be under the control of, white people. Recent experimental work demonstrates that the association between black people and apes still exists in non-verbal, non-conscious reactions to visual stimuli depicting human faces: subliminal presentation of black faces, but not white faces, facilitates the recognition of degraded images of apes (Goff *et al.*, 2008). Using archival data and newspaper coverage of trials eligible for the death penalty in Philadelphia between 1979 and 1999, Goff *et al.* also demonstrate that language connoting ape-like associations was more frequent when the defendant was black rather than white. Furthermore, the extent of ape-related language in the press was directly related to the likelihood of black defendants being sentenced to death. The work therefore demonstrates that a supposedly antiquated form of signification and devaluation still operates, and may even contribute to the disproportionate use of the death penalty against black people in the US.

In Europe, the Swiss People's Party has been particularly adept at using 'old fashioned' visceral symbols in its populist platform. In support of a recent referendum on banning Islamic minarets, the party used a poster showing eight black minarets sprouting like mushrooms (or missiles) across the Swiss flag. In the foreground stood a woman covered in a Niqab. Underneath it all, in large letters, simply 'Stop'. In their victorious 2007 election, the party became infamous for a poster regarding immigration that contained the caption 'for more security'. It pictured three white sheep standing on the Swiss flag and one black sheep who had just been kicked off it. In an Italian town controlled by the Italian far-right Northern League Party, a house-to-house search to identify and remove illegal immigrants in 2009 was framed in similar terms: this undertaking was to end on Christmas Day and thus became known as 'operation white Christmas'. These three examples suggest that the blatant and 'old fashioned' use of black as a sign of foreboding and foreignness can be deployed in new, modern forms; the deployment of black as a sign of 'race' is both old and new at the same time.

Theories of contemporary racism and the 'prejudice problematic'

Theorists of modern/symbolic racism argue that changes in the political climate brought about by the civil rights movement have led to corresponding cognitive and behavioural changes among white Americans, but that the negative affect towards black people acquired through childhood socialization is more enduring. Thus, the supposedly new forms of racism are thought to entail a stubborn residue of antipathy towards black people:

Conformity pressures, as well as the intrinsic strength of early-learned attitudes, promote the persistence of prejudice through the vicissitudes of later life. Realistic threats may come and go, but the solid core of prejudice remains, no matter how anachronistic it may become. (Kinder and Sears (1981, p. 416))

From this perspective, then, prejudice is an anachronistic residue that is resistant to change and must be projected onto new beliefs that are seen as more legitimate in a post-civil rights political culture. Beliefs about the innate inferiority of black people and explicit endorsement of regimes of segregation (such as the Jim Crow laws) that fit a popular prototype of racism are seen as a thing of the past, having been replaced by the newer forms.

Advocates of the 'symbolic racism' perspective are especially keen to argue that new forms of racism are no longer functional for contemporary group or individual interests. Residual antipathy from an earlier era stubbornly outlasts its political utility. Debates about policies such as busing and affirmative action then act as triggers that arouse this latent prejudice and serve as the medium through which it can be expressed without being recognized for what it is (Henry and Sears, 2002; Sears and Henry, 2003; Sears *et al.*, 1979, 1997). As Bobo (2004) puts it, the symbolic racism theory sees racism as a personal prejudice that '*intrudes into politics*' with no '*instrumental or rational objective*' of its own (p. 27). A related approach, based on the notion of 'aversive racism', similarly points to a contradiction between contemporary norms and prejudice (Gaertner and Dovidio, 2000, 2005; Pearson *et al.*, 2009). In this case, the tension is between sincerely endorsed egalitarian principles and automatic evaluative biases arising from mere categorization. Such approaches imply that while our social milieu endows us with a commitment to equality, our cognitive and motivational nature is a source of prejudice, and is therefore in conflict with that commitment. As such, all of these approaches are rooted in the prejudice problematic as identified and critiqued in this volume and elsewhere (e.g. Billig, 1985; Leach, 1998, 2002b; Reicher, 2007; Wetherell and Potter, 1992).

The merit of the work described above should not be denied. A considerable threat to struggles for racial justice comes from a belief that racism is no longer a problem, that it is confined to politically marginal extremists, and that it no longer affects the way most people relate to one another in any substantive way. Empirical work demonstrating that this is not the case is therefore of real value. Such work includes, for example, evidence for the continued role of negative evaluations of black people in the formation of public opinion and voting in the US (e.g. Sears *et al.*, 1997). It also includes demonstrations of routine, unacknowledged discrimination in employment and legal decision-making (Gaertner and Dovidio, 2000, 2005; Pearson *et al.*, 2009).

However, the theoretical framework within which this work has been carried out lacks an adequate conceptualization of racism itself. As we have explained, it could be argued that conceptualization of racism as antipathy towards black people has the advantage of not being tied to specific doctrines or ideological content, and therefore allowing for the possibility that racism persists while being expressed through novel discourses under new conditions. However, because the transforming content of racism is understood merely as a progressively subtle expression of the same old prejudice, there is no interest in ideological shifts per se (Leach, 1998, 2005). This renders the investigation closed to questions of how white privilege is made sense of and defended or how anti-racist mobilization is responded to through changing political circumstances (Bobo, 2004). Conceptualizing racism as a residue from the past that is expressed through subtler forms in current, more egalitarian, times obscures its role as part of an *active* practice of subordination directed towards a *future* reality (for a similar point see Reicher, 2007). Thus, there is a price to be paid for the redefinition of racism from the doctrine of genetic inferiority to the various expressions of anti-black prejudice.

There is also a vast social psychological literature on prejudice that does not conceptualize it as irrational or divorced from material or social relational conditions. Accounts pointing to macro-social conditions rather than intrapsychic distortions have proved just as popular with scholars of prejudice over several decades. The classic work of Muzafer Sherif (e.g. Sherif *et al.*, 1961), which treats individual-level antipathy as a consequence of negative interdependence between groups, rather than a cause of it, has left a lasting impression on the field. Ongoing work on zero-sum competition and intergroup threat, for example, can be placed in this lineage (e.g. Green, in press; Stephan and Renfro, 2003), as can recent work on relative deprivation (Leach *et al.*, 2007; Pettigrew *et al.*, 2008).

Tajfel's (1978) pioneering contributions on the social functions of stereotypes, whereby derogatory beliefs about social categories are understood in terms of their legitimating and explanatory utility, rather than as cognitive distortion, have also left their mark (see McGarthy *et al.*, 2002). For example, social dominance theory (Sidanius and Pratto, 1999) advances the notion of 'legitimizing myths' through which the privileged seek to perpetuate and extend their subjugation of others. And, a great deal of research on stereotype content focuses on its potential to explain and legitimate inequality and malevolence (for a review, see Mackie and Smith, 2002). So too does recent work on prejudice-as-emotion emphasize the ways in which emotions make sense of intergroup relations and suggest how they should be dealt with (for reviews, see Mackie and Smith, 2002; Tiedens and Leach, 2004). None of these contributions have entailed the abandonment of the notion of prejudice as antipathy. Thus, there is a long history of research that retains the concept of prejudice while viewing it, broadly speaking, as *functional*. This being so, it would be mistaken to characterize the prejudice paradigm as having pursued a crude individualism, or as having ignored the purposeful nature of derogatory feelings and beliefs and discriminatory behaviour.

Yet, we do not consider a shift from a dysfunctional to functional, or intrapsychic to social, view of prejudice sufficient to bring about an adequate social psychology of racism. The 'race relations' paradigm in sociology has been criticized, most notably by Miles (1988; see also Solomos and Back, 1994), for incorporating racial categories into its theorizing as though their ontological status was unproblematic, and a parallel point can be made about the psychology of intergroup relations. By incorporating racial categories directly into the analysis and asking how 'whites' feel about 'blacks', we generally fail to ask what it means to construe one's social relations in terms of race in the first place, or how we come to do this. What is needed before work on intergroup relations can fully inform our understanding of racism is a psychology of racialization as a particular kind of social categorization. By developing this, we would put ourselves in a much stronger position to make sense of both the unity and diversity of racist ideology (Leach, 1998, 2002b; Miles and Brown, 2003; Reicher, 2001).

It has been pointed out that in its emphasis on generic processes, social psychology has largely neglected the particularity of social categories such as nationality (Billig, 1995; Reicher and Hopkins, 2001), ethnicity (Betancourt and Regeser Lopez, 1993; Leach and Brown, 1999; Zagefka, 2009) and gender (Cameron and Lalonde, 2001; Hare-Mustin and Maracek, 1988). In the same way, race and racialization have not been investigated in their own right in intergroup relations research (Hopkins *et al.*, 1997; Leach, 1998). Indeed, the description of particular intergroup contexts as 'racial' involves importing common-sense racial categories into the analysis: for example, the relations between white and black Americans would be understood as race relations while those between science and humanities students would not. This might seem reasonable enough, but the point is that without any theoretical account of why 'race' is an appropriate theoretical category in the former context and not the latter, all we can do is to mirror common sense about some groups being races and others not. This means that the processes of racialization itself can never be scrutinized. A further consequence of the disinterest in the particularity of social categories is that the way in which, for example, race and nation are articulated together cannot be comprehended. Scholars of racism since the 1980s have noted the centrality of nationhood to racist discourses and practices (Balibar, 1991; Barker, 1981; Gilroy, 1987/ 2002). Yet, as far as most psychological theory on prejudice and intergroup relations is concerned, 'race' and 'nation' are simply two examples of social categories to which their theories apply equivalently, so the significance of the interface of national and racial categorization is missed.

In short, we are suggesting that social psychological research on prejudice has largely failed to adequately theorize racism in its own right. This applies as much to theories that attribute a functional role to prejudice in intergroup relations as to those that reduce it to the dysfunction of bigoted individuals or the inevitable outcome of universal cognitive mechanisms (Leach, 1998). Consequently, we are left with no tools with which to trace the continuity of racism as it is transformed into new forms, or as supposedly antiquated racist tropes reappear. Our task in the next section is to outline the features of racism that a future social psychology of racism must attend to.

For a social psychology of racism

Our social psychological conceptualization of racism starts with noting the particular representational qualities of racist ideology and then suggests that the analytic focus needs to be on the semiotic and phenomenological forms through which these representations are instantiated in psychological and social life. While this approach follows that of some scholars (e.g. Benedict, 1942/1983; Miles and Brown, 2003), it has been criticized by others. Specifically, discursive psychologists have criticized this approach on the grounds that racist discourse is fluid, variable and situated, such that it is impossible to specify a priori what kind of representational content will be drawn upon in support for racist practices (e.g. Wetherell and Potter, 1992). Instead, these authors label discourse as racist to the extent that it legitimizes and perpetuates oppressive power relations; it is the effects of discourse rather than its content that determines whether it is racist or not. Yet, while racist discourse is indeed fluid, variable and situated, the same could be said of forms of racist oppression. Slavery is not the *same thing* as Jim Crow segregation, which in turn is not the same as excluding indigenous minority languages from school curricula or locking up families in immigration detention centres. Therefore, if racist discourse is to be defined on the basis of the practices that are sustained by it, then one still needs a definition that makes sense of the continuity of racism through its varied instances. Shifting the object of definition from content to consequence does not solve this problem. Furthermore, in their study of racism in New Zealand, Wetherell and Potter (1992) specify racist practice to entail oppressive relations between those defined '*as Māori and those defined as Pākehā*' (p. 70). This highlights the difficulty of attempting to define racist practice in advance of the content of representations, but at the same time needing to refer to elements of those representations ('those defined as *Māori* . . .') in order to characterize a given social relationship as 'racial'.

Specifying representational features that constitute racism, as Miles and Brown (2003) advocate, does not negate the variety of forms that those features can take. It is not specific doctrinal content such as pseudo-scientific theories about race, genes and intelligence that is specified, but rather the representational processes of racialization and devaluation. These can operate through pseudo-scientific theories about race but also work in other ways. It is by attending to these representational processes, rather than by reconceptualizing racism as any discourse that legitimizes oppression, that both the continuity and variability of racism can be understood. Thus, we believe that for a social psychology of racism, scholarship must attend to the process of racialization, the importance of devaluation, and a conceptualization of discourse and prejudice as signs with a particular social psychological appeal.

Racialization   Racism attributes social importance to human characteristics (Miles and Brown, 2003; see also Hall, 1996) by signifying populations as naturally and immutably different from one another. These characteristics have often fallen within Hall's (1996) triad of 'skin, hair and bone' – visible features of the body. However, racialization is not primarily about visible difference. For example, anti-Semitism constructs Jews as a racial category (the term 'racism' was first applied to Nazi anti-Semitism; Balibar, 1991) without necessarily focusing on obvious visible difference. Indeed, the possibility of Jews passing unrecognized served to make them seem more threatening, necessitating deliberate measures to render them visible (e.g. the Nazi's yellow star). Nevertheless, in many cases phenotypical features are often presumed to indicate a deeper, more fundamental racial essence that is more than 'skin deep'. The notion of essentialism is pertinent here because an object's essence does not reside in its surface features, but is merely indicated by them. Thus, racialization, as a particular form of social categorization, entails the essentialization of human characteristics.

Understood in these terms, racialization does not have to entail any explicit concept of 'race'. For example, nationhood can sometimes be represented as a quasi-biological category (Barker, 1981; Gilroy, 1987), and the term 'ethnic' is frequently used in both social scientific and 'everyday' discourse to signify what is in fact understood as racial (Hill, 2008; Zagefka, 2009). Furthermore, racialization does not entail a specific doctrine or theory: signification and essentialization can be done in a variety of both formal and informal ways. The representational features of racist ideology can therefore be specified without being limited to the definition of a particular kind of scientific doctrine.

Devaluation   Whether it is put in biological, cultural or other terms, what is achieved in racism is to signify a particular group as inferior in a way that implies inferior regard or treatment (e.g. Leach *et al.*, 2000;

for discussions, see Balibar, 1991; Leach, 2002a; Todorov, 1984). Benedict's (1942/1983) definition of racism as the ascription of 'congenital' inferiority (p. 97) is favoured by Leach (2005), precisely because (1) it makes clear that inferiority is the central claim in racism, and (2) it does not assume that genetics is the only basis for this inferiority. Congenital inferiority is present at birth, but need not be genetic. It is another way of claiming that the inferiority claimed in racism relies on an essentialist view of its target.

The inferiority ascribed to outgroups can rarely be understood in isolation from representations of the ingroup (Leach et al., 2000; Reicher, 2001, 2007). 'Their' attributes are seen as inferior relative to some semi-absolute standard of what good people are like. The devaluation in racism can also be more relative in quality. 'Their' attributes are seen as problematic by virtue of what they mean for 'us'. So it is that attributes that are positive in some contexts (sexual potency, intelligence, power) can be construed as negative when they are ascribed to an outgroup that is viewed as problematic for the ingroup in some way. For example, sexual potency signifies a threat when it is ascribed to those who spark fears of rape or miscegenation.

Devaluation is also tied to the particular meaning of the ingroup category. For example, while immigrant minorities may in some cases be constructed as culturally different and therefore alien to the dominant majority, this alien-ness is a problem only because the majority construe themselves in terms of a national community whose nationhood is threatened by the presence of aliens. Similarly, the sentiment conceptualized as part of the 'symbolic racism' construct that black leaders have pushed too hard and that black people get more than they deserve (e.g. Sears and Henry, 2003) rests on a sense of violated ingroup entitlement or, as Blumer (1958) puts it, 'sense of group position'. Blumer emphasizes that prejudice researchers need to attend to the social processes through which a sense of group position and entitlement is constructed; that it is not a straightforward perception of one's structural position in relation to others, but an active, creative and collective process of construal. Thus, the devaluation of outgroups is fundamentally bound up with the construction of collective ingroup identities. Recent attention to notions of whiteness and nativeness in the human sciences has sparked renewed social psychological attention to the importance of ingroup identity in racism (see Reicher, 2007). Studies of white privilege and feelings about relative advantage seek to make explicit the ways in which membership in dominant or normative groups enable racism (e.g. Leach et al., 2007; for discussions, see Leach and Brown, 1999; Sidanius and Pratto, 1999). This work has also examined the ways in which explicit group identity may enable efforts against racism where individuals come to view their membership as immoral or politically problematic (e.g. Leach *et al.*, 2006).

Discourse and prejudice as signs with a social psychological appeal   While we view racism as ideology, it does not necessarily follow that this is in all cases linguistic. Racialization and problematization do happen importantly through language, but they operate through other phenomena as well, including antipathetic mental and affective states. For this reason, there is no need to jettison the concept of prejudice. For example, non-conscious associations between a social category and negativity of the sort indicated by implicit measures of prejudice can be interpreted as a form of signification, as people read, say, black skin as a cue to fear and African appearance or urban dialect as a sign of inferiority (Hall, 1996). The point is that ideology is instantiated in ways other than words (Durrheim and Dixon, 2005). A fuller account of racism, beyond prejudice, requires a reconceptualization of prejudice and of discourse as particular semiotic forms. One may think, feel, act, talk and imagine racism with the use of a wide array of signs rendered meaningful through such social action. A similar argument has been made regarding the need to account for the visceral, somatic aspects of racism (Hook, 2006). If it were to more directly examine the particular signs at work in the emotions that people use to represent the meaning given to groups, work on emotion in intergroup relations could fit well within a broader semiotic approach (see Tiedens and Leach, 2004).

Rigidly exorcizing mental or affective states from the analysis of racism is not necessarily the solution to the disciplinary failings that we have identified. While the study of discourse will continue to be crucial (see Chapters 7 to 10 in this volume, for example), the construct of prejudice, together with the various measurement technologies associated with it, also has its place when conceptualized as part of a broader representational phenomenon. The work cited above on ape associations is a good example of how this can be done (Goff *et al.*, 2008). Making a place for prejudice does not necessitate assuming that prejudice exists prior to discourse, or that discourse should be interpreted as merely reflective of prejudiced mental states. Like all other signs, including the iconography of black sheep or missile-like mushrooms threatening the nation (shown as a flag), discourse and prejudice are particular ways of representing human experience and meaning. A social psychology of racism, and of all ideology, can be quite open to the many and varied forms in which such signs come if they are conceptualized as signs mobilized in the social psychological process of representation. Although discourse, prejudice, stereotypes, attitudes, emotions, etc. are grounded in semi-autonomous theories and methods, they may be integrated within a broader notion of racialized signification.

Note

1. 'Busing' is the term used to describe the controversial practice of transporting children attending black schools (usually in city centres) by bus to white schools (usually in the suburbs).

References

Adorno, T. W., Frenkel-Brunswik, E., Levinson, D. J. and Sanford, R. N. (1950). *The Authoritarian Personality*. New York: Harper.

Allport, G. W. (1954). *The Nature of Prejudice*. Reading, MA: Addison-Wesley.

Balibar, E. (1991). Is there a 'neo-racism'? In E. Balibar and I. Wallerstein (eds.), *Race, Nation, Class: Ambiguous Identities*. London: Verso.

Barker, M. (1981). *The New Racism: Conservatives and the Ideology of the Tribe*. Frederick, MD: University Publications of America.

Benedict, R. (1942/1983). *Race and Racism*. London: Routledge and Kegan Paul.

Betancourt, H. and Regeser Lopez, S. (1993). The study of culture, ethnicity, and race in American psychology. *American Psychologist*, **48**(6), 629–37.

Billig, M. (1985). Prejudice and particularization: from a perceptual to a rhetorical approach. *European Journal of Social Psychology*, **15**, 79–103.

(1995). *Banal Nationalism*. London: Thousand Oaks.

Blumer, H. (1958). Race prejudice as a sense of group position. *Pacific Sociological Review*, **1**, 3–7.

Bobo, L. D. (2004). Inequalities that endure? Race ideology, American politics, and the peculiar role of the social sciences. In M. Krysan and A. E. Lewis (eds.), *The Changing Terrain of Race and Ethnicity*. New York: Russell Sage Foundation.

Bobo, L. D. and Kluegel, J. R. (1997). Status, ideology and dimensions of whites' racial beliefs and attitudes: progress and stagnation. In S. A. Tuch and J. K. Martin (eds.), *Racial Attitudes in the 1990s: Continuity and Change*. Westport, CT: Praeger.

Cameron, J. E. and Lalonde, R. N. (2001). Social identification and gender-related ideology in women and men. *British Journal of Social Psychology*, **40**, 59–77.

Carmichael, S. and Hamilton, C. V. (1967). *Black Power: the Politics of Liberation in America*. Harmondsworth, UK: Pelican Books.

Duckitt, J. (1992). *The Social Psychology of Prejudice*. Westport, CT: Praeger.

Durrheim, K. and Dixon, J. (2005). Studying talk and embodied practices: toward a psychology of materiality of 'race relations'. *Journal of Community and Applied Social Psychology*, **15**, 446–60.

Fanon, F. (1967/2008). *Black Skin, White Masks*. London: Pluto Press.

Gaertner, S. L. and Dovidio, J. F. (2000). *Reducing Intergroup Bias: the Common Ingroup Identity Model*. Philadelphia, PA: Psychology Press.

(2005). Understanding and addressing contemporary racism: from aversive racism to the common ingroup identity model. *Journal of Social Issues*, **61**, 615–39.

Gilroy, P. (1987/2002). *There Ain't no Black in the Union Jack: the Cultural Politics of Race and Nation.* Abingdon, UK: Routledge.

Goff, P. A., Eberhardt, J. E., Williams, M. J. and Jackson, M. C. (2008). Not yet human: implicit knowledge, historical dehumanisation, and contemporary consequences. *Journal of Personality and Social Psychology*, **94**, 292–306.

Goldberg, D. T. (2002). *The Racial State.* Oxford, UK: Blackwell.

Green, E. G. T. (in press). Who can enter? A multilevel analysis on public support for immigration criteria across 20 European countries. *Group Processes and Intergroup Relations.*

Hall, S. (1996). Race: the floating signifier. A videotaped lecture from the Open University. Milton Keynes.

Hare-Mustin, R. T. and Marecek, J. (1988). The meaning of difference: gender theory, postmodernism, and psychology. *American Psychologist*, **43**, 455–64.

Henry, P. J. and Sears, D. O. (2002). The symbolic racism 2000 scale. *Political Psychology*, **23**, 253–83.

Hill, J. H. (2008). *The Everyday Language of White Racism.* Oxford, UK: Wiley-Blackwell.

Hook, D. (2006). 'Pre-discursive' racism. *Journal of Community and Applied Psychology*, **16**, 207–32.

Hopkins, N., Reicher, S. and Levine, M. (1997). On the parallels between social cognition and the 'new racism'. *British Journal of Social Psychology*, **36**, 305–29.

Jayaratne, T. E., Ybarra, O., Sheldon, J. P., Brown, T. N., Feldbaum, M., Pfeffer, C. A. and Petty, E. M. (2006). White Americans' genetic lay theories of race and differences and sexual orientation: their relationship with prejudice towards blacks, and gay men and lesbians. *Group Processes and Intergroup Relations*, **9**, 77–94.

Kevles, D. (1985). *In the Name of Eugenics: Genetics and the Uses of Human Heredity.* New York: Knopf.

Kinder, D. R. and Sears, D. O. (1981). Prejudice and politics: symbolic racism versus racial threats to the good life. *Journal of Personality and Social Psychology*, **40**, 414–31.

Kundnani, A. (2007). *The End of Tolerance: Racism in 21st Century Britain.* London: Pluto Press.

Leach, C. W. (1998). Toward a social psychology of racism? Comments on 'On the parallels between social cognition and the "new racism"' by N. Hopkins, S. Reicher and M. Levine. *British Journal of Social Psychology*, **37**, 255–8.

(2002a). Democracy's dilemma: explaining racial inequality in egalitarian societies. *Sociological Forum*, **17**, 681–96.

(2002b). The social psychology of racism reconsidered. *Feminism and Psychology*, **12**, 439–44.

(2005). Against the notion of a 'new racism'. *Journal of Community and Applied Social Psychology*, **15**, 432–45.

Leach, C. W. and Brown, L. M. (1999). Ethnicity and identity politics. In L. Kurtz (ed.), *Encyclopedia of Violence, Peace, and Conflict* (Vol. 1, pp.765–75). New York: Academic Press.

Leach, C. W., Iyer, A. and Pedersen, A. (2006). Anger and guilt about in-group advantage explain the willingness for political action. *Personality and Social Psychology Bulletin*, **32**, 1,232–45.

(2007). Angry opposition to government redress: when the structurally advantaged perceive themselves as relatively deprived. *British Journal of Social Psychology*, **46**, 191–204.

Leach, C. W., Peng, T. R. and Volkens, J. (2000). Is racism dead? Comparing (expressive) means and (structural equation) models. *British Journal of Social Psychology*, **39**, 449–65.

Lentin, A. (2005). Replacing 'race', historicizing 'culture' in multiculturalism. *Patterns of Prejudice*, **39**, 379–96.

Mackie, D. M. and Smith, E. R. (eds.) (2002). *From Prejudice to Intergroup Emotions: Differentiated Reactions to Social Groups*. New York: Psychology Press.

McConahay, J. B. (1981). Has racism declined in America? It depends on who is asking and what is asked. *Journal of Conflict Resolution*, **25**, 563–79.

(1983). Modern racism and modern discrimination: the effects of race, racial attitudes, and context on simulated hiring decisions. *Personality and Social Psychology Bulletin*, **9**, 551–8.

McGarthy, C., Yzerbyt, V. Y. and Spears, R. (eds.) (2002). *Stereotypes as Explanations: the Formation of Meaningful Beliefs about Social Groups*. Cambridge, UK: Cambridge University Press.

Miles, R. (1988). Racism, Marxism, and British politics. *Economy and Society*, **17**, 428–61.

Miles, R. and Brown, M. (2003). *Racism*. London: Routledge.

Pearson, A. R., Dovidio, J. F. and Gaertner, S. L. (2009). The nature of contemporary prejudice: insights from aversive racism. *Social and Personality Psychology Compass*, **3**, 314–38.

Pehrson, S., Brown, R. and Zagefka, H. (2009). When does national identification lead to the rejection of immigrants? Cross-sectional and longitudinal evidence for the role of essentialist in-group definitions. *British Journal of Social Psychology*, **48**, 61–76.

Pettigrew, T. F. (2007). The social science of American race relations in the twentieth century. *Social and Personality Psychology Compass*, **2**, 1–28.

Pettigrew, T. F., Christ, O., Wagner, U., Meertens, R. W., van Dick, R. and Zick, A. (2008). Relative deprivation and intergroup prejudice. *Journal of Social Issues*, **64**, 385–401.

Reicher, S. (2001). Studying psychology, studying racism. In M. Augostinos and K. J. Reynolds (eds.), *Understanding Prejudice, Racism and Social Conflict*. London: Sage.

(2007). Rethinking the paradigm of prejudice. *South African Journal of Psychology*, **37**, 820–34.

Reicher, S. and Hopkins, N. (2001). Psychology and the end of history: a critique and a proposal for the psychology of social categorization. *Political Psychology*, **22**, 383–407.

Sears, D. O. and Henry, P. J. (2003). The origins of symbolic racism. *Journal of Personality and Social Psychology*, **85**, 259–75.

Sears, D. O., Hensler, C. P. and Speer, L. K. (1979). Whites' opposition to 'busing': self-interest or symbolic politics? *The American Political Science Review*, **73**, 369–84.

Sears, D. O., van Laar, C., Carrillo, M. and Kosterman, R. (1997). Is it really racism? The origins of white Americans' opposition to race-targeted policies. *Public Opinion Quarterly*, **61**, 16–53.

Sherif, M., Harvey, O. J., White, B. J., Hood, W. R. and Sherif, C. W. (1961). *Intergroup Cooperation and Competition: the Robbers Cave Experiment*. Norman, OK: University Book Exchange.

Sidanius, J. and Pratto, F. (1999). *Social Dominance: an Intergroup Theory of Social Hierarchy and Oppression*. New York: Cambridge University Press.

Smedley, A. and Smedley, B. D. (2005). Race as biology is fiction, racism as a social problem is real. *American Psychologist*, **60**, 16–26.

Solomos, J. and Back, L. (1994). Conceptualising racisms: social theory, politics and research. *Sociology*, **28**, 143–61.

Stephan, W. G. and Renfro, C. L. (2003). The role of threat in intergroup relations. In D. M. Mackie and E. R. Smith (eds.), *From Prejudice to Intergroup Emotions: Differentiated Reactions to Social Groups*. New York: Psychology Press.

Stoler, A. L. (1995). *Race and the Education of Desire: Foucault's History of Sexuality and the Colonial Order of Things*. Durham, NC: Duke University Press.

Tajfel, H. (1978). *Differentiation Between Social Groups: Studies in the Social Psychology of Inter-group Relations*. London: Academic Press.

Tiedens, L. Z. and Leach, C. W. (eds.) (2004). *The Social Life of Emotions*. New York: Cambridge University Press.

Todorov, T. (1984). *The Conquest of America: the Question of the Other* (Richard Howard, trans.). New York: Harper & Row.

UNESCO (1952). *The Race Concept: Results of an Inquiry*. Paris: UNESCO.

Wetherell, M. and Potter, J. (1992). *Mapping the Language of Racism: Discourse and the Legitimation of Exploitation*. New York: Columbia University Press.

Williams, M. J. and Eberhardt, J. L. (2008). Biological conceptions of race and the motivation to cross racial boundaries. *Journal of Personality and Social Psychology*, **94**, 1,033–47.

Zagefka, H. (2009). The concept of ethnicity in social psychological research: definitional issues. *International Journal of Intercultural Relations*, **33**, 228–41.

7 The notion of 'prejudice': some rhetorical and ideological aspects

Michael Billig

Introduction

A recent issue of a magazine published by the National Front contained an article entitled 'Patterns of prejudice'. It began with the statement: 'Perhaps the favourite accusation thrown at the National Front by its multi-racialist critics is that we are simply a bunch of bigots, that our stance on Race, the very heart and core of our political being, is no more than ignorant prejudice against Coloured people' (*Vanguard*, April 1987). The tone of the article was pseudo-academic. The author, in the style of a scholar, defines 'prejudice' in his second paragraph: 'it is generally taken to mean forming an opinion, especially about an issue or person or group of people, without knowing, or without taking into account, all the relevant facts'. The main part of the article was devoted to arguing that the National Front had taken into account 'the relevant facts' in coming to its conclusions that Britain should be populated solely with white-skinned people. The author cited psychological books, which claimed that black people were intellectually inferior on average to white people: 'Read *The Inequity of Man* by H. J. Eysenck, Professor of Psychology at the University of London for the facts here.' A couple of paragraphs of lay anthropology were added to suggest that black people in Africa had accomplished 'virtually nothing' before 'the White Man came'. The references to professors and their books led to the predictable conclusion: 'On the Black issue our verdict is based on the facts, we have judged the case on the evidence, fairly, and come to the only just conclusions.' It was the National Front's liberal opponents, who were avoiding the 'facts': 'They can't site [sic] a mass of scientific evidence to support their beliefs.' Having defined the key term and having cited the relevant facts, the author's final sentence points the accusing finger at liberals: 'Dare we say it – it is they, not we, who are prejudiced.'

In an obvious sense, this article is an unremarkable piece of fascist writing. Pre-war German Nazi propaganda cited academic, and pseudo-academic, sources in elaborating racial themes. In fact, the individuals

139

who wrote the 'academic' pieces were often the people who drew the political conclusions (for analyses, see Cohn, 1967; Lutzhöft, 1971; Poliakov, 1974). Similarly, post-war fascists have been using psychological and anthropological material in their racist ideology (Billig, 1978, 1981; Seidel, 1986). The book lists of post-war fascist groups have long stocked the sources cited in the article. However, the theme which deserves more attention is the basic argument of the article: the author is claiming not to be prejudiced and is attributing prejudice to those who oppose the National Front. In other words, the author is turning round an obvious accusation made against fascists. In so doing, he is not denying the value at the root of the accusation – namely, that prejudice is wrong. In fact, one might say that the article, with its defence of National Front thinking and its attack on liberalism, is reinforcing the value that one should be unprejudiced, for both the attack and defence are based, in essence, upon deciding who should be called 'prejudiced'.

Denial of prejudice

In the way that the author of the National Front article denied his own prejudice, his writing resembled much other discourse on race in contemporary politics. Those who argue against black interests or against non-white immigration typically deny that they are prejudiced. Reeves (1983), in his study of contemporary British political discourse, uses the term 'discursive deracialisation' to describe the strategy by which politicians avoid using racial categories. Acts of Parliament, designed to restrict immigration of non-whites, are phrased in such a way that race is never mentioned. Other criteria are used, and it is, as if by magic, that these 'fair-minded' criteria result in the exclusion of non-whites. Denials of prejudice and racism are made by politicians on the New Right (Gordon and Klug, 1986; see also Studlar, 1974, and Schoen, 1977, for examples from Enoch Powell's speeches). On the New Right the denial is often accompanied by the claim that it is the anti-racists who are the *real* racists (Barker, 1981).

It is not only in the discourse of politicians that one finds the denial of prejudice. There is evidence, from a variety of sources, that ordinary people voicing anti-black sentiments typically deny their own prejudices. American researchers have referred to the 'new racism', which denies being racist, in contrast to 'old-fashioned red-necked racism', which unambiguously trumpeted racial values (McConahay and Hough, 1976; Kinder and Sears, 1981; McConahay, 1981, 1982; McConahay *et al.*, 1981; Jacobson, 1985; Kinder, 1986). The attitudes held by the modern racists are deracialized in that the attitudes are justified by traditional values, such as equality and fairness, and not by overt racial themes. It has been suggested that the racism of the new racist is not so new and that even so-called red-necks justified segregation in deracialized terms (Weigel and Howes, 1985; see also the criticisms of Sniderman and Tetlock, 1986a, 1986b). Certainly, Gunnar Myrdal's great work *An American Dilemma* (1944) provides evidence that, even in the deep South during the days of segregation, the expression of racism was not completely uninhibited. Myrdal found that Southern whites, defending discrimination, picked their words with care, showing an indirectness in the way they talked about blacks: 'When talking about the Negro problem, everybody – not only the intellectual liberals – is thus anxious to locate race prejudice outside himself' (1944, p. 37).

Myrdal was able to pick up this anxiety from unstructured conversations he held with Americans. In this respect his research resembles modern studies of discourse, which aim to capture the flow and tone of remarks as they are made, rather than confine respondents within a narrow matrix of pre-set response. Van Dijk's studies of discourse of the Dutch white working class show a similar pattern to that of the American studies of 'modern racism', in that racist sentiments are simultaneously expressed and denied (for example, van Dijk, 1983, 1984, 1985a). For example, one respondent declared: 'I have nothing against foreigners. But their attitude, their aggression is scaring' (van Dijk, 1984, p. 65). The same pattern was found in the discourse of white, middle-class New Zealanders, when they talked of Maoris (McFayden and Wetherell, 1986; Wetherell and Potter, 1986). Similarly, Cochrane and Billig (1984) and Billig *et al.* (1988) also report working-class white youths in Britain, who deny prejudice (they have nothing against blacks) as a preface to complaining about blacks. One complaint, which often occurred, was that it is the blacks who hold the real prejudices. Even some young supporters of the National Front showed this pattern of ambivalence in their discourse. Billig (1986) describes a similar pattern in groups of young middle-class Conservatives, who also attribute the *real* prejudice to blacks. The same pattern is also to be found in the discourse of parliamentary debates about apartheid (Seidel, 1988).

Evidence from different nationalities and different class backgrounds suggests an overall pattern to discourse about race and prejudice. There is a denial of prejudice, which fits the pattern of a 'disclaimer' (Hewitt and Stokes, 1975): 'I'm not prejudiced.' This statement does not stand unqualified: it is typically followed by a 'but', which announces the expression of anti-black sentiments or anecdotes. All this suggests the obvious, but perhaps rather neglected, point that there is a general cultural norm against 'prejudice'. So general is the norm that the value of not being 'prejudiced' is even shared by the fascist writer who is at pains to deny his own prejudice but to pin the label upon liberal opponents. If this value has permeated even the discourse of fascist ideologists, then its importance should not be underestimated when attempting to understand the ideology of modern racism. Above all, we should not expect the ideology to be straightforward, for it is an ideology, which includes the word 'prejudice' and the associated value attached to the word. Thus any analysis of modern racism should not be focused entirely upon majority groups' images and stereotypes of minority groups. It should also include an analysis of what modern people understand by the very concept of 'prejudice', for it is a concept not only used by social scientists, but which is also significant in ordinary discourse.

The norm against prejudice

The phraseology 'I'm not prejudiced but . . .', and its variants, suggest a cognitive, or attitudinal, ambivalence, for the phraseology simultaneously expresses two contrary themes. From a theoretical point of view, social psychologists have often been unhappy in dealing with cognitive ambivalence. Influenced by balance theories, they have often tended to assume that ambivalence must be resolved into a cognitively unitary consonance (see Billig, 1982, and Billig *et al.*, 1988, for such criticisms of mainstream social psychological theory). There has been a temptation to assume that there is an underlying cognitive consonance. This can be seen in attempts to divide the contrary themes of 'I'm not prejudiced but . . .' into separate levels; by claiming that one of the contrary themes possesses a deeper psychological significance, one resolves the apparent contradiction. For instance, it has been suggested that the prejudiced themes exist at a psychologically deeper level than the denial of prejudice. Therefore, the prejudiced themes are held to indicate the 'genuine' attitudinal structure. Such a division into higher and lower (genuine and superficial) themes can be seen in the classic work on the psychology of prejudice, *The Authoritarian Personality* (Adorno *et al.*, 1950). Recognizing that authoritarians did not phrase their bigotry in unqualified statements, Adorno *et al.* suggested that they were playing lip-service to the wider social norms of tolerance, which conflicted with their inner psychological motives. In arguing thus, Adorno *et al.* were in effect suggesting that the inner psychological motivations for racism existed at a deeper level of social reality than the socially shared norms of tolerance.

The drawback of this sort of analysis is that it distinguishes between the superficial norms of society, and the deeper, perhaps partially hidden, forces of the psyche. Such a distinction can lead to an over-psychologization of the study of ideology, for obvious social norms are seen to possess less significance than personal motivations. There is also the assumption that an ideology must possess an internal unity. Paradoxically this assumption of ideological unity was not made by Adorno when collaborating with Horkheimer to write *Dialectic of Enlightenment* (1973). This work probed the fact that the ideology of modern capitalist society expressed the philosophy of the Enlightenment in a way that simultaneously proclaimed and negated liberalism.

The work of discourse analysis also shows that the denials of prejudice should not be dismissed so facilely as lacking social significance. Van Dijk has analysed the language of racism, thereby building up a picture of modern ideology which pays particular attention to the way that elite messages can be transformed into ordinary discourse (van Dijk, 1985b, 1987). There is no doubt that this work has been enormously fruitful in pointing out the detailed strategies and rhetorical manoeuvres involved in the expression of racism. Moreover, it is socially important for the way it demystifies such manoeuvres. Van Dijk raises the question as to whether the denials of prejudice should be treated as expressions of impression-management rather than of genuine attitudes. For example, van Dijk (1983) distinguishes between 'the effective expression of semantic macro-structures (themes)' and the 'interactional and social goal' of creating the desired impression in the hearer. He goes on to assert that 'these two different sets of goals may be sometimes in conflict: a direct or "honest" expression of the beliefs or the opinions from the speaker's situation model may lead to negative social evaluation of the speaker by the hearer' (1983, p. 384). The disjunction between honest attitudinal expression and impression-management is again expressed in van Dijk (1984) when discussing linguistic devices involved in the denial of prejudice. The denial of prejudice is strategic, but 'we thereby want to convey that the move is strategical only relative to the goal of "making a good impression", rather than to the goal of being "sincere and honest"' (p. 127).

Although this might sometimes occur in discourse, and van Dijk's own data reveals the complexity of racial discourse, it cannot be the full story. Van Dijk's analyses, with their emphasis upon the creation of ideology (e.g. van Dijk, 1986b, 1987), do not make the mistake of assuming that impression-management follows culturally universal laws (e.g. Tedeschi, 1981). It cannot be assumed that in all cultures and historical epochs the expression of disparaging remarks about other peoples creates a bad impression. Such an impression can only be created when there are social norms. This is clearly recognized by van Dijk, who writes that 'on the one hand people want to express possibly negative experiences or evaluations, but on the other hand social norms force them to make a good impression, and not appear as racists' (1985a, pp. 69–70). Yet, again there is the contrast between personal inclinations and social norms. From a social psychological perspective, there is a further step to be taken, in order to link the social norms to individual consciousness. The social norms cannot merely exist as constraints existing outside individuals. For social norms to function as social pressures, they must be internalized, and thereby form part of the individual's cognitive beliefs. Thus the conflict behind 'I'm not prejudiced but . . .' is not merely the conflict between the individual and extraneous social customs (or perhaps, other people), but a conflict within individuals, who have two contrasting ideological themes upon which to draw. To use Althusser's (1971) terminology it is this ideological contradiction which 'interpellates' the subject.

Evidence for this comes from the fact that the ambivalent expression does not seem to be confined to a limited range of situations, in which individuals find themselves on public display, especially to an audience from a higher social class or more advanced educational attainment. Billig's (1986) study is based on ethnographic observation of Young Conservatives relaxing in their own social environment. In this situation, where all participants are presumed to have similar viewpoints, prejudice is still not freed from its ambivalent expression. All have accepted the social norm, which they would use to condemn others and by which they would not wish to be condemned. The article in the fascist publication also shows the ideological force of the concept of 'prejudice'. This article was primarily directed at fellow members of the National Front. Within a social circle in which direct expression of crude prejudice is not discouraged, one can find, nevertheless, an argument which draws upon the prevailing images, or social norms, of prejudice. Its author was keen that neither himself nor his readership should be considered prejudiced. In order to understand the force of this social norm, it is necessary to look beyond social presentation. The ideological roots of the concept also need to be explored, for it is one half of an ideology, an internalized consciousness, which doubly sanctions prejudice. It is sanctioned to the extent that it is allowed and it is sanctioned to the extent that it is penalized.

The meaning of 'prejudice'

Much of the research into the social psychology of racism has been narrow to the extent to which it has concentrated upon the images of outgroups, rather than on the image of 'prejudice' or 'racism' itself. Social psychologists have conducted thousands of studies about stereotypes of outgroups or desired social distance from outgroup members, etc. They have built up an enormous collection of data about the images which subjects, especially white male Americans, have about outgroups. The more recent studies of discourse analysis have captured the tones which people use to talk of others. In the main, such studies, especially the traditional stereotype research, are narrowly focused, in that they seek to examine respondents' views on a narrow topic, or towards a single 'stimulus object'. With the exception of the discourse studies, they do not seek to construct an image of the contemporary ideology of racism, by which is meant the socially shared pattern of ideas about race and nationality circulating in contemporary society. If analysis of this wider ideology is sought, then the focus of attention must be directed beyond the restricted studies of stereotypes or social distance. It must be directed towards the images of 'prejudice'.

The very phrase 'I'm not prejudiced but . . .' indicates the connection between the concept of 'prejudice' and those views of outgroups, which social psychologists typically accept as indicators of prejudice. The fact that the social desirability of not appearing to be prejudiced is linked in discourse to its expression means that an analysis of the ideology, or the wider pattern of ideas, should not avoid the theme of 'prejudice'. To use the language of Moscovici and his coworkers (Moscovici, 1982, 1983, 1984; Jodelet, 1984) social psychologists need to gather information about the social representation of 'prejudice' in majority discourse, just as they have studied the social representation of minority groups. As has been suggested, 'prejudice', as an everyday concept, as well as a social-scientific one, represents a strong cultural value; even racist theorists of a fascist party appear to wish to avoid being labelled as prejudiced and do not care to think of themselves as prejudiced. Consequently, the ideological and social psychological significance of the concept needs to be examined, in the context of the ideology of race.

In order to do this, a rhetorical perspective is recommended. The central feature of the rhetorical perspective proposed by Billig (1985 and 1987) is that it studies the argumentative aspects of discourse (see also Shotter, 1987). Central to this perspective is the analysis of 'common-places', or those everyday phrases which express values (Rokeach, 1973; Ehninger and Hauser, 1984), and which, according to Aristotle in *The Rhetoric*, add a 'moral quality to our speech' (Aristotle, 1909). Typically these common-places are not employed untendentiously, but are used to justify the self against actual, or potential, criticisms of others. A rhetorical approach would point directly at the argumentative nature of racist discourse. This is an aspect which has been emphasised by Van Dijk (1984, 1986a; see also Schiffrin, 1985). Argumentative discourse is to be found in the context of justification and criticism (Perelman and Olbrechts-Tyteca, 1971). The stories told by respondents are used to justify a particular position, as well as to criticize the characters in the stories. Similarly, the phrase 'I'm not prejudiced but . . .' represents an advanced justification (or *prolepsis*) against the criticism of being prejudiced (see Billig, 1987, for further discussion of this point). By using the formula, the speaker not only seeks to deflect criticism, but also lays claim to be a member of the moral community of the unprejudiced. Even the fascist author is laying claim to membership of this community, as he seeks to rebut 'the favourite accusation thrown at the National Front'.

More is involved in the denial of prejudice than the rebuttal of actual criticisms, which might be made by specific others. It is not merely that the speaker wants to create a good impression in the sight of others, who might have a different set of values. Speakers also justify themselves to those who might be perceived as being similar to the self. Thus, Billig's (1986) ethnographic study of Young Conservatives showed that the denial of prejudice occurred in a situation where all shared similar views. Similarly, the National Front writer was addressing fellow members of his party. Since the audience is presumed to possess similar views to the speaker, the speaker, in a real sense, is literally engaging in self-justification: the self is being justified by the self to the self. In this respect, the internal discourses of the self resemble external arguments between selves (Billig, 1987). In order to engage in such self-justification, the speaker must possess the ideological and argumentative tools for criticizing 'prejudice', for the speaker wishes to escape from criticisms which could come equally from both self and audience. It is this aspect of the speaker's self-justification and criticism of 'prejudice' which is omitted in any explanation which relies exclusively on the notion of impression-management.

The ideological basis of this self-justification lies in a claim to being rational, and, as such, the semantic use of 'prejudice' involves lay notions of the philosophy and psychology of rationality. This can be seen by considering the concept of 'prejudice' itself and its transformation from being a concept of Enlightenment philosophy to a concept which permits, by its apparent criticism, the expression of prejudice in everyday discourse. It can be argued that the ordinary use of the word 'prejudice' indicates that the traditions of liberalism have passed into everyday discourse. On the other hand, the frequent use of the concept in the formula 'I'm not prejudiced but . . .' implies the limits of these traditions, at least as instantiated in everyday reality.

The word 'prejudice' attracted the meaning of irrationality during the Enlightenment, as philosophers adapted a legal term in their dispute with unreasoning faith. Gadamer has claimed that 'it is not until the Enlightenment that the concept of prejudice acquires the negative aspect we are all familiar with' (1979, p. 240). He goes on to connect the semantic change with 'the general tendency of the Enlightenment not to accept any authority and to decide everything before the judgement seat of reason' (p. 241). Voltaire provides a good example of the way in which the philosophy of rationality implied a theory of irrationality, which was based upon psychological ideas about the source of erroneous thought. In his *Philosophical Dictionary* Voltaire included an item for 'prejudice'. The entry started with the statement that 'prejudice is an opinion without judgement' (Voltaire, 1929, p. 351): i.e. the processes of reasoning have not been applied to the prejudiced opinion. In this way, an opinion is prejudiced if the judgements on which the opinion is based are faulty or even totally lacking.

The person who uses the phrase 'I'm not prejudiced but . . .' implies some image of what the 'prejudiced' person is like, and this image is similar to that held by Voltaire, in that the prejudiced person is presumed to hold views which have not been formed rationally. The semantic influence of the Enlightenment can even be seen in the discourse of the fascist writer quoted earlier. Although ostensibly criticizing the traditions of liberalism, the fascist writer, nevertheless, employs the discourse of these traditions when discussing 'prejudice'. His definition of this Enlightenment concept is similar to Voltaire in that he suggests that the prejudiced person comes to a conclusion without bothering about the facts of the matter. There was a distinction between positions which were 'merely expressions of bigoted dislike' and those which are 'solidly buttressed by reality'. In making this distinction the writer was upholding the Enlightenment philosophy that conclusions should be based upon reality and not upon psychological dispositions.

The distinction between the rationality of the self and the irrationality of the 'prejudiced' also appears in the comments of the teenagers interviewed by Cochrane and Billig (1984) and Billig *et al.* (1988). Even supporters of the National Front, and its policy of expelling non-whites, felt impelled to justify their views. The persons claiming to lack prejudices, but who oppose the presence of non-white immigrants, offer justifications for their positions. As van Dijk (1984) has shown, they typically tell stories about immigrants or use abstract reasonings, such as that 'if there were less blacks, there would be more jobs or housing'. Either way, the prejudiced persons are attempting to justify their position by adopting either a theoretical or empirical perspective. The reasons for the position are externalized, as the speaker, in effect, says that it is the empirical nature of the world, rather than the preferences of the self, which has led to the conclusion. In speaking thus, there is a claim to rational discourse and an implicit defence against any criticism of being irrational. In this way, the discourse is argumentative in both senses of the term: arguments are given to bolster a conclusion and these arguments are justifications against the potential criticism of being irrational.

The speaker's self-image (or rather, self-justification) of reasonableness depends upon a contrast with what is unreasonable. The fascist writer exemplified his image of unreasonableness with examples of anti-racists. Similarly, Billig *et al.* describe 'reasonable' white teenagers, some of whom were sympathizers of the National Front, as distancing themselves from the 'skinheads' or 'lunatics'. The very term 'lunatic', which was widely used in this discourse, implies a lay psychological theory: the term denotes people whose thinking is disrupted from logicality by personality or stupidity. The 'lunatics', in contrast to those who proclaimed their rationality, offered no justifications beyond a dislike for non-whites or a liking for violence. In this way, the use of justifications itself was the defence against attribution of irrational 'lunacy', for, if speakers were unable to offer 'factual' justifications for their views on immigrants, they too would be irrationally 'lunatic'.

Voltaire's use of 'prejudice' differs from the current use in two ways, in that it was less firmly tied to negative evaluations and to images of outgroups. Because the negative evaluation was not as strong as it is now, Voltaire was able to talk about justifiable prejudices, such as those that a child might have in favour of a teacher. The target of the Enlightenment philosophers was the prejudices of religion and it is possible to find the term being used in other contexts without the negative connotation. Two examples, neither taken from philosophical discourse, but both from English sources, will illustrate this usage. *The Annual Register* for 1787 included a short essay entitled 'On prejudice', reprinted from the third volume of the *Observer*. The essay was quite clear in condemning the prejudices of religions, while distinguishing these from other prejudices. Thus, the author asserted that the 'prejudices of education are less dangerous than religious ones' (1788, p. 182) and even that 'national prejudice' should be seen as a 'virtue' (p. 181). The second example is taken from the early years of the nineteenth century. It concerns the reaction of the Whig politician, Lord Brougham, to the Prince Regent's sympathy for the House of Stewart. Lord Brougham reminded His Majesty of the misdemeanours of the Stewart kings, which had included 'thwarting the prejudices and opposing wishes' of the nation (quoted in Priestley, 1971, p. 159).

Semantically these quotations must appear curious to the modern reader, who would see a contradiction of terms in the notion of virtuous prejudice and who would expect the thwarting of prejudices to be a matter for praise not blame. Both Brougham and the author in *The Annual Register*, as supporters of the liberal Enlightenment's battle with traditional religious authority, were prepared to defend national, and nationalist, sentiments. Yet these are feelings which seem to contradict the universalist, rational aspirations of liberalism. This is not a contradiction which has been resolved. Nowadays such national sentiments are also defended by those who place themselves within the traditions of liberalism. As Barker (1981) has shown, this combination is typical of thinkers on the new conservative right. However, there has been a shift of semantics, concerning the notion of 'prejudice'. Among the writers of the new right, it would be untypical to find an explicit defence of 'national prejudice', for the concept of prejudice has largely been conceded in the wish to avoid the criticism of being irrationally bigoted. National sentiment, instincts, feelings, etc., might be defended, and indeed be given a 'rational' (non-instinctual, etc.) justification in terms of biology, social function or whatever (Seidel, 1985). In outlining an argument against multi-racial immigration, such New Right authors might justify themselves in terms of so-called 'national feelings', but argumentative rhetoric and semantic history combine to leave such a phrase as 'national prejudices' to their opponents.

One reason why the modern reader has difficulty with a positive evaluation of the term 'national prejudices' is that, in the twentieth century, prejudice has taken on a substantive meaning. Its prototype is not any opinion formed without judgement, but nationalist, or racist, opinions in particular. As such, the phrase 'I'm not prejudiced but . . .' is not merely a defence of rationality in general, but is a defence against that particular sort of irrationality which leads to hostility against individuals based upon the colour of their skin or the provenance of their passport. Samelson (1978) has documented the growth of interests by social scientists in the topic of 'prejudice'. In the early years of the century the term prejudice was rarely left unqualified: for instance, psychologists would study 'race prejudice' or 'national prejudice'. In the early post-war years, a semantic change is detectable. When Gordon Allport wrote his classic work *The Nature of Prejudice* (1958), he left 'prejudice' unqualified as he wished to include general principles of psychological functioning in his analysis. Nevertheless, the main emphasis of the book is upon the prejudices of racism, anti-Semitism and nationalism, so much so that the unqualified term is sufficient to evoke these exemplifications. Had Voltaire used such a title as *The Nature of Prejudice*, his readers may have expected criticism of clerics. In the mid-twentieth century, Allport's title invites his readers to expect the arguments of liberalism to be directed against different targets.

This semantic shift should not necessarily be interpreted as indicating a decline in nationalism or racism. What it does indicate is the demands of liberal ideology that the virtues of 'national prejudice' be justified and thereby translated from the category of 'prejudice'. The contradictory demands of justifying and criticizing national prejudice can be seen in the everyday discourse of racism.

Justification and denial of prejudice

If there is a social taboo against expressing unjustified negative views against outgroups, then the speaker who wishes to express discriminatory views must be ready to search for, and find, suitable reasons. Considerable ingenuity may be required to discover non-racial criteria for racial discrimination and non-racial reasons for criticizing other races. In consequence, one should not expect the discourse of racism to be necessarily marked by the ponderous unsubtlety of thought described by Adorno *et al.* (1950). In fact, there are good reasons for supposing that the classic authoritarians of the study by Adorno *et al.* (1950) were much more cognitively supple than was supposed (Billig, 1982a, 1985). Similarly, the distinction between 'old-fashioned' and 'modern' racism may not always be a distinction in kind, but may reflect an ability to provide justifications, often post hoc, for views and positions. Education may enhance the ability to produce justifications, rather than eliminate racism *tout court*. Thus there is evidence that the better educated do not show a greater consonance between general principles of fairness and particular stances on racial issues, but may show greater flexibility in justifying the laying aside of abstract principles (Sniderman *et al.*, 1984).

In addition, if in modern times racism has become the prototypical instantiation of the concept of 'prejudice', then similar justificatory strategies can be expected, when people deny racism and prejudice: in denying that one is racist, one is denying that one is prejudiced, and vice versa. The images, or social representations, of prejudice and racism will be similar. The racist will be seen as being irrationally prejudiced, harbouring irrational violence and hatred. Those who deny their own prejudice and racism will need this image, for their protestations of rationality depend upon a contrast with irrationality. Thus right-wing politicians will use the image of irrationally violent Nazis, in order that their own policies on race will appear reasonable by contrast (Billig, 1982b).

These themes can be illustrated in a newspaper report about discrimination in the British Army. *The Observer* newspaper published a lengthy investigation, which claimed that there was substantial discrimination by elite regiments against potential black recruits. It followed a report by the Commission of Racial Equality on the same topic. *The Observer* reported that 'seven regiments of the Household Division – protectors of the Royal Family, Colonel-in-Chief, Her Majesty the Queen – operate an unofficial colour bar' (8 August 1986). The newspaper recorded the comments of some serving Guardsmen:

One serving senior Guards NCO [Non-Commissioned Officer] told us: 'There are no Blacks in the Guards. There never have been and never will be. People do not want to see a black face under a bearskin. Blacks are generally persuaded to go elsewhere.'

A Guards officer who left recently told us: 'Blacks do not get to the depot. It has become a tradition not to have Blacks.' He added, apparently unaware of the illogicality of his statement: 'There is no racial discrimination.'

The Director of Army Recruiting . . . denied last week there was any colour bar on black or Asian Guardsmen. 'The Guards have the same requirements for recruits as any infantry or Royal Armoured Corps regiment,' he said. He believed that there were 'some', but he couldn't name a Guards regiment with a black soldier in it. (*The Observer* (8 August 1986))

There are several points which can be noted about these quoted remarks. In an obvious respect all three are similar: all seek to justify the same discriminatory practice and all three have emerged from the same institution that practises discrimination. This similarity should caution against making too firm a distinction between the three; for example, one might have sought to make distinctions in terms of being instances of either 'new' or 'old' racism, especially on the grounds that new racists, unlike old racists, will justify their position by citing non-racial general principles (Sniderman and Tetlock, 1986a, 1986b; see also Potter and Wetherall, 1987, for arguments against deducing 'true' attitudes from discourse). Nevertheless, there are differences in the ways that the speakers express their views, particularly with respect to the justifications they offer. The three were presented in ascending order of rank, and this order matches the extent to which the views are given 'non-prejudiced' justification.

The NCO does not seek to deny prejudice. In fact, his comments seemingly invite the charge, for he describes the lack of black guardsmen in terms of feelings rather than in terms of the disclosure of external factuality: 'People do not want to see a black face under a bearskin.' The speaker is not criticizing 'people' for having these wants, nor is a justification given for them. He is, of course, assuming that 'people' are white. Without a justification being given, these 'wants' constitute the sort of psychological state which is said to characterize prejudice. The teenage respondents of Cochrane and Billig (1984) and Billig *et al.* (1988) implied that it was the prejudiced people who did not 'like' black people or did not 'want' them in Britain. By contrast, they implied that the unprejudiced personally did not mind black people (some of their best friends were black. . .), but there were all sorts of other reasons, beyond their personal feelings, why regrettably it was better if there were no black people in Britain. The quoted comments of the NCO are too short to indicate whether he might in fact justify his comments in this way, if he were personally accused of prejudice. It should be noted that he remarks that 'people' do not want to see a black face, not that he personally objects to such a sight.

The second quoted soldier, unlike the first one, actually denies prejudice: 'There is no discrimination,' he contends. This comment depends upon having some rough idea what would count as racial discrimination. Unfortunately, the newspaper reporter did not press him on the point. More crucially there is little social scientific work to fall back upon, in order to demonstrate what people consider to be prototypical examples of prejudice and discrimination. There is survey evidence that, whatever people imagine 'racial prejudice' to be, they conceive that it is others, not themselves, who are prejudiced (Airey, 1984). The ex-soldier's comment suggests, contrary to the interpretation of the reporter, that there might be a perceived connection between tradition and the absence of discrimination. If the speaker identifies discrimination with irrational feelings of hostility against blacks, then there exists the basis for a denial of prejudice: if the regiment is motivated by the desire to uphold tradition, then it is not motivated by feelings of antipathy towards blacks, and therefore it is not prejudiced. More detailed questioning might have revealed whether the soldier's discourse would have taken this argumentative tack.

The third comment of the three gives the most sophisticated defence. An account is given which explains present practices without recourse to justifying the feelings of anyone who might be implicated in the practices. In fact, the account is a lay 'sociological' one: it describes how a system works, and all those psychological states, which might be indicative of a prejudiced mentality, have no place in this system. There was no colour bar, because normal rules are applied for the selection of recruits, and it just happens that black and Asian people fail the tests. Here is an example of the deracialization of discourse (Reeves, 1983). The rules are deracialized, for they do not forbid black and Asian success. Those who operate the rules are not racist, for they merely follow procedures in a colour blind way. In fact, it is something of a mystery how black and Asian people fail the test. The unstated implication is that there is something about the aptitude of the potential recruits themselves which leads to their failure. Sometimes, in this sort of deracialized discourse, the speaker can reveal racist assumptions and unexamined stereotypes. A senior London police officer was attempting to attract black recruits into the police force, while denying that racism in the force might have deterred black people from joining in the past: 'Racism in the force is not the main reason for black people preferring not to apply. Being a police officer entails working long and difficult hours' (*The Guardian*, 3 June 1986).

The police officer, like the Director of Army Recruiting, offers an explanation, which specifically seeks to rule out racist motivations. In this way there is a denial of prejudice, not only on the part of the speaker, but also on the part of the institution which the speaker is justifying. By equating 'prejudice' or 'racism' with individual psychological states, 'institutional racism' becomes a logical impossibility: for how can institutions harbour irrational hatreds? By making institutional racism an impossibility in theory, this sort of discourse justifies it in practice. The line of argument depends upon two principal features: (a) there is a need to produce an overt justification for practices which might be criticized and this justification must explain racial discrimination in terms of anything other than irrational preferences; (b) the discourse implies that irrational preference would be morally bad and the good intentions of the speaker, and those whom the speaker justifies, are guaranteed if they are shown to differ from those who might act on the basis of irrational prejudices.

Both these two factors can be seen in an editorial in the right-wing newspaper *The Daily Telegraph* (12 June 1976) on the same issue of discrimination in the army. Like the army officers, the writer attempted to justify the recruitment practices of the Guards, and, as might be expected from a serious organ of right-wing opinion, more ingenuity was shown in the search for justificatory reasons than was by the lower-ranking quoted officers. The main direction of the editorial's argument was that positive discrimination was 'dangerous muddling'. There was also the defence of present practices. It was true, conceded the newspaper, that black faces were not to be found in the ranks of the Household Division of the Guards. But this was not racism, because there are 'reasons' for the non-recruitment. By 'reasons', the newspaper meant reasons which were 'reasonable' and, thus, other than prejudiced preferences. An explanation was needed, and one was: 'What seems to inhibit the Guards from varying their recruiting policy is a concern to preserve the uniform appearance of the ranks on ceremonial occasions.' However, as the writer recognized, perhaps this was no longer a convincing reason. The newspaper concluded: 'Soldiers might take time to consider whether in this attitude they are not just fixed in the past' (*Daily Telegraph*, 12 June 1986). In other words, the worst criticism which could be levelled against the failure to recruit blacks was that of failing to move with the times. In this instance, the discourse of prejudice, with its mixture of simultaneous denial and justification, ended with a declaration of the classic liberal imperative of historical progress.

Conclusion

Horkheimer and Adorno in *Dialectic of Enlightenment* (1973) insisted upon seeing the development of irrational racism as being the development of liberalism, as practised in an illiberal society. In the phrase of Horkheimer, it is the 'tendency of liberalism to tilt over into fascism' (1947, p. 20). Whether this diagnosis is historically or sociologically true is one matter, but the relations between liberalism and racism cannot be dismissed. The fascist writer, denying all prejudice, shows how the discourse of liberalism can tilt over into that of fascism. Moreover, one should not expect the liberal ideology of today, as revealed in ordinary discourse, to reflect the universalistic aspirations of the Enlightenment. Marx and Engels may have predicted in *The Communist Manifesto* (1968) that capitalism would abolish the particularities of nations and make outdated narrow national consciousness. However, international economic arrangements have not totally superseded national ones. If ideology reflects economic organiza-tion, then one might expect that modern consciousness should contain its universalistic and its particularistic common-places. There are the toler-ant themes of international brotherhood (and nowadays of sisterhood) to draw upon, to add the moral flavour of liberalism to arguments. Again, there are narrower considerations to be justified in terms of other common-places. If liberalism has triumphed, then it is not in eradicating the prejudices of the nation, except in name. Its triumph in everyday discourse is the demand for rational or empirical justification. The para-dox is that the more prejudices are criticized, the more the prejudices of liberalism are justified.

References

Adorno, T. W., Frenkel-Brunswik, E., Levinson, D. J. and Sanford, R. N. (1950). *The Authoritarian Personality.* New York: Harper.

Airey, C. (1984). Social and moral values. In R. Jowell and C. Airey (eds.), *British Social Attitudes: the 1984 Report* (pp.121–56). Aldershot, UK: Gower.

Allport, G. W. (1958). *The Nature of Prejudice.* Garden City, NY: Anchor Books.

Althusser, L. (1971). *Lenin and Philosophy, and Other Essays* (B. Brewster, trans.). London: NLB.

Anonymous (1788). On prejudice. *Annual Register,* **1,787**, 181–4. London: G. G. J. and G. Robinson.

Aristotle (1909). *The Rhetoric of Aristole: a Translation.* Cambridge, UK: Cambridge University Press.

Barker, M. (1981). *The New Racism: Conservatives and the Ideology of the Tribe.* London: Junction Books.

Billig, M. (1978). *Fascists: a Social Psychological View of the National Front.* London: Academic Press; European Association of Experimental Social Psychology.

  (1981). *L'Internationale Raciste: de la Psychologie à la Science des Races.* Paris: François Maspero.

  (1982a). *Ideology and Social Psychology: Extremism, Moderation and Contradiction.* Oxford, UK: Blackwell.

  (1982b). Anti-Semitism in the eighties. *Month,* **15**, 125–30.

  (1985). Prejudice, categorization and particularization – from a perceptual to a rhetorical approach. *European Journal of Social Psychology,* **15**(1), 79–103.

  (1986). Very ordinary life and the Young Conservatives. In H. Beloff (ed.), *Getting into Life.* London: Methuen.

  (1987). *Arguing and Thinking: a Rhetorical Approach to Social Psychology.* Cambridge, UK: Cambridge University Press.

Billig, M., Condor, S., Edwards, D., Gane, M., Middleton, D. and Radley, A. (1988). *Ideological Dilemmas: a Social Psychology of Everyday Thinking.* London: Sage.

Cochrane, R. and Billig, M. (1984). I'm not National Front, but . . . *New Society,* **68**, 255–8.

Cohn, N. (1967). *Warrant for Genocide: the Myth of the Jewish World Conspiracy and the Protocols of the Elders of Zion.* London: Eyre and Spottiswoode.

Ehninger, D. and Hauser, G. A. (1984). Communication of values. In C. C. Arnold and J. W. Bowers (eds.), *Handbook of Rhetorical and Communication Theory.* Boston, MA: Allyn and Bacon.

Gadamer, H.-G. (1979). *Truth and Method* (2nd edn). London: Sheed and Ward.

Gordon, P. and Klug, F. (1986). *New Right New Reaction.* London: Searchlight.

Hewitt, J. P. and Stokes, R. (1975). Disclaimers. *American Sociological Review,* **40**, 1–11.

Horkheimer, M. (1947). *Eclipse of Reason.* New York: Oxford University Press.

Horkheimer, M. and Adorno, T. W. (1973). *Dialectic of Enlightenment* (John Cumming, trans.). London: Allen Lane.

Jacobson, S. K. (1985). Resistance to affirmative action: self-interest or racism? *Journal of Conflict Resolution,* **29**, 306–29.

Jodelet, D. (1984). Représentation sociale: phénomènes, concept et théorie. In S. Moscovici (ed.), *Psychologie Sociale* (pp.367–78). Paris: Presses Universitaires de France.

Kinder, D. R. (1986). The continuing American-dilemma – white resistance to racial change 40 years after Myrdal. *Journal of Social Issues,* **42**(2), 151–71.

Kinder, D. R. and Sears, D. O. (1981). Prejudice and politics – symbolic racism versus racial threats to the good life. *Journal of Personality and Social Psychology,* **40**(3), 414–31.

Lutzhöft, H.-J. (1971). *Der Nordische Gedanke in Deutschland 1920 bis 1940.* Stuttgart, Germany: Klett.

Marx, K. and Engels, F. (1968). *The Communist Manifesto: Selected Works.* London: Lawrence and Wishart.

McConahay, J. B. (1981). Reducing racial prejudice in desegregated schools. In W. D. Hawley (ed.), *Effective School Desegregation* (pp.35–53). Beverly Hills, CA: Sage.

(1982). Self-interest versus racial attitudes as correlates of anti-busing attitudes in Louisville: is it the buses or the blacks? *Journal of Politics*, **44**, 692–720.

McConahay, J. B. and Hough, J. C. (1976). Symbolic racism. *Journal of Social Issues*, **32**, 23–45.

McConahay, J. B., Hardee, B. B. and Batts, V. (1981). Has racism declined in America? *Journal of Conflict Resolution*, 563–79.

McFayden, R. and Wetherall, M. (1986). Categories in discourse. Paper presented at the Social Psychology Section, British Psychological Society Conference.

Moscovici, S. (1982). The coming era of representations. In J. P. Codol and J. P. Leyens (eds.), *Cognitive Analysis of Social Behaviour*. The Hague: Martinus Nijhoff.

(1983). The phenomenon of social representations. In R. M. Farr and S. Moscovici (eds.), *Social Representations* (pp.3–69). Cambridge, UK: Cambridge University Press.

(1984). The myth of the lonely paradigm: a rejoinder. *Social Research*, **51**, 939–67.

Myrdal, G. (1944). *An American Dilemma: the Negro Problem and Modern Democracy*. New York: Harper.

Perelman, C. M. and Olbrechts-Tyteca, L. (1971). *The New Rhetoric: A Treatise on Argumentation* (J. Wilkinson and P. Weaver, trans.). Notre Dame/London: University of Notre Dame Press.

Poliakov, L. (1974). *The Aryan Myth*. London: Chatto Heinemann.

Potter, J. and Wetherell, M. (1987). *Discourse and Social Psychology*. London: Sage.

Priestley, J. B. (1971). *The Prince of Pleasure and His Regency, 1811–1820*. London: Sphere Books.

Reeves, F. (1983). *British Racial Discourse: a Study of British Political Discourse about Race and Race-related Matters*. Cambridge, UK: Cambridge University Press.

Rokeach, M. (1973). *The Nature of Human Values*. London/New York: Collier-Macmillan/Free Press.

Samelson, F. (1978). From race psychology to studies in prejudice – some observations on thematic reversal in social-psychology. *Journal of the History of the Behavioral Sciences*, **14**(3), 265–78.

Schiffrin, D. (1985). Everyday argument: the organization of diversity in talk. In T. A. van Dijk (ed.), *Handbook of Discourse Analysis* (Vol. 3, pp.35–46). London: Academic Press.

Schoen, D. E. (1977). *Enoch Powell and the Powellites*. London: Macmillan.

Seidel, G. (1985). Culture, nation and 'race' in the British and French New Right. In R. Levitas (ed.), *The Ideology of the New Right* (pp.107–35). Oxford, UK: Polity Press.

(1986). *The Holocaust Denial*. Leeds: Beyond the Pale.

(1988). 'We condemn Apartheid, BUT ...': a discursive analysis of the European Parliament debate on sanctions (July, 1986). *Sociological Review Monograph*, **36**, 222–49.

Shotter, J. (1987). Rhetoric as a model for psychology. *Proceedings of the 'Future of Psychology' Conference*. Leicester, UK: British Psychological Society.

Sniderman, P. M. and Tetlock, P. E. (1986a). Symbolic racism: problems of motive attribution in political analysis. *Journal of Social Issues*, **42**, 129–50.

(1986b). Reflections on American racism. *Journal of Social Issues*, **42**, 173–87.

Sniderman, P. M., Brody, R. A. and Kulinsky, J. H. (1984). Policy reasoning and political values: the problem of racial equality. *American Journal of Political Science*, **28**, 75–94.

Studlar, D. T. (1974). British public opinion, colour issues, and Enoch Powell – longitudinal analysis. *British Journal of Political Science*, 4(Jul), 371–81.

Tedeschi, J. T. (1981). *Impression Management Theory and Social Psychological Research*. New York/London: Academic Press.

van Dijk, T. A. (1983). Cognitive and conversational strategies in the expression of ethnic prejudice. *Text*, **3**(4), 375–404.

(1984). *Prejudice and Discourse: an Analysis of Ethnic Prejudice in Cognition and Conversation*. Amsterdam: Benjamins.

(1985a). Cognitive models in discourse production: the expression of ethnic situations in prejudiced discourse. In J. P. Forgas (ed.), *Language and Social Situations* (pp. 61–79). New York: Springer.

(1985b). *Elite Discourse and Racism*. Paper presented at the Utrecht Summer School on Critical Theory, Utrecht.

(1986a). When majorities talk about minorities. In M. L. McLaughlin (ed.), *Communication Yearbook* (Vol. 9, pp.57–83). Beverly Hills, CA: Sage.

(1986b). Mediating racism: the role of the media in the reproduction of racism. In R. Wodak (ed.), *Language, Power and Ideology*. Amsterdam: Benjamins.

(1987). Discourse and power. Unpublished manuscript. Department of General Studies, University of Amsterdam.

Voltaire (1929). *Dictionnaire Philosophique*. Paris: Werdet et Lequien Fils, Firmin Didot frères.

Weigel, R. H. and Howes, P. W. (1985). Conceptions of racial prejudice: symbolic racism reconsidered. *Journal of Social Issues*, **41**, 117–38.

Wetherell, M. and Potter, J. (1986). Discourse analysis and the social psychology of racism. *Social Psychology Section Newsletter*, **15**, 24–9.

8   The prejudice problematic

Margaret Wetherell

> It required years of labour and billions of dollars to gain the secret of the
> atom. It will take a still greater investment to gain the secrets of man's
> irrational nature.   G. W. Allport (1954)

This chapter identifies and explores a discursive ordering which I shall call
the 'problematic of prejudice'.[1] I intend to study this problematic in two of
its guises: as a theoretical and analytic practice within social psychology
and as a form of accounting within the discourse of Pakeha (white
European) New Zealanders. I shall argue that the prejudice problematic,
contrary to some of the avowed intentions of its advocates within the social
sciences, fulfils some important ideological roles for Pakeha New
Zealanders. Accounting in terms of prejudice can draw attention away
from immediate social reform towards utopian visions; it can provide a
logic and method for justifying individual conduct; and it can establish a
positive identity and a benevolent 'vocabulary of motives' vis à vis other,
supposedly less enlightened, individuals.

I use the term 'problematic' in this context because it suggests we are
dealing with a relatively integrated framework of distinctive assumptions,
intellectual strategies, questions and problems. The most integrated form
of prejudice talk appears, of course, within the texts of social psychology.
The 'lived ideology' is, as usual, much more fragmented, piecemeal and
contradictory, caught up as it is in the kaleidoscope of common sense. In
this chapter I use the intellectuals' version to help chart a coherent path
through the lay discourse.

At several points in the interviews the sample was asked about forms
of racism, discrimination and disadvantage in New Zealand. When I
looked at how this topic was handled, the responses seemed immediately familiar. Here was the social psychology of irrational attitudes and

beliefs, the social psychology of 'racial prejudice', transposed from the lecture room to the kitchen table. This diffusion of science into common sense, or equally of common sense into science, is interesting. Why does this particular set of argumentative resources form the basis of everyday stories of motives, injustice and contact between groups as well as populating the papers and monographs of professional social scientists?

It is easy to be scathing about the problematics of the past in the attempt to demonstrate that one's own distinctive set of assumptions, strategies and questions represent a superior and advanced mode of analysis. Rereading some of the classic texts of prejudice from the 1950s and then again from the 1970s (Adorno *et al.*, 1950; Allport, 1954; Ehrlich, 1973; Jones, 1972), what is most apparent is the moral and political frame in which the concept of prejudice was proposed and investigated in social psychology.

G. W. Allport's belief in the power of science to produce technical solutions to the problems of human relations is evident in his words which introduce this chapter. Allport's texts display obvious respect for the values of 'civilised men [sic]', for the potential of the 'human family' and the democratic ideals of America – to a degree which seems naive and quaint when viewed through the lens of the postmodern 1990s. Yet moral fervour and a passion to remedy racism also shine through his text.

This chapter, therefore, is concerned with what is becoming a familiar paradox or pattern. Argumentative resources are varied and fragmented, drawn upon in an ad hoc and promiscuous manner. Their ideological thrust can be exceedingly difficult to predict in abstract, or in advance, as it depends on the details of the practice. This flexibility of argumentative and discursive resources was again evident as I compared the social psychology of prejudice, sometimes radical and typically reformist in its stance, with the justificatory and legitimating talk of Pakeha New Zealanders which seemed, on the whole, to bolster their position of privilege.

The first few sections of this chapter try to clarify the characteristic tensions in the prejudice problematic to show its ideological potential. I then look at some of the typical discursive moves found in prejudice talk. My aim in both cases is to indicate how prejudice discourse escapes the confines of academic textbooks and itself becomes part of ideological practice. Finally, towards the end of the chapter I will attempt to pull out the implications for anti-racist strategies, focusing on attempts by psychologists and others to develop educational programmes based on prejudice theory and research.

Prejudice in social psychological and lay discourse

Unlike the concept of 'race', the intellectual history of the concept of prejudice has not, as far as I am aware, been traced to the same extent. But, as with other elements of Pakeha New Zealanders' discourse, its roots seem to lie in the classic traditions of the Enlightenment. Billig in Chapter 7 points out, following the analysis of Gadamer (1979), that it was as a result of the shifts in thought associated with the Enlightenment that the term 'prejudice' began to acquire a negative connotation. Prejudice became firmly associated with the mischief of irrationality which all decent post-Enlightenment citizens would wish to avoid. The contrast established between prejudice and rationality then became specified more narrowly during the twentieth century, appearing as a contrast between prejudice and tolerance as the term gradually became a convenient shorthand for 'racial prejudice' and 'racial stereotypes'.

The particular ethical flavour of the prejudice problematic and its characteristic modes of explanation thus reflect some dilemmas, fractures and blind alleys within Enlightenment traditions of thought more broadly. The impression is often given in social psychology that concepts spring newly minted from rigorous empirical research. In contrast, I shall assume that the conceptual apparatus of social psychology closely reflects the discursive history of Western culture.

This section focuses on the main themes in accounts of prejudice within both social psychology and lay discourse. I will move back and forth between the academic texts and our interviews to highlight the nodes around which the prejudice problematic revolves. And, I begin with some anecdotes. One set comes from G. W. Allport, while the other story was told by one of our interviewees.

In Rhodesia, a white truck driver passed a group of idle natives and muttered, 'They're lazy brutes.' A few hours later he saw natives heaving two-hundred pound sacks of grain onto a truck, singing in rhythm to their work. 'Savages,' he grumbled. 'What do you expect?'

In Boston a dignitary of the Roman Catholic Church was driving along a lonesome road on the outskirts of the city. Seeing a small Negro boy trudging along, the dignitary told his chauffeur to stop and give the boy a lift. Seated together in the back of the limousine, the cleric, to make conversation, asked, 'Little Boy, are you a Catholic?' Wide-eyed with alarm, the boy replied, 'No sir, it's bad enough being coloured without being one of those things.' (Allport, 1954, p. 3)

Mills: Yes, although there was um, this is diverging a bit, there was a guy at the shows today, er last week, helping with the my husband's firm's stall they had there, and he was a salesman with the firm, he was what I thought was a typical salesman, he was raving on about how there's no way he was going to be turned into a Maori against his will, he came from Britain you know, and he was only my age or younger, would have been about thirty (yeah). I couldn't believe it, I just looked at him in horror (yeah). You know, got all on his high horse with all these Polynesians that were going to make him go back to the grass skirts ha. Oh it was really weird.

Allport's carefully constructed anecdotes appear on the first page of his text and serve an exemplificatory purpose. He uses them to delineate the nature of the problem which will be the subject of his book. The story from Mills is part of an argument about how intergroup relations in New Zealand are changing for the worse.

Our purpose in introducing these anecdotes is also illustrative and to make a point. Both extracts work by turning a spotlight on the character and motives of particular individuals. Further, they identify weak points in that character – emotionality, lack of moderation and extremity in the salesman, inconsistency, stupidity and disingenuous naivety in the case of Allport's various narrative characters. This stress on the failings of individuals is probably the most crucial distinguishing feature of what I wish to identify as the prejudice problematic.

Prejudice accounts are psychological accounts. Allport and his colleagues do not neglect the importance of socio-cultural factors in racism and may even see the social domain as the principal cause of prejudice (e.g. Ehrlich, 1973). But, argues Allport, 'it is only within the nexus of personality that we find the effective operation of historical, cultural and economic factors' (1954, p. xviii). For this reason it is possible to put together a string of anecdotes from different parts of the globe – Boston, Rhodesia, India, London, Auckland and so on. The local manifestations of prejudice might vary but it can be analysed as a universal human failing. Explanations within the problematic thus tend to focus on this root cause – the deformation of human feelings – before turning outwards to look at how particular social conditions channel its expression.

Social psychologists and Pakeha New Zealanders agree that the difficulty concerns particular sorts of people who suffer from a 'problem'. Strangely, these people are usually always someone else, although there is also scope within this discourse for particular kinds of confessions and self-accusations. One of the typical tensions in prejudice discourse emerges when we try to specify this moral judgement further. Are the prejudiced a special, notably blame-worthy, group, or can we all be prejudiced from time to time? Lay discourse and socio-psychological theory swing backwards and forwards between these two options.

Individual bigotry and collective guilt

The psychodynamic strand in the socio-psychological analysis of prejudice emphasizes the distinctive character weaknesses of the prejudiced – their rigidity, emotional needs, reluctance to respond to new information and pattern of vindictive gratification. As Jones (1972) notes, for many theorists, 'race' prejudice becomes seen as a symptom of a basic adaptive inferiority, the sign of a person who is low down in the homo sapiens hierarchy (p. 66). In comparison, the social cognition strand of prejudice work suggests a much more inclusive picture. The prejudiced are not necessarily different from other individuals. We can all be guilty of prejudgement, this perspective argues, and we can't help it because life is short and our minds are limited. People are built this way for perfectly sensible reasons, the social cognition researcher might suggest, and so constantly judge in advance of the facts.

These two possibilities – the particular and the universal – provide, in lay discourse, for a range of rhetorical options: magnanimity and victimization, self-distancing and limited apology.

Stones: I think there's prejudice both ways (yes? uhum). Um (.) I think prejudice is something that uh everybody has. I don't think anybody can honestly sit back and say you don't have some prejudice. Uh in fact uh I I used to think I had very little prejudice, I think, I think colour prejudice, I'm colour blind and I suppose that helps hahaahaha uh 'cos I don't, colour doesn't mean as much to me (yeah, right). So if I see somebody that's dark I I don't even think of colour because I'm colour blind and I switch off colours, because of that, but I found that uh you know this the Canadian election was fought on and uh um you know I started to find that really I'm quite anti-French, without really realizing. And um I suppose I find at times I'm anti-American, having lived next door to them and seen, so you know we all have these prejudices. Irrespective of whether they're colour, or even, uh religion or creed or anything.

Wetherell: Right. What do you think about, what do you think most New Zealanders' attitudes are to Maoris? Positive or negative?

Bradman: Gee I don't know. I I um when you first said that I thought, yeah um it's hard to say I I I guess um a lot of it must be negative, yeah (mmhm) um uh like I know a guy who is quite quite bigoted, irrationally bigoted you know (mmhm) and um that sort of point of view to a lesser degree perhaps than this guy, to a greater or lesser degree perhaps yes overall, um I guess there is a lot of um a sort of stereotyping (mm) I mean they think of the Maori as being um thick and and lethargic (mmhm) and um no-hoper and poor and so forth, whereas this is not necessarily the case (case, mmhm).

Boardman: Yes (mm). We've got both, we've got both sort of mental prejudice and verbal prejudice. Um, and both fairly heavily represented (yeah). There is a colossal amount of prejudice some of it, I was almost going to say justified but the word prejudice excludes that (yes). Um, one can understand the basis in some instances but not in others (yes). Uh but one thing that always amuses me cos I happen to have an interest in people and their appearance and their mannerisms and their way of speech, is the number of people who are apparently anti-Maori who quite clearly have Maori blood! (yes) And they seem to consider, well I say quite clearly, no not quite clearly but you could be (mm) fairly sure that what they're doing in fact is reacting against part of their own character (mmhm). They're not at war with the rest of the community, they're at war with themselves (yes). Um, they haven't come to terms with both parts of their make-up (mmhm) and as a result they try to banish one part by um denigrating it. I think you will find that's very common amongst people of mixed blood, whether it be coloured to white or um two different European races, two different African races or whatever (yes). Anyone who has two cultural backgrounds, one part usually stronger than the other uh has difficulty balancing themselves (yes). And often it comes out in the form of a racial intolerance against what actually is part of themselves (yes).

Stones, a Canadian now living in New Zealand, argues that he personally has no racial prejudice because he is 'colour blind' but that prejudice of this kind is understandable because everybody has prejudices, and he gives the example of his own attitude to French Canadians. In the other extracts, the prejudiced are displayed as more separated from oneself – they are the irrationally bigoted or, in Boardman's case, some of the prejudiced are seen, albeit in rather an unusual manner, as suffering from a psychological disturbance generated by self-hate at their own part-Maori ancestry. But whether understood as particular or as universal, prejudice discourse locates the problem within the psychological make-up of the individual.

Irrationality and prejudgement

The 'cognitive' theme in the prejudice problematic, which stresses mis-judgement and problems of information processing rather than character structure and psychopathology, creates another form of tension. It high-lights the classic dilemma of positivism: facts versus values. The difficulty is this – what counts as a rational judgement? When is a description merely factual and when is it an interested account? If prejudice is 'thinking ill of others without sufficient warrant' (Allport, 1954, p. 6), then what is an adequate warrant? Here, of course, issues of authenticity and facticity arise.

Jones (1972) suggests three criteria for prejudice. Prejudice, as opposed to 'justified denigration', involves prior judgement. Secondly, prejudice is indicated when an individual continues to hold an opinion despite being confronted with contradictory information. Finally, a prejudiced individual will be someone who promulgates their view even when aware, before they judge, of those contradictory facts. However, Jones then becomes tangled in the fact/value dilemma when he notes that good judgement is also often a normative assessment.

Allport similarly stresses the importance of being able to reverse one's judgement in the face of inconsistent information. The failure to do so indicates some 'emotional resistance'. However, in the end he, too, is unable to resolve the fact/value dilemma, arguing that prejudice is also a moral evaluation placed by a culture on some of its own practices and is usually a probabilistic decision. Allport concludes that social psychology needs to draw a distinction between prejudice and realistic group conflict. Prejudice is where there is a low probability that the judgement is rational, whereas in realistic group conflicts there is a high probability that a negative reaction to another group is warranted. The distinction is vital for Allport, because he wants to maintain grounds for justifying some collective group actions, such as the Allied response to Hitler while castigating other responses. In other words, he wants to keep open the move of 'you are prejudiced, while I am simply responding to the real negative features of my opponent'.

It is easy to see how this fact/value dilemma of Enlightenment thought could lead social psychologists straight into all the absurdities of the 'kernel of truth' investigations in stereotyping research conducted from the 1930s onwards. The logic of the dilemma is such that it becomes sensible to try and discover whether white Americans' image of the 'Negro', for example, might be based on the 'real characteristics' of 'Negros'.

Again, this fact/value dilemma is not merely academic and I shall show in the next section how 'factual accounting' is a useful rhetorical device for mitigating the offence of prejudice. Many of those I interviewed implied that their hostility was not in fact prejudice but a realistic description of the actual characteristics of Maori people. And, one interviewee's response was uncannily reminiscent of Allport's insight that group conflict over scarce resources provides a more normatively acceptable justification of negative actions than appeals to prejudiced motives. Sedge, in the next extract, justifying the former apartheid regime in South Africa, argues that defence of one's group's interests is perfectly legitimate.

Sedge: Um and er if they want to, you know they say they're doing, they're getting sport just to to keep apartheid going (mmhmm). I don't think it is, they're keeping apartheid going because as they see it over there, it's the only way that they're going to keep the good way of life (yes). I mean, you know, if somebody came round to me and said, 'look we're going to move a whole pile of these Maoris off Bastion Point and they're going to take over this part of Remuera, just this corner here, going round this block of houses here', I'd say, 'no they're not' (yes). And, you know, no matter what happens they're not going to do it. I shall take such steps as are necessary to avoid it (yes). Now if somebody says, 'oh yes, but this is how it's going to be' (mm), I'd go flat out, I mean I don't care whether it's apartheid or whatever you call it. Build the barricades up there and you know and put machine guns on the top (mmhmm) and that is what I see that they're just preserving (mmhmm) um what they've got. Okay maybe it isn't the best but it's far from being the worst.

Because prejudice is usually conceived as an individual or personal reaction primarily concerning private moral standards and rationality, it can be separated from collective group reactions caused by competition for scarce resources, for instance. Prejudice can be distinguished from responses brought about by social processes wider than the individual such as economic recession. Prejudice remains a personal pathology, a failure of inner-directed empathy and intellect, rather than a social pathology, shaped by power relations and the conflicting vested interests of groups.

The manifest and the latent

So far, I have identified two sources of tension within the prejudice problematic – between the particular and the universal and between facts and values. The problematic also supplies a third tension – between appearances and reality or between the surface and the underneath. Unlike the first two tensions, which provide for contrasting forms of analysis, this tension is spotted within the object of study and can be located either within individuals or within societies.

Andrews: I think er the um it's like the racist it's like the class problem again. There are things like race problems, class problems all bubbling away under the surface and to a far greater degree than what than would be sort of officially acknowledged by a lot of people, but you only have to go to a Rotary club meeting or somewhere and hear the sort of pet prejudices that are trotted out week after week and everybody gets them out, gives them a little polish, 'hey mates isn't that nice?' and puts them back in their pocket (haha yes).

Reed: I'm trying to think of that with the racist thing so there's a tremendous amount um, you know, when you boil the kettle and the water gets very hot? (yes) But it's not until it's boiling that it breaks the surface (yes), the smoothness of the top of the water? (yes) And I think that's what's happening here.

The prevailing metaphor, therefore, is almost geological in character – of forces under the surface of society which from time to time break through into normal social intercourse, revealing the true state of affairs. Relations between the conscious and the unconscious of the prejudiced person may be seen as operating in similar ways with prejudice as the repressed or latent force and rationality and reasonableness as the superficial ego traits.

Tolerance and harmony

The ideal identity which contrasts with prejudice is very clearly expressed both in social psychology and in the discourse of Pakeha New Zealanders. 'Racial harmony' comes from the considerate and unbiased treatment of all fellow human beings. All should be treated without prejudgement – treated equally, on the basis of individual merits, regardless of race. If the prejudiced person is the fallen angel, speaking with bias and lack of sympathy and acting out an insensitive and perverse irrationality, the tolerant individual:

> . . . is on friendly terms with all sorts of people . . . He makes no distinction of race, colour, or creed. He not only endures but, in general, approves his fellow men . . . Tolerant children . . . come from homes with a permissive atmosphere. They feel welcomed, accepted and loved, no matter what they do . . . The greater mental flexibility of the tolerant person (even in childhood) is shown by his rejection of two-valued logic. He seldom agrees that 'there are only two kinds of people: the weak and the strong'; or that 'there is only one right way to do anything'. He does not bifurcate his environment into the wholly proper and the wholly improper. For him there are shades of gray. (Allport, 1954, pp. 425–6)

The prejudice problematic feeds into and reinforces a utopian vision of society as well as of the individual personality. The tolerant society is based around rationality, justice and caring feelings for others. I have noted elsewhere the various manifestations of equivalent ideals in the discourse of Pakeha New Zealanders – in talk of 'one nation', for example; in the trope of 'two cultures, one people'; in the formulation of tolerant understanding and respect for differences found in the discourse of culture; in the functionalist emphasis on a coherent and integrated society working as a productive machine, with all parts in harmony; and in the discourse which imagines history progressing towards a more just and better world.

This vision is both part of the rhetoric of public figures and the private dream of ordinary New Zealanders. In the public domain it has been most evident in the views expressed by church authorities over the years. For there is a common focus in both Christianity and in the prejudice problematic on self-examination, individual weakness and moral reform.

> . . . suspicion, fear and hostility have tended to characterize relationships between different human groupings. Human sinfulness is a divisive power encouraging notions of prejudice, disrespect and superiority.
>
> However, Christians believe that the grace of God can overcome human divisions and sinful attitudes, and make unity and harmony possible. This is illustrated at Pentecost by the 'reversal of Babel'. People of different races were able to understand each other.

Racial prejudice is an individual problem that makes it impossible for a person of one race to meet a person of another with openness and love.

The Christian church ... overcomes the alienation between races. As a community of faith its members are meant to enjoy a unity that transcends racial differences. However, because it is a community of fallible and sinful people, the Church can distort the Gospel and fail to be the sign of reconciliation God intends it to be. (Extracts from Te Kaupapa Tikanga Rua: bicultural development: report of the Anglican Church on the Treaty of Waitangi, 1984, p. 36)

As Charlie Husband has argued, taking a critical perspective on this ideal, one of the problems with tolerance is that it represents 'a largesse of the powerful' (1986). It is a form of talk which hazily suggests unity of interests, charitable beneficence and a positive atmosphere without any detailed examination of ends and means or questioning of the exact nature of the compromises which might be required between opposed vested interests.

This failure to engage with social structural change is encouraged by the focus within the prejudice problematic on changing people's attitudes rather than modes of social organization. A great deal of emphasis is placed on the importance of contact between individuals, 'black and white together, united, but not in struggle'. This is often articulated as a feeling that if only we could get at children when they are young, before they are 'contaminated' by prejudice, then the world would be a better place. The innocent and naive reactions of children, in fact, serve within the prejudice problematic as a model for us all.

Ben Couch (Former Minister of Maori Affairs): Well at one stage he er he I was often wondering why do we need a Race Relations Conciliator? And er but we are er made up of a hotch potch, of course, er a mixture of many races in this country and er someone thought of the idea of the Race Relations and mainly because of in the last twenty years, as I've said, everything's become words and trying to make people er aware who you are (yes). Reminds me of a story of young Jimmy going to school and er coming home and telling his Mummy, 'oh I made a friend today', and er they said, 'oh well what's his name?', he said 'oh it's Johnny', Jimmy and Johnny, and the Mother said to him, 'oh is he a Maori or is he a Pakeha?' (yes) The kid didn't know (hahaha). You see what I mean? (yes) He said 'eh?'

Similarly the benefits of proper information and education are frequently stressed. In social psychology this optimistic face of the prejudice problematic has led to a great deal of research on the benefits of intergroup contact. The theoretical paucity of the contact tradition in social psychology and its reliance on individualistic analyses of racism has been well documented (Hewstone and Brown, 1986; Reicher, 1986).

As in other aspects of the prejudice problematic, there is a tension and possible contradiction in these visions of various remedies for racism. Optimism about the reform of deviant individuals can be contrasted with conservative pessimism. Prejudice can be seen as a conscious choice for a harsh view on another 'race' and thus as morally accountable and alterable. But, if prejudice is framed as a natural and unavoidable human reaction, an unconscious and even instinctive aversion to differences which reflects an inbuilt preference for one's own kind, then the only possible response is scepticism about reforming fallible human nature.

The moral identity of tolerance, as we have seen, tends to be portrayed as the proper state while prejudice becomes the deviant or fallen state: blameworthy and accountable. A tolerant identity does not usually have to be explained. Its moral value provides sufficient accountability and a rationale for the motivation. The whole thrust of the prejudice problematic, therefore, encourages a discourse characterized by circumambulation and avoidance. Everybody wants to be tolerant and nobody wants to be prejudiced.

Across our interviews argumentative and rhetorical work was oriented towards dodging the identity and imputation of prejudice. If possible, prejudice was recharacterized as something less noxious and this description was most definitely not accepted without negotiation and justification. I shall examine some of the patterns of these very common discursive moves in the next section and I will continue my attempt to describe how the prejudice problematic actually turns back on itself, empowering Pakeha New Zealanders, becoming part of the arguments for the status quo.

But it is worth noting, first, that the tensions within the prejudice problematic and the ambivalence it produces entirely weaken this discourse as a crusading force for anti-racism. Blaming individuals has been a weapon with mixed effects. It is one of the ironies of the social psychology of racism that perhaps the most earnest and sustained attempt in the history of the discipline to mount a critique of racism should have this paradoxical edge.

Dodging the identity of prejudice: how to deal with accusations

Talk of prejudice and tolerance is always talk to some purpose. I turn now to look at how Pakeha New Zealanders have used the problematic of prejudice strategically in their everyday accounts, as the dominant majority group acting in relation to the minority group.

The pattern of careful negotiation and identity construction around the topic of prejudice has been documented many times (Billig, 1985; Cochrane and Billig, 1984; Potter and Wetherell, 1987, 1988; Van Dijk,

1984, 1987). Van Dijk describes in detail the pragmatic and semantic moves which structure this discourse, and how lay people simultaneously speak 'prejudice' while attempting to avoid being described as prejudiced. This phenomenon has been described as an example of the rhetorical strategy of prolepsis (Billig *et al.*, 1988). It is an 'on the one hand, on the other hand' discursive move that acknowledges but deflects potential criticism. The pattern of credentialling or disclaiming involved is also evident in the formulations that begin 'I'm not prejudiced but...' (Hewitt and Stokes, 1975; Potter and Wetherell, 1987, ch. 2; van Dijk, 1991).

During the course of the interview, most of our sample was asked the following question or some variant of it: do you think Pakeha New Zealanders are prejudiced? Is there much discrimination against Maori people? Our introduction of the topic and typical question format presented an accounting problem for our respondents. Given the negative identity attributed to prejudice, it sets up a certain kind of accusation, or was interpreted in this way. I could thus treat responses to this question as a set which oriented to a commonly occurring discursive situation: dealing with an unwelcome evaluation.

What are the standard discursive moves for coping with a negative evaluation? Crudely, one can (a) admit the offence but offer mitigations or excuses, or (b) deny the offence and claim that one is wrongly accused, or (c) accept the blaming in entirety and perhaps intensify or expand on it by giving other examples (ask for other offences to be taken into account, if you like). One could also (d) undermine the accusation itself by renegotiating the nature of the offence, recategorizing it as something less negative and more excusable, or (e) redirect the accusation to another group of people, carefully separating or distancing oneself from the accusation.

In our sample, very few took up option (c). A small number did argue that Pakeha New Zealanders were prejudiced but the form of their argument followed the academic pattern: prejudice was identified as a virulent character fault in other people, not in oneself. The majority of those I interviewed thus tried to rebut or renegotiate the accusation. They usually combined several of the possible moves described above, frequently in a dense form, as can be seen below:

Wetherell: Um, yes, we were talking about Maori culture and so on. What er (.) do you think there's any racial prejudice in New Zealand, that people aren't (.) are prejudiced against Maoris (.) or not really?

Bickerstaff: I don't really think so, I think that we have grown up with the knowledge that the Maoris are our neighbours and our friends and er I feel that this (.) we've never been at a point where we have had to accept them so to speak, they've been part of us, yes, and ride in the buses, in the cinemas, er, you don't think of them as Maoris, it's just until there's some nasty (.) aggressive types that you feel you must avoid (yes) that the question even arises. Er I feel er in the last few years it's been blown out of proportion.

Wetherell: Do you think there's much sort of racial discrimination in New Zealand, say by the European majority against particular Maoris, or for employment, or you know?

Ackland: Um, I don't think it's so much a bias against them, it may be more a behaviour bar in a way (mm), and unfortunately some Maoris tend to give their whole people a bad name. But I don't really think there's uh, a bias, the same with the renting you know the properties and that (yes), if you've had a tenant, if you've been a Maori tenanter and mistreated or neglected a place, you'd think twice before letting it to another one (yes). I say I'm totally neutral, a lot of Europeans live like that (yes), they have poor standards.

Ackland's discourse combines several of the strategies identified above (b, d, a, e). He disagrees with the suggestion that Pakeha New Zealanders might show racial discrimination (e.g. 'I don't really think there's a bias'), but also recategorizes any possible offence as a 'behaviour bar' distinguished from what he describes in another part of the interview as a 'colour bar'. Thus the offence becomes not racial prejudice per se but a reaction to the behaviour of the minority group, he then mitigates this 'weaker' offence by explaining why this bias is a justifiable reaction to unacceptable actions, and finally Ackland distances himself from the accusation of bias by noting that he himself is totally neutral.

Similarly Bickerstaff denies the imputation of prejudice, but also provides a truncated mitigation by the categorization 'nasty, aggressive types' which suggests that any prejudice against such people would be a 'reasonable' response, and ends by undermining or trivializing the possible offence, claiming the issue is 'blown out of proportion'. This extract also could be read as implying that Pakeha New Zealanders might be magnanimous in not thinking of Maoris as 'Maoris' and thus overlooking their status as members of what she seems to assume are an inevitably inferior group. Alternatively, she could be read as suggesting that she and others do not think in 'racial' terms, but think instead along 'people are just people, not races' lines.

Both Bickerstaff and Ackland can also be read as orienting to the issues discussed by Jones (1972), and similar specifications of what counts as prejudgement, and what counts as justified comment. Both Ackland and Bickerstaff break up the category 'Maori', are careful to particularize ('some Maoris', some nasty aggressive types), avoiding the impression of sweeping generalization, and both give a factual version, leaving safeguards against critique. There is considerable scope for back-tracking introduced into these accounts.

In general, our sample seemed to regard it as effective rhetoric to weave different strategies together, denying an offence, while also accounting for or explaining a version of that offence and, perhaps too, separating oneself from those being accused. The point I wish to make here is that these conversational gambits do not occur in a vacuum. There is a complex interaction between the nature of the interpretative resources within the prejudice problematic, their ideological thrust and the practical conversational moves of those I interviewed.

Some forms of conversation analysis seem to lack a vital dimension to the extent they ignore aspects of this interaction, especially cases where conversational moves remain the focus rather than the broader ideological dimensions of argumentative resources. Similarly, attention to the interpretative resource alone misses the flexible application of that resource in practice. When we look at practice it becomes clear how prejudice discourse begins to double back on itself so that what was once an accusation or critique of racism becomes mobilized as an important part of the rhetorical work which maintains a racist status quo. We can see in these extracts how the ideological potential evident in individualistic, positivistic and utopian framings of the 'problem' becomes realized in practice as the members of a society struggle to justify the conduct of the group with which they have become aligned.

We can see how skilful and inventive ripostes to prejudice accusations could become a familiar part of the discursive habits of Pakeha New Zealanders. The social psychologist and the lay person become like two sides of the same coin. The social psychologist accuses and the Pakeha New Zealander defends, but both draw on the same resources to mount their arguments. The forms of both accusation and defence are structured by the tensions within the prejudice problematic.

So, what are the ideological advantages of prejudice discourse in its lay formulation? How does prejudice talk help in the task of legitimation? Some of these advantages have been discussed already – talk of prejudice pathologizes the issue and postpones investigation of concrete grievances, substituting high-minded waffle about the joys of living in harmony. But the principal benefit lies in the positive/negative contrast in the prejudice problematic which allows for 'splitting'. A bestial other can be constructed who is different from self. The other is presented as driven by 'id-type' forces of irrational emotion and illogical dislike. While the self, in contrast, becomes all ego – a rational, thoughtful and reflective subject who speaks with the authority of facts. Sometimes the split can be placed within oneself ('we are all prejudiced'), but more commonly the splitting is externalized, creating a *dramatis personae* of malevolent and benevolent actors.

In other words, Pakeha New Zealanders become empowered by this difference. They acquire a voice and subject position of authority partly through projecting the problem elsewhere but also because the association between prejudice and values allows those who rebut the accusation to more easily construct their own descriptions as merely factual. Value, interested motivation, and the grinding of axes lie elsewhere with the prejudiced other, removed from oneself. The prejudice problematic effectively pushes the debate from values to the 'kernel of truth'.

The prejudice problematic within social psychology depends on being able to categorize individuals as prejudiced or tolerant types. But, in practice, people are adept at upsetting the dichotomy and muddying the categorizations and, when all of us become skilled at exploiting the rhetorical possibilities of the prejudice problematic, who is to say just which of us are the tolerant sheep and which the prejudiced goats?

Reforming the prejudiced

In the last part of this chapter I wish to examine some of the substantial suggestions for anti-racist practice which have emerged from the prejudice problematic, to consider, that is, some concrete suggestions for the reform of the prejudiced. I will focus on one instantiation – Judy Katz's (1978) *Handbook for Anti-racism Training* – as an exemplar of a broader movement. Katz's work is particularly apposite as it has been applied extensively within New Zealand (Spoonley, 1988), as well as elsewhere. This critical examination also gives me an opportunity to lay out an alternative framework for anti-racism.

Katz combines the social psychology of prejudice with humanistic psychology, a common move in some forms of anti-racist training. In effect, she argues that racism is a health hazard for white and black alike. Blacks may suffer more but whites are also 'ill' with racism. It can be seen, from this perspective, as a form of white schizophrenia. The remedy is seen as lying in the administration of a good dose of painful self-probing and hard work on oneself, systematically identifying and eradicating stereotypes, guilt and delusions of white superiority.

Katz outlines a series of exercises for group workshops which will allow whites to confront the reality of their racism, deal with their feelings and come to terms with their own ethnicity. The workshops seek to encourage the psychological and intellectual development of the people who take part and, since these participants are also members of institutions, since they talk to friends and neighbours and are capable of translating their attitudes into behaviours, Katz hopes that society may change also.

The short autobiography with which she prefaces her book indicates the flavour of this approach.

The issue of racism is one of very deep concern to me. Becoming aware of racism and owning my whiteness has been a long process. It is a process that I have often fought and rejected inside myself. It is a process that has been marked by intro-spection, confrontation, anger, frustration, confusion, and guilt on the one hand and the joy of discovering another level in me and finding a new sense of personal freedom on the other. (Katz, 1978, p. v)

Katz's assumptions and her personal conviction demonstrate some of the specific strengths and weaknesses of the prejudice problematic when it becomes applied to anti-racist practice.

One strength of this form of anti-racist practice lies in the moral fervour and passion the prejudice problematic allows. The enemy is clear-cut and they are obviously evil – it may be other people or oneself – but the locus is plain and action is relatively straightforward. An armoury of techniques for self-improvement also becomes available, so the focus is immediately practical. There is also a clear and sensible logic to the principle of work-ing with individuals in order to change societies. Individuals are, indeed, members of institutions and, as Katz says, highly motivated and anti-racist individuals take an active part in introducing equal opportunities pro-grammes, examining school curricula, tracking down instances of harass-ment and in reforming from within.

But are these strengths undermined by the weaknesses of the prejudice problematic? And what are those weaknesses in this context? In common with many other social psychologists, Katz defines racism narrowly. Racism is seen as a delusion of white superiority. It is a set of mental habits and emotions circulating within individuals. Racism is a creation of white people, not 'white societies'.

Her approach assumes a relatively simple model of social process and social structure. Society can be divided into two communities – a white ethnic group and a black ethnic group – each with a distinctive cultural and 'racial' essence. Whites belong together because they share the same history, the same perspectives and the same skin colour. It is assumed that this shared cultural, ethnic and phenotypical heritage gives white people common interests and so it is meaningful to talk of whites en masse. Racism is thus conceptualized as a form of group antipathy: the mutual distrust of two contrasting communities. In this way, the prejudice prob-lematic displays a strong tendency to 'naturalize' racism; it becomes a ubiquitous phenomenon deriving inexorably from obvious differences.

My analysis of racism is rather different. The problem is not that one ethnic community has irrational delusions in relation to another ethnic community. The problem lies in the way a society, like New Zealand, has been systematically structured and organized around one particular nexus and concentration of power (cf. also Spoonley, 1988). Indeed, the problem consists in the way rationality (economic, individual, group and 'good sense') has been constructed in New Zealand society. Racism is a manifestation of the pattern of uneven power relations in New Zealand.

Discourse analysis and anti-racism

During most of New Zealand's short colonial history the people involved in this history have been described as 'races' and as separate 'cultures'. But I have tried to analyse this intergroup description as one method in the social construction of difference, rather than as a reflection of natural category differences. The 'racialization' of groups has been seen as just one 'node' within the ideological pattern which sustains and maintains the pattern of power relations.

In contrast to Katz, therefore, I wish to examine how the construction and categorization of groups and communities, including the assumption of shared culture, might be part of the problem. Moreover, I see racism as rooted in the social and structural rather than in the personal and psychological. Of course, the personal and psychological reflect the shape of the social and structural, and I have tried, through discourse theory, to indicate how that relation works in practice, but human psychological peculiarities do not dictate the ideological atmosphere and its shifting pattern.

As I have tried to demonstrate through several different discourse analyses now, the ideological justification of exploitative social relations is not necessarily based on emotions of distaste, on anti-black affect, on ideas of hierarchies of civilization or on white people's concepts of innate superiority and inferiority. This form of racist discourse has proved an extraordinarily effective legitimating tool in the past, and I have documented its uses, but its days may well be numbered. Justification also involves other forms of argument and, perhaps to an increasing degree, types of discourse and practical politics which seem much less objectionable and much more familiar, such as the rhetoric of equal opportunities itself. Without an analysis of power and shifting ideological forms it is very difficult to tackle this opening of a second front.

It is comforting and sometimes crucial to be able to point to moral weaknesses in other members of society. But we need to ask whether racism (which I have tried to study as a collective discursive practice) is solely the province of the inadequate and poorly developed individual. I found much of the discourse of those I interviewed odious and the feeling would probably have been mutual. That is, no doubt they would have found my views equally offensive, if I had explicated them at length. Nonetheless, in common human terms, many of those I interviewed could be described as decent, likeable, well-balanced and well-meaning people. They might not want to return the compliment and find me similarly sane and sound, but the point is that the psychologizing of racism seems to misplace the problem.

Katz's solution sidesteps the issue that many of the 'self-actualized' (in the terminology of humanistic psychology) also happen to be racist. Is it possible that if Pakeha New Zealanders became much less 'neurotic' about Maori issues and generally more fulfilled as human beings, power relations would change overnight? Perhaps there would be some important effects within particular institutions and within some arenas. But in the end I am not convinced that individual psychological change generates economic and social change.

A very similar debate occurs within feminism. Men are clearly guilty, who can deny that? But is it their weakness as human beings, their non-endearing traits and unpleasant little habits that cause the oppression of women? Some would argue that these failings are precisely the problem, and a bit of painful self-probing is exactly what is called for, and certainly these traits are constituted through patriarchy. But can men be 'reconstructed' so easily without large-scale changes in the social relations of gender? While self-critique, confession and soul searching are important and make life better for individual women and men, do these therapeutic practices overthrow patriarchy? Will the growth of a cadre of 'new men' or cleansed Pakeha New Zealanders be sufficient in itself to change the lot of substantial groups of women and men or substantial groups of Maori and Pakeha? From a different perspective, it could be argued that, as with the social mobility afforded the working class within the education system, a few can move 'upwards', but mobility is not possible for the working class as a whole without a radical change in social organization.

The discourse analysis presented in this chapter clearly demonstrates this particular weakness in the prejudice approach to anti-racism. How would this approach go about working with the people I interviewed? These people would first need to be convinced that, despite their protestations, they were actually prejudiced or racist. Then, once they had begun to attend workshops, the process of self-confrontation and dealing with feelings could begin. I take the point that workshops may sometimes radically change the discourse of the selected individuals attending. Workshops might well provide participants with a new vocabulary of motives, a new set of identity narratives and so on, and that can be a powerful benefit.

But, it is clear that this route involves working within the logic and the positive/negative dialectic of prejudice talk I identified in the previous section. It doesn't question the prejudice problematic and its particular framing of the problem; it reinforces its hold. In particular, it firmly instantiates the distinction between the prejudiced and the enlightened, through the blaming of individuals, and gives prejudice discourse immense credibility as a model of racism. There is a vicious circle at work here. Katz and her colleagues wish us all to acknowledge our prejudice and I agree this is necessary. But the form of acknowledging precisely sustains the kinds of discursive moves, disclaimers, mitigations and factual accounting we have witnessed.

I am not trying to argue, as an alternative to the anti-racist practice described above, that people should not be held accountable for their discourse. And, I also agree with Katz that individuals can make a difference within institutions. My work more generally has developed a sustained critique of the discourse of those I interviewed. I have assumed that Pakeha New Zealanders are accountable for their framing of their situation and, equally, that my account should similarly be open to attack and ridicule. The conscious adoption of the problematic of ideology puts me within the same orbit as those I interviewed; obviously I, also, have been 'political' and taken up a stance.

But this emphasis on accountability differs from the claim that white individuals create racism and it leads to different strategies for anti-racist practice. I have argued that Pakeha New Zealanders articulate in their discourse a collectively shared set of resources for legitimating their social position. They are responsible for the articulation but not in the sense that racism always reflects character weakness or illogical thought. A few people I interviewed could draw on counter-ideological discourse, of the kind I adopt in this book, for instance, and were cross-cut by socialist and feminist interpellations. People were not consistent, either, across the field of debate. Anti-racist arguments became meshed together with support for racist policies. An argument would be mobilized in one direction only to veer back on itself.

From my perspective, then, an important part of anti-racist practice is identifying the forms legitimation takes, and charting also the fragmented and dilemmatic nature of everyday discourse, because it is at those points of fracture and contradiction that there is scope for change and the redirection of argument.

But I am not suggesting, however, that discourse is everything and should be the sole site for action. The conclusions from my analyses could be read as depressing for discourse analysts or, rather, for the thesis of the partial autonomy of ideological discourse and its independent effectivity. The pattern could be interpreted as showing how the fluidity of racist discourse provides resilience. The forms of legitimation are varied, florid and forever changing in remarkable ways, yet material disadvantage continues in much the same old direction. Ideological discourse sometimes seems simultaneously crucial and trivial. It is crucial to maintaining certain practices and yet trivial as an agent of social change.

But this reading is in danger of clumsily reinstating an infrastructure and superstructure distinction. We begin to see, once again, real life chugging along 'underneath' discourse which dances along, 'on top', changing its shape and forever donning new guises in tune to the tug of the real, but powerless to act back on the repressed base. If nothing else, Foucault's work suggests that the relation between discourse, social structures, practices and processes is more complex than that. The semiotic intrudes into more places than the structuralist can imagine, shaping the habits of institutions, disciplining bodies through social practices, redefining simple distinctions between talk and action and so on. Interventions in the discursive, therefore, as the history of anti-racism itself demonstrates, are never interventions in the ethereal.

One final weakness with the anti-racism proposed within the prejudice problematic is its tendency towards global ambitions. The vision, as I noted earlier, is utopian. It is for harmony on a grand scale. Paul Gilroy (1987) has argued that, in contrast, the appropriate anti-racist strategy is both more extensive and more modest.

> More modest because these struggles define themselves by their relationship to the everyday experience of their protagonists and the need to address and ameliorate concrete grievances at this level; more extensive because an elaborate and sophisticated critique of social structure and relations of contemporary capitalism has been a consistent if not a continuous feature of the 'racial' politics and culture from which these struggles have sprung. These two tendencies shape each other and their reciprocity dissolves the old distinction between reformist and revolutionary modes of political action. (Gilroy, 1987, p. 116)

These proposals are based on Gilroy's experience of black politics within the UK. It is easy for me to develop ideas about the aims of anti-racist practice in New Zealand from the UK, a safe distance of 12,000 miles. But the strategy of critique and local action around specific issues, which Gilroy recommends, seems preferable to Katz's rather solemn self-examination. Indeed, this is a strategy that some Maori and Pakeha groups have successfully practised for many years, particularly around opposition to South African rugby tours. Anti-racism is not just a white task or, indeed, a matter for Maoris, although our forms of practice may sometimes diverge. As Witi Ihimaera puts it: 'A *Maori* affair? Like heck it is. We're both in this *waka* together' (1977, p. 10). And debate must continue about the best way to steer the canoe.

Note

1. This is a slightly modified version of Chapter 8 of Wetherell and Potter's *Mapping the Language of Racism* (1992).

References

Adorno, T. W., Frenkel-Brunswik, E., Levinson, D. J. and Sanford, R. N. (1950). *The Authoritarian Personality*. New York: Harper and Row.

Allport, G. W. (1954). *The Nature of Prejudice*. Reading, MA: Addison-Wesley.

Billig, M. (1985). Prejudice, categorisation and particularisation: from a perceptual to a rhetorical approach. *European Journal of Social Psychology*, **15**, 79–103.

Billig, M., Condor, S., Edwards, D., Gane, M., Middleton, D. and Radley, A. (1988). *Ideological Dilemmas: a Social Psychology of Everyday Thinking*. London: Sage.

Cochrane, R. and Billig, M. (1984). 'I'm not National Front but . . .'. *New Society*, **68**, 255–8.

Ehrlich, H. J. (1973). *The Social Psychology of Prejudice*. New York: John Wiley and Sons.

Gadamer, H. (1979). *Truth and Method*. London: Sheed and Ward.

Gilroy, P. (1987). *There Ain't no Black in the Union Jack*. London: Hutchinson.

Hewitt, J. P. and Stokes, R. (1975). Disclaimers. *American Sociological Review*, **92**, 110–57.

Hewstone, M. and Brown, R. (1986). Contact is not enough: an intergroup perspective on the 'contact hypothesis'. In M. Hewstone and R. Brown (eds.), *Contact and Conflict in Intergroup Encounters*. Oxford, UK: Blackwell.

Husband, C. (1986). The concepts of attitude and prejudice in the mystification of 'race' and 'racism'. Paper presented at the British Psychology Society, Social Psychology Section Annual Conference, University of Sussex.

Ihimaera, W. (1977). The Maori affairs syndrome. *The New Zealand Listener*, **27**, August, 10–11.

Jones, J. M. (1972). *Prejudice and Racism*. Reading, MA: Addison-Wesley.

Katz, J. (1978). *White Awareness: Handbook for Anti-racism Training*. Norman, OK: University of Oklahoma Press.

Potter, J. and Wetherell, M. (1987). *Discourse and Social Psychology*. London: Sage.
(1988). Accomplishing attitudes: fact and evaluation in racist discourse. *Text*, **8**, 51–68.

Reicher, S. (1986). Contact, action and racialization: some British evidence. In M. Hewstone and R. Brown (eds.), *Contact and Conflict in Intergroup Encounters*. Oxford, UK: Blackwell.

Spoonley, P. (1988). *Racism and Ethnicity*. Auckland, New Zealand: Oxford University Press.

Van Dijk, T. A. (1984). *Prejudice and Discourse*. Amsterdam, the Netherlands: Benjamins.
(1987). *Communicating Racism*. Newbury Park, CA: Sage.
(1991). *Racism and the Press*. London: Routledge.

Wetherell, M. and Potter, J. (1992). *Mapping the Language of Racism: Discourse and the Legitimation of Exploitation*. London: Harvester Wheatsheaf.

9   Implicit prejudice in mind and interaction

Kevin Durrheim

In recent years there has been a sea-change in social psychology: away from theories of conscious, deliberate or explicit processing to theories and research of unconscious, automatic or implicit processing. Social information processing of all sorts has been discovered to proceed more or less automatically (Bargh, 1996). Dual process models of information processing propose that 'effortful conscious reasoning takes place only under relatively rare circumstances, when people possess both cognitive capacity and strong motivation' (Smith, 1996, p. 905).

From early on (Gaertner and McLaughlin, 1983), these theories of implicit cognition have been applied to understanding negative stereotypes and prejudice that people have for outgroups and their members. The research shows that stereotyping typically proceeds automatically as attention is drawn to race, gender and other characteristics of people unconsciously and unintentionally; and that this in turn shapes social judgements and evaluations of all sorts, also in automatic and unconscious ways (Banaji and Hardin, 1996; Dovidio *et al.*, 1986; Fazio and Dunton, 1997; Greenwald and Banaji, 1995; Wittenbrink *et al.*, 1997).

For example, in her now classic study, Devine (1989) used nonconscious priming to elicit automatic stereotype activation. To prime race, she first had subjects participate in a vigilance task in which they were asked to identify the location of words that flashed on a screen so quickly that the content of the words was not recognizable. The content of the words served as unconscious primes. In two experimental conditions, either 20 per cent or 80 per cent of the words presented were related to the racial stereotype (blacks, niggers, poor, lazy, athletic, busing, Harlem) while the remainder were neutral (water, then, would, etc.). After this, in an ostensibly unrelated impression formation task, subjects read a paragraph describing a race-unspecified target person's ambiguously hostile behaviours. Subjects then rated the target on several trait scales. Even though the primes were inaccessible and the whole experimental scenario had no explicit references to race, the primed unconscious stereotypes prompted both high and low prejudiced subjects to interpret the behaviour of the target in race-based terms. Devine (1989) concludes that 'even for subjects who honestly report having no negative prejudices against Blacks, activation of stereotypes can have automatic effects that if not consciously monitored produce effects that resemble prejudiced responses' (p. 13).

Banaji *et al.* (1993) showed that such stereotypical associations and evaluations can be set in motion by unconscious stereotypical information in implicit memory. Common sense associations are part of cultural knowledge, and can have a subtle and unconscious effect on our perceptions, whether we personally subscribe to the stereotype or not. To prime the implicit stereotype of male aggressiveness and female dependence, Banaji *et al.* (1993) asked their subjects to unscramble sentences that indicated either aggression (e.g. never backs down) or dependence (e.g. won't go alone) or were neutral. Then, in a second unrelated study, they asked the subjects to evaluate the behaviour of ambiguously aggressive or dependent men and women. The earlier unconscious prime differentially influenced their evaluations of men and women, encouraging subjects to see the behaviour in gender stereotypical terms. For example, both male and female subjects rated females as more dependent after the dependent but not the neutral prime. Stereotypical information influenced judgements in a task in which the stereotypes were not conscious to the subjects, even among subjects who were themselves prejudiced by the stereotype.

This work on implicit cognition has been argued to have two different sets of implications for research on prejudice and stereotyping. On the one hand, Fazio and his colleagues have argued that implicit measures are a 'bona fide pipeline' (Fazio and Dunton, 1997; Fazio *et al.*, 1995). In this view, implicit prejudice measures are genuine measures of attitudes because they are not susceptible to the self-presentational demands that influence people's explicit reports of their stereotypes and attitudes about outgroups. Since these measures tap into stereotypical associations that are automatic, uncontrolled and unconscious, they must reflect the true underlying attitudes. This conclusion is further bolstered by findings that implicit and explicit measures do not always correlate, and that implicit measures show predictable black–white differences in prejudice and that they correlate significantly with other unobtrusive measures, such as a black experimenter's rating of the quality of interaction with the subject. Mitchell *et al.* (2003) comment that this approach has been 'offered up as the chameleon's mirror for social cognition' (p. 468) because to use implicit measurement techniques is to see past obscuring influences of conscious impression management to true underlying attitudes.

Alongside this view that automatic stereotyping and prejudice are more genuine than their explicit counterparts is the dual process model advocated by Dovidio, Gaertner and their colleagues (Dovidio, 2001; Dovidio and Gaertner, 2004; Dovidio *et al.*, 1997). In this model, both implicit and explicit attitudes are treated as genuine but dissociated. They have different origins and modes of expression. Implicit attitudes and stereotyping have their roots in early experiences in the family, and operate in the unconscious mode, being automatically activated (cf. Wilson *et al.*, 2000). Later, as an adult, the person adopts egalitarian views which are expressed in the conscious mode, as exemplified by self report measures. These later, explicit, attitudes replace but do not eradicate the earlier implicit racism, and the two operate alongside each other, each having different sets of effects. In their replication and extension of the classic study by Word *et al.* (1974), Dovidio *et al.* (1997, 2002) showed that implicit attitudes primarily predicted more spontaneous race-related behaviours such as non-verbal features of interracial interaction (blinking, eye contact) which were not open to conscious control. In contrast, self-reported racial prejudice primarily predicted more deliberative responses, such as verbal expressions of friendliness in interracial interaction, which were consciously controlled and shaped by normative pressures.

Theories of implicit prejudice and stereotyping provide useful explanations for the kinds of attitudinal variation that have come to characterize contemporary prejudice. First, it can account for the patterns of individual cross-situational variation that contemporary observers have noted (Durrheim and Dixon, 2004). This variation is a defining feature of aversive racism (Dovidio and Gaertner, 2004), which characterizes the attitudes of whites who regard themselves as nonprejudiced and who consciously and sincerely endorse egalitarian values. However, they continue to harbour unconscious negativity towards blacks, and this is manifest in subtle and rationalizable acts of discrimination, such as hiring decisions where the candidates are ambiguously qualified for the job, and where the decision can be attributed to nonracial factors (see Dovidio and Gaertner, 2000). Aversive racism theory can also explain why black and white interlocutors often disagree about the existence of white racism. Whites typically judge themselves to be nonracist on the basis of the manifest content of their interaction (what they say), whereas their black interlocutors judge them to be racist on the basis of the subtle cues they give by way of uncontrollable and unconscious nonverbal behaviour (how they say it) (Dovidio *et al.*, 1997).

Overall, the study of implicit cognition has made an important contribution to our understanding of prejudice and stereotyping. It has shown how deeply meaningful race, gender and other social category information is to people, and how little prompting it takes for people to think in stereotypical ways. It can also account for the persistence of racial bias in the contemporary context where levels of prejudice among whites have rapidly declined since the mid-twentieth century. Prejudice has 'gone underground' as it is avoided in public expressions or conscious deliberations, but is prevalent in the unconscious mind, ever ready to be activated and used in subtle ways in responding to members of stereotyped groups (Monteith *et al.*, 2001).

Critique of implicit prejudice

The theory and measurement of implicit prejudice mark a major shift in the way social psychologists think about prejudice (Banaji *et al.*, 2004). The Allportian view, which dominated an earlier epoch, assumed that prejudice was irrational, motivated by negative affect and operated largely in conscious mode. In contrast, Greenwald and Banaji (1995, p. 8) define implicit attitudes as 'Introspectively unidentified (or inaccurately identified) traces of past experience that mediate favourable or unfavourable feeling, thought, or action toward social objects' (p. 268). These residues are theorized to be associations between concepts in memory, where one concept has the potential to activate another when the associations are strong. These associations are 'automatically activated in the presence of a triggering stimulus' (Macrae and Bodenhousen, 2001, p. 242) and have an effect in mediating reactions outside the consciousness or will of the observer. Thus, in what has been seen as a radical break with the Allportian tradition, implicit attitudes do not require that the individual endorses the prejudiced beliefs. The theory of implicit prejudice views prejudiced attitudes as operating unconsciously or automatically, outside the ambit of individual awareness, will or intention, and they are consequently not necessarily motivated by (consciously experienced) negative affect or hostility.

Implicit measurement techniques have the ability to detect these unconscious associations by using reaction time measures to determine the strength with which the priming of one category activates a second category. In the implicit association test (IAT), for example, anti-black prejudice is indicated when the reaction times on 'incompatible' trials (e.g. the pairing of stereotypical black names and positive words such as 'love') are longer than reaction times on 'compatible' trials (e.g. the pairing of stereotypical black names with negative words such as 'evil'). In this way prejudice may be detected without asking the participant to say whether or not they agree to, endorse or support the association between blackness and negative traits. The mental association is measured directly.

Consequently, implicit measures are thought to be more valid measures of attitudes – thus *bona fide* pipeline – because they are nonreactive. In contrast, responses to older self-report measures are likely to be influenced by factors such as demand characteristics, evaluation apprehension and subject role-playing (Greenwald *et al.*, 2002).

Despite these apparent advances and the enthusiasm with which the theory and methods have been embraced in social psychology, the idea of implicit prejudice has not been universally accepted as a panacea. Arkes and Tetlock (2004) reject the non-Allportian notion of prejudice without endorsement for both political and psychological reasons. Politically, they argue that the theory lowers the 'thresholds for labelling citizens as racist' (Tetlock and Arkes, 2004, p. 312) by gauging prejudice 'not by what people do, or by what people say, but rather by milliseconds of response facilitation or inhibition in implicit association paradigms' (Arkes and Tetlock, 2004, p. 275). Arkes and Tetlock worry that this lower threshold of prejudice will lead to labelling people racist who should not be. An individual may be accountable as a 'racist' because they 'fail' an implicit test, and yet they may disavow racism, reject racial stereotypes and support equality between groups. Thus Tetlock and Arkes (2004) suggest that 'indictments for changing implicit racism take us precariously close to the realm of thought crimes' (p. 316).

Not only is this expanded definition of racism evident in the implicit measures, but it is also evident in kinds of 'discrimination' that have been of interest in experimental work. Implicit prejudice is thought to be manifest in nondeliberative spontaneous behaviours, and so researchers have typically focused on such innocuous behaviours as eye blink frequency, eye gaze duration and body language (e.g. Dovidio *et al.*, 1997, 2002; McConnell and Leibold, 2001). According to Tetlock and Arkes (2004) this focus is a *reductio ad absurdium* 'in a world that has seen, comparatively recently, the massacres of Armenians by Turks, Jews by citizens of most European nations, Tibetans by Chinese, Tutsis by Hutus, Bosnians by Serbs and vice versa' (Suedfield, 2004, p. 301).

The criticism that Arkes and Tetlock make of the psychological foundation of implicit prejudice also has a dual focus on the attitudes themselves and the kinds of discrimination that they are supposed to produce. They argue that without individual endorsement of the attitudes it is not clear that the reaction time measures of unconscious association can properly be conceived as measuring prejudice. In particular, associations like those between black people and criminality may reflect social reality or cultural stereotypes rather than personal prejudice (cf. Karpinski and Hilton, 2001). It may be for this reason that many African Americans manifest anti-black prejudice on the IAT: although they are not personally prejudiced against their own group, they have been exposed to a culture of racist beliefs and these associations are reflected in their responses to the implicit measures.

In a similar vein, Arkes and Tetlock (2004) suggest that the proposed outcomes of implicit prejudice – blinking, gaze aversion, etc. – may be motivated by factors other than prejudice: 'A white person who is genuinely ashamed of society's treatment of African Americans by Whites might well be scored as prejudiced by raters in many validation studies that probe links between prejudice and non-verbal behaviour such as gaze aversion and body language. Yet, a person who is ashamed of white's treatment of African Americans is not likely to be a bigot, the opposite is more likely' (p. 265). Rather than being motivated by Allportian antipathy, these behaviours may be motivated by shame, guilt, stereotype threat or some other factor. Their validity as outcomes of racial prejudice are in doubt, for such nonverbal behaviours are 'probably not what most people think of when they think of discriminatory behaviour' (Banks *et al.*, 2006, pp. 1,187–8).

These political and psychological problems with implicit prejudice research potentially undermine the utility of the research endeavour. The severity of the trouble is perhaps best seen in reflections about the policy implications of implicit attitude research as demonstrated in the questions set to Banaji by the author of a *Washington Post* article: 'Might it [IAT scores] predict, for example, which police officers are likely to mistakenly shoot an unarmed black man? ... Should such tests be used to cull juries of people with high bias scores? Might employers use such tests to weed out potential racists? Might employees trying to prove discrimination demand that their bosses take bias tests?' (Vedantam, 2005, p. 12). Banaji's response was staggering, for it betrayed a lack of confidence in the validity of the measures: she would 'testify in court against any attempt to use the test to identify biased individuals' because it is false to 'assume that someone who shows bias on the test will always act in a biased manner' (Vedantam, 2005, p. 12).

In the light of Banaji's confession, perhaps the political problems are the opposite of those that Arkes and Tetlock anticipate. Rather than helping to identify racism, the lowered threshold of prejudice may broaden the scope of its applicability so much that the concept loses its political edge and is no longer useful in the real world. How, after all, can you hold people accountable for beliefs that they don't endorse? The implicit prejudice explanations may excuse racism by explaining it away: *tout comprendre c'est tout pardoner* (cf. Billig, 2002). By explaining discriminatory behaviour in terms of unconscious cognitive processes that are outside individual control, these theories 'present perpetrators in an understandable light that wittingly or unwittingly invites empathy' (Billig, 2002, p. 176).

The subject of prejudice

Amid the controversy surrounding Arkes and Tetlock's (2004) critique of implicit prejudice there was widespread agreement that the theory of implicit prejudice marked a fundamental departure from the traditional conception of prejudiced attitudes. In this section I will argue that, on the contrary, the theory of implicit prejudice is a direct continuation of the theoretical tradition of cognitive social psychology and, as such, it bears all the hallmarks of the prejudice problematic. The real innovation is in technique. As Banaji *et al.* (2004) recognize, 'The historical reliance on self-report measures may have been more from convenience and a lack of alternative measures than a strong theoretical commitment that attitudes operate only as conscious entities' (p. 280). Priming methodology and reaction time measures provided a technology to observe cognitive associations directly, without the conscious mediation of the research participant.

New implicit measurement techniques allowed social psychologists to explore for the first time the lower limits of the reach of culture into individual minds, its 'capacity to reach toward the regions of human experience which appear as immediately given, as the incontrovertible evidence of our senses' (Tajfel, 1969, p. 322). This project had long been of interest to cognitive psychologists because, like the subsequent generation of implicit theorists, they always believed that cognitive processes functioned automatically in the background and took primacy over conscious deliberations and motives. Consciously endorsed attitudes had to rely on raw materials of sensory perception that had already been filtered through a cognitive mechanism, and it was these more immediate processes that social psychologists hoped to explain.

Jerome Bruner provided the most famous statement of this deterministic and mechanistic view of the prejudiced subject: 'perception acts sometimes as a welcoming committee and sometimes a screening committee. It now appears as though both of these committees are closer to the entrance port than previously conceived' (Bruner, 1957, p. 139). Perception was of interest because it provided the 'incontrovertible evidence of our senses' that could then be subject to more deliberative processes. The prejudiced subject is, in the first instance, a perceiver. The act of categorization takes place immediately in perception, as we see the world of 'objects' such as tables, chairs, furniture and black and white people in culture's terms. It is for this reason that early cognitive theorists like Bruner viewed perception as continuous with cognition. In perception, raw sense data is subject to categorization, as the cognitive mechanism acted as a welcoming or screening committee, inviting some outcomes while denying others. Thus, 'A theory of perception ... needs a mechanism capable of inference and categorizing as much as one is needed in the theory of cognition' (Bruner, 1957, p. 124). By situating cognition in the context of perception, as the mechanism that has already processed information and made it available for conscious deliberation, cognitive psychologists of half a century ago anticipated implicit cognition: 'In no sense need the process be conscious or deliberate' (Bruner, 1957, p. 124).

In this theory, it makes no sense to think of perceptions as veridical, and hence the foundation of prejudice as irrational overgeneralization falls away. We don't perceive the world as it actually is but we always see it in culture's terms. In this way, the cognitive tradition provides a highly deterministic view of the prejudiced subject as a cultural dupe. This same view is presumed in the theory of implicit prejudice: 'Implicit attitudes, as I see it, reflect traces of experience *within* culture that have become so integral a part of the individual's own mental and social makeup that it is artificial, if not patently odd, to separate such attitudes into "culture" versus "self" parts' (Banaji, 2001, p. 139). The unconscious nature of the cognitive/perceptual process renders the theory a highly mechanistic one. 'In its simplest form, then, an automatic process can be conceptualized as an IF–THEN relation . . . IF certain conditions hold in the cognitive environment, THEN the process in question will run to completion' (Bargh, 1996, p. 177; cf. Bargh, 1999).

This theory of the prejudiced subject has had two consequences in terms of the focus of research on attitudes that are partly definitive of the prejudice problematic. The social psychology of prejudice research has been very much interested in individual minds and very little interested in the social expressions of stereotypes and prejudice. The interest in the mind comes from the theory that categorization is a mental act, a cognitive accomplishment of the individual perceiver. Thus, the proper focus of research is on the mechanics, situational influences and outcomes of this process. How, in Bruner's terms, do the welcoming and screening committees function, under what conditions, and with what effects? Any expressions of prejudice are understood to be downstream consequences of the mental events that take causal primacy.

Most commonly, the conditions and effects of prejudice have been studied by requiring research participants to make judgements of one kind or another in experimental situations. As an illustrative example of many studies of the effects of implicit cognition, Hugenberg and Bodenhausen (2003) asked participants to watch computer-generated faces morph from one facial expression (hostility) to another (happiness) and say when hostility was no longer apparent. Black faces were seen to be hostile for longer, and this was associated with implicit bias (IAT). The cause of the biased face perception was presumably the implicit association between black people and hostility. In this model, stereotyping is something that occurs in the mind before social interaction, and which determines the individual perceptions and judgements, which are the downstream consequences of the underlying biased perspective.

Notice how this approach stops short of studying social life. What is missing is how this perception translates into interaction with others. How would a white perceiver respond to a black person after seeing their face as hostile? What would they say to a white or black peer? This occlusion is no coincidence. As discussed above, such expressions are presumed to be subject to self-presentational and other social influences. They are not to be fully trusted and they have consequently not been the focus of much research. The mechanistic unfolding of the 'if . . . then process', the effect of the cultural imprint on mind, is best observed without the distorting influence of the perceiver having to make known their expressions to others and thus be accountable for them.

Implicit prejudice research has contributed to this research agenda by not requiring research participants to endorse attitudes. Response time measures cast an 'experimental veil' over prejudice by eliminating two audiences from witnessing the perceiver's attitude, namely the researcher and the perceiver themselves (Steel and Morawski, 2002). The dual process model of prejudice makes a further contribution towards removing social audiences from the research context by directing attention to forms of expression which, like implicit attitudes, are themselves outside conscious awareness and deliberation. Instead of having people make judgements in the experimental context that could be interpreted as being racist (e.g. saying when the black face starts to look hostile), the primary interest in implicit prejudice research is the 'behavioural leakage' – the downstream effect – of implicit prejudice into unconscious, automatic and spontaneous behaviours (Dovidio et al., 1997).

Thus, research which has sought to establish the validity of implicit prejudice by studying its effects has looked for these effects in non-verbal behaviour which 'generally lies outside of conscious awareness and control' and can thus 'be considered less subject to social desirability effects than are verbal attitude reports' (Crosby et al., 1980, cited in Dovidio et al., 1997). These are the nonverbal behaviours such as blinking, forward body lean, expressiveness of arms or eye gaze duration, that were of so much concern to Arkes and Tetlock. In practice, these nonverbal behavioural outcomes are determined by asking independent judges to count the incidence of the behaviours (e.g. Dovidio et al., 1997) or, more typically, to provide global overall ratings of the nonverbal behavioural interaction (Dovidio et al., 2002; Fazio et al., 1995; McConnell and Leibold, 2001; Richeson and Shelton, 2005; Shelton et al., 2005).

For example, Dovidio *et al.* (2002) had white subjects converse with either black or white confederates about a non-racial, mundane topic: 'Dating in the current era has some advantages and disadvantages to dating in earlier periods'. The videotaped conversations were rated by independent judges for verbal friendliness (what they said, e.g. agreements, greetings, invitations and so on) and nonverbal friendliness (how they said it, e.g. eye contact, smiling, blinks, nods). As hypothesized by dual process theory, verbal friendliness was correlated with an explicit measure of racism but nonverbal friendliness was correlated with a response latency implicit racism measure.

There are two consequences of this research tradition that has sought to study implicit attitudes and their implicit expressions. First, the research reinforces the deterministic and mechanistic view of the prejudiced subject. The primary concerns are private individual categorical associations and their effect on uncontrolled behaviour. Research participants must endorse neither the attitude nor their behavioural responses and are consequently accountable for neither. Thus, the prejudiced subject is not a fully social subject who can expect to justify their attitudes or behaviours and who must therefore tailor their views to the demands of the social context. Second, the actual expression of stereotypes and prejudice is elided completely in research where the focus of attention is on the mental processes and their implicit effects on unconscious behaviour. By getting raters' global impression of nonverbal or verbal friendliness, the research does not study those aspects of the performance that are rated as prejudiced or not. By counting frequencies of events in interactional behaviour, the research ignores the interactional meaning of the behaviour – e.g. a smile or a blink/wink may be positive or negative!

Implicit prejudice research has continued and extended the cognitive tradition of prejudice studies, being suspicious of individual endorsements of prejudiced attitudes and behaviours. New implicit cognition measurement technologies have allowed researchers to explore the full implications of cognitive theories of prejudice by focusing on unconscious and automatic forms of prejudice and their expression. The work has moved the focus on prejudice deeper and deeper into the recesses of the unconscious mind and automatic processes, away from ordinary social contexts where prejudice and discrimination are manifest in everyday life in terms of accountable avowals and behaviours (Banaji *et al.*, 2001). As Arkes and Tetlock (2004) show, this newer research has exposed serious political and psychological problems with prejudice research. How do we know that these implicit associations and nonverbal behavioural correlates actually are valid indices and manifestations of prejudice? And if we say they are, don't we risk lowering the bar of racism or explaining racism away as an inevitable and understandable consequence of living in an unequal society?

In addition, the cognitive tradition of prejudice research in social psychology begs the question about how prejudice is expressed in social contexts such as jury deliberations, selection committees and ordinary conversations where individuals can certainly be held accountable for what they say and do. Or, as Suedfield (2004) asks, how can prejudice be expressed to rally support for genocide? To date, the main emphasis in the social psychology of stereotypes has been on the psychological side of the equation. Stereotypes are increasingly seen as automatic and inevitable category–feature associations that are mental residues of exposure to cultural prejudice. Current theory and measurement remove stereotypes from the flux of social life and place them firmly in mind as unconscious mental associations. This work has been very good at showing how such stereotypes influence individual judgements and uncontrolled behaviours in interaction. However, the voluminous literature on implicit prejudice and stereotyping tells us very little about how stereotypical associations are made in social contexts, how stereotypes and prejudice are communicated, taken up or resisted by others.

So the problem left over is to explain how prejudiced attitudes are expressed and function in social interaction. In addition to being mental associations that emerge downstream in uncontrolled behaviours and automatic judgements, attitudes need to be expressed in social interaction if they are to be the basis for coordinated collective judgements and activities. For example, in making decisions about the hiring of a candidate or in jury deliberations, the stereotypes need to be communicated for them to influence the behaviour of others and for a group to collectively make a prejudiced decision. Likewise, hate has to be communicated if genocide is to be committed. If it is true that most people today genuinely believe themselves to be nonprejudiced and will no longer express crude stereotypes, how is prejudice communicated? How do people coordinate their actions so that public policies, hiring decisions and jury court decisions come to reflect the influence of the stereotypes? And, how are the next generation learning to stereotype?

The implicit prejudice in talk-in-interaction: stereotyping by implication

Besides looking for prejudice in the silent and hidden recesses of the mind, the cognitive processes associated with prejudice can be studied in the noisy rhetorical contexts of 'talk-in-interaction' (Billig, 1997; Edwards, 1997). This change of focus can help to restore the view of the prejudiced subject as a social agent rather than a cultural dupe who mechanistically applies stereotypes. Certainly, stereotypes and prejudiced attitudes are widely shared cultural phenomena, but this does not mean that individuals must deliberately repress them or are doomed to repeat them as they 'leak' into public view. There is a middle way between thoughtful repression and thoughtless expression of prejudice proposed by dual process models.

Personal accountability is the defining feature of the expression of prejudice and stereotypes in social settings. Because such expressions may be socially sanctioned or blameworthy, people attend to these possible social ramifications when expressing their attitudes. In expressing prejudice we need to be sure that we do not open ourselves to criticism. We need to make sure that our interlocutors see the world in the same way as we do so that our expressions don't stand out as being racist or bigoted (cf. Billig, 1988). This is precisely the social dimension of prejudice that underpinned concerns about reactive measurement and that drove the implicit measurement project. However, rather than something to be eliminated, efforts to adapt prejudice to the social audience are precisely the phenomenon that needs to be studied. It is critical if we are to understand how prejudice can achieve social effects, how we can enlist others to accept our prejudices and to understand how our actions are properly motivated by them. In expressing our stereotypes and prejudices we are able to justify our actions, criticize other actions, and so enjoin others to share in our stereotypes and world view.

In this section I present two interview extracts to demonstrate how prejudiced attitudes may be expressed in subtle, even implicit, ways in talk-in-interaction. The extracts come from an interview I conducted on the beach with a white family who were on summer vacation. The interview was about their attitudes towards desegregation of the beaches in post-apartheid South Africa. On the basis of these pieces of talk-in-interaction, I will show that stereotypes are formulated in the context of social interaction and that they can take an implicit form in which the hearer must help the speaker to stereotype. As such, the expression of prejudice is a genuinely collaborative activity which is not accomplished in the mind of a lone individual.

Extract (1)

KEVIN: And have you ever been to Durban for a holiday? I know that used to be a
          big um tourist attraction.
JULIE: We used to go there ja but that that
KEVIN: Used to?
MARIE: Not any more
JULIE: Years ago
MARIE: You can't get on the beaches now

JULIE: Ja because you can't even go to the public toilets there you get mugged
KEVIN: [ja]
MARIE: [ja] they actually warn you before you go in
JULIE: And that was
MARIE: Wednesday (the) other day
JULIE: we were (.) warned by black people there not to go there

Extract (2)

KEVIN: So if um (.) a black family came and sit sort of next to you (.) or maybe
           up there
JULIE: It won't bother us
KEVIN: How do you feel about that?
JULIE: Nothing
LYNDA: We won't do anything it's just
JULIE: It won't bother us as long as they behave themselves
JULIE: It won't bother us at all (.) as long as they just leave the place in a (.)
           good conditions and don't get drunk here and (.) things like that
           then it's fine
KEVIN: Then it's fine?
JULIE: No problem
KEVIN: No problem (.) And would you go and talk
JULIE: The un e... (.) the/the unwanted the (.) the how can I say it
CHARL: [=elements]
KEVIN: [=uninvited]
JULIE: Ja those people (Kevin: oh) That's all (.) As he said we're not racists not
           at all (.) but um
JULIE: Do you think we're not racists?
           [hhhh   ]
MARIE: [hhhh   ]
KEVIN: [Good question hhhh   ]

Both of these passages of talk-in-interaction show that stereotypes are
formulated in the context of social interaction (see also Condor and
Figgou's analysis in Chapter 10). Racial stereotypes are socially occasioned. In Extract (1) stereotypes about black people are needed to
explain why the family no longer holiday in Durban, and in Extract
(2) stereotypes about blacks are used to explain why they would object
to having black neighbours on the beach. The preference for segregation in both of these contexts is likely to be blameworthy and the
stereotypes are used to account for these potentially discrediting acts
of racial discrimination. This is no occasion to repress racial stereotypes: they are needed to do the rhetorical work of justification and
criticism.

As can be seen from the extracts, stereotype expression has a number of
features that allow it to do the work of explaining and justifying

discrimination and the preference for segregation. First, stereotypes are typically not abstract statements of negativity towards a group in general but focus on a particular feature of a group as it pertains to the issue or topic at hand. For example, the account of segregation is justified by the stereotype that black beachgoers may include a criminal element (Extract 1) or may make a mess and become drunk and unruly on the beach (Extract 2). In other interviews concerns were raised about black beach-goers potentially not respecting personal space, overcrowding, or behaving or dressing in an uncivilized manner. Such stereotypes of black people are likely to be less useful in other contexts such as criticizing governments in Africa or explaining why some sports teams or university professors should not be racially representative. On the beach, representations of blacks as filthy, criminal, drunkards can do the work of explaining why white people prefer to stick to themselves. It is noteworthy that these are not the subtle covert expressions of racism that modern racism theorists might expect (e.g. Sears and Henry, 2005). On the contrary, crude and negative stereotypes are required to do the job of explaining preferences for segregation.

Racial stereotypes are not simply repressed anachronistic remnants that leak, undetected, into behaviour. They are also rhetorical resources that are used to account for one's preferences and behaviours. Although there are rhetorical demands both for the specific and crude stereotype content, there are also risks involved in expressing them, for they are themselves potentially discrediting indicators of prejudice. While solving one rhetorical problem – explaining racial discrimination – the expressed stereotypes can create other rhetorical problems. So, in expressing racial stereotypes, speakers must navigate between the Scylla of discrimination and the Charybdis of prejudice!

It is for this reason that great care has to be taken in how the stereotypes are expressed. The offensiveness of their content cannot be toned down as this would undermine their power as explanations of segregation. The extracts above reveal three features of stereotype expression that allow speakers to deploy stereotypes while at the same time distancing themselves from them. Their expression is implicit, not in the sense of being automatic or unconscious, but by taking the form of an implication.

First, the expressed stereotype takes a noncategorical form. While 'the assessment target of most implicit prejudice research has been attitudes toward Whites and African Americans as undifferentiated wholes' (Arkes and Tetlock, 2004, p. 174), this is not the way people stereotype others in real life. On the contrary, in talk-in-interaction we can observe explicit attempts to indicate that the characterization does not apply to the group as a whole. For example, in Extract (2) the concern is about unwanted elements, not black people in general. Other interviewees explained that their objection was to behaviours such as drunkenness and unmannerly conduct, that they would find equally objectionable among white neighbours.

Second, the target of the stereotype is a vague and underspecified subject. The category of person to whom the stereotype applies is often not explicitly stated. In Extract (1), for example, we are not told who the muggers in the public toilets are. This is left unstated but implied. In Extract (2) we observe the difficulty the speaker has in saying who the objectionable people are. In the first part of the extract the interviewees refer to the undefined 'they' but later the interviewer, Kevin, was set to probe further about their attitudes towards black neighbours, asking whether their family would interact with the neighbours. Julie warded off this possible reference to race by interjecting to define the objectionable neighbours as unwanted people, not as black people. She struggles to qualify the unwanted character of the neighbours and is assisted both by Charl and Kevin who also avoid references to race. As is the case here, the subject of the stereotype is often only implied.

Third, the category–feature associations are often indirect. Not only is the categorical subject of the stereotype presented in a noncategorical and vague manner but the association between this category and the offensive attribute is often indirect. This association typically relies on metaphor or metonym, using place, occasion or topic to convey a sense of who the features may apply to. For example, Extract (1) is ostensibly not about race at all. The question is about going to the Durban beaches. It requires insider knowledge to understand that whereas Durban was previously the prime destination for white holidaymakers, since desegregation, it had 'become black'. This insider knowledge would help the hearer understand why a white beachgoer might now get mugged in the public toilets there.

Given all this indirection one may well ask whether these extracts provide instances of stereotyping at all. Does all this focus on individual differences and denial of the relevance of categorical responses mean that we have progressed beyond race stereotyping and prejudice expression? Now that racial prejudice is counter-normative in post-apartheid South Africa, does this mean that it is banished from expression and is only to be found in the recesses of the unconscious mind? A detailed study of race talk, such as that recorded in the two extracts above, would suggest not. Although there is no evidence of explicit stereotyping, of positive statements of associations between categories and attributes, evidence of an implicit form of stereotyping by implication abounds.

In both extracts, the speakers imply that certain traits are characteristic of blacks. The primary way in which the implication is done is by introducing a particular topic of concern in the context of talking about race contact. In Extract (1), the topic of the potential mugging in the public toilets is introduced in a context of talking about going to Durban beach. Why this topic and not the infinite number of other topics, for example, about the quality of the sand, sea or ice cream? A stereotypical association is implied by raising particular concerns and not others in the context of talking about race.

In addition to this researcher-initiated interpretation of stereotyping by implication, the extracts also provide evidence of the participants hearing the stereotypical implications, recognizing that they might be heard by others, and attempting to manage this hearing. In Extract (1), Julie tells the researcher that the family had been warned by black people not to go to Durban beach. Why was it necessary to introduce race when it had not been raised as being relevant to the deliberations about visiting Durban? This may be an attempt at self-presentation, showing that their preferences for segregation are not informed by potentially racist white perspectives, but on advice from black people. Julie recognizes that Kevin and the other participants may have heard her talk about the dangerousness of Durban to imply a racial stereotype about the black people who are understood to frequent the beach. In Extract (2), despite not stating stereotypes explicitly, Julie explicitly denies racism, and then asks the interviewer whether he heard what they had said as racist. By so denying racism, the speaker recognizes that their talk – stereotypical implication – could be heard as being racist.

Stereotyping by implication depends on the existence of common sense cultural knowledge of stereotypes that serves as the 'background' to the racial expression (Durrheim *et al.*, 2009). It is this common sense that links speakers and hearers and makes it possible for speakers to gesture towards the stereotype in implicit ways, knowing that the hearer will be able to do the rest of the work of understanding. Thus speakers need not articulate stereotypes in all their florid detail for them to be effective. Although people need objectionable stereotypes to justify discrimination, these need not be stated explicitly. Stereotyping by implication can be likened to an act of telling public secrets. The unutterable stereotypes are gestured in forms of expression in which they are simultaneously revealed and hidden. It is left up to the hearer to understand what has been said, by completing the picture of the stereotype. Stereotyping by implication is genuinely collaborative, 'joint action' (Shotter, 1993). It is not something individuals can do by themselves and it is certainly not something that can be achieved in the isolation of the individual unconscious mind. Implicit expressions require listeners to do the work of understanding the racial implication. It requires the hearer who is a cultural insider, who knows, for example, that Durban beaches have 'become black'.

Edwards (1997) argues that such collaboration characterizes all language usage. Because words are inherently always potentially polysemic, an act of interpretation is required to understand the meaning of expressions in the context in which they are uttered. Thus, 'hearers must perform active contextualizing work in order to see what descriptions mean, and speakers rely upon hearers performing such work in order that their utterances will make definite sense' (Heritage, 1984, p. 148). Speakers also have the responsibility of ensuring that hearers hear correctly. This is done through a process of gesturing towards the intended meaning – for example, linking being on Durban beach with the risk of mugging – while drawing attention away from unintended meanings – for example, that the speaker believes that blacks are criminal. As competent members of a culture, hearers know the metaphorical and metonymic associations that populate the narratives of societies with their particular histories and contexts. To stereotype by implication it is not necessary to go into the details. All that is required is to gesture towards these narratives by reference to (racially unspecified) people frequenting certain places and doing stereotypically objectionable things.

This collaborative interaction serves specific rhetorical functions for stereotyping. The fact that speakers do not have to make explicit associations between social categories and negative attributes means that racism can always be denied. Further, since it is up to hearers to do active contextualizing work and meaning-making, the hearer may actually be accountable for hearing a stereotype where none was intended. Stereotyping by implication means both that the speaker need not articulate the stereotype in all its florid detail and that hearers may become responsible for their share in 'hearing a stereotype' where none was stated. Thus, critics of racism beware!

Conclusion

Reaction time measures of implicit prejudice have taken us to the logical endpoint of the cognitive approach to prejudice. They have allowed researchers to explore the capacity for prejudice to reach deep into the inner recesses of the mind and to give structure to the 'incontrovertible evidence of our senses' (Tajfel, 1969, p. 322) outside the will and control of the person. This has reinforced the determinist and mechanistic view of the prejudiced subject that has long been the foundation of the prejudice problematic. Implicit prejudice research has also brought problems with the cognitive approach to prejudice in social psychology into clearer relief. As Arkes and Tetlock (2004) argue so well, reducing prejudice and discrimination to automatic associations that require no endorsement

raises serious psychological questions about the validity of these perform-
ances as indices of prejudice. Such lowering of the bar of racism also raises
political consequences of either blaming too many people for racism or
excusing too many people by explaining racism away as a natural mental
function.

Tetlock and his colleagues hope to salvage the concept of prejudice by
relying on Allport's definition to identify crude expressions that betray
faulty categorization and antipathy (Arkes and Tetlock, 2004; Sniderman
and Tetlock, 1986; Tetlock and Arkes, 2004). Implicit researchers are
correct to portray this as a 'quaint' view, given the subtlety of racial
expressions today (Banaji *et al.*, 2004). As the two extracts above show,
racial projects such as the commitment to segregation in post-apartheid
South Africa are not defended by irrationally hostile rhetoric. As
Durrheim and Dixon (2004) argued, 'by focusing on a narrow class of
supposedly unequivocal racist expressions, researchers risk overlooking
forms of racist evaluation that operate precisely via equivocation, contradiction, and subtlety' (p. 360). We suggested, then, that prejudice can be
studied in terms of its expressions in the 'fibre of everyday life: in the
conversational and physical contexts of social interaction' (p. 635). The
research on implicit prejudice has taken us further away from this focus.

This chapter has demonstrated that implicit prejudice and stereotyping
can be treated as interactional accomplishments. Viewed in this way, we
can now appreciate how cultural shared stereotypes can be communicated
to others in implicit and indirect ways in order to shape collective practices, policies and decisions; and how such implicit stereotypes can thus be
learned by the next generation. People learn how to stereotype through
innuendo, irony and implication, making implicit associations between
race categories and racial attributes. These routines of talking are taught
in the same way as other routines such as greetings, question–answer
exchanges and so on. In stereotyping by implication, speakers can align
their views with those of others and thus coordinate their actions to bring
about the effects of racial discrimination in a society which ostensibly does
not use race stereotypes.

This interactional approach to studying prejudiced cognition restores
agency and sociality to the prejudiced subject. People use cultural stereotypes in resourceful and creative ways to express prejudice and defend
racial discrimination. It is not due to romantic views about the agentic
subject that talk-in-interaction should be the focus of social psychological
research on prejudice. It is because accountable social interaction forms
such an important part of human life and is critical for launching and
managing racial projects. People do certainly engage in many routine
activities like somnambulists, where their mental associations may leak

into their behaviour outside of consciousness. However, people are also very careful to act in accountable ways in expressing their beliefs and practices about race, and we need a social psychology of prejudice that is equipped to study these expressions.

References

Arkes, H. R. and Tetlock, P. E. (2004). Attributions of implicit prejudice, or 'Would Jesse Jackson "fail" the Implicit Association Test?'. *Psychological Inquiry*, **15**, 257–78.

Banaji, M. R. (2001). Implicit attitudes can be measured. In H. L. Roediger, III, J. S. Nairne, I. Neath and A. Surprenant (eds.), *The Nature of Remembering: Essays in Honor of Robert G. Crowder* (pp.117–50). Washington, DC: American Psychological Association.

Banaji, M. R. and Hardin, C. D. (1996). Automatic stereotyping. *Psychological Science*, **7**, 136–41.

Banaji, M. R., Hardin, C. and Rothman, A. J. (1993). Implicit stereotyping in person judgement. *Journal of Personality and Social Psychology*, **65**, 272–81.

Banaji, M. R., Lemm, K. M. and Carpenter, S. J. (2001). The social unconscious. In A. Tesser and N. Schwartz (eds.), *Blackwell Handbook of Social Psychology: Intraindividual Processes* (pp.134–58). Oxford, UK: Blackwell.

Banaji, M. R., Nosek, B. A. and Greenwald, A. G. (2004). No place for nostalgia in science: a response to Arkes and Tetlock. *Psychological Inquiry*, **15**, 279–310.

Banks, R. R., Eberhardt, J. L. and Ross, L. (2006). Discrimination and implicit bias in a racially unequal society. *California Law Review*, **94**, 1,169–90.

Bargh, J. A. (1996). Automaticity in social psychology. In E. T. Higgins and A. W. Kruglanshi (eds.), *Social Psychology: a Handbook of Basic Principles* (pp.169–83). New York: Guilford.

(1999). The cognitive monster: the case against controllability of automatic stereotype effects. In S. Chaiken and Y. Trope (eds.), *Dual Process Theories in Social Psychology*. New York: Guilford.

Billig, M. (1988). The notion of 'prejudice': some rhetorical and ideological aspects. *Text*, **8**, 91–111.

(1997). *Arguing and Thinking: a Rhetorical Approach to Social Psychology* (2nd edn). Cambridge, UK: Cambridge University Press.

(2002). Henri Tajfel's 'Cognitive aspects of prejudice' and the psychology of bigotry. *British Journal of Social Psychology*, **41**, 171–88.

Bruner, J. S. (1957). On perceptual readiness. *Psychological Review*, **64**, 123–52.

Crosby, F., Bromley, S. and Saxe, L. (1980). Recent unobtrusive studies in black and white discrimination and prejudice: a literature review. *Psychological Bulletin*, **87**, 546–63.

Devine, P. G. (1989). Stereotypes and prejudice: their automatic and controlled components. *Journal of Personality and Social Psychology*, **56**, 5–18.

Dovidio, J. F. (2001). On the nature of contemporary prejudice: the third wave. *Journal of Social Issues*, **57**, 829–49.

Dovidio, J. F. and Gaertner, S. L. (2000). Aversive racism in selection decisions: 1989 and 1999. *Psychological Science*, **11**, 319–23.

(2004). Aversive racism. *Advances in Experimental Social Psychology*, **36**, 1–51.

Dovidio, J. F., Evans, N. and Tyler, R. B. (1986). Racial stereotypes: their contents and cognitive representations. *Journal of Experimental Social Psychology*, **22**, 22–37.

Dovidio, J. F., Kawakami, K. and Gaertner, S. L. (2002). Implicit and explicit prejudice in interracial interaction. *Journal of Personality and Social Psychology*, **82**, 62–8.

Dovidio, J. F., Kawakami, K., Johnson, C., Johnson, B. and Howard, A. (1997). On the nature of prejudice: automatic and controlled processes. *Journal of Experimental Social Psychology*, **33**, 510–40.

Durrheim, K. and Dixon, J. (2004). Attitudes and the fibre of everyday life: the discourse of racial evaluation and the lived experience of desegregation. *American Psychologist*, **59**, 626–36.

Durrheim, K., Hook, D. and Riggs, D. (2009). Race and racism. In D. Fox, I. Prilleltensky and S. Austin (eds.), *Critical Psychology: an Introduction* (2nd edn). Thousand Oaks, CA: Sage.

Edwards, D. (1997). *Discourse and Cognition*. London: Sage.

Fazio, R. H. and Dunton, B. C. (1997). Categorization by race: the impact of automatic and controlled components of racial attitudes. *Journal of Experimental Social Psychology*, **33**, 451–70.

Fazio, R. H., Jackson, J. R., Dunton, B. C. and Williams, C. J. (1995). Variability in automatic activation as an unobtrusive measure of racial attitudes: a bona fide pipeline. *Journal of Personality and Social Psychology*, **69**, 1,013–27.

Gaertner, S. L. and McLaughlin, J. P. (1983). Racial stereotypes: associations and ascriptions of positive and negative characteristics. *Social Psychology Quarterly*, **46**, 23–30.

Greenwald, A. G. and Banaji, M. (1995). Implicit social cognition: attitudes, self-esteem and stereotypes. *Psychological Review*, **102**, 4–27.

Greenwald, A. G., Banaji, M. R., Rudman, L. A., Farnham, S. D., Nosek, B. A. and Mellot, D. S. (2002). A unified theory of implicit attitudes, stereotypes, self-esteem and self-concept. *Psychological Review*, **109**, 3–25.

Heritage, J. C. (1984). *Garfinkel and Ethnomethodology*. Cambridge, UK: Polity.

Hugenberg, K. and Bodenhausen, G. V. (2003). Facing prejudice: implicit prejudice and the perception of facial threat. *Psychological Science*, **14**, 640–3.

Karpinski, A. and Hilton, J. L. (2001). Attitudes and the implicit association test. *Journal of Personality and Social Psychology*, **81**, 774–88.

Macrae, C. N. and Bodenhausen, G. V. (2001). Social cognition: categorical person perception. *British Journal of Psychology*, **92**, 239–55.

McConnell, A. R. and Leibold, J. M. (2001). Relations among the implicit association test, discriminatory behaviour, and explicit measures of racial attitudes. *Journal of Experimental Social Psychology*, **37**, 435–42.

Mitchell, J. P., Nosek, B. A. and Banaji, M. R. (2003). Contextual variations in implicit evaluation. *Journal of Experimental Psychology: General*, **132**, 455–69.

Monteith, M. J., Voils, C. I. and Ashburn-Nardo, L. (2001). Taking a look underground: detecting, interpreting and reacting to implicit racial biases. *Social Cognition*, **19**, 395–417.

Richeson, J. A. and Shelton, J. N. (2005). *Journal of Nonverbal Behavior*, **29**, 75–86.

Sears, D. O. and Henry, P. J. (2005). Over thirty years later: a contemporary look at symbolic racism and its critics. *Advances in Experimental Social Psychology*, **37**, 95–150.

Shelton, N. J., Richeson, J. A. and Salvatore, J. (2005). Expecting to be the target of prejudice: implications for interethnic interactions. *Journal of Personality and Social Psychology*, **31**, 1,189–202.

Shotter, J. (1993). *Conversational Realities*. London: Sage.

Smith, E. R. (1996). What do connectionism and social psychology offer each other? *Journal of Personality and Social Psychology*, **70**, 893–912.

Sniderman, P. M. and Tetlock, P. E. (1986). Symbolic racism: problems of motive attribution in political debate. *Journal of Social Issues*, **42**, 129–50.

Steel, R. S. and Morawski, J. G. (2002). Implicit cognition and the social unconscious. *Theory and Psychology*, **12**, 37–54.

Suedfield, P. (2004). Racism in the brain; or is it racism on the brain? *Psychological Inquiry*, **15**, 298–302.

Tajfel, H. (1969). Social and cultural factors in perception. In G. Lindzey and E. Aronson (eds.), *Handbook of Social Psychology* (Vol. 3). Reading, MA: Addison-Wesley.

Tetlock, P. E. and Arkes, H. R. (2004). The implicit prejudice exchange: islands of consensus in a sea of controversy. *Psychological Inquiry*, **15**, 311–21.

Vedantam, S. (2005). See no bias. *Washington Post* (23 January), available at www. washingtonpost.com/wp-dyn/articles/A27067-2005Jan21.html

Wilson, T. D., Lindsey, S. and Schooler, T. Y. (2000). A model of dual attitudes. *Psychological Review*, **107**, 101–26.

Wittenbrink, B., Gist, P. L. and Hilton, J. L. (1997). Structural properties of stereotypic knowledge and their influences on the construal of social situations. *Journal of Personality and Social Psychology*, **72**, 526–43.

Word, C. O., Zanna, M. P. and Cooper, J. (1974). Non-verbal mediation of self-fulfilling prophecies in interracial interaction. *Journal of Experimental Social Psychology*, **10**, 109–20.

10 Rethinking the prejudice problematic: a collaborative cognition approach

Susan Condor and Lia Figgou

> Prejudice is understood as the human individuals' psychological tendency to make unfavorable evaluations about members of other social groups.
>
> Ibanez *et al.* (2009, p. 81)

> It blunts the thinking to speak of the participants in the social scene as 'individuals'.
>
> Asch (1952, p. 180)

The vagueness of prejudice

As Pawlik and d'Ydewalle (2006) have noted, psychologists generally tend to refer to their research objects in common-language terminology. Consequently, authors of academic texts often start out by providing formal definitions of any key terms in order to establish a clear boundary between their own scientific understanding and the imprecise, inaccurate, forms of conceptualization typical of 'mere' common sense (cf. Billig, 1990; Shapin, 2001). Social psychological work on prejudice is, of course, no exception, and most authors offer their readers a definition of the term 'prejudice', which they typically distinguish from purportedly less accurate or precise everyday uses of the word.

Academic terminology is, of course, subject to change over time. Psychologists originally used the term 'attitude' to refer to a physiological condition (Danziger, 1997), and although contemporary social psychologists like to trace their definitions of 'stereotype' to Lippmann's (1922) text *Public Opinion*, Lippmann's original use of the term was actually more akin to the current construct of schema (Newman, 2009).

When introducing the construct of 'prejudice', social psychologists often point to historical shifts in nonscientific usage of the term (Allport, 1954; Billig, 1988), and suggest that psychological definitions have gradually developed in line with advances in scientific theory and research (e.g. Stagnor, 2009). However, detailed attention to published work in social psychology actually indicates a high level of consistency in formal definitions of prejudice over the past century. When originally employed in academic psychology, the term 'prejudice' was used to refer to a general affective 'prepossession' towards any kind of object or idea (e.g. Morse, 1907). In social psychology, however, the word quickly came to refer specifically to antipathy towards members of a social category. In the first decades of the twentieth century, US social psychologists often adopted the ordinary language term 'race prejudice', defined by W.O. Brown (1933, p. 294) as 'the tendency to react with varying degrees of hostility to a group regarded as racial'. It is instructive to compare this definition with Stangor's (2009, p. 1) claim that, 'We *now* define prejudice as a negative attitude towards a group or towards members of the group' (our emphasis). In fact, we can appreciate that – apart from the substitution of the concept of 'attitude' for 'react[ion]' – Stangor's own definition of 'prejudice' is essentially identical to the definition of 'race prejudice' offered by W.O. Brown three quarters of a century earlier.

Similarly, social psychologists' claims concerning the distinctiveness of their formal scientific usage of the term 'prejudice' do not necessarily withstand critical scrutiny. Admittedly, some aspects of contemporary social psychological theorizing on prejudice are, to borrow Borgida and Fiske's (2008) formulation, 'beyond commonsense'. Nevertheless in many respects the definitions, normative concerns, prototypes and theories of prejudice employed by ordinary social actors display distinct parallels with the more elaborate, formalized, models employed in the reified universe of social psychological science (Billig, 1988; Figgou and Condor, 2006; Hodson and Esses, 2005; Wetherell, Chapter 8, this volume).

In particular, we may note that although social psychologists often claim that their definitions of 'prejudice' have been carefully formulated with a view to scientific precision, in practice their accounts are often no more specific than common language versions. For example, Stangor's description of prejudice as 'a negative attitude towards a group or towards members of the group' leaves the terms 'negative', 'attitude' and 'group' open to a range of interpretations.

The vagueness of social psychological definitions of 'prejudice' need not be regarded as a problem. On the contrary, it is possible that the enduring popularity of prejudice as an object of social psychological theory and research may be in part attributable to the 'permanent imprecision' (cf. Lowy, 1992) of both the term and the construct to which it refers.[1] Although social psychologists typically treat precision as the *sine qua non* of scientific language, in fact loose, fluid, vague constructs often facilitate empirical innovation (Lowy, 1992), by enabling researchers in one field to make use of ideas and methods developed by people working on different topics or in different academic disciplines (Galison, 1999).

The history of social psychological work on prejudice certainly bears witness to a quite extraordinary level of intellectual customization. At various points in time researchers have adapted their understanding of prejudice to capitalize upon changing social psychological fashions, interests and technological developments. Theorists have been able to approach prejudice variously as a matter of instinct, drive, motivation, emotion, categorization, social identity, attribution, personality, executive control, or rhetoric. Researchers have been able to customize the prejudice problematic to enable them to employ almost every technique in the toolbox of social psychological methods: field experiments; sociograms; direct self-report questionnaires (including Thurstone and Likert scales, semantic differential scales, adjective check-lists and social distance scales); repertory grids; bogus pipelines; nonreactive self-report measures (e.g. the California E Scale and the Modern Racism Scale); projective tests (e.g. the Thematic Apperception Test, sentence completion tests); clinical (or 'insight') interviews; qualitative interviews and focus groups; galvanic skin response; pupil dilation; eye blinking; eye contact; response latency; and functional magnetic resonance imaging, to name but a few.

The taxonomic imagination

Faced with the diversity of social psychological work on prejudice, it has become common for authors to attempt to impose some overarching order by formulating classificatory schemes. On the one hand, authors have developed taxonomies of *academic perspectives*, ordered roughly chronologically (e.g. Dovidio, 2001; Dovidio and Gaertner, 1986; Gaertner and Dovidio, 2005) or according to level of analysis (see Duckitt, 1992). On the other hand, authors have formulated taxonomies *of prejudices*, subclassifying the construct into distinguishable types, including: old fashioned, classical, modern, new, contemporary, symbolic, blatant, aversive, subtle, overt, benign, public, private, explicit, implicit, indirect, covert, automatic, controlled, latent, ambivalent, hostile, benevolent, instrumental, negative, everyday, complementary and colour blind. Once distinguished, the relationships between these different forms of prejudice may be described through various types of integrative model (e.g. Cuddy *et al.*, 2007; Duckitt and Sibley, 2009; Ekehammar *et al.*, 2009; Gawronski *et al.*, 2008; Nail *et al.*, 2003, 2008; Son Hing *et al.*, 2008).

While some theorists attempt to develop an overarching integrative account of the various ways in which prejudice may be manifested, others contend that the prejudice construct has evolved into a conceptual monster. Authors question, for example, whether subtle prejudice is 'really' prejudice; whether implicit association test (IAT) responses are in fact indicative of negative attitudes; or whether 'prejudice' should be distinguished from constructs such as 'bias', 'stigma', 'stereotyping', 'discrimination' or 'ingroup favouritism'. Going further, critical social psychologists have questioned the general adequacy of what Wetherell and Potter termed the 'prejudice problematic' for the conceptualization and explanation of macrosocial conflict, racist social processes and societal structures of social inequality (e.g. Adams *et al.*, 2008; Henriques, 1984; Wetherell, Chapter 8, this volume; Wetherell and Potter, 1992).

Compared to many current discussions of the social psychology of prejudice, our objective in this chapter is comparatively modest. We will not be presenting a new integrative model, nor will we offer a swinging critique of past work. Rather, taking advantage of the scope for innovation afforded by the vagueness of the prejudice construct, we will advocate a new approach that draws upon contemporary cognitive science perspectives on collaborative cognition.

Reconceiving the agent of prejudice: from methodological individualism to collaborative cognition

Our point of conceptual departure is based on the observation that, notwithstanding their evident differences, existing social psychological approaches to prejudice share a tendency towards methodological individualism, defined by Weber ([1913] 1981, p. 158) as the tendency to treat 'the single individual and his action as the basic unit, as [the] "atom"' of a social event or process.

Some social psychological approaches to prejudice are quite clearly individualistic in focus. This is true both of attempts to account for individual differences with reference to personality variables such as right wing authoritarianism or social dominance orientation, and also of approaches which emphasize the role of universal, lower-level, cognitive processes in the formation or suppression of prejudiced attitudes.[2] However, we would argue that methodological individualism is not confined to this kind of work.

Social identity theorists tend in principle to oppose 'individualistic' approaches to social psychology in general (Turner and Oakes, 1986), and to prejudice in particular (Reynolds and Turner, 2006; Reynolds *et al.*, 2001; Reynolds *et al.*, Chapter 2, this volume).[3] However, although these authors eschew forms of accounting which focus on individual differences, or which emphasize the role of dispositional over situational factors in the genesis of intergroup hostility, they nevertheless tend to subscribe to *methodological* individualism, in so far as they accept Turner's (1987, p. 4) claim that 'psychological processes reside only in individuals'. Methodological individualism is also evident when social identity theorists conceptualize collective behaviour as the outcome of the coincidence of individual psychological states of social identity (characterized by Turner as 'a "socially structured field" *within the individual mind*', 1987, p. 207, our emphasis). This kind of perspective is reflected, for example, in research that treats the individual social actor (albeit one who may be 'acting in terms of group') as the analytic case, and which operationalizes 'shared' stereotypes as statistical aggregates of individual responses (e.g. Haslam and Wilson, 2000; Haslam *et al.*, 1999; Hornsey and Hogg, 2000).

Similarly, discourse analytic approaches are often associated with anti-individualist epistemological perspectives. In practice, however, a good deal of research on racist or prejudiced discourse has tended to focus on the ways in which culturally available interpretative repertoires are reflected in the accounts produced by individual speakers. Discourse analysts typically treat hate speech and more subtle forms of verbal discrimination as rhetorical phenomena. Verbal acts of discrimination are hence construed as attempts on the part of one individual to persuade another (e.g. Augoustinos and Every, 2007; Reisigl and Wodak, 2001).[4] Alternatively, theorists may prefer to stress the way in which individual thought takes the form of internal dialogue between prejudiced and tolerant themes (Billig, Chapter 7, this volume; Billig *et al.*, 1988).

In this chapter, we consider how social psychologists might avoid methodological individualism by reconceiving of prejudice as a matter of collaborative cognition. Developed in cognitive science, the construct of collaborative cognition incorporates three key premises. The first is the simple observation that, in everyday life, human cognition 'mostly takes place in the context of other people' (Smith, 2008, p. 24). The second premise is that cognitive processes may be effectively *distributed* (Hutchins, 1995) between individuals, and that social networks may constitute dynamical information processing systems (Gureckis and Goldstone, 2006). Cognitive scientists hence suggest that 'the boundaries of cognition extend beyond the boundaries of individual organisms' (Robbins and Aydede, 2009, p. 3).

Third, collaborative cognition is often understood to be *emergent* in so far as interacting networks of social actors are able to accomplish things that individuals would be unable to do alone. This can involve coordinated effort aimed at the implementation of complex planned action (Rogoff *et al.*, 2002; cf. Asch, 1952), but can also result in ironic outcomes, unanticipated by the social actors concerned (Suchman, 1987).

A concern over processes of collaborative cognition has a number of general implications for the way in which social psychologists understand person perception and social judgement (Semin and Cacioppo, 2008; Smith, 2008; Smith and Collins, 2009). In the following pages we will develop some of our own work on the expression and suppression of prejudice in dialogue (Condor, 2006; Condor *et al.*, 2006; cf. Condor, 1990) to consider some of the ways in which a collaborative cognition perspective may shed new light on the processes involved in the construction, expression and suppression of public prejudice.

Studying collaborative processes

Rediscovering public prejudice

In principle, a collaborative cognition approach is quite compatible with most existing definitions of prejudice. However, as Stahl (2006, p. 5) noted, 'Whereas individual cognition is hidden in private mental processes, group cognition is necessarily publicly visible. This is because any ideas involved in a group interaction must be displayed in order for the members of the group to participate in the collaborative process.' Since it makes sense for a collaborative cognition approach to focus on public forms of prejudice, for the purposes of this chapter, we will be adopting Rupert Brown's (1995, p. 8) definition of prejudice as 'the holding of derogatory social attitudes or cognitive beliefs' and also 'the *expression* of negative affect, or the *display* of hostile or discriminatory behaviour towards members of a group on account of their membership of that group' (our emphasis).

This principled focus on public prejudice itself represents a departure from most current social psychological theory and research. Contemporary social psychologists are often inclined to assume that 'genuine' prejudice can be equated with an individual's private – often implicit – evaluations of social groups (see also Durrheim, Chapter 9, this volume). For example, Crandall and Eshleman (2003) describe 'genuine' prejudice as 'primary, primal, underlying, powerful, early-learned, automatic, cognitively simple, and relatively effortless' (p. 415). Accordingly, social psychologists are inclined to view public expressions of intergroup attitudes as – in Crandall and Eshleman's terms – 'inauthentic prejudice' (or, more properly, inauthentic tolerance). In contrast, it is interesting to note that earlier generations of social psychologists did not generally treat public attitudes as less genuine, or as less social psychologically important, than private attitudes. As Donald Katz and Floyd Allport (1931) argued:

The popular distinction between what [people] 'actually' think or feel and what they report when they attempt a rational or public accounting of attitudes is often misconceived. From a psychological as well as a logical standpoint, there is no justification for asserting that the attitude which [a person] reveals privately and confidentially ... is his *real* or *true* opinion, whereas the attitude which he expresses on the same subject to a professor or to an audience is a pure fiction significant only as an evasion or as a means of securing popularity ... [S]ince much of human behavior is social, and so many of the situations in which we find ourselves are public or institutional in character, we shall miss a great deal that is important in understanding both the social order and the part which the individual plays in it if we do not consider ... 'public' as well as ... 'private' attitudes. (Katz and Allport (1931, pp. ix–x))

In considering the ways in which prejudice can be occasioned, displayed and suppressed collaboratively in the course of situated social interaction, one of our aims is to reinstate public prejudice as a legitimate object for social psychological enquiry in its own right.

Beyond the laboratory: prejudice in the wild

The processes by which cognitive processes may operate through complex dynamical social systems may be studied using computational modelling (e.g. Goldstone and Janssen, 2005; Smith and Collins, 2009). However, as Stahl (2006) noted, it is perfectly possible to observe collaborative cognition in action. Consequently, studies of collaborative and distributed cognition generally use qualitative, observational methods, involving some form of interaction analysis (Jordan and Henderson, 1995), including techniques drawn from conversation analysis.[5]

Work on collaborative and distributed cognition generally emphasizes the situated character of human thought and reasoning. Consequently, researchers typically question the wisdom of assuming that 'basic' research can be adequately conducted in laboratory contexts (Resnik, 1991; cf. Tajfel, 1972), and stress the necessity of studying cognitive processes as they are manifested 'in the wild' (Hutchins, 1995). Applied to the issue of prejudice, this kind of perspective calls for a measure of methodological innovation. As we have noted, social psychologists have used an enormous variety of methods to interrogate the prejudice problematic. However, they have not generally been disposed to study prejudice 'in the wild'.[6] Apart from La Piere's (1928) comparative analysis of race prejudice in France and England, and Minard's (1952) rather better remembered analysis of race relations in West Virginian mining communities, social psychologists have generally been disinclined to analyse prejudice as it is manifested in ordinary social life.[7]

For the purposes of this chapter, we will be considering forms of public prejudice that, while not entirely wild, were at least born and reared in semi-captivity. Specifically, our data generally come from informal research encounters, in which the participants are aware of the presence of the researcher, and of the recording device, but have not been specifically prompted to produce reports of their attitudes towards particular outgroups. In these settings, claims to, or displays of, racial, ethnic or national antipathy are typically produced by the respondents as a form of side-play. In all of these cases, the research is taking place on the respondents' 'home turf', and the recorded interactions are taking place between individuals who (apart from the researcher) have an established relationship with each other. The informality of the conversations is marked by jocularity, profanity and sub-standard speech (cf. Goffman, 1959, p. 128).

Collaboration in action

To the extent that social psychologists have been concerned to study the expression of prejudice in social encounters, they have generally been inclined to focus on the ways in which a particular individual may moderate his or her expression of prejudiced thoughts and sentiments in public settings. A consideration of the ways in which people actually express views concerning racial, ethnic or national outgroups in relatively naturalistic conversational contexts suggests that this kind of focus may be, at best, partially, and, at worst, positively, misleading. When people are engaged in (relatively) informal conversations with friends, workmates and family, they are often less inclined to suppress, mitigate or justify expressions of prejudice than social psychologists have been wont to suppose. In these kinds of settings, copresent social actors rarely adopt the role of passive audience, but tend rather to actively engage in a multiparty conversation. In the following pages, we will draw attention to three particular ways in which the expression or suppression of prejudiced views may be collaboratively accomplished, which we will term *interactional scaffolding, joint construction* and *distributed inhibition*.

Interactional scaffolding I: entrainment

The concept of scaffolding was introduced to psychology by Bruner, to describe the ways in which an adult can support a child's acquisition of concepts or skills (Bruner, 1978; Wood *et al.*, 1976). More generally, the term refers to the processes by which one individual's acquisition of understanding or skills is supported by prompts and models provided by more experienced coactors.

The strip of conversation reported in extract (1) illustrates a case in which one individual is helped to produce a racist narrative by two of his friends. The context was an informal interview conducted over drinks in the respondent's ('local') public house. At the point at which this extract starts, Frank is extemporizing about his views on immigration and multi-culturalism, a topic which he had introduced in response to an earlier question about national identity.[8] Although the researcher's (R) questions are addressed directly to Frank, his friends Jim and Chris (who, unlike Frank, were both members of the far right British National Party) provide prompts and 'model answers', encouraging Frank to voice a particular form of racist account.

Extract (1)

1	FRANK	I don't mind the Indians, I think the Indians are quite all right,
2		actually. Because they fought in the war with us and everything.
3		So, got a bit of respect for the Indians. I don't like them all, but I got
4		respect for them, cos they fought in the war with us. But Pakis.
5	R	What's up with them?
6	FRANK	What's up with them? They fucking stink.
7	JIM	No. It's not that. It's just, they like, they hate us (.) an' all that.
8	FRANK	And they come and live in this country and they
9		say they hate =
10	CHRIS	They come to this country, and they say, 'Yeah, we hate,
11		we hate the English' and all that. Well, why do you wanna come
12		and live here? Why do they wanna sponge off us? Why, why should
13		I pay my taxes every week to give them some money out of my
14		taxes, so they can go and fucking open a Paki shop, on a corner?
15		And they're saying they hate the English.
16	FRANK	And at the end of the day we've made a home for them.
17		They've got a home, they've got a nice corner street [sic] and all that,
18		if they lived over in Pakistan, they'd mostly probably have nothing.
19		When we've treated them, I think we've treated them fair dos, all the
20		way through.
21	JIM	We civilized them.
22	FRANK	Well, we did. We civilized them didn't we? (.)
23	R	What, though, if, if they're born here, are they not English anyway?
24	CHRIS	No. Are they fuck.
25	FRANK	No, are they fuck.
26	R	Why not?
27	CHRIS	Get out.

The first thing to note about this stretch of talk is the presence of explicit expressions of ethnic hostility indicated, among other things, by the use of the recognizably pejorative term, *Paki*. In this case, the presence of an audience does not prime normative concerns to suppress displays of prejudice. On the contrary, at various points we see the speakers treating the expression of *positive* views of ethnic others as normatively accountable. Early in the extract Frank presents a relatively positive assessment of '*the Indians*' (lines 1–4), whom he positions as a model minority. Significantly, immediately after producing this utterance he attends to the possibility that his account might be interpreted as positively favourable towards '*the Indians*', and qualifies his original assessment with the disclaimer, '*I don't like them all, but* . . .' (line 3).[9] When the researcher asks whether people of Pakistani origin are English, the three men treat this question as provocative banter, to which '*are they fuck*' and '*get out*' are responses in kind.

The second thing to note is the way in which Jim and Chris actively support Frank's attempt to formulate a prejudiced narrative about people in England of Pakistani ethnic heritage. Frank's original response to the researcher's query '*What's up with them?*' (line 5) is dismissive and cursory ('*They fucking stink*', line 6). At this stage Jim intervenes to 'correct' Frank's account, and to prompt a preferable line of argument ('*they hate us*', line 7). Frank accepts this assistance, and takes the narrative forward by substituting Jim's generic '*an' all that*' (line 7) with the specific '*they come and live in this country*' (line 8). At this point Frank's account peters out. Chris then helps out by reinforcing Frank's offering, and then contributing the additional consideration that '*they . . . sponge off us*' (line 12) in order to run '*a Paki shop, on a corner*' (line 14). Frank again accepts the offering, adding the evaluative gloss, '*we've treated them fair dos*' (line 19). Jim finally offers an upgrade assessment ('*We civilized them*', line 21) which Frank then echoes.

Interactional scaffolding II: facilitation and reinforcement

In psychology, the scaffolding metaphor generally refers to situations in which more experienced people provide a supportive structure for another individual's development of conceptual skills and narrative reasoning. However, Clark (1997) has extended the notion of 'external scaffolding' to encompass a variety of situations in which an individual's cognitive work is supported by bodily functions (as is the case, for example, when we count on our fingers), objects and symbols (as is the case when we perform calculations using a paper and pencil) and by other people in the environment. Understood in this more general sense, we can see scaffolding at work in many mundane forms of social interaction. Work on the choreography of dialogic interaction has pointed to the ways in which any particular actor's behaviour will be contingent upon the responses of others. Even when an individual appears to be producing a monologue, in practice the occasioning, content and prosody of their talk will be shaped by other coactors, who afford a suitable conversational opening, permit them to retain the floor, and provide ongoing feedback through back-channel responses (Bavelas *et al.*, 2000) and postural and gaze coordination (Bavelas and Gerwing, 2007; Goodwin, 2000; Shockley *et al.*, 2009).

When we consider the form of prejudiced talk in actual social encounters, we can appreciate the role routinely played by copresent social actors in supporting and reinforcing the narrator's account. This is illustrated in extract (2), in which we see an exchange between a researcher and two couples, the Abbotts (Gwen and Larry, both in their 80s) and the Bishops (Pete and Sheila, both in their 70s). The researcher had initially approached the Abbotts and the Bishops as they were chatting over their garden fence, and requested their help for a study about 'people's attitudes to where they live'. The exchange reproduced below was occasioned by the researcher asking about how London (where they had lived previously) had 'changed':

Extract (2)

1 GA	I'm not – I'm not prejudiced, a- about [coloured] people
2 SB	[No, no]
3 R	Uhuh?
4 GA	But, when you've been living in a house, we lived in a house for
5	nearly fifty years, and you had neighbours, Pakistani neighbours
6 R	Uhuh?
7 GA	Frying all their stuff –
8 PB	What's wrong with the Pakis?
9 GA	No –
10 SB	No, [listen to her!]
11 GA	[Nothing wrong] with them
12 SB	Wait, wait, wait.
13 GA	They were very friendly
14 SB	Yes
15 R	[Uhuh?]
16 GA	[But], they weren't us.
17 R	Uhuh?
18 GA	You know what I mean, they're a different =
19 LA	They've got their own =
20 GA	= race.
21 LA	Yeah. They've got their own side, yeah.
22 GA	As I say, I'm not prejudiced against them, um –
23 PB	Yes you are!
24 GA	No I'm [not].
25 SB	[No] she's not actually.
26 PB	You're not allowed to shoot them any more, you realize that

```
27      don't you?
28      ((all laugh))
29 SB   [((laughing)) Shut up!]
30 GA   [((inaudible))] I gave my gun up!
31 SB   Can I take him away?
32      ((all laugh))
33 GA   I said I gave my gun up!
34 SB   Yes
35 LA   I'll tell you something –
36 GA   It's the same with people that are not even black people. [I've got a
37      grandchild who's married =]
38 LA   [We're the only ones to be married in a submarine.]
39 GA   = to a Jamaican boy.
40 R    ((to LA)) Really?
49 SB   We're not even married.
50 LA   During war time ((inaudible))
51 R    That's fantastic.
```

The conversation reported in extract (2) does not involve the kind of explicit collaboration between speakers evident in extract (1). Pete, Sheila and Larry do not prime Gwen with particular considerations, nor do they add anything substantive to her line of argument. However, once we consider the details of the exchange, we can appreciate how Gwen's Pakistani neighbours narrative is in fact being sustained and promoted through the effective support of others. The unfolding of the story is not simply contingent upon Gwen Abbott's own intentions and discursive efforts, but also upon the other participants who (in the case of the researcher) provide a suitable conversational opening, allow her to take and to retain the floor and provide reinforcement through markers of continued attention (from the researcher, until line 40), agreement (in the case of Sheila Bishop), cooperative completion and echoing (from her husband, Larry) and heckling banter (from Pete Bishop).[10]

Improvisation and joint construction

Up to this point, we have considered how in everyday social encounters displays of prejudice may represent the product of collaborative social interaction. However, we have not considered how the content of these accounts may represent an emergent product of social interaction. Extract (3) has been taken from an informal research conversation conducted on the beach with three young women aged between 15 and 16 (see Condor, 2006). The extract starts at the point when the researcher poses a question about their opinions concerning a current political policy issue.

Extract (3)

1	R	So wh – what do do you think about Scotland having their own
2		parliament?
3	CHLOE	What?
4	R	You know, eh Scottish people, they've recently got got their own
5		parliament uh and Wales have got an Assembly.
6	GEM	I hate the Welsh.
7		((laughter))
8	KATIE	Yeah. Sheep-shaggers.
9		((laughter))
10	CHLOE	They're not as as bad as the French though.
11	R	What's wrong with the French?
12	CHLOE	[I dunno]
13	KATIE	[They eat] horses.
14	GEM	An' frogs. An' they are frogs so that makes them cannibals.
15		((laughter))
16	CHLOE	Yeah. And the Chinese, they eat dogs [and stuff].
17	KATIE	[Yeah]
18		((laughter))
19	CHLOE	Sweet and sour Doberman.
20	GEM	Tastes like dog shit anyway.
21		((laughter))
22	KATIE	Yeah. They're terrible, the Chinkies.
23	GEM	Not as bad as the Pakis though. [I hate Pakis].
24	KATIE	[No. Yeah] They're the worst. Cos the
25		Chinkies they just stay in in their house and places, but the Pakis
26		they're everywhere you go fucking harassing you an' an' =
27	GEM	them fucking Pakis is well outa order.
28	KATIE	Perverts. An' they smell [an' all]
29	GEM	[An' they] smell an' all. Y'know that boy,
30		Naheed, I sat next to in maths. He smelt like piss an' that.
31		((laughter))
32	CHLOE	Poo vindaloo.
33		((laughter))
34	GEM	I dunno [I hate em all]
35	KATIE	[An' they got] little dicks.
36	GEM	Well you'd know you slag.
37		((laughter))

Once again, we can appreciate how the public character of this encounter does not apparently prime norms of tolerance. Gemma, Katie and Chloe openly advertise their hostile attitudes: '*I hate the Welsh*', '*I hate Pakis*', '*I hate them all*'. The respondents are clearly expending a good deal of effort in an attempt to trump each other's display of prejudice. This observation might lead us to question the assumption that expressions of prejudice reflect relatively 'automatic' responses, and it is only the suppression of prejudice that requires 'controlled' forms of behaviour.

This exchange also demonstrates how pejorative representations of others need not simply involve giving voice to pictures that pre-exist in the heads of the participants. There is a clear improvisational quality to this fast-paced banter, and the conversation displays the moment-to-moment contingency, whereby each actor's contribution sets a context for other participants' subsequent response. The eventual catalogue of ethnic and national stereotypes represents an emergent phenomenon in so far as it could not have been anticipated or formulated by any of the individual participants in isolation.

Distributed inhibition

Social psychologists commonly suggest that the act of suppressing, justifying or otherwise mitigating public expressions of prejudice is likely to be cognitively effortful. In recent years, social psychologists have paid a good deal of attention to the motivations for, and techniques used to accomplish, prejudice inhibition (Plant and Devine, 2009). To date, most of this work assumes that the motives and resource-intensive cognitive techniques required to inhibit explicit expressions of prejudice are necessarily located within the heads of discrete individuals.

In contrast, a collaborative cognition perspective would allow for the possibility that the work of prejudice inhibition, like other complex multistage cognitive processes, may be distributed between agents.[11] Clarke and Chalmers (1998) coined the term 'cognitive offloading' to refer to the process of devolving some aspects of a complex cognitive task to other people, symbols or objects. Once we move beyond the circumscribed universe of the psychological laboratory or formal research interview, we can begin to appreciate how the 'brakes' (cf. Allport, 1954) on public expressions of prejudice can be applied by people other than the primary speaker (see also Condor et al., 2006).

On occasions, individuals may rely on others to undertake some of the labour of 'self'-monitoring. In particular, we have often witnessed husbands offloading the task of monitoring their talk for (potential) public displays of prejudice onto their wives. In the following extract, for example, we see Sheila alert her husband to the fact that he is about to utter the taboo term, 'Paki':

Extract (4)

BARRY   It was just across the road from the Pak
SHEILA   BARRY
BARRY   corner shop.

In extract (4), Barry accepts his wife's assistance with the task of 'self'-monitoring, and self-corrects accordingly. In other cases of the social division of cognitive labour (cf. Lutz and Keil, 2002), we find the responsibility for 'modernizing' the expression of racism distributed between social interactants. In extract (5), Julie inhibits her mother's articulation of the term '*negro*' and substitutes '*Afro Caribbean*':

Extract (5)

DIANA   I'm appalled – appalled at *The Guardian*, the adverts in *The Guardian*.
        A team of something or other, to join a team, ethnic and so and so, and –
        I remember reading something about the lesbian and gay ones in – and
        the town hall ones, and then it has to be for the ne–
JULIE   Afro Caribbean
DIANA   Afro Caribbean and my friend's boss had to be sacked because he wasn't
        willing to go along with the trend.

In extract (6), similarly, we see Alan's teenage children attempt to inhibit his expression of prejudice by changing the subject and, when this fails, open admonishment:

Extract (6)

ALAN   And this country's too small, we can't cope. And as a country I mean
        there are these people coming in and saying um 'we've just come from
        Pakistan and we've taken up er residence here, we insist the government
        start an Urdhu school' or whatever
ELLIE   Have you seen what they've done to the old High School, Dad?
BEN   They've made it into flats.
ELLIE   Yeah.
ALAN   And what I ask myself is why are they here? Because you know the rule is
        they are meant to claim asylum in the first safe country they come to. And
        they have to pass through other countries to get here. So why aren't they in
        France, saying, 'we don't' –
BEN   – you and Mum thought of moving to France once, didn't you Dad?
ELLIE   Why didn't you? It would have been great with all that wine and sunshine
        and we could of –
ALAN   The reason they're not in France is because the French won't put up with
        this. They say that if you're living in France you have to like accept the way
        of life. You can't just come in and start –
ELLIE   – give it a rest, Dad.

Concluding comments

Social psychologists are apt to regard vagueness in terminology or conceptualization as an impediment to scientific progress. In contrast, we have suggested that the fact that prejudice has been, and remains, a vague construct has enabled social psychological research to capitalize on general innovations taking place in psychological science. In this chapter, we have attempted to continue in this tradition, by taking advantage of some contemporary developments in cognitive science. The construct of collaborative cognition draws attention to the self-evident fact that in everyday life neither thinking nor speaking are typically solitary activities. The tendency on the part of social psychologists to trace prejudice to cognitions, emotions or actions of discrete individuals has distracted our attention from the ways in which pejorative representations of social outgroups may be collaboratively formulated, mobilized or inhibited.

A concern over the ways in which public displays of prejudice unfold over the course of social interaction has allowed us to rethink some aspects of the conventional social psychological wisdom concerning the nature of prejudice. First, a consideration of prejudice 'in the wild' demonstrates the current persistence of blatant displays of ethnic, racial or national antipathy (see also Pehrson and Leach, Chapter 6, this volume), and leads us to question Sears's (2005, p. 351) assessment of explicit forms of racism as now 'nearly non-existent'. Second, this work has led us to question the common presumption that individuals are generally inclined to moderate the views that they voice in the presence of others. In cases in which social actors are familiar and comfortable with the other people present, an individual's expression of both subtle and blatant prejudiced views may in fact be prompted and facilitated by others, through coaching, reinforcement or merely tacit permission.

Third, we questioned the common assumption that public expressions of prejudice represent the (possibly censored) articulation of sentiments and images that pre-exist in the minds of the individual speakers. We showed how public prejudice can constitute an emergent product of social interaction.

Finally, on a more positive note, the capacity to inhibit public expressions of prejudice need not, in practice, be limited by an individual's motivations or executive function. When prejudiced talk emerges in everyday social encounters, a dual-braking system can operate, with the responsibility for 'self'-monitoring and correction becoming effectively distributed between participating social actors.

Notes

1. In addition, the enduring appeal of the construct also undoubtedly stems from the fact that prejudice has typically been regarded as a psychological defect and/or pressing social problem (cf. Krueger and Funder, 2004), meaning that researchers can readily justify an interest in the topic through forms of utility accounting (cf. Potter and Mulkay, 1982).

2. The former perspective (which emphasizes the uniqueness of the individual) corresponds to Simmel's (1917) construct of 'Germanic' individualism, whereas the latter (which considers individuals to be exemplars of a general human type) corresponds with Simmel's notion of 'romantic' individualism.

3. We are using the term 'social identity theory' to refer both to intergroup theory and to self-categorization perspectives.

4. It is common for social psychologists to treat rhetorical perspectives as compatible with Bakhtinian dialogic approaches to communication (e.g. Billig, 1987). However, in so far as Bakhtin focused on dialogue as communicative interaction, his work in fact challenged individualistic rhetorical approaches (Kent, 1998).

5. These 'noncognitivist' perspectives in cognitive science, which '[avoid] speculating on psychological processes hidden in the heads of individuals and instead looks to empirical observable group processes of interaction and discourse' (Stahl, 2006, p. 5), have evident parallels with the kind of approach advocated by discursive psychologists (e.g. Edwards and Potter, 2005).

6. Even research on the formation and maintenance of stereotypes in conversation has tended to be conducted in laboratory rather than naturalistic conversational contexts (e.g. Karasawa *et al.*, 2007; Kashima, 2000; cf. Ruscher, 1998, 2001; Semin, 2007).

7. Apart from matters of habit and pragmatics (it is, after all, relatively cheap and easy to conduct research on a captive subject-pool of university undergraduates) there are good reasons why social psychologists may have shied away from studying prejudice 'in the wild'. Most ethnographic accounts are rather anecdotal for empirical social psychological tastes, and contemporary field research on 'everyday' racism (e.g. Eliasoph, 1999) has not collected the kind of audio or video recordings that would afford detailed analyses of the precise content, and dynamics, of prejudiced talk in interaction.

8. All names in the extracts are pseudonyms.

9. This extract also exemplifies how symbolic racist arguments are not always employed as a 'subtle' form of prejudice. Most of the arguments against Pakistanis proffered by Chris, Jim and Frank focus on 'their' failure to comply with 'our rules', and 'their' tendency to take advantage of the 'fair' treatment that they have received. However, in this case the speakers are clearly using these symbolic racist arguments to work up their collective display of hostility towards Pakistanis, rather than to disguise or to sanitize their own negative attitudes.

10. This exchange was promoted by what the research team termed a 'trigger question', designed to afford a conversational opening for talk about race and ethnicity. On the basis of pilot work we had learned that white people who had moved from urban to rural areas often had 'white flight' explanations available, but could be reluctant to voice these in response to direct questions. The researcher's question about how London has changed was strategically designed to provoke precisely the kind of talk that followed.

11. The networks across which complex cognitive operations are distributed are typically hybrid in form, including both human actors and nonhuman agents, including symbols and technologies (Latour, 1993; see Condor, 1996). For the purposes of this chapter, however, we will confine our attention to the distribution of the task of prejudice suppression between interacting human subjects.

References

Adams, G., Edkins, V., Lacka, D., Pickett, K. and Cheryn, S. (2008). Teaching about racism: pernicious implications of the standard portrayal. *Basic and Applied Psychology*, **30**, 349–61.

Allport, G. (1954). *The Nature of Prejudice*. Reading, MA: Addison.

Asch, S. (1952). *Social Psychology*. Englewood Cliffs, NJ: Prentice-Hall.

Augoustinos, M. and Every, D. (2007). The language of 'race' and prejudice. *Journal of Language and Social Psychology*, **26**, 123–41.

Bavelas, J. and Gerwing, J. (2007). Conversational hand gestures and facial displays in face to face dialogue. In K. Fieldler (ed.), *Social Communication* (Ch. 10). New York: Psychology Press.

Bavelas, J., Coates, J. and Johnson, T. (2000). Listeners as co-narrators. *Journal of Personality and Social Psychology*, **79**, 941–52.

Billig, M. (1987). *Arguing and Thinking*. Cambridge, UK: Cambridge University Press.

(1988). The notion of prejudice: some rhetorical and ideological aspects. *Text*, **8**, 91–110.

(1990). Rhetoric of social psychology. In I. Parker and J. Shotter (eds.), *Deconstructing Social Psychology* (Ch. 3). London: Routledge.

Borgida, E. and Fiske, S. (2008). *Beyond Common Sense*. Oxford, UK: Blackwell.

Brown, R. (1995). *Prejudice: Its Social Psychology*. Oxford, UK: Blackwell.

Brown, W. O. (1933). Rationalization of race prejudice. *International Journal of Ethics*, **43**, 294–306.

Bruner, J. S. (1978). The role of dialogue in language acquisition. In A. Sinclair, R. Jarvella and W. Levelt (eds.), *The Child's Conception of Language*. New York: Springer-Verlag.

Clark, A. (1997). *Being There: Putting Brain, Body and World Together Again*. Cambridge, MA: MIT Press.

Clark, A. and Chalmers, D. (1998). The extended mind. *Analysis*, **58**, 10–23.

Condor, S. (1990). Social stereotypes and social identity. In D. Abrams and M. Hogg (eds.), *Social Identity Theory* (pp.230–48). London: Harvester Wheatsheaf.

(1996). Social identity and time. In P. Robinson (ed.), *Social Groups and Identities: Developing the Legacy of Henri Tajfel* (pp.285–315). Oxford, UK: Butterworth Heinemann.

(2006). Public prejudice as collaborative accomplishment: towards a dialogic social psychology of racism. *Journal of Community and Applied Social Psychology*, **6**, 1–18.

Condor, S., Figgou, L., Abell, J., Gibson, S. and Stevenson, C. (2006). 'They're not racist …' Prejudice denial, mitigation and suppression in dialogue. *British Journal of Social Psychology*, **44**, 441–62.

Crandall, C. and Eshleman, A. (2003). A justification-suppression model of the expression and experience of prejudice. *Psychological Bulletin*, **129**, 414–46.

Cuddy, A., Fiske, S. and Glick, P. (2007). The BIAS map: behaviors from intergroup affect and stereotypes. *Journal of Personality and Social Psychology*, **92**, 631–48.

Danziger, K. (1997). *Naming the Mind: How Psychology Found its Language*. London: Sage.

Dovidio, J. (2001). On the nature of contemporary prejudice: the third wave. *Journal of Social Issues*, 57, 829–49.

Dovidio, J. and Gaertner, S. (1986). Prejudice, discrimination and racism: historical trends and contemporary approaches. In J. Dovidio and S. Gaertner (eds.), *Prejudice, Discrimination and Racism* (pp.1–34). Orlando, FL: Academic Press.

Duckitt, J. (1992). Psychology and prejudice: a historical analysis and integrative framework. *American Psychologist*, 47, 1,182–93.

Duckitt, J. and Sibley, C. (2009). A dual-process motivational model of ideology, politics, and prejudice. *Psychological Inquiry*, 20(Apr), 98–109.

Edwards, D. and Potter, J. (2005). Discursive psychology, mental states and descriptions. In H. te Molder and J. Potter (eds.), *Conversation and Cognition* (pp.241–59). Cambridge, UK: Cambridge University Press.

Ekehammar, B., Akrami, N. and Yang-Wallentin, F. (2009). Ethnic prejudice: a combined personality and social psychology model. *Individual Differences Research*, 7, 255–64.

Eliasoph, N. (1999). 'Everyday racism' in a culture of political avoidance: civil society, speech, and taboo. *Social Problems*, 46, 479–502.

Figgou, L. and Condor, S. (2006). Irrational categorization, natural intolerance and reasonable discrimination: lay representations of prejudice and racism. *British Journal of Social Psychology*, 44, 1–29.

Gaertner, S. and Dovidio, J. (2005). Understanding and addressing contemporary racism: from aversive racism to the common ingroup identity model. *Journal of Social Issues*, 61, 615–39.

Galison, P. (1999). Trading zone: coordinating action and belief. In M. Biagioli (ed.), *The Science Studies Reader*. London: Routledge.

Gawronski, B., Peters, K., Brochu, P. and Strack, F. (2008). Understanding the relations between different forms of racial prejudice. *Personality and Social Psychology Bulletin*, 34, 648–65.

Goffman, E. (1959). *The Presentation of Self in Everyday Life*. New York: Doubleday.

Goldstone, R. and Janssen, M. (2005). Computational models of collective behavior. *Trends in Cognitive Sciences*, 9, 424–30.

Goodwin, C. (2000). Action and embodiment within situated human interaction. *Journal of Pragmatics*, 32, 1,489–522.

Gureckis, T. and Goldstone, R. (2006). Thinking in groups. *Pragmatics and Cognition*, 14, 293–311.

Haslam, S. A. and Wilson, A. (2000). In what sense are prejudicial beliefs personal? The importance of an in-group's shared stereotypes. *British Journal of Social Psychology*, 39, 45–63.

Haslam, S. A., Oakes, P., Reynolds, K. and Turner, J. (1999). Social identity salience and the emergence of stereotype consensus. *Personality and Social Psychology Bulletin*, 25, 809–18.

Henriques, J. (1984). Social psychology and the politics of racism. In J. Henriques, W. Hollway, C. Urwin, C. Venn and V. Walkerdine (eds.), *Changing the Subject: Psychology, Social Regulation and Subjectivity* (pp.60–89). London: Methuen.

Hodson, G. and Esses, V. (2005). Lay perceptions of ethnic prejudice. *European Journal of Social Psychology*, **35**, 329–44.

Hornsey, M. and Hogg, M. (2000). Subgroup relations: a comparison of mutual intergroup differentiation and common ingroup identity models of prejudice reduction. *Personality and Social Psychology Bulletin*, **26**, 242–56.

Hutchins, E. (1995). *Cognition in the Wild*. Cambridge, MA: MIT Press.

Ibanez, A., Haye, A., González, R., Hurtado, E. and Henríquez, R. (2009). Multilevel analysis of cultural phenomena. *Journal for the Theory of Social Behaviour*, **39**, 81–110.

Jordan, B. and Henderson, A. (1995). Interaction analysis. *Journal of the Learning Sciences*, **4**, 39–103.

Karasawa, M., Asai, N. and Tanabe, Y. (2007). Stereotypes as shared beliefs. *Group Processes and Intergroup Relations*, **10**, 515–32.

Kashima, Y. (2000). Maintaining cultural stereotypes in the serial reproduction of narratives. *Personality and Social Psychology Bulletin*, **26**, 594–604.

Katz, D. and Allport, F. (1931). *Students' Attitudes: a Report of the Syracuse University Reaction Study*. Syracuse, NY: Craftsman Press.

Kent, T. (1998). Hermeneutics and genre: Bakhtin and the problem of communicative interaction. In F. Framer (ed.), *Landmark Essays on Bakhtin, Rhetoric, and Writing* (pp.33–49). Mahwah, NJ: Hermagoras-Erlbaum.

Krueger, J. and Funder, D. (2004). Towards a balanced social psychology. *Behavioral and Brain Sciences*, **27**, 313–27.

LaPiere, R. (1928). Race prejudice: France and England. *Social Forces*, **7**, 102–11.

Latour, B. (1993). *We have Never been Modern*. London: Longman.

Lippmann, W. (1922). *Public Opinion*. New York: Free Press.

Lowy, I. (1992). The strength of loose concepts. *History of Science*, **30**, 371–96.

Lutz, D. and Keil, F. (2002). Early understanding of the division of cognitive labor. *Child Development*, **73**, 1,073–84.

Minard, R. (1952). Race relationships in the Pocahontas coal field. *Journal of Social Issues*, **8**, 29–44.

Morse, J. (1907). The psychology of prejudice. *International Journal of Ethics*, **17**, 490–506.

Nail, P., Harton, H. and Barnes, A. (2008). A test of Dovidio and Gaertner's integrated model of racism. *North American Journal of Psychology*, **10**, 197–220.

Nail, P., Harton, H. and Decker, B. (2003). Political orientation and modern versus aversive racism. *Journal of Personality and Social Psychology*, **84**, 754–70.

Newman, L. S. (2009). Was Walter Lippmann interested in stereotyping? Public opinion and cognitive social psychology. *History of Psychology*, **12**, 7–18.

Pawlik, K. and d'Ydewalle, G. (eds.) (2006). *Psychological Concepts*. New York: Psychology Press.

Plant, E. and Devine, P. (2009). The active control of prejudice: unpacking the intentions guiding control efforts. *Journal of Personality and Social Psychology*, **96**, 640–52.

Potter, J. and Mulkay, M. (1982). Making theory useful: utility accounting in social psychologists' discourse. *Fundamenta Scientiae*, **4**, 259–78.

Reisigl, M. and Wodak, R. (2001). *Discourse and Discrimination*. London: Routledge.

Resnick, L. B., Levine, J. M. and Teasley, S. D. (eds.) (1991). *Perspectives on Socially Shared Cognition*. Washington, DC: American Psychological Association.

Reynolds, K. and Turner, J. (2006). Individuality and the prejudiced personality. *European Review of Social Psychology*, **17**, 233–70.

Reynolds, K., Turner, J., Haslam, S. A. and Ryan, M. (2001). The role of personality and group factors in explaining prejudice. *Journal of Experimental Social Psychology*, **37**, 427–34.

Robbins, P. and Aydede, M. (2009). A short primer on situated cognition. In P. Robbins and M. Aydede (eds.), *The Cambridge Handbook of Situated Cognition*. Cambridge, UK: Cambridge University Press.

Rogoff, B., Topping, K., Baker-Sennett, J. and Lacasa, P. (2002). Mutual contributions of individuals, partners, and institutions: planning to remember in Girl Scout cookie sales. *Social Development*, **11**, 266–89.

Ruscher, J. B. (1998). Prejudice and stereotyping in everyday communication. *Advances in Experimental Social Psychology*, **30**, 241–307.

(2001). *Prejudiced Communication*. New York: Guilford Press.

Sears, D. (2005). Inner conflict in the political psychology of racism. In J. Dovidio, P. Glick and L. Rudman (eds.), *On the Nature of Prejudice* (pp.343–58). New York: Blackwell.

Semin, G. R. (2007). Stereotypes in the wild. In Y. Kashima, K. Fiedler and P. Freytag (eds.), *Stereotype Dynamics: Language-based Approaches to Stereotype Formation, Maintenance, and Transformation* (pp.11–28). Mahwah, NJ: Lawrence Erlbaum.

Semin, G. R. and Cacioppo, J. T. (2008). Grounding social cognition: synchronization, entrainment, and coordination. In G. R. Semin and E. R. Smith (eds.), *Embodied Grounding: Social, Cognitive, Affective, and Neuroscientific Approaches* (pp.119–47). New York: Cambridge University Press.

Shapin, S. (2001). Proverbial economies. *Social Studies of Science*, **31**, 731–69.

Shockley, K., Richardson, D. and Dale, R. (2009). Conversation and coordinative structures. *Topics in Cognitive Science*, **1**, 305–19.

Simmel, G. (1917). Individualismus. In G. Simmel (ed.), *Gesamtausgabe*. Frankfurt am Main, Germany: Suhrkamp.

Smith, E. (2008). Social relationships and groups: new insights on embodied and distributed cognition. *Cognitive Systems Research*, **9**, 24–32.

Smith, E. and Collins, E. (2009). Contextualizing person perception: distributed social cognition. *Psychological Review*, **116**, 343–64.

Son Hing, L. S., Chung-Yan, G. A., Hamilton, L. K. and Zanna, M. P. (2008). A two-dimensional model that employs explicit and implicit attitudes to characterize prejudice. *Journal of Personality and Social Psychology*, **94**, 971–87.

Stahl, G. (2006). *Group Cognition*. Cambridge, MA: MIT Press.

Stangor, C. (2009). The study of stereotyping, prejudice and discrimination within social psychology. In T. Nelson (ed.), *Handbook of Prejudice, Stereotyping and Discrimination* (Ch. 1). New York: Psychology Press.

Suchman, L. (1987). *Plans and Situated Actions*. Cambridge, UK: Cambridge University Press.

Tajfel, H. (1972). Experiments in a vacuum. In J. Israel and H. Tajfel (eds.), *The Context of Social Psychology* (pp.69–121). London: Academic Press.

Turner, J. (1987). A self-categorization theory. In J. Turner, M. Hogg, P. Oakes, S. Reicher and M. Wetherell (eds.), *Rediscovering the Social Group*. Oxford, UK: Blackwell.

Turner, J. C. and Oakes, P. (1986). The significance of the social identity concept for social psychology with reference to individualism, interactionism and social influence. *British Journal of Social Psychology*, **25**, 237–52.

Weber, M. (1981 [1913]). Essay on some categories of interpretative sociology. *Sociological Quarterly*, **56**, 145–80.

Wetherell, M. and Potter, J. (1992). *Mapping the Language of Racism*. London: Sage.

Wood, D., Bruner, J. and Ross, G. (1976). The role of tutoring in problem-solving. *Journal of Child Psychology and Psychiatry*, **17**, 89–100.

Part II

Prejudice and social change revisited

11 Models of social change in social psychology: collective action or prejudice reduction? Conflict or harmony?

Stephen C. Wright and Gamze Baray[1]

How could it be that creating more liking between members of different groups could be a bad thing? Only a bigot or a reactionary would question the value of intergroup harmony and encourage a positive view of intergroup conflict. Not too many years ago, no sensible social psychologists would propose that there could be too much concern about prejudice reduction. Social psychology has dedicated thousands of research articles to understanding the nature, the causes, the consequences and, of course, the reduction of prejudice (see Dovidio *et al.*, 2010; Paluck and Green, 2009 for reviews). Underlying virtually all of this work is the assumption that reducing stereotyping and prejudice is essential to improving intergroup relations; that negative attitudes are at the heart of intergroup inequality; and that social justice is inextricably tied to strengthening intergroup harmony. Yet, there appears to be a growing number of us who have begun to question this 'full speed ahead on prejudice reduction' approach.

Nearly a decade ago, one of us (Wright, 2001, p. 415) proposed, although quite briefly, the possibility that although the strategies that effectively reduce prejudice might have very positive effects on members of the advantaged group,

from the perspective of disadvantaged groups, the same mechanism that serves to reduce the problems associated with advantaged group prejudice also weaken the impetus for members of the disadvantaged group to take collective action designed to reduce existing intergroup inequalities. *Cross-cutting categorization* effects (e.g., Brown and Turner, 1979), *superordinate goals* (e.g., Sherif, 1967), *intergroup contact* effects (e.g., Pettigrew, 1998), and many other strategies improve intergroup attitudes in part by changing the degree of differentiation between the groups and, thus, each of these might also reduce collective action by disadvantaged group members.

This idea sprung from the recognition that there had been little conversation between the literature on prejudice and the literature on collective action and social change. However, there are a number of inklings in the literature that have set the stage for a number of us (e.g. Dixon *et al.*, 2007) to consider the limits of prejudice reduction as the sole, or even the most promising, route to meaningful social change.

A number of theoretical perspectives have pointed out that low status groups are seldom uniformly devalued and that positive characterizations of, and warm feelings towards, the outgroup can coexist with high levels of intergroup inequality. Some have gone so far as to describe positive regard as a useful tool for maintaining inequality (e.g. Jackman, 1994). Yet, the usual response to the revelations that disadvantaged groups can be described in subjectively positive terms, and can even be loved and cared for, has been to modify the definition of prejudice. So, prejudice can be 'ambivalent', or it need not involve antipathy at all. While this broadening of the meaning of prejudice has been useful in developing a clearer understanding of how inequality is maintained, it has done little to dampen the discipline's enthusiasm for creating positive outgroup characterizations and cross-group liking as the best way to combat social inequality. It seems to us that perhaps the time has come to wonder openly about whether prejudice is really at the heart of the problem at all.

Certainly, antipathy, hostility and active denigration of the other must be dealt with if we are to maintain liveable multi-group societies. It would simply be foolish to suggest otherwise. Thus, our claim is not that prejudice reduction is unnecessary or irrelevant, but rather that a unitary focus on the promotion of positive attitudes and intergroup liking has obscured considerations of what may be more critical features of intergroup inequality such as structural inequalities and associated differences in power and privilege. This focus has also led to near unquestioned support for integration and contact and a stark aversion to segregation. Finally, the focus on cross-group liking and 'getting along' has led to an exaggerated veneration of intergroup harmony and a corresponding exaggerated vilification of intergroup conflict. What we propose is that successful social change emerges out of a balance of harmony and conflict, segregation and contact, and antipathy and positive regard.

The concerns with the emphasis on prejudice reduction become more apparent when this approach is contrasted with an alternative strategy for creating change. There is a smaller, but no less vibrant, social psychological literature that considers the psychology of collective action and social movement participation. This research tradition considers, among other things, the question of why members sometimes will act on behalf of their group in efforts to improve the ingroup's status and treatment (Wright, 2001, 2010). This literature has described the value of these actions in altering the normative understanding of the intergroup inequalities (from legitimate to illegitimate) and in forcing advantaged groups to relinquish some of their power or to improve the treatment of the disadvantaged group. The point is, social change can be facilitated by direct confrontation by those who are disadvantaged.

Thus, the literatures on prejudice reduction and collective action both consider efforts to strengthen social justice and reduce inequality, and both are psychological, in that they consider the motives, thoughts, feelings and actions of individuals. However, these two literatures have for the most part developed in isolation from each other. There are at least three key divergences between the two approaches that may account for their lack of connection: the focus on harmony versus conflict; the focus of the advantaged versus disadvantaged groups; and the focus on psychological versus structural change. In this chapter, we explore these divergences.

Can there be too much harmony?

Prejudice reduction has been very clearly connected to the broader goal of promoting *intergroup harmony* and *social cohesion*. In fact, in this literature *intergroup harmony* and *positive intergroup relations* have often been used synonymously, as have the terms *intergroup conflict* and *negative intergroup relations*. From this perspective, conflict between groups should be prevented, avoided and halted quickly when it does occur, and harmony should be vigorously pursued and nurtured when it occurs. However, when we consider intergroup relations from the perspective of collective action, this harmony/good and conflict/bad dichotomy becomes clearly problematic. A collective action perspective concerns itself with *equality across groups*, not harmony, and focuses on *social justice*, not social cohesion. From a collective action perspective, conflict is essential. It is through conflict that inequalities and injustices are exposed, challenged and perhaps reduced. Tajfel and Turner (1979) described collective action as 'social competition', directly implicating conflict between groups over social status. Rather than avoided, conflict is to be embraced, nurtured and sustained.

In fact, intergroup harmony can be orthogonal to intergroup equality. In a model describing how the content and valence of group stereotypes can combine to produce different patterns of intergroup relations, Taylor and Moghaddam (1994) describe two very different types of intergroup harmony. The first is the positive kind of harmony most often envisioned. Here there is consensus between the groups about the content of group stereotypes – that is, Group A believes that Group B has a set of attributes and Group B agrees that these are their attributes. Simultaneously, there is the same consensus about the attributes of Group A. Harmony arises from this shared consensus, and arrangement is positive because both groups also value the attributes of the outgroup. Thus, the two groups hold similar status positions within the intergroup context. There is a shared vision of group differences and both groups are accorded admirable attributes – agreement, positive valence, harmony and equality.

However, there is a second kind of harmony: one based on legitimized intergroup inequality. Again, there is agreement between the groups about both the content and the evaluation of each group's attributes. However, the consensus is that the attributes of one group – the dominant group – are positively valued, and the attributes of the other – the subordinate group – are not. The result, a consensual relationship of dominance and subordination that is legitimized by agreement about the superiority of one group's attributes. This kind of legitimization of an unequal system is reflected in other theoretical approaches like system-justification (Jost *et al.*, 2004). In this case, the harmony that emerges serves the dominant group very well, and they should actively promote the consensual representations of the two groups. As long as the consensus remains, so too does their enviable position in a stable harmonious group hierarchy.

A full elaboration of harmony's shortcomings and the benefits of conflict is not possible here, but it appears that work in intergroup relations might benefit from an examination of the organizational psychology literature (see, for example, De Dreu, 2011), which has moved beyond the unitary view of conflict as entirely negative, has vigorously explored the benefits of conflict and has focused on conflict management and change through conflict resolution. The result is an evolving understanding of when, why and how conflict can produce beneficial outcomes for the broader organization and for the conflict participants. We suggest that the intergroup relations literature might benefit from the adoption of a similar agenda, considering the productive as well as destructive outcomes of intergroup conflict.

Prejudice reduction or collective action? Focusing on different targets

Work on collective action and prejudice reduction have, for the most part, focused on different target groups. Certainly, advantaged group members engage in reactionary collective action to protect their privilege and stabilize their high-status position (e.g. Simon and Klandermans, 2001), and some members of privileged groups will, at times, break from their collective self-interest and act on behalf of the disadvantaged group (see Iyer and Leach, 2010). However, for the most part, the psychological analyses of collective action have focused on those with the most to gain from social change – the disadvantaged groups.

In contrast, although most theories of prejudice recognize that members of all groups can (and do) harbour negative views of other groups, prejudice reduction has primarily been a project directed at advantaged group members (see Pettigrew and Tropp, 2006; Reicher, 2007). This is not surprising, as focusing on the attitudes of those who have the power to turn prejudice into discrimination makes tremendous sense. However, although prejudice reduction has primarily been about 'fixing' the advantaged group, many strategies require the direct participation of disadvantaged group members. The clearest example of this is social psychology's most prominent perspective on prejudice reduction – *contact theory* (Allport, 1954). Emerging from an initial assumption that negative intergroup attitudes stem from unfamiliarity and ignorance, contact theory posits that interpersonal contact between members of different groups, under specified conditions, can reduce prejudice. Over the last fifty-five years, a great deal of research and theorizing has examined the conditions under which contact is most effective, and the numerous processes underlying the attitude change that results from interpersonal cross-group interactions (see Brown and Hewstone, 2005; Pettigrew and Tropp, 2006; Wright, 2009).

At first glance, it may seem unproblematic that prejudice reduction efforts require the active participation of disadvantaged group members. Why not improve the thoughts and feelings of both groups simultaneously? However, when one contrasts the underlying psychological processes thought to be the catalyst for prejudice reduction with those thought to be essential for collective action participation, one finds some glaring and fundamental contradictions, as captured in Figure 11.1 (see Wright and Lubensky, 2009).

Comparing the psychology of prejudice reduction and collective action

Prejudice reduction	Collective action
➢ **Low** salience of category membership	➢ **High** salience of category membership
➢ **Weak** collective identification	➢ **Strong** collective identification
➢ **Low** salience of group-based inequality	➢ **High** salience of group-based inequality
➢ Perceive group boundaries to be **permeable**	➢ Perceive group boundaries to be **impermeable**
➢ Generally **positive** characterizations of the outgroup	➢ Generally **negative** characterizations of the outgroup

Figure 11.1: Two models of social change

Contradictory psychologies for the disadvantaged

Category salience and ingroup identification. Two critical psychological requirements of collective action participation are high salience of, and strong identification with, one's ingroup (e.g. Simon and Klandermans, 2001). In order to act on behalf of the ingroup, one must be keenly aware of one's membership in that group, and that membership must be a meaningful part of one's identity. The importance of identification for collective action participation is nicely summarized by Doosje and Ellemers (1997): '"die-hard" members are more predisposed to act in terms of the group, and make sacrifices for it, than are "fair-weather" members' (p. 358). Conversely, many models of prejudice reduction strongly advocate for the need to reduce the salience of collective identity. Participants in prejudice reduction efforts should be focused on the similarities across groups, or should strengthen their identification with a larger superordinate category that blurs the distinction between 'us' and 'them'.

Admittedly, Brown and Hewstone's (2005) model of intergroup contact, and Wright and colleagues' inclusion of other in the self model (e.g. Wright *et al.*, 2005), call for maintaining some salience of group memberships during cross-group contact. However, even in these models, maintaining the salience of collective identity is primarily concerned with maintaining the salience of the other's (the interaction partner's) collective identity as a means of ensuring that the positive feelings generated towards that individual will generalize to the group as a whole. The intention is not that contact participants should be focusing on their own collective identity in an effort to bolster their feelings of connection and commitment to their ingroup. Rather, both of these models propose that high salience of the other's collective identity is needed in order to strengthen one's positive feelings towards the outgroup.

Thus, effective prejudice reduction is thought to benefit from a reduction in the degree to which individuals focus on their connection and commitment to their ingroup, while collective action relies on high ingroup identification and group salience. Thus, immersion of disadvantaged group members in prejudice reduction contexts should directly impede the development and maintenance of a critical determinant of the collective action participation.

Status inequality. Collective action emerges in response to perceived inequality in the status or treatment of the ingroup. Members of the disadvantaged group compare their collective condition to that of the outgroup, and find it lacking. Of course, it is possible that group members may subsequently justify their current low status or see little chance that the situation can change, and thus decide against collective action (e.g. Jost et al., 2004; Tajfel and Turner, 1979; Wright, 2001). However, recognition of the group-based inequality is an essential first step on the road to collective action.

Conversely, prejudice reduction approaches, and contact theory specifically, call for reductions in the salience of group status differences. Astutely realizing that existing group status difference would influence social interaction in ways that would confirm rather than alter existing negative stereotypes, Allport's (1954) original formulation of contact theory described *equal status* interactions as critical to prejudice reduction, and structuring contact situations to temporarily erase group status differences has been a cornerstone of contact interventions (e.g. the jigsaw classroom; Aronson and Patnoe, 1997).

Again, the psychology of collective action stands in clear contrast to the preferred psychology of prejudice reduction – one requiring high salience of intergroup inequalities and the other advocating a perception of equal status.

Boundary (im)permeability. Another critical psychological prerequisite of collective action is a perception that the boundary between the disadvantaged ingroup and the advantaged outgroup is impermeable, preventing individual movement from one's disadvantaged position to a more enviable position in the advantaged group. In other words, collective action occurs when upward individual mobility is impossible (see Tajfel and Turner, 1979; Wright et al., 1990).

The perception that group boundaries are firmly closed increases feelings of shared fate with other ingroup members. Also, a system that allows no possibility of improving one's personal position is likely to be perceived as less legitimate than one that allows for even minimal individual mobility. Thus a perception that the boundaries are impermeable leads to higher ingroup identification and stronger feelings of injustice, both of which are strong motivators of collective action (see van Zomeren et al., 2008; Wright, 2010).

Again, prejudice reduction prefers the opposite perception. Improved intergroup attitudes are often described as resulting from perceiving greater similarity between groups and 'blurring of group boundaries' (e.g. Rosenthal and Crisp, 2006). This can be done, for example, by focusing attention on a broader superordinate category that includes both groups – a *common ingroup identity* (Gaertner and Dovidio, 2000); by focusing on recategorizing individuals such that some of those who were outgroup members are now seen as ingroup members (and some previous ingroup members are now outgroup members) – *cross-cutting categorization*; and by having groups work together to accomplish shared goals or meet shared challenges – *superordinate goals, cooperative learning* (see Paluck and Green, 2009). So, while collective action emerges when boundaries are clear and immutable, prejudice reduction benefits from the blurring of these boundaries.

Characterizing the outgroup. Finally, prejudice reduction strategies, by definition, seek to improve the characterizations and evaluations of the outgroup. Collective action, on the other hand, is facilitated by identifying the outgroup as the villain whose actions and attitudes are directly responsible for 'my' group's unfair position (see Simon and Klandermans, 2001; Wright and Tropp, 2002). Holding negative stereotypes about them provides the ideological justification for direct group action against them (Stott and Drury, 2004).

Thus, prejudice reduction and collective action participation require members of the disadvantaged group to hold entirely opposite views of the outgroup. Participation in prejudice reduction efforts (e.g. serving as a partner in cross-group contact) should produce liking and respect for the outgroup, while participation in collective action is facilitated by seeing them as malevolent agents of oppression. Again, there is a clear contradiction between the psychological requirements of these two.

Summary. At first glance, prejudice reduction and collective action might appear quite complementary: one offers methods for improving the attitudes of the advantaged; the other offers insights into strengthening social movements by the disadvantaged. However, when we consider those cases where disadvantaged group members are required to participate in the prejudice reduction process, we find that the psychological requirements of prejudice reduction are, in numerous ways, directly antithetical to those that facilitate and sustain collective action participation. To be effective in both, disadvantaged group members must simultaneously: (a) have high and low identification with the ingroup; (b) be highly aware and largely unaware of their collective identity; (c) be unaware of the inequalities between groups but recognize their group's clear disadvantage; (d) see the boundaries between groups as clear and impenetrable but also blurred and unimportant; and finally, (e) feel respectful and cooperative towards the advantaged outgroup while seeing them as discriminating exploiter. The obvious conclusion is that it will be extremely difficult to simultaneously be an optimal participant in prejudice reduction efforts and an assertive facilitator of collective action. Stated more provocatively, perhaps: 'however well-intentioned they may be, many procedures used to reduce prejudice may also serve to undermine collective action by the disadvantaged group' (Wright and Lubensky, 2009, p. 303).

Implications for contact and separation

Taken together, these variables also have direct implications for the concepts of integration and separation. As mentioned earlier, the strong focus on prejudice reduction (and its close affiliates harmony and social cohesion) has led to a championing of *integration* of disadvantaged and advantaged groups. Conversely, separation of the groups and a preference for spending time with the ingroup have been seen as evidence of poor intergroup relations. However, when there are clear intergroup inequalities, minority groups often are not able to assert their collective identity (culture, language, etc.) in integrated settings. The structural reality created by the differential power of the two groups to influence the content and context when integration occurs means that integration may represent *de facto* assimilation for the low-status minority group.

From a prejudice reduction perspective this may be a good thing. Members of the disadvantaged/minority group act in ways that are familiar and positive for advantaged group members (because they assimilate to the advantaged group norms, values, etc.). This will lead to interpersonal liking which, according to theories of cross-group contact, should then generalize to produce more positive attitudes towards the outgroup as a whole (see Brown and Hewstone, 2005; Wright *et al.*, 2005). However, the cost paid for these positive attitudes may be the strength of the distinctive identity of the disadvantaged ingroup. There are a number of reasons why this sacrifice of collective identity may be harmful. Strong collective identity, for example, has been convincingly shown to be an important buffer for self-esteem and well-being in the face of discrimination (see Schmitt and Branscombe, 2002). However, in this chapter we have focused on how a strong collective identity arms the disadvantaged minority for the struggle for collective equality by fostering a collective action orientation (Wright and Lubensky, 2009).

From this perspective, too much integration, just like too much harmony, may not be a good thing. Again, the solution to advantaged group prejudice and the means by which to reduce tensions between groups can undermine the very group these efforts are designed to benefit. The single-minded pursuit of prejudice reduction and harmony may sacrifice the collective identity of the minority group by strongly discouraging the separation needed to cultivate and strengthen that unique identity. While complete separation may not seem justified, when we look beyond prejudice reduction and accept that positive intergroup relations must also include opportunities for disadvantaged groups to openly challenge existing inequalities, some degree of group separation may be absolutely necessary (see also Hopkins and Kahani-Hopkin, 2006).

Who is the agent of change?

Although our focus here is on critiques of the model, we would be completely remiss if we did not acknowledge that the emergence of the prejudice reduction model more than sixty years ago was an extremely important advancement in the understanding of intergroup inequality. Describing advantaged group prejudice as the cause of social inequality was a huge step forward. Rather than the problem being with the character or habits of those who were disadvantaged, social inequality was recast as resulting, at least in part, from the flawed reasoning and unreasonable beliefs of the advantaged. This view 'placed' the problem squarely in the heads of those who benefited from the existing inequality, making the situation and treatment of the disadvantaged much harder to justify or legitimize. Members of the disadvantaged group were now characterized as undeserving targets of malicious mistreatment by wrong-thinking members of the advantaged group.

The importance of this shift in explanation cannot be exaggerated. It had enormously positive implications for social change. However, more than half a century since this change really began to take hold, it is perhaps time to wonder if it has shifted things far enough. The focus on advantaged group prejudice shifts the blame for group-based inequality from the disadvantaged to the advantaged group, but it does not shift the agency of the solution from the advantaged group to the disadvantaged group. When the problem was defined in terms of the inadequacies of the disadvantaged group, the solution to inequality was, of course, equally patronizing. Well-meaning members of the advantaged group would 'educate' or 'civilize' members of the disadvantaged group. By teaching them the ways of the advantaged, these agents of change would provide the resources needed to at least begin to compete and succeed (as much as was possible) in the world of the superior advantaged group. With the emergence of the prejudice reduction model and the shifting of the problem into the heads of the advantaged, the target of remediation changed. Education (perhaps even 'civilizing') was needed for the advantaged group. However, the implicit message about who would solve the problem of inequality has remained the same. Once rid of their bad ideas and inappropriate attitudes, it is the members of the advantaged group who will now stop discriminating against the disadvantaged and open the doors of equality and opportunity to the disadvantaged. Although relieved of the responsibility for inequality, members of the disadvantaged group remain, for the most part, passive targets of advantaged group actions, which will now change from discriminatory to egalitarian as their prejudices are removed.

Collective action, on the other hand, puts agency for change squarely in the hands of the disadvantaged group. The thoughts, emotions, motives and actions of disadvantaged group members are the key catalysts that will alter the status quo. The question of whether change will occur or not depends as much on the disadvantaged group's level of motivation and resolve and the appropriateness of the tactics they choose, as it does on the resistance mounted by the advantaged group (or any assistance that some advantaged group members might offer). As a model of social change, collective action requires that we consider the disadvantaged not only as targets of injustice who will be treated unfairly or fairly depending on the psychology (prejudice) of the advantaged group, but also as causal agents who play a direct and decisive role in improving their status.

Thus, taking the collective action perspective moves us another step forward in the study of intergroup inequality. The advantaged group may be the problem; thus understanding the psychology of advantaged group prejudice gives us important insights into the causes and perpetuation of intergroup inequality. However, this does not mean that the solution to the problem need emanate from the same source as the cause. In order for our analysis to promote the full emancipation of the disadvantaged group, it needs to consider that movement towards real change will very likely emerge from assertive resistance and intergroup conflict initiated and sustained by the disadvantaged group, rather than actions initiated by (or allowed by) a reformed advantaged group.

Prejudice reduction or collective action? Focusing on different levels of analysis

Not only do the prejudice reduction and collective action models focus on different targets, these two approaches have very different points of departure. The underlying premise of prejudice reduction is that changing 'hearts and minds' (improving attitudes) will be the catalyst for social change. Changes in individual psychology (reduced prejudice) should lead to change in interpersonal cross-group behaviour (less discrimination) and this in turn should lead to greater equality in the opportunities and outcomes and status provided to members of the two groups. A collective action approach seeks social change by directly challenging the existing group status hierarchy. This approach seeks structural change in the opportunities, outcomes and status of the two groups and, by implication, sees improvements in interpersonal relations and individual attitudes as secondary and perhaps as a consequence of greater equality.

This difference in orientation is nicely captured in a model of 'levels of analysis' described by Pettigrew (1996). Pettigrew uses the term 'micro-level' to describe analyses of intergroup relations that focus on intrapersonal phenomena (cognitions, emotions etc. within individual people), the term 'meso-level' to describe those that focus on interpersonal phenomena (the interactions between individual people) and 'macro-level' to describe analyses that focus on broader social institutions and the structural relations between groups in societies. While both the prejudice reduction and collective action models involve consideration of all of these levels, they have a decidedly different view of the causal flow. Prejudice reduction seeks to alter micro-level phenomena to spark reductions in interpersonal acts of discrimination (meso-level change), and as these more positive interpersonal behaviours proliferate, they should reduce macro-level structural and status inequalities. The collective action model describes actors' efforts to change the macro-level intergroup relations as the starting point, and to the degree that it is concerned with interpersonal (meso-level) and intraindividual (micro-level) phenomena at all, this view would propose that greater equality at the macro-level might then alter the dynamics of interpersonal cross-group interactions and individual psychological processes. This difference between the models in terms of the causal flow of social change exposes a number of rather serious concerns with the prejudice reduction approach.

Of course, this levels-of-analysis discussion might remind us of the important (but often unspoken) question of what level of change is most desirable or important. In this chapter, we have privileged macro-level change as most important. Reducing the degree of group-based inequality in treatment, opportunities and outcomes has been presented as the critical determinant of positive 'social change'. Perhaps a more detailed consideration of this assumption is warranted. First, we suspect that most advocates for change would not be satisfied with change solely at the micro-level. If changes in the heads of individuals do not lead to measurable change even in the way that these individuals interact with outgroup members, then there would be little benefit to anyone (except perhaps the individual who has changed), and it would seem a stretch to call this 'social change'.

However, whether improvements at the macro-level are necessarily always more important than meso-level change is less obvious. We human beings live much of our lives through and in interpersonal interactions with the individuals who share our physical spaces. It is true that the content and nature of these interpersonal interactions are strongly influenced by broader status inequalities between groups and by larger institutional rules, so that changes at the macro-level should alter these interpersonal interactions. However, the quality of these daily interpersonal exchanges are also determined by the emotional valence, the warmth and the comfort internal to these specific interactions. If we like, feel close to and interact easily with the specific others in our local/ personal world, our life is decidedly better than if our daily interpersonal interactions are effortful, uncomfortable and with people who we neither like nor who like us (e.g. Headey *et al.*, 1991). In fact, it might not be unreasonable to hypothesize that, under many circumstances, the closeness and friendliness of our daily interactions may well be more important to our happiness than whether the individuals we interact with have more or less social status, opportunities or material resources than us. Put another way, we might not trade our positive, caring, meso-level interactions across unequal groups for macro-level, group-based equality that was associated with tense or even negative interpersonal interactions. For example, a daughter with a wonderful, warm, loving relationship with her sexist father may prefer to live with the consequences of the obvious inequality of the male/female relations within her home in order not to jeopardize the psychological closeness and positive interpersonal experiences with her father – positive meso-level, cross-group relations trump equality in macro-level, intergroup relations.

However, as our earlier discussion of harmonious intergroup inequality makes clear, positive interpersonal interactions without structural change in group status is not what most of us who theorize about intergroup relations would see as the preferred goal of social change. More interestingly, there may be disagreement between members of the two groups about what level of positive change demonstrates that the intergroup relations are positive. For example, Saguy and colleagues (2009) provide laboratory evidence that members of high status groups may interpret positive meso-level interactions with outgroup members that result in positive feelings about the outgroup as evidence of positive intergroup relations, and thus see no need to alter the resource inequalities between the two groups. However, members of the low status group, while just as satisfied and pleased with positive meso-level interactions with the outgroup, subsequently expect that these positive interpersonal exchanges should lead the advantaged group to relinquish some of their power and share resources more equally. Thus, while both groups share a positive view of their convivial cross-group interpersonal interactions, only the disadvantaged group sees this as an indication that there should, or will, be macro-level structural change in the relative status of the two groups.

However, the general point here is that we need to remind ourselves to be explicit in what we mean by social change. Prejudice reduction that leads to more positive, civil and respectful interpersonal cross-group interactions is certainly 'positive social change' at one level. However, there are many, especially members of low status groups who have questions about the legitimacy of their low status, who would be very interested in the degree to which (and exactly how) these more positive meso-level cross-group interactions will produce meaningful change in the macro-level intergroup relations.

Challenges for the micro→meso→macro causal sequence

First, and perhaps most obvious, there is considerable evidence in the psychological literature demonstrating the disconnect between attitudes and actions. Although attitudes are surely one important determinant of action, there are numerous other situational and psychological variables that might lead one to unintentionally or unknowingly act in attitude-inconsistent ways. It is clearly beyond the scope of this chapter to review the literature on how and why we might act in ways that are inconsistent with our attitudes. However, the call by many reviewers and editors in our scholarly journals for prejudice researchers to include 'behavioural measures' seems evidence (although clearly not scientific evidence) of two things: (a) that some social scientists care whether attitude change produces behavioural change, and (b) that some social scientists are sceptical about whether attitude change will necessarily produce behavioural change. Suffice to say that reducing prejudice should only reduce interpersonal acts of discrimination to the degree that changing attitudes influences behaviour.

However, the concern with this causal sequence is not just the possibility of slippage in the effectiveness of change as we move up from the micro to the meso level. There are also a number of reasons why an emphasis on creating positive cross-group interpersonal interactions and encouraging members of both groups to 'be nice' and 'get along' may result in the perpetuation of the current intergroup inequalities rather than their reduction. Several theories, and associated research, describe how the content and nature of the interpersonal dynamic that often emerge in interactions between members of groups holding different status positions can be experienced as subjectively pleasant and friendly, while simultaneously serving to legitimize and stabilize the hierarchical intergroup structure.

One process by which this can happen is elaborated by Ridgeway and colleagues in what has been called status construction theory (e.g. Ridgeway, 2001; Ridgeway and Correll, 2006). Generally, this theoretical perspective describes how group status beliefs are formed and spread in a society through local, interpersonal, cross-group social interactions. Much of the theory is dedicated to explaining how direct interactions between members of different groups can translate real group differences in material resources and power into beliefs about which groups possess the characteristics 'that count' and are thus deserving of more social status. A full review of the theory is beyond the scope of this chapter, but what is of clear interest here is the theory's discussion of how these status beliefs, once developed, are reified, legitimized and spread to others through the same mechanism by which they are formed – through local interpersonal interactions between members of the two groups.

Ridgeway and colleagues argue that, once formed, beliefs about the relative status of groups serve as 'implicit, often unconscious assumptions about the worthiness of particular actors', and these assumptions are the basis for behaviour in subsequent cross-group encounters. Individuals who hold these beliefs will engage in subtle (and not so subtle) patterns of behaviour that communicate to and 'teach' their partners, and any observers of the interaction, the relative position of members of the two groups. Since these status beliefs are understood to be consensual, the actor will also expect his or her partner to respond with patterns of behaviour consistent with the partner's relative status position as well. Through this process of teaching and enacting of status roles in specific interpersonal interactions, these beliefs about the relative worthiness of advantaged and disadvantaged group members become engrained in the social reality of both groups. Members of both groups come to understand their respective role in subsequent cross-group interactions, and they play this role relatively unconsciously and effortlessly; and, because they are playing mutually compatible roles, the interactions can often go smoothly and pleasantly. In fact, the existence, and the appropriate performance, of an agreed-upon script may imply to the participants, and to the observers, the presence of positive intergroup attitudes. Thus, these interactions can generate positive and warm feelings, even genuine liking, while at the same time reifying, not undermining, the status inequalities.

The ideas presented by status construction theory are echoed in other social psychological theories. For example, shared reality theory (e.g. Hardin and Higgins, 1996) examines the ways in which interpersonal interactions shape individuals' self-views. Based on the assumption that cultural stereotypes are known and shared, the theory posits that cultural stereotypes will not only guide people's expectations about others' and their own behaviour, but can also shape the individual's self-views – leading the individual to take on the group stereotypes (to self-stereotype) – during social interactions. The interesting additional claim of shared reality theory is that this self-stereotyping will occur more strongly when affiliative motivations are strong. That is, when the desire to form and maintain social bonds with the interaction partner is high, people will describe themselves and act in ways that are consistent with the culturally shared stereotypes of their ingroup. Similarly, Sinclair and colleagues (e.g. Sinclair *et al.*, 2005) further posit that effective social interactions require perspective-taking that allows interaction partners to formulate a mutual understanding of the social world. Their research shows that people will adjust or 'tune' their understandings of themselves and their social reality when interacting with valued others. This social tuning is an attempt to maintain a sense of shared reality with that other. Thus, individuals will adopt what they believe to be the shared stereotypic representations of their group if they want to form and maintain social bonds with outgroup others. Like status construction theory, then, this perspective does not conceive a strong desire to have positive cross-group interactions as necessarily something that will reduce the legitimacy of group-based inequality.

The process proposed by status construction theory and the evidence for social tuning present a view of cross-group interactions that is diametrically opposite to that implied by the prejudice reduction approach, in terms of the expected impact of pleasant cross-group interactions on macro-level intergroup inequalities. More positive intergroup attitudes may indeed increase interest in positive and warm interactions with outgroup members (i.e. increase cross-group affiliative motives), but status construction theory and social tuning effects would predict that raising these cross-group affiliative motives should only increase the degree to which partners will interact in ways that represent, and thus confirm and strengthen, the existing, culturally shared status inequalities.

It might appear, on the surface at least, that some prejudice reduction theories, most notably intergroup contact theory, had already accounted for this concern about the possible negative implications of existing status differences between the groups. For example, Allport (1954), and many others since, have argued that cross-group contact situations should be constructed to ensure equal status within the local context. However, status construction theory holds that it is precisely these kind of situations – situations where individuals from groups that are widely known to hold unequal status meet in circumstances where they have equal access to resources and power – that serve to most clearly reify the legitimacy of the status inequalities. Let's go back to our example of the recent immigrant/host national interaction. When the interaction context is one where the host nationals' superior knowledge, language proficiency and superior access to institutional resources are highly salient, this sets the stage for building the belief that host nationals deserve more status than recent immigrants. However, it is still possible that the differences in status demonstrated in this interaction could be attributed to the individual people or to the current local context, thus reducing the degree to which this experience contributes to the 'teaching' of a wildly accepted belief about the status of the two groups. However, if these same individuals later interact in a situation that is constructed to ensure that the recent immigrant and the host national have equal access to needed resources (half the discussion is in their respective language, their cultural knowledge is made important, etc.) and equal power, but despite this reality of equality they continue to subtly enact higher and lower status roles – the roles they have practised in other contexts where power and resources were unequally distributed – then now there is no explanation for their demonstrated inequality than their group membership. Thus, it is when the local reality is that the two are equal and yet they continue to act as though they are not that group-based status differences are most strongly communicated. As Ridgeway puts it, 'rich women do not learn women's lower status position from poor men, they learn it from rich men'. Similarly, poor women do not learn women's lower status from rich men (where their treatment as lower status can be explained by real differences in resources and power), they learn it from poor men (where the clearest explanation for their treatment as lower status is their gender).

As a second example we might examine more closely the jigsaw classroom technique, introduced in the 1970s as a means to reduce ethnic and racial prejudice among children (Aronson and Patnoe, 1997). Although there are variations in its practice, one approach involves forming five- to six-child groups that vary in terms of gender, race and ethnicity. Each child is then given part of the needed information to accomplish the task at hand. The children then take turns presenting the pieces of information that each has to the rest of the group. This local interaction is explicitly designed to ensure equality of resources and power across group members. The first criticism might be that – despite very valiant attempts to structure the task to create equality and more broadly to make the classroom a 'group status free zone' – there will remain real differences in the objective resources available to students from different groups, or differences in language proficiency or less obvious disparities in knowledge of the seemingly banal, yet culture-specific, codes of interpersonal communication among children. Children who are relatively less familiar with these codes are unlikely to take leadership roles. As these more subtle forms of resource inequality manifest themselves in very positive but nonetheless unequal interactions, status beliefs are being learned.

Moreover, and even more disappointing, even if a teacher was able to create a local interaction context that entirely removes even these more subtle resource differences (e.g. in a bilingual classroom, doing a task that equally required both groups' cultural competencies), status construction theory would predict that this experience would be the one that would most clearly and strongly reify children's existing status beliefs about the two groups. Given that children in this type of classroom would almost certainly have participated in and observed numerous cross-group interactions outside the classroom in situations where group-based differences in resources were highly relevant, they would have had lots of opportunities to learn how to enact these unequal interactions and may have begun to acquire the broader culturally shared beliefs about the relative status of the groups. So now, as they watch themselves and their outgroup partners interact on a task where there are no real bases for inequality (no resource differences), and yet members of both groups still show subtle behavioural cues of the superiority of majority children over minority children, the most reasonable conclusion would be that these status differences can be legitimately attached to the categories themselves.

Again, we need to make clear the distinction between engaging in friendly, pleasant, positive, prosocial cross-group interactions – the kinds that might result from a lack of prejudice – and equal interactions free of even subtle behavioural cues of status differences between groups. Together, status construction theory and research on social tuning provide a compelling explanation for why reducing prejudice across unequal status groups might effectively create strong motivation to engage in pleasant, warm cross-group interactions, and also why these strong affiliative motives and the interactions they inspire may serve to reify status differences, not undermine them.

Conclusions and resolutions

Based on this analysis, we believe that it is reasonable to question whether or not there can be too much prejudice reduction, harmony and integration, and further, we believe that the answer is 'yes'. Although it is clear that efforts to reduce rampant antipathy, overt expressions of hostility and active denigration of other groups would need to be part of any scheme to improve many intergroup relations, it also appears reasonable to consider the limitations of a focus on prejudice reduction. Social psychologists need to recognize that prejudice reduction may directly conflict with another important means through which positive social change occurs – collective action. Failure to recognize these limitations will very likely lead us into the trap into which many members of advantaged groups fall – assuming that because interpersonal interactions across groups are convivial and warm that intergroup inequalities are either gone or are acceptable.

However, we do not wish to conclude this chapter on an entirely pessimistic note. The contradictions and divergences between these two broad views of how to achieve positive intergroup relations can be (and at times are) ameliorated and perhaps entirely overcome. Although it is beyond the scope of the current chapter to elaborate how this might be accomplished, we will offer a few brief comments. Previously (see Wright and Lubensky, 2009), suggestions have been made about ways that individual members of disadvantaged groups might overcome the psychological incongruities of having positive relations with individual members of the advantaged group while maintaining active participation in collective action. For example, by subtyping outgroup friends in ways that distance them from the rest of the advantaged ingroup, positive feelings about the friend need not undermine perceptions of the rest of the outgroup as oppressive agents of discriminatory mistreatment. In addition, this 'exception to the rule' position also imposes (provides) an alternative identity for the advantaged group friend. They are offered the alternative identity as an ally or co-conspirator in the fight to reduce inequality. If the advantaged group member accepts, or even promotes, this kind of subtyping, taking on the proffered alternative identity, interpersonal (meso-level) interactions between these two individuals are unlikely to model the kind of status construction effects described by Ridgeway, or to represent the kind of harmony that will divert attention from the group-level (macro-level) inequalities.

Individual-level solutions like this also mirror some broader group-level solutions. Recently, Subašić et al. (2008) proposed a political solidarity model of social change which posits that some advantaged group members will seek to form an alliance with the disadvantaged group when they cease to experience a shared feeling of group identity with members of their own group who are represented as the authority responsible for the unjust decisions, actions and policies. When those who control resources engage in actions or enact policies that are seen by other members of the advantaged ingroup to be contrary to their own ingroup norms, then this subgroup ceases to be seen as part of the ingroup. At this point, direct challenge to this authority, in collaboration with the disadvantaged group, becomes possible. Although this model focuses primarily on the psychology of the advantaged group and when they may be willing to act against unjust authority, it does articulate an active role for the disadvantaged group and its members.

Apparent in models that describe possible coalitions including both advantaged and disadvantaged group members is recognition that conversations between the two groups need to include clear and open discussions not only of what they share in common and why they should get along, but also about the inequalities and the past and current discrimination faced by the disadvantaged. Thus, unlike common models of intergroup contact, for example, these models see the need to represent the advantaged group in ways that are not complementary and for there to be frank and open discussion of how the experiences of the two groups differ. The practical accomplishment of this goal might be informed by a number of current programmes that focus on 'critical intergroup dialogue' (e.g. Zuniga *et al.*, 2002). These programmes use structured discussion between advantaged and disadvantaged group members to raise awareness about group differences, consider issues of group-based inequality and collective justice, talk about the cultural, political and historical causes of intergroup tension and encourage participants to take an active role in social change. A potentially fruitful avenue for future enquiry would be an elaboration of the psychology that might motivate both advantaged and disadvantaged group members to participate in these programmes: how the programmes might alter the participants' perceptions of themselves, their own group, the outgroup and the larger society in which these two groups exist; and whether and how these changes might motivate and sustain action designed to reduce inequality.

In short, we must continue to investigate how cross-group cooperation in service of justice and social change occurs. However, for group-based equality to be cultivated and maintained, we need to move beyond a model dominated by a focus on prejudice reduction, and recognize that efforts to change unjust and unequal social structures will require both harmony and managed conflict, a recognition of group differences as well as similarities, open discussion of existing inequalities that exposes both discrimination and privilege and enough animus and acrimony to stimulate assertive action.

Note

1. We would like to acknowledge the contributions of Micah Lubensky, Antoinette Semenya, Joseph Comeau, Leo Kiu and Shelly Zhou to our continued research efforts to investigate these processes. We would also like to thank the Simon Fraser University Community Trust Endowment Fund for support provided to the second author and the Social Science and Humanities Research Council of Canada for funding provided to the first author.

References

Allport, G. W. (1954). *The Nature of Prejudice*. Reading, MA: Addison-Wesley.
Aronson, E. and Patnoe, S. (1997). *The Jigsaw Classroom: Building Cooperation in the Classroom*. New York: Longman.

Brown, R. and Hewstone, M. (2005). An integrative theory of intergroup contact. In M. P. Zanna (ed.), *Advances in Experimental Social Psychology* (Vol. 37, pp.255–343). San Diego, CA: Academic Press.

Brown, R. J. and Turner, J. C. (1979). The criss-cross categorization effect in intergroup discrimination. *British Journal of Social and Clinical Psychology*, **18**, 371–83.

De Dreu, C. (2011). Conflict at work: basic principles and applied issues. In S. Zedeck (ed.), *American Psychological Association Handbook of Industrial and Organizational Psychology: Maintaining, Expanding, and Contracting the Organization* (Vol. 3, pp.461–93). Washington, DC: American Psychological Association.

Dixon, J. A., Durrheim, K. and Tredoux, C. (2007). Intergroup contact and attitudes toward the principle and practice of racial equality. *Psychological Science*, **18**, 867–72.

Doosje, B. and Ellemers, N. (1997). Stereotyping under threat: the role of group identification. In R. Spears and P. J. Oakes (eds.), *The Social Psychology of Stereotyping and Group Life* (pp.257–72). Oxford, UK: Blackwell.

Dovidio, J. F., Hewstone, M., Glick, P. and Esses, V. M. (eds.) (2010). *Handbook of Prejudice, Stereotyping, and Discrimination*. Thousand Oaks, CA: Sage Publications.

Gaertner, S. L. and Dovidio, J. F. (2000). *Reducing Intergroup Bias: the Common Ingroup Identity Model*. Philadelphia, PA: Psychology Press.

Hardin, C. D. and Higgins, E. T. (1996). Shared reality: how social verification makes the subjective objective. In R. Sorrentino and E. T. Higgins (eds.), *Handbook of Motivation and Cognition* (Vol. 3, pp.28–84). New York: Guilford.

Headey, B., Veenhoven, R. and Wearing, A. (1991). Top-down versus bottom-up theories of subjective well-being. *Social Indicators Research*, **24**(1), 81–100.

Hopkins, N. and Kahani-Hopkins, V. (2006). Minority group members' theories of intergroup contact: a case study of British Muslims' conceptualizations of 'Islamophobia' and social change. *British Journal of Social Psychology*, **45**, 245–64.

Iyer, A. and Leach, C. (2010). Helping disadvantaged out-groups challenge unjust inequality: the role of group-based emotions. In S. Stürmer and M. Snyder (eds.), *The Psychology of Prosocial Behavior: Group Processes, Intergroup Relations, and Helping* (pp.337–53). Malden, MA: Wiley-Blackwell.

Jackman, M. R. (1994). *The Velvet Glove: Paternalism and Conflict in Gender, Class, and Race Relations*. Berkeley, CA: University of California Press.

Jost, J. T., Banaji, M. and Nosek, B. A. (2004). A decade of system justification theory: accumulated evidence of conscious and unconscious bolstering of the status quo. *Political Psychology*, **25**, 881–919.

Paluck, E. and Green, D. (2009). Prejudice reduction: what works? A review and assessment of research and practice. *Annual Review of Psychology*, **60**, 339–67.

Pettigrew, T. (1996). *How to Think Like a Social Scientist*. New York: HarperCollins.

(1998). Intergroup contact theory. *Annual Review of Psychology*, **49**, 65–85.

Pettigrew, T. F. and Tropp, L. R. (2006). A meta-analytic test of intergroup contact theory. *Journal of Personality and Social Psychology*, **90**(5), 751–83.

Reicher, S. (2007). Rethinking the paradigm of prejudice. *South African Journal of Psychology*, **37**, 820–34.

Ridgeway, C. (2001). The emergence of status beliefs: from structural inequality to legitimizing ideology. In J. Jost and B. Major (eds.), *The Psychology of Legitimacy: Emerging Perspectives on Ideology, Justice, and Intergroup Relations* (pp.257–77). New York: Cambridge University Press.

Ridgeway, C. L. and Correll, S. J. (2006). Consensus and the creation of status beliefs. *Social Forces*, **85**, 431–53.

Rosenthal, H. S. and Crisp, R. J. (2006). Reducing stereotype threat by blurring intergroup boundaries. *Personality and Social Psychology Bulletin*, **32**(4), 501–11.

Saguy, T., Tausch, N., Dovidio, J. F. and Pratto, F. (2009). The irony of harmony: intergroup contact can produce false expectations for equality. *Psychological Science*, **20**, 114–21.

Schmitt, M. T. and Branscombe, N. R. (2002). The meaning and consequences of perceived discrimination in disadvantaged and privileged social groups. In W. Stroebe and M. Hewstone (eds.), *European Review of Social Psychology* (Vol. 12, pp.167–99). Chichester, UK: Wiley.

Sherif, M. (1967). *Group Conflict and Cooperation: their Social Psychology*. London: Routledge and Kegan Paul.

Simon, B. and Klandermans, B. (2001). Politicized collective identity: a social psychological analysis. *American Psychologist*, **56**(4), 319–31.

Sinclair, S., Hardin, C. D., Lowery, B. S. and Colangelo, A. (2005). Social tuning of automatic racial attitudes: the role of affiliative motivation. *Journal of Personality and Social Psychology*, **89**, 583–92.

Stott, C. and Drury, J. (2004). The importance of social structure and social interaction in stereotype consensus and content: is the whole greater than the sum of its parts? *European Journal of Social Psychology*, **34**, 11–23.

Subašić, E., Reynolds, K. and Turner, J. (2008). The political solidarity model of social change: dynamics of self-categorization in intergroup power relations. *Personality and Social Psychology Review*, **12**, 330–52.

Tajfel, H. and Turner, J. C. (1979). An integrative theory of intergroup conflict. In W. G. Austin and S. Worchel (eds.), *The Social Psychology of Intergroup Relations* (pp.33–48). Monterey, CA: Brooks/Cole.

Taylor, D. M. and Moghaddam, F. M. (1994). *Theories of Intergroup Relations: International and Social Psychological Perspectives* (2nd edn). Westport, CT: Preager.

van Zomeren, M., Postmes, T. and Spears, R. (2008). Toward an integrative social identity model of collective action: a quantitative research synthesis of three sociopsychological perspectives. *Psychological Bulletin*, **134**, 504–35.

Wright, S. C. (2001). Strategic collective action: social psychology and social change. In R. Brown and S. L. Gaertner (eds.), *Intergroup Processes: Blackwell Handbook of Social Psychology* (Vol. 4). Oxford, UK: Blackwell.

(2009). Cross-group contact effects. In S. Otten, T. Kessler and K. Sassenberg (eds.), *Intergroup Relations: the Role of Emotion and Motivation* (pp.262–83). New York: Psychology Press.

(2010). Collective action and social change. In J. F. Dovidio, M. Hewstone, P. Glick and V. M. Esses (eds.), *Handbook of Prejudice, Stereotyping, and Discrimination* (pp.577–96). Thousand Oaks, CA: Sage Publications.

Wright, S. C. and Lubensky, M. E. (2009). The struggle for equality: collective action versus prejudice reduction. In S. Demoulin, J. P. Leyens and J. F. Dovidio (eds.), *Intergroup Misunderstandings: Impact of Divergent Social Realities* (pp.291–310). New York: Psychology Press.

Wright, S. C. and Tropp, L. (2002). Collective action in response to disadvantage: intergroup perceptions, social identification and social change. In I. Walker and H. Smith (eds.), *Relative Deprivation: Specification, Development, and Integration*. Cambridge, UK: Cambridge University Press.

Wright, S. C., Brody, S. M. and Aron, A. (2005). Intergroup contact: still our best hope for improving intergroup relations. In C. S. Crandall and M. Schaller (eds.), *Social Psychology of Prejudice: Historical and Contemporary Issues* (pp.115–42). Seattle, WA: Lewinian Press.

Wright, S. C., Taylor, D. M. and Moghaddam, F. M. (1990). Responding to membership in a disadvantaged group: from acceptance to collective protest. *Journal of Personality and Social Psychology*, **58**, 994–1,003.

Zuniga, X., Nagda, B. A. and Sevig, T. D. (2002). Intergroup dialogues: an educational model for cultivating engagement across differences. *Equity and Excellence in Education*, **35**, 7–17.

12   From attitudes to (in)action: the darker side of 'we'

John F. Dovidio, Tamar Saguy, Samuel L. Gaertner and Erin L. Thomas[1]

The study of intergroup relations has traditionally focused on the role of individual prejudice in motivating discrimination and creating disparities. Prejudice has been classically defined as a negative attitude, in Allport's (1954) terms 'an antipathy based on faulty and inflexible generalization. It may be felt or expressed. It may be directed toward a group as a whole, or toward an individual because he [sic] is a member of that group' (p. 9). Over the past fifty years, in particular, psychologists have invested considerable energy in exploring how interventions, such as appropriately structured intergroup contact, can reduce prejudice (Pettigrew and Tropp, 2006). In addition, stimulated by the classic work of Tajfel and Turner (1979), recent approaches have also examined how group perceptions and identity can influence intergroup prejudice (Brown, 1996) and inform strategies for reducing bias (Gaertner and Dovidio, 2010). Extending the line of analysis presented by Wright and Baray in the previous chapter, this chapter acknowledges the benefits of these frameworks for improving intergroup attitudes and relieving immediate tensions but also suggests that such approaches, in isolation, may have unintended consequences that inhibit action by members of disadvantaged and advantaged groups towards social structural changes towards equality in the longer term.

We focus our analysis in this chapter on a line of research that we initiated over twenty years ago on the common ingroup identity model (Gaertner and Dovidio, 2000, 2009; Gaertner *et al.*, 1989, 1993). Previous research on prejudice reduction had, over an extended period, identified positive intergroup contact as a potent intervention for reducing prejudice and investigated the parameters (e.g. equal status and cooperative interaction) that moderated the effectiveness of contact (Pettigrew and Tropp, 2006, 2008). The common ingroup identity model, in contrast, considered the psychological processes – specifically, cognitive representations of social groups – that *mediate* the impact of various conditions of contact on reductions in prejudice.

Drawing on the theoretical foundations of social identity theory (Tajfel and Turner, 1979) and self-categorization theory (Turner *et al.*, 1987), the model emphasizes the process of recategorizing individuals formerly seen as members of different groups within a common, superordinate, ingroup identity. The basic premise is that if members of different groups are induced to conceive of themselves as a single, more inclusive group rather than as two completely separate groups, attitudes towards former outgroup members will become more positive through processes involving pro-ingroup bias. That is, the model directs the processes that lead to ingroup favouritism towards former outgroup members, as well (see Gaertner and Dovidio, 2000, 2009).

The present chapter extends, and in some ways challenges, the original common ingroup identity model by examining the different preferences, functions and consequences of positive contact and common identity for members of advantaged and disadvantaged groups. Specifically, we propose that intergroup contact focusing on commonality can reinforce the status quo, which benefits the advantaged group, and undermine collective action for equality by members of the disadvantaged group. We thus explore the potential 'darker side of we' for disadvantaged-group members.

We first briefly review the basis of and evidence for the common ingroup identity model. We then discuss the different forms of recategorization, as a one-group representation or a dual identity. We next examine the importance of understanding advantaged- and disadvantaged-group perspectives on intergroup relations and how these views relate to preferences for and effectiveness of different types of group representations, including a dual identity recategorization, in which both the original group boundaries and the superordinate identity are salient. The sections that follow explore the different motivations and preferences of members of advantaged and disadvantaged groups and how they operate to shape intergroup interactions and influence intergroup relations in the short and long term. The concluding section discusses practical implications and directions for future research.

The common ingroup identity model

The common ingroup identity model assumes that intergroup biases are rooted in the universal human tendency to simplify complex environments by classifying objects and people into groups or categories. This process of categorization often occurs spontaneously on the basis of physical similarity, proximity, or shared fate. Though social categorization helps to simplify the world and make it more understandable, it also produces motivational and cognitive intergroup biases (Fiske and Taylor, 2007). In the process of categorizing people into groups, individuals typically classify themselves *into* one of the social categories and *out of* the others.

Ingroup/outgroup social categorization has immediate and profound impacts on the way people think and feel about others (see Dovidio and Gaertner, 2010, for a review). Cognitively, when people or objects are categorized into different groups, extant differences between members of the same category tend to be perceptually minimized, and differences between members of different groups become exaggerated or over-generalized. Moreover, people retain more positive information about ingroup than about outgroup members, discounting negative information about the ingroup. Motivationally, because people derive their self-esteem in part from the prestige of groups to which they belong, they are driven to regard the group to which they belong (their ingroup) and its accomplishments in a positive light compared to other groups (outgroups) (Tajfel and Turner, 1979). Although ingroup favouritism can evolve into a more destructive, anti-outgroup attitude (i.e. prejudice), the cognitive and motivational processes that drive ingroup favouritism can also provide a means to reduce prejudice and discrimination. This latter point is the essence of the common ingroup identity model.

The common ingroup identity model (Gaertner and Dovidio, 2000, 2009) recognizes the fluidity of social categorization processes and the reality that people simultaneously belong to a variety of social groups (e.g. families, neighbourhoods, cities, regions and nations). These groups are often hierarchically organized in terms of inclusiveness, with some social categories (e.g. nations) inclusive of others (e.g. regions). Different goals, motives, expectations or emphases in the immediate context can shift the level of category inclusiveness that will dominate the situation. Specifically, the model proposes that inducing people to recategorize ingroup and outgroup members within a common category boundary (a one-group representation based, for example, on a common school, city or national identity) redirects those motivational and cognitive processes that produce ingroup-favouring biases to increase positive feelings, beliefs and behaviours towards others who were previously regarded primarily in terms of their outgroup membership.

The common ingroup identity model has received considerable empirical support (see Gaertner and Dovidio, 2000, 2009). Experimental interventions that emphasize common identity through visual cues (e.g. integrated seating and common dress; Gaertner *et al.*, 1989), by requiring cooperative interdependence between groups (Gaertner *et al.*, 1990), or by making common aspects of identity highly salient (see Gaertner and Dovidio,

2000), reduce intergroup bias in large part by changing people's representations of group memberships from two groups to one group. Investigations across a variety of intergroup settings (e.g. students from different racial groups, banking executives who had experienced a corporate merger and college students from blended families; Gaertner *et al.*, 1999; West *et al.*, 2009) offer converging support for the idea that the features specified by contact theory (Allport, 1954; Pettigrew and Tropp, 2006) reduce intergroup bias because they transform people's representations of the memberships from separate groups to a single, more inclusive group.

Recategorization as one group or a dual identity: a functional approach

Recent research on the common ingroup identity model reveals that recategorization does not always require each group to forsake its less inclusive group identity completely to effectively reduce intergroup bias. It is possible for members to conceive of two groups (e.g. blacks and whites) as distinct units within the context of a superordinate identity (e.g. school). Thus, people can think about both different-group and superordinate-group identities at the same time in terms of a 'subgroups-within-a-common-group' or a 'dual-identity' representation. Consistent with the hypothesis that a dual identity represents a viable alternative form of recategorization, experimental interventions to induce different representations of groups have demonstrated that creating a dual identity can be just as effective as producing a one-group identity and, potentially even more so, for reducing bias between groups as a whole (González and Brown, 2003). However, whereas the creation of a singular common identity consistently elicits more positive intergroup attitudes, the relative effectiveness of a dual identity is much more variable. Although the strength of a dual identity typically also predicts lower levels of prejudice, it sometimes relates to higher levels of bias (Gaertner and Dovidio, 2009).

We have hypothesized that one factor that determines the relative effectiveness of a one-group or a dual-identity representation is the perceived impacts these different approaches will have for advancing the interests of one's group (see Dovidio *et al.*, 2009). From this functional perspective, members of advantaged groups, who are motivated to maintain their higher social status (Blumer, 1958; Tajfel and Turner, 1979), are generally expected to prefer a one-group representation because it deflects attention away from disparities between groups and reduces subgroup identification. These conditions reduce the likelihood of collective action among disadvantaged-group members that challenges the status quo (Wright and Lubensky, 2009). Key elements necessary for collective action by members of disadvantaged groups to occur are (a) perception of the status difference between the disadvantaged and advantaged group as illegitimate, and (b) salient group identity (Ellemers and Barreto, 2001; van Zomeren *et al.*, 2008; Wright, 2001). Thus, if disadvantaged-group members adopt a one-group perspective at the expense of their previous group identity, they may attend less to group-based disparities and, when they do consider disparities, may perceive them as more legitimate (Huo, 2003). These processes can undermine minorities' motivations to initiate action to challenge the status quo and thus further contribute to the stability of existing social structures (Doosje *et al.*, 1999; Wright *et al.*, 2008; Wright and Baray, Chapter 11 of this volume).

In contrast, members of disadvantaged groups are expected to prefer a dual identity because it recognizes group distinctiveness by drawing attention to group disparities and simultaneously facilitates moral inclusiveness. Specifically, the advantage of a dual identity for disadvantaged-group members is that it affirms the distinctiveness of their subgroup identity but in a context of connection and potential cooperation with the advantaged group (Brown and Hewstone, 2005). People often fail to extend their principles or morality and justice to members of other groups, whereas the common group component of a dual identity helps to establish a context of 'moral inclusion' (Opotow, 1995). Thus, group-based inequity and injustice are more likely to be recognized by majority group members and responded to as moral violations, which can motivate the majority group toward action for equality (Tyler and Blader, 2003). Shared group identity also provides common ground for intergroup interaction and exchange. Recognition of dual identities can therefore stimulate both members of disadvantaged and advantaged groups to mobilize to address injustices.

We consider the implications of this functional perspective in the following sections. We first explore different group preferences for one-group representations and dual identities and then discuss different consequences of the representations for motivations and actions to change relations between groups towards greater equality.

Group preferences for one-group and dual-identity representations

Our functional analysis of group representations suggests that members of advantaged groups and members of disadvantaged groups will (a) have different preferences for one-group and dual-identity representations;

(b) be more satisfied with the nature of intergroup relations when their preferred representations are achieved; and (c) seek to manipulate intergroup situations to achieve these representations through their own actions and reinforce desired responses from members of other groups.

Representation preferences. Although not identical, one-group and dual-identity representations are closely related to assimilation and multicultural ideologies, respectively. Assimilation requires minority group members to conform to dominant values and ideals, often requiring the abandonment of inconsistent racial or ethnic group values, to achieve full acceptance in society. Assimilation often stresses singular allegiance to a common national identity. In contrast, multicultural integration strives to be inclusive by recognizing, and often celebrating, intergroup differences and their contributions to a common society. In general, preference for a one-group representation is highly correlated with support for an assimilative ideology, whereas preference for a dual identity is significantly related to endorsement of a multicultural ideology (Dovidio *et al.*, 2000).

Consistent with our functional perspective, members of advantaged groups generally prefer a one-group representation and an assimilative ideology across a range of intergroup settings, whereas members of disadvantaged groups prefer a dual identity and a multicultural ideology. For example, in the US, whites express a specific preference for a one-group representation in intergroup relations and more strongly support an assimilative ideology, whereas racial and ethnic minorities prefer a dual identity and a multicultural ideology (Dovidio *et al.*, 2000; Ryan *et al.*, 2007). Additional research also reveals that members of the host society and members of immigrant groups have different preferences for assimilation and multicultural integration. In the Netherlands, van Oudenhoven *et al.* (1998) found that Dutch majority group members preferred an assimilation of minority groups (in which minority group identity was abandoned and replaced by identification with the dominant Dutch culture), whereas Turkish and Moroccan immigrants most strongly endorsed integration (in which they would retain their own cultural identity while also valuing the dominant Dutch culture). Verkuyten (2006) summarized the results of eight studies of adolescents and young adults in Europe and found that minority group members supported multiculturalism (integration) more than did majority group members.

Representation preference and intergroup attitudes. To the extent that members of advantaged and disadvantaged groups prefer representations that best promote their group's interests, we further hypothesize that one-group and dual-identity representations will differentially influence their satisfaction with the intergroup climate. Specifically, we posited that the relation between intergroup contact and perceptions of positive intergroup relations, as predicted by contact theory, would be differentially mediated by one-group and dual-identity representations for whites and racial/ethnic minorities. We anticipated that the relation for whites would be mediated by one-group representations and the relation for racial and ethnic minorities would be mediated by a dual-identity representation, which recognizes both racial/ethnic group identity and a superordinate identity (see Dovidio *et al.*, 2000).

The results confirmed our hypothesis. For whites, more positive perceptions of intergroup contact related to stronger perceptions of one group, a dual identity and separate individuals, as well as weaker perceptions of different groups. However, when considered simultaneously, only the one-group representation significantly mediated satisfaction with intergroup relations. Also, as predicted, favourable conditions of contact predicted each of the representations for racial and ethnic minorities but, in contrast to the pattern for whites, this effect was mediated primarily by the dual-identity representation. Moreover, this pattern of differential mediation was stronger for people higher in racial/ethnic identification, both for whites and for members of racial and ethnic minority groups.

Shaping group representations. The third implication considered in this section of the strategic function of advantaged- and disadvantaged-group members' preferred representations is that members of these groups are motivated to influence intergroup relations in ways that emphasize their desired representations. This influence occurs through manipulation of the content of intergroup discourse, the systematic reinforcement of outgroup members' orientations, or support for policies that promote the preferred representation.

In a pair of studies, one with laboratory groups varying in control over a valued resource (extra credit for experimental participation) and the other with ethnic groups varying in status in Israel (Ashkenazim, high status; Mizrahim, low status), Saguy *et al.* (2008) investigated how members of advantaged and disadvantaged groups may attempt to steer intergroup discourse in different ways. In particular, we hypothesized that whereas members of advantaged groups would prefer discourse that focuses virtually exclusively on commonality, members of disadvantaged groups would be more balanced in their preference to discuss group differences and commonalities (the two critical elements of a dual identity). Across both studies, members of advantaged and disadvantaged groups showed an equivalently strong interest in discussing topics of commonality. However, members of advantaged groups exhibited significantly less interest than did members of disadvantaged groups in discussing differences between the groups. Members of disadvantaged groups showed equivalently strong preferences for talking about commonality *and* difference. Moreover, the effect of group status on desire to talk about differences between the groups was mediated by motivation for changing group positions towards equality. That is, disadvantaged-group members' greater preference to discuss points of difference, relative to advantaged-group members, occurred because they had a greater motivation for a change in the power structure.

In general, these studies converge to reveal that hierarchical relations between groups systematically lead to different contact preferences and strategies for members of advantaged and disadvantaged groups. Members of advantaged groups, who are motivated to maintain the status quo, show a preference for focusing on commonalities to the exclusion of differences. Members of disadvantaged groups, who desire to alter the status quo to improve their group's hierarchical position, exhibit a greater desire to talk about differences between the groups but, at the same time, to discuss commonalities between the groups.

To the extent that members of advantaged and disadvantaged groups strategically attempt to influence the representations of members of the other group, then they would be expected to respond particularly positively to members of the other group who appear to endorse the preferred representation of one's own group. Consistent with this reasoning, Nier *et al.* (2001, Study 2) demonstrated that white fans attending an American football game were significantly more helpful in response to a black interviewer's attempt to survey them about their food preferences when they shared common university affiliation (apparent by their respective university signature clothing) than when they had different university affiliations. For white interviewers, with whom they already shared racial group membership, the effect was much less pronounced. In a recent study (Thomas *et al.*, 2009), we further found that whites were responsive to indications of common identity by blacks, whether or not that identity was directly relevant to the immediate context. Across a number of sporting events (basketball as well as football), white fans were more helpful to black interviewers when they displayed a cap that indicated common national identity (USA) or university identity than when they wore a cap with the name of a different nation (France) or the rival university. In contrast, white fans showed elevated helping for white interviewers only when they displayed a situationally relevant common identity – common university identity versus rival university identity. In both of these field studies, the sizes of the samples of black fans were too small to permit meaningful analyses.

These field studies with fans at sporting events support our expectations that whites respond particularly positively to blacks who display common identity in a naturalistic setting. These findings, however, do not directly distinguish between whites' responses to blacks revealing a one-group identity or a dual identity. We found evidence in support of this distinction in a laboratory experiment (Dovidio *et al.*, 2010). White college students from Colgate University viewed a videotape that portrayed an interview with a black male student (actually a confederate) with whom they anticipated interacting in a subsequent session. The confederate responded to the questions posed to him using a script developed based on pilot testing to make a positive impression. After a series of questions intended to create this positive impression (e.g. about college activities and educational goals), the interviewer asked the confederate, 'And how do you see yourself?' The response was constructed to reflect one of the four representations outlined in the common ingroup identity model: (a) 'I see myself primarily as a Colgate student' (one group); (b) 'I see myself primarily as a black person' (different group); (c) 'I see myself primarily as a black Colgate student (or a Colgate student who is black)' (dual identity); or (d) 'I see myself primarily as a unique individual' (separate individuals). We tested how the different representations communicated by the black confederate influenced both liking for the confederate and attitudes toward blacks as a group.

White participants responded most positively in the condition in which the black confederate advocated common university identity (the one-group representation). In this condition, they liked the confederate the most and displayed the lowest level of prejudice towards blacks as a whole. The other three conditions did not significantly differ from one another. Liking for the confederate tended to be least favourable and attitudes towards blacks tended to be the most negative when the black confederate expressed a dual identity, but this condition was not significantly different than when the confederate emphasized only his black identity.

In another experiment involving majority group members (Dutch in the Netherlands), we again tested how different representations communicated by a minority-group member (a Moroccan immigrant, who acted as a confederate) influenced attitudes towards that individual and towards the outgroup as a whole (Scheepers *et al.*, 2010). As in the previous study, responses were more negative when the minority-group member communicated a dual identity, compared to a one-group representation. However, when participants, majority-group members, were induced to adopt a dual-identity representation, their attitudes towards the individual communicating a dual identity and towards Moroccans generally were significantly more positive. Overall, these findings indicate that expressions of subgroup identity by a member of a disadvantaged group is responded to negatively by members of the advantaged group (see also

Kaiser and Pratt-Hyatt, 2009), whose default preferred representation is that of one group. These negative responses are attenuated, however, once advantaged-group members themselves learn to believe in the benefits of a dual identity, a finding that supports the functional argument of intergroup responses.

In this section, we have argued that members of advantaged and disadvantaged groups have different preferences for common and dual identities, that their satisfaction with intergroup relations is differentially influenced by these alternative representations and that they appear to strategically influence members of the other group to attend to and potentially adopt their preferred representation. In the next section, we address the central assumption of our position – that the preference of advantaged-group members to establish a common, one-group identity may effectively reduce prejudice and immediate intergroup tension, but in the longer term it may impede social change towards equality between groups.

Common identity, intergroup attitudes and action for change

While acknowledging the demonstrated value of creating a common identity for improving attitudes (Gaertner and Dovidio, 2000), fostering more personalized and intimate interaction (Dovidio *et al.*, 1997) and promoting prosocial behaviour across group lines (Nier *et al.*, 2001), we acknowledge that another consequence of a focus on commonality is distracting attention away from group disparity and inequity, thereby reinforcing the status quo that advantages the majority group. Even apparently positive forms of action, such as helping, can be executed strategically to maintain status differences between groups and promote the dependency of the disadvantaged group (Nadler and Halabi, 2006).

Dixon *et al.* (2005, 2007) have questioned the traditional focus of social psychological research on intergroup attitudes as the ultimate measure of positive intergroup relations without adequate attention to the impact of attitudes on actual structural change towards equality. Dixon *et al.* 'accept that contact may transform interpersonal attitudes and stereotypes, but caution that it may leave unaltered the ideological beliefs that sustain systems of racial discrimination' (Dixon *et al.*, 2007, p. 868). They further argue that 'it is possible that the emotional benefits of contact may be offset by its tendency to promote acceptance of broader patterns of discrimination' (Dixon *et al.*, 2005, p. 707).

In support of this proposition, they document a general 'principle-implementation gap' between majority group members' widespread endorsement of equality in principle and their weaker, less consistent support for policies for creating concrete social change between the groups in society (Dixon *et al.*, 2005, 2007; see also Dovidio and Gaertner, 1996). This position dovetails with our hypothesis that when original group boundaries are degraded and replaced by a superordinate identity, majority group members are likely to respond more positively to an *individual* originally viewed as a member of another group, but they may be less likely to extend support to the other group as an *entity*. Thus, individual mobility may be facilitated but without a change in social structure or relative status between the groups.

From this perspective, if positive contact (or an emphasis on common identity) reduces attention to structural inequality as it promotes positive attitudes towards members of the outgroup, it can have consequences for group members' expectations regarding intergroup relations and hierarchy. Specifically, such outcomes may inflate perceptions of the fairness of the advantaged group among disadvantaged-group members and thus produce optimism about prospects of equality and relax their motivation to take direct action for social change.

We conducted three studies that explored these implications (Saguy *et al.*, 2009). The first study experimentally examined the causal effect of a commonality-focused encounter, relative to a difference-focused interaction, on disadvantaged-group members' outgroup attitudes, attention to inequality and expectations of outgroup fairness, as well as on advantaged-group members' intergroup orientations and resource allocation. The second and third studies generalized and extended the findings, specifically with respect to disadvantaged groups, by examining the relation of positive intergroup contact to attitudes, perceptions of inequality and outgroup fairness and support for social change in two naturalistic intergroup contexts.

The laboratory study (Saguy *et al.*, 2009, Study 1) manipulated power between two randomly assigned groups by giving the advantaged group the position of assigning extra course credits to the two groups (see also Saguy *et al.*, 2008). Before the members of the advantaged group allocated the credits, members of both groups interacted with instructions to focus on either intergroup commonalities or differences.

As expected, commonality-focused interaction produced more positive intergroup attitudes for both advantaged- and disadvantaged-group members than did difference-focused contact. In addition, for both groups, attention to inequality between groups was lower in the commonality-focused condition. Moreover, members of the disadvantaged group expected the advantaged group to be fairer in allocating the resources and to distribute the credits in a more equitable fashion following commonality-focused, rather than differences-focused, interaction. These effects were mediated by more positive intergroup attitudes and decreased attention to inequity during the interaction.

However, when the disadvantaged-group members' expectations were compared to the advantaged groups' actual allocation, there was a significant discrepancy. As the members of the disadvantaged groups anticipated, advantaged groups were substantially biased against the disadvantaged groups in the allocation of credits after differences-focused contact but, unexpectedly from the perspective of disadvantaged-group members, advantaged groups were just as biased in allocating the credits after commonality-focused interaction. The more positive intergroup attitudes of advantaged-group members in the commonality-focused, versus differences-focused, condition did not translate into more material support to achieve equality, and the advantaged groups' allocation fell significantly below what disadvantaged groups anticipated.

We found further support for the proposition that members of advantaged groups are primarily motivated by a proximal goal of achieving intergroup harmony, which reinforces the status quo, than by an ultimate objective of creating equality between groups. Earlier we described a study (Dovidio et al., 2010) in which white participants responded more positively to a black confederate who emphasized his common ingroup identity. In particular, white students showed greater liking for him personally and lower levels of prejudice towards blacks generally when the black confederate indicated that he primarily thought of himself in terms of the common university than when he emphasized a dual identity (as a black university student), his racial identity alone, or his uniqueness as an individual. After measuring these attitudes, under the guise of a separate study, we also assessed participants' support for policies that emphasized colour-blind assimilationist or colour-conscious multicultural policies that would potentially meet the particular needs of black students on campus. An example of an assimilationist policy was 'Students in their first year should be assigned roommates on a random basis'; an example of a multicultural policy was 'Minority students should be able to choose to have a roommate of the same race or ethnicity in their first year, but there should not be separate minority dormitories'.

The pattern of policy support (see Figure 12.1) revealed that support for colour-blind assimilationist policies was greatest in the condition in which the black confederate primarily emphasized his common university identity, whereas support for colour-conscious multicultural policies was lowest in this condition. Support for multicultural policies that benefited minority groups particularly was highest when the confederate expressed a dual identity. Overall, white participants' lower levels of prejudice

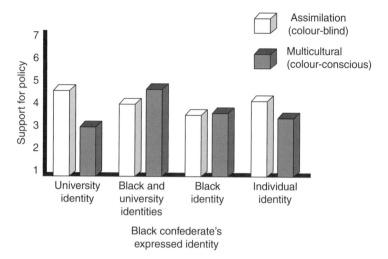

Figure 12.1: White participants displayed particularly strong support for colour-blind, assimilationist policies when a black confederate expressed primarily common university identity; they showed support for colour-conscious, multicultural policies mainly when the black confederate emphasized his dual identity

predicted support for assimilationist policies. That is, those expressing lower prejudice after being exposed to the black confederate more strongly endorsed policies that deemphasized group boundaries and identification. Lower levels of prejudice, however, were unrelated to support for multicultural policies that would offer particular benefits to blacks on campus. Taken together, these findings suggest that white participants may be less prejudiced when they encounter blacks who endorse common identity and respond to them personally in quite positive ways; however, these more positive orientations are more likely to translate into initiatives that deemphasize group membership than to efforts to benefit blacks as a group in the longer term.

In both this study and the Saguy *et al.* (2009) study of resource allocations, there appears to be an inconsistency between creating more positive attitudes towards members of disadvantaged groups and a willingness to promote their group interests. On the one hand, recognition of this inconsistency might arouse feelings of betrayal among members of disadvantaged groups that would increase intergroup tensions and facilitate their collective action. On the other hand, the immediate salience of shared positive attitudes and enhanced individual acceptance might obscure the lack of longer-term commitment to equality for members of disadvantaged groups (see also Jost *et al.*, 2004, on system justification). To explore these possibilities, two subsequent studies focused on the responses of members of two different disadvantaged groups, Arabs in Israel and Muslims in India, in terms of naturalistic intergroup relations.

In the study of Arabs in Israel (Saguy *et al.*, 2009, Study 2), we examined the statistical associations among friendships with Jews (a type of positive contact that is particularly likely to involve a focus on commonalities; Aron *et al.*, 2005), attitudes towards Jews, awareness of inequality and perceptions of Jews as fair. We further measured Arabs' support for social change towards equality. We hypothesized that, because less attention to illegitimate aspects in the inequality and positive outgroup orientations may undermine both the mobilization of disadvantaged-group members towards social action (Simon and Klandermans, 2001), and perceptions that progress may be made through outgroup fairness can reduce personal motivations for action, such factors would relate to *weaker* support for social action for change among Arabs.

Consistent with the results of our laboratory experiment, more positive contact with Jews was associated with more positive attitudes towards Jews and with reduced awareness of inequality between Jews and Arabs. In addition, improved attitudes were associated with increased perceptions of Jews as fair. Moreover, and consistent with our theorizing, both perceptions of Jews as fair and reduced awareness of inequality were associated with reduced support for social change. Thus, through its effects on the way disadvantaged-group members viewed social inequality and members of the other group, contact was associated with a *decrease* in support for social change. The overall model testing the proposed links between variables fit the data very well and better than alternative models (see Figure 12.2).

Results of the study of Muslims in India (see Saguy *et al.*, 2011) replicated these findings. Having more Hindu friends was related to the improved attitudes of Muslims towards Hindus, but it also reduced awareness of inequality between Muslims and Hindus. In addition, these outcomes predicted stronger perceptions of Hindus as fair, which in turn were related to weaker collective action tendencies (measured as intentions to participate in various actions that could improve the position of Muslims in India).

Wright and Lubensky (2009), who examined data from a survey of African-American and Latino/a students at a predominantly white university, produced compatible findings. Positive intergroup contact was associated with more favourable attitudes towards whites and with less support for collective action. In addition, mediation analyses revealed that the negative effect of contact on collective action was in part the result of a reduction in ethnic identification. In addition, Wright *et al.* (2008), using

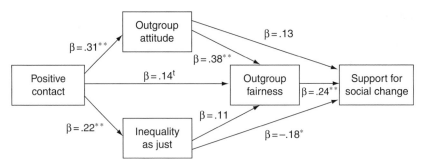

Figure 12.2: More positive attitudes towards Jews and greater perceptions of their fairness mediate the effects of positive intergroup contact on Arabs' lower level of support for social change

methodologies designed specifically to create common group identity (e.g. Gaertner *et al.*, 1989), found that these interventions not only improved intergroup attitudes but also reduced the motivation of minority group members to actively and collectively take action to improve their disadvantaged social position. Thus, because it improves attitudes and blurs group differences, positive contact and a focus on commonality can undermine the conditions necessary for collective action to occur. Similarly, Dixon *et al.* (2007), in a survey study of black and white respondents in South Africa, found that more positive intergroup contact was associated with black South Africans' decreased support for social policies that might enhance racial equality. Black South Africans who reported more positive contact with whites were less supportive of compensatory policies promoting the interests of blacks in education and employment.

Summary and implications

Previous work on the common ingroup identity model reveals the impressive power of 'we'. Conceiving of others in terms of common-group identity, rather than separate-group identities, harnesses the forces of ingroup favouritism and redirects them to produce more positive thoughts and feelings towards others in ways that have immediate impact for reducing intergroup bias. In this chapter, however, we further considered a potential 'darker side of we'. That is, thinking of members of disadvantaged groups only in terms of common identity can distract attention away from group-based inequities, undermining motivations of members of the advantaged group to benefit the disadvantaged group collectively. Moreover, the findings we have reported suggest that experiences of positive, commonality-focused contact can affect the way disadvantaged-group members view social inequality and their own disadvantage. These perceptions, which reflect an overly optimistic view of intergroup relations, can reduce motivation to challenge existing social inequality.

We further proposed, and attempted to document, that members of advantaged and disadvantaged groups prefer different recategorized representations, one-group or dual-identity, because these representations best promote the particular interest of their respective groups. Specifically, we found that members of advantaged groups generally prefer a one-group representation, whereas members of disadvantaged groups prefer a dual identity. However, to the extent that these relations are functionally motivated, they are not invariant. For instance, we found that when intergroup tensions are high and group interests are threatened, members of advantaged groups emphasize common identity more, whereas members of disadvantaged groups emphasize multicultural interests to an even greater degree (Dovidio et al., 2008). In addition, there may be cultural variation in group orientations. In cultural contexts in which the status of minorities is tenuous because of the nature of immigration policies (e.g. in Portugal; see Guerra et al., 2010), minority groups may prefer a one-group representation, whereas majority group members may prefer a dual identity in which the different group memberships remain identifiable so as to favourably differentiate higher- from lower-status groups. Guerra et al. (2010) found that in Portugal an intervention that emphasized one common group identity was more effective for producing positive intergroup attitudes among African Portuguese children, whereas an intervention that highlighted dual identity had more positive impact on European Portuguese children. Future research might thus productively consider how the stability and legitimacy of intergroup relations could critically moderate preferences for different representations and their intergroup consequences.

In addition, although ideologies such as assimilation and multiculturalism are commonly viewed as oppositional (Wolsko et al., 2006), we note that in practice commonality need not preclude concern for the particular needs and interests of members of disadvantaged groups. The critical factor likely involves the nature of positive contact and how this harmony is achieved. For instance, whereas emphasis on commonality topics that are unrelated to group inequalities may deflect attention from disparities and thereby lead group members to relax their motivation for achieving equality, common identity constructed around a sense of morality and humanity would likely bring the illegitimacy of disparities to light. Such a commonality focus can both bring members of advantaged and disadvantaged groups together and motivate them, perhaps in coordinated fashion, to eliminate social inequities.

In conclusion, research on intergroup relations has traditionally focused on prejudice reduction as a primary metric for improved intergroup relations. Work on contact theory, for example, has generally used prejudice reduction as the main (albeit not exclusive) criterion measure of intervention effectiveness (Pettigrew and Tropp, 2006). We acknowledge the importance of prejudice reduction as an important outcome; intergroup antipathy often needs to be ameliorated before other interventions, such as cooperation and common goals, can be implemented. However, reducing prejudice is not sufficient to ensure equitable and enduring positive intergroup relations. Empirically, prejudice is only modestly related to discrimination ($r = .26$ to $.32$; see Dovidio *et al.*, 1996; and Talaska *et al.*, 2008).

Moreover, reductions in prejudice that promote intergroup harmony may meet the immediate needs of members of advantaged and disadvantaged groups for being liked and respected, but may not translate to sustained efforts to challenge the status quo to create structural social change. We note, though, that commonality, positive intergroup contact and intergroup harmony do not *necessarily* undermine efforts towards equality, but it is important to recognize that commonality and intergroup harmony per se do not necessarily lead to intergroup equality. The challenge, both theoretically and practically, is thus to extend the analyses of intergroup relations to understand more fully the dynamics not just about feeling good about others but also doing good for them.

Note

1. Preparation of this chapter was supported by NSF Grant BCS-0613218 awarded to the first two authors and Spencer Grant 200900193 awarded to the first author.

References

Allport, G. W. (1954). *The Nature of Prejudice*. Cambridge, MA: Addison-Wesley.
Aron, A., McLaughlin-Volpe, T., Mashek, D., Lewandowski, G., Wright, S. C. and Aron, E. N. (2005). Including others in the self. In W. Stroebe and M. Hewstone (eds.), *European Review of Social Psychology* (Vol. 15, pp.101–32). Hove, UK: Psychology Press.
Blumer, H. (1958). Race prejudice as a sense of group position. *Pacific Sociological Review*, **1**, 3–7.
Brown, R. (1996). *Prejudice: its Social Psychology*. Malden, MA: Blackwell.
Brown, R. and Hewstone, M. (2005). An integrative theory of intergroup contact. In M. P. Zanna (ed.), *Advances in Experimental Social Psychology* (Vol. 37, pp.255–343). San Diego, CA: Academic Press.

Dixon, J. A., Durrheim, K. and Tredoux, C. (2005). Beyond the optimal strategy: a 'reality check' for the contact hypothesis. *American Psychologist*, **60**, 697–711.

(2007). Intergroup contact and attitudes toward the principle and practice of racial equality. *Psychological Science*, **18**, 867–72.

Doosje, B., Ellemers, N. and Spears, R. (1999). Commitment and intergroup behaviour. In N. Ellemers, R. Spears and B. Doosje (eds.), *Social Identity: Context, Commitment and Content* (pp.84–107). Oxford, UK: Blackwell.

Dovidio, J. F. and Gaertner, S. L. (1996). Affirmative action, unintentional racial biases, and intergroup relations. *Journal of Social Issues*, **52**(4), 51–75.

(2010). Intergroup bias. In S. T. Fiske, D. Gilbert and G. Lindzey (eds.), *Handbook of Social Psychology* (Vol. 2, pp.1,084–121). New York: Wiley.

Dovidio, J. F., Brigham, J. C., Johnson, B. T. and Gaertner, S. L. (1996). Stereotyping, prejudice, and discrimination: another look. In C. N. Macrae, M. Hewstone and C. Stangor (eds.), *Foundations of Stereotypes and Stereotyping* (pp.276–319). New York: Guilford.

Dovidio, J. F., Gaertner, S. L. and Kafati, G. (2000). Group identity and intergroup relations: the common in-group identity model. In S. R. Thye, E. J. Lawler, M. W. Macy and H. A. Walker (eds.), *Advances in Group Processes* (Vol. 17, pp.1–34). Stamford, CT: JAI Press.

Dovidio, J. F., Gaertner, S. L. and Saguy, T. (2008). Another view of 'we': majority and minority group perspectives on a common ingroup identity. *European Review of Social Psychology*, **18**, 296–330.

(2009). Commonality and the complexity of 'we': social attitudes and social change. *Personality and Social Psychology Review*, **13**, 3–20.

Dovidio, J. F., Gaertner, S. L., Shnabel, N., Saguy, T. and Johnson, J. D. (2010). Recategorization and prosocial behavior: common identity and a dual identity. In S. Stürmer and M. Snyder (eds.), *The Psychology of Prosocial Behavior* (pp.191–208). Malden, MA: Wiley-Blackwell.

Dovidio, J. F., Gaertner, S. L., Validzic, A., Matoka, K., Johnson, B. and Frazier, S. (1997). Extending the benefits of re-categorization: evaluations, self-disclosure and helping. *Journal of Experimental Social Psychology*, **33**, 401–20.

Ellemers, N. and Barreto, M. (2001). The impact of relative group status: affective, behavioral, and perceptual consequences. In R. Brown and S. L. Gaertner (eds.), *Blackwell Handbook of Social Psychology: Intergroup Processes* (pp.324–43). Oxford, UK: Blackwell.

Fiske, S. T. and Taylor, S. E. (2007). *Social Cognition: from Brains to Culture*. New York: McGraw-Hill.

Gaertner, S. L. and Dovidio, J. F. (2000). *Reducing Intergroup Bias: the Common Ingroup Identity Model*. Philadelphia, PA: The Psychology Press.

(2009). A common ingroup identity: a categorization-based approach for reducing intergroup bias. In T. Nelson (ed.), *Handbook of Prejudice* (pp.489–506). Philadelphia, PA: Taylor and Francis.

(2010). Social categorization. In J. F. Dovidio, M. Hewstone, P. Glick and V. M. Esses (eds.), *Handbook of Prejudice, Stereotyping, and Discrimination* (pp.526–43). Thousand Oaks, CA: Sage.

Gaertner, S. L., Dovidio, J. F., Anastasio, P. A., Bachman, B. A. and Rust, M. C. (1993). The common ingroup identity model: recategorization and the reduction of intergroup bias. In W. Stroebe and M. Hewstone (eds.), *European Review of Social Psychology* (Vol. 4, pp.1–26). New York: John Wiley and Sons.

Gaertner, S. L., Dovidio, J. F., Nier, J., Ward, C. and Banker, B. (1999). Across cultural divides: the value of a superordinate identity. In D. Prentice and D. Miller (eds.), *Cultural Divides: Understanding and Overcoming Group Conflict* (pp.173–212). New York: Russell Sage Foundation.

Gaertner, S. L., Mann, J. A., Dovidio, J. F., Murrell, A. J. and Pomare, M. (1990). How does cooperation reduce intergroup bias? *Journal of Personality and Social Psychology*, **59**, 692–704.

Gaertner, S. L., Mann, J. A., Murrell, A. J. and Dovidio, J. F. (1989). Reduction of intergroup bias: the benefits of recategorization. *Journal of Personality and Social Psychology*, **57**, 239–49.

González, R. and Brown, R. (2003). Generalization of positive attitude as a function of subgroup and superordinate group identification in intergroup contact. *European Journal of Social Psychology*, **33**, 195–214.

Guerra, R., Rebelo, M., Monteiro, M. B., Riek, B. M., Maia, E. W., Gaertner, S. L. and Dovidio, J. F. (2010). How should intergroup contact be structured to reduce bias among majority and minority group children? *Group Processes and Intergroup Relations*, **13**, 445–60.

Huo, Y. J. (2003). Procedural justice and social regulation across group boundaries: does subgroup identity undermine relationship-based governance? *Personality and Social Psychology Bulletin*, **29**, 336–48.

Jost, J. T., Banaji, M. and Nosek, B. A. (2004). A decade of system justification theory: accumulated evidence of conscious and unconscious bolstering of the status quo. *Political Psychology*, **25**, 881–919.

Kaiser, C. and Pratt-Hyatt, J. (2009). Distributing prejudice unequally: do whites distribute their prejudice toward strongly identified minorities? *Journal of Personality and Social Psychology*, **96**, 432–45.

Nadler, A. and Halabi, S. (2006). Intergroup helping as status relations: effects of status stability in-group identification and type of help on receptivity to help from high status group. *Journal of Personality and Social Psychology*, **91**, 97–110.

Nier, J. A., Gaertner, S. L., Dovidio, J. F., Banker, B. S. and Ward, C. M. (2001). Changing interracial evaluations and behavior: the effects of a common group identity. *Group Processes and Intergroup Relations*, **4**, 299–316.

Opotow, S. (1995). Drawing the line: social categorization, moral exclusion, and the scope of justice. In B. B. Bunker and J. Z. Rubin (eds.), *Conflict, Cooperation, and Justice: Essays Inspired by the Work of Morton Deutsch* (pp.347–69). San Francisco, CA: Jossey-Bass.

Pettigrew, T. F. and Tropp, L. R. (2006). A meta-analytic test of intergroup contact theory. *Journal of Personality and Social Psychology*, **90**, 751–83.

(2008). How does contact reduce prejudice? A meta analytic test of three mediators. *European Journal of Social Psychology*, **38**, 922–34.

Ryan, C. S., Hunt, J. S., Weible, J. A., Peterson, C. R. and Casas, J. F. (2007). Multicultural and colorblind ideology, stereotypes, and ethnocentrism among black and white Americans. *Group Processes and Intergroup Relations*, **10**, 617–37.

Saguy, T., Dovidio, J. F. and Pratto, F. (2008). Beyond contact: intergroup contact in the context of power relations. *Personality and Social Psychology Bulletin*, **34**, 432–45.

Saguy, T., Tausch, N., Dovidio, J. F. and Pratto, F. (2009). The irony of harmony: intergroup contact can produce false expectations for equality. *Psychological Science*, **29**, 114–21.

Saguy, T., Tausch, N., Dovidio, J. F., Pratto, F. and Singh, P. (2011). Tension and harmony in intergroup relations. In P. R. Shaver and M. Mikulincer (eds.), *Understanding and Reducing Aggression, Violence, and their Consequences* (pp.333–48). Washington, DC: American Psychological Association.

Scheepers, D., Saguy, T., Dovidio, J. F. and Gaertner, S. L. (2010). The challenge of multiculturalism. Unpublished manuscript, University of Leiden, Netherlands.

Simon, B. and Klandermans, B. (2001). Politicized collective identity: a social-psychological analysis. *American Psychologist*, **56**, 319–31.

Tajfel, H. and Turner, J. C. (1979). An integrative theory of intergroup conflict. In W. G. Austin and S. Worchel (eds.), *The Social Psychology of Intergroup Relations* (pp.33–48). Monterey, CA: Brooks/Cole.

Talaska, C. A., Fiske, S. T. and Chaiken, S. (2008). Legitimating racial discrimination: emotions, not beliefs, best predict discrimination in a meta-analysis. *Social Justice Research*, **21**, 263–96.

Thomas, E. L., Saguy, T., Dovidio, J. F. and Gaertner, S. L. (2009). The many hats we wear: the influences of identity commonality and relevance on intergroup helping behavior. Poster presented at the *Groups Preconference at the Annual Meeting of the Society for Personality and Social Psychology* (Feb). Tampa, FL.

Turner, J. C., Hogg, M. A., Oakes, P. J., Reicher, S. D. and Wetherell, M. S. (1987). *Rediscovering the Social Group: a Self-categorization Theory*. Oxford, UK: Blackwell.

Tyler, T. and Blader, S. L. (2003). The group engagement model: procedural justice, social identity, and cooperative behavior. *Personality and Social Psychology Review*, 7, 349–61.

van Oudenhoven, J. P., Prins, K. S. and Buunk, B. (1998). Attitudes of minority and majority members towards adaptation of immigrants. *European Journal of Social Psychology*, **28**, 995–1,013.

van Zomeren, M., Postmes, T. and Spears, R. (2008). Toward an integrative social identity model of collective action: a quantitative research synthesis of three socio-psychological perspectives. *Psychological Bulletin*, **134**, 504–35.

Verkuyten, M. (2006). Multicultural recognition and ethnic minority rights: a social identity perspective. In W. Stroebe and M. Hewstone (eds.), *European Review of Social Psychology* (Vol. 17, pp.148–84). Hove, UK: Psychology Press.

West, T. V., Pearson, A. R., Dovidio, J. F., Shelton, J. N. and Trail, T. (2009). Superordinate identity and intergroup roommate friendship development. *Journal of Experimental Social Psychology*, **45**, 1,266–72.

Wolsko, C., Park, B. and Judd, C. M. (2006). Considering the Tower of Babel: correlates of assimilation and multiculturalism among ethnic minority and majority groups in the United States. *Social Justice Research*, **19**, 277–306.

Wright, S. C. (2001). Strategic collective action: social psychology and social change. In R. Brown and S. L. Gaertner (eds.), *Blackwell Handbook of Social Psychology: Intergroup Processes* (pp.223–56). Oxford, UK: Blackwell.

Wright, S. C. and Lubensky, M. E. (2009). The struggle for social equality: collective action versus prejudice reduction. In S. Demoulin, J.-P. Leyens and J. F. Dovidio (eds.), *Intergroup Misunderstandings: Impact of Divergent Social Realities* (pp.291–310). New York: Psychology Press.

Wright, S. C., Kiu, L., Semenya, A. and Comeau, J. (2008). *Prejudice Reduction and Collective Action: When Strategies for Reducing Social Inequality Collide.* Paper presented at the Meeting of the European Association for Experimental Social Psychology (June). Optija, Croatia.

13 Contact and social change in an ongoing asymmetrical conflict: four social-psychological models of reconciliation-aimed planned encounters between Israeli Jews and Palestinians

Ifat Maoz

Introduction

This chapter focuses on reconciliation-aimed intergroup encounters – between Israeli Jews and Palestinians – that attempt to reduce hostility and increase understanding and cooperation between the two nationalities. Like other contact interventions conducted in settings of intergroup conflict, encounters between Israeli Jews and Palestinians represent a paradoxical project aiming to produce equality and cooperation between groups that are embedded in a protracted, asymmetrical conflict. Though existing research teaches us valuable lessons on the effectiveness of contact conducted under optimal conditions (Pettigrew, 1998; Pettigrew and Tropp, 2000, 2006), little is said about contact between groups involved in an acute dispute (Dixon and Durrheim, 2003; for important exceptions see Salomon, 2004, 2006).

The study presented here is inspired by a recent school of thought that looks at processes and effects of contact in non-optimal conditions of deeply divided societies (Dixon and Durrheim, 2003; Dixon *et al.*, 2005, 2007; Hewstone, 1996). It also joins a growing number of studies presenting a critical approach to planned encounters between Israeli Jews and Palestinians (Abu-Nimer, 1999, 2004; Bekerman, 2002, 2009, in press; Halabi and Sonnenschein, 2004; Helman, 2002; Salomon, 2004; Suleiman, 2004).

Building on these traditions of research, this chapter follows the evolution of reconciliation-aimed contact interventions between Israeli Jews and Palestinians in the past twenty years. It identifies and traces the evolvement of four social-psychological models of intergroup encounters, discusses the mechanisms used within these models to cope with the reality of conflict and inequality and discusses the extent to which the different models actually aim at inducing social change.

Planned encounters between Israeli Jews and Palestinians constitute a useful case in point. Observing their encounters enables us to learn about models and mechanisms through which intergroup contact interventions – conducted in realistic situations of conflict – attempt to address barriers to conflict resolution and assist the transition to peaceful reconciliation. It also enables us to explore the strengths and limits of a model of social change based around prejudice reduction, i.e. designed to promote harmony and diffuse negative feelings towards, and thoughts about, members of other groups (see also Wright and Baray, Chapter 11 of this volume).

Planned encounters between Israeli Jews and Palestinians: an overview

Attempts at improving intergroup relations through organized encounters between Israeli Jews and Palestinians began sporadically in the 1950s, when the Palestinian Arab population in Israel was still under military rule, and continued through the 1960s and 1970s – when several large-scale programmes of planned encounters between Israeli Jews and Palestinians were established (Maoz, 2006). Planned encounters between Israeli Jews and Palestinians went through rapid expansion and redefinition of their form and goals in the early 1980s, in the harsh political climate that followed the Lebanon war. A series of public-opinion surveys indicated growing right-wing extremism and increased anti-democratic and anti-Arab tendencies among Israeli Jews (Maoz, 2000a, 2009). These trends evoked concern among Jewish educators and served as a strong trigger for the initiation, expansion and institutionalization of contact interventions between Israeli Jews and Palestinians (Maoz, 2000a). School curricula concerning Jewish–Arab relations were endorsed and supported by the Ministry of Education, and encounter workshops targeted at school students and teachers became part of these curricula (Maoz, 2000a, 2009).

Thus, planned encounters between Israeli Jews and Palestinians became part of a fast-expanding category of intergroup contact interventions widely used since the last decades of the twentieth century to address different conflicts and intergroup tensions around the world, as means of improving intergroup attitudes, reducing prejudice and hostility and fostering respect and understanding between rival ethnic and national groups (Bar-Tal, 2002, 2004; Salomon, 2002, 2004, 2006; Stephan and Stephan, 2001).

Since the mid-1980s, dozens of encounter programmes between Israeli Jews and Palestinians have been conducted each year. These range from one-shot meetings to long-term and continuous series of meetings, and include youth encounters, dialogues between university students, university professors and other professionals (Maoz, 2004). Planned encounter programmes typically include eight to twelve participants from each nationality, are facilitated by a Jewish and an Arab facilitator and are conducted in the framework of educational and communal institutions and organizations (Maoz, 2009).

A series of public-opinion surveys of representative samples (N = 500) of the Jewish Israeli population in the years 2002, 2003 and 2005 (Maoz, 2009) indicate that about 16 per cent of the Jewish Israeli population have participated in at least one programme of planned encounters between Israeli Jews and Palestinians in their lifetime. This rate of reported participation was consistent beyond the specific surveys and became even larger (21 per cent of Israeli Jews) when taking into account only the secular Jewish population. Although not a very large percentage, these data clearly show that planned encounters have reached, over the years, a considerable number of Israeli Jews. About one in every six Israeli Jew has participated in their lifetime in an encounter with Palestinian Arabs (Maoz, 2009).

The contact hypothesis and planned encounters between Israeli Jews and Palestinians

In many cases, planned encounters between Israeli Jews and Palestinians derive their rationale from the contact hypothesis popularized by the American social psychologist Gordon Allport (1954), and further developed and transported to the Israeli context by the educator and social psychologist Yehuda Amir (1969). This theory states that intergroup contact can be effective in reducing negative intergroup stereotypes and mutual prejudices, provided that certain conditions are met (Pettigrew, 1998). The primary conditions for effective intergroup contact are: (1) equal status of both groups in the contact situation; (b) ongoing personal interaction between individuals from both groups; (c) cooperation in a situation of mutual dependence, in which members of both groups work together towards a common goal; and (d) institutional support – consensus among the authorities and the relevant institutions about norms that support equality.

Although research findings generally support the effectiveness of contact in improving intergroup relations (Pettigrew, 1998; for recent extensive meta-analyses see Pettigrew and Tropp, 2000, 2006), much of this research relates to contact conducted under relatively favourable conditions as defined by the contact hypothesis (see Dixon and

Durrheim, 2003; Dixon *et al.*, 2005, 2007 for elaborate criticism on the limitations of focusing on the study of optimal intergroup contacts).

The majority of existing research does not study intergroup contact interventions in conditions of acute, asymmetrical violent conflict (for important exceptions, see Salomon, 2004, 2006). Moreover, little attention has been given to the conceptual definition of social-psychological mechanisms through which intergroup encounters – conducted in settings of active conflict between the sides – attempt to address psychological barriers to conflict resolution and assist the transition to peaceful reconciliation.

This chapter is based on empirical data derived from several research programmes on planned intergroup encounters – conducted in the context of the acute, ongoing asymmetrical conflict between Israeli Jews and Palestinians – and aimed at improving relations between the sides. The chapter traces the evolution in the field of four social-psychological models of encounters between Israeli Jews and Palestinians, explicates the mechanisms through which these models attempt to address the existing reality of Jewish–Arab conflict and achieve reconciliation, and elaborates on the dilemmas and limitations that are associated with operating each of these models. A focal question regarding contact interventions in settings of institutionalized discrimination, such as exists towards the Palestinian Arab citizens of Israel (Al-Haj, 2002, 2005), is the extent to which these interventions aim at actual socio-political change, as opposed to simply promoting more positive attitudes towards others (Dixon *et al.*, 2005; Wright and Lubensky, 2009). To address this question, the analysis presented here places the models described on a continuum ranging from approaches that fully or partially support the existing status quo (or at least do not openly challenge it) to models that implicitly or explicitly call for socio-political change.

Different models of planned encounters between Israeli Jews and Palestinians

The model that initially guided planned contact interventions between Israeli Jews and Palestinians and is still the most dominant model in this field is the coexistence model. This model closely adheres to the principles of the contact hypothesis, emphasizing interpersonal interaction as leading to individual-level social change (Dixon *et al.*, 2005), while largely ignoring the protracted intergroup conflict between Israelis and Palestinians as well as the asymmetrical structural relations between Israeli Jews and Palestinians (Suleiman, 2004).

However, the coexistence model is by no means the only model of structured encounters between Israeli Jews and Palestinians. One of the most intriguing phenomena related to encounter activities between Israeli Jews and Palestinians is the evolution of several different models of intergroup encounters in terms of goals, ideology and major conflict transformation practices used. It seems that the paradoxical project of striving for symmetry and cooperation in a reality of protracted, asymmetrical conflict has led those involved in encounter activities to gradually depart from the initial coexistence model of Jewish–Arab encounters and form new models that more directly address the problematics of the relations between the Jewish majority and the Palestinian Arab minority in the state of Israel.

The study presented in this chapter traces the evolution of four different social-psychological models of planned encounters between Israeli Jews and Palestinians: the coexistence model, the joint projects model, the confrontational model and the narrative-story-telling model (Maoz, 2011).

Method

This analysis is based on empirical data derived from a series of research programmes conducted by the author from the mid-1980s until 2008, tracing the evolution of models of planned contact interventions between Israeli Jews and Palestinians through the subjective perceptions of those involved in shaping, enacting and participating in planned Jewish–Arab encounter activities. The research tools used were largely qualitative (Glaser and Strauss, 1967; Strauss and Corbin, 1998) and included the following: (1) in-depth interviews, discussions and conversations with organizers, planners, directors, facilitators and participants of Jewish–Arab encounter programmes; (2) observations of encounter activities and encounter programme staff meetings; and (3) analyses of documents related to encounter programmes such as proposals, plans and programmes, activity summaries and reports (see also Maoz, 2011).

The coexistence model

The coexistence model draws its rationale directly from major theories of intergroup relations such as the contact hypothesis (Allport, 1954; Pettigrew, 1998), and is a prevalent encounter model used in several conflict-sites around the world. It was imported to Israel from the US in the 1980s and constituted the first major model of planned contact interventions between Israeli Jews and Palestinians. Today it remains the dominant model and guides the majority of these contact interventions.

The coexistence model seeks to promote mutual understanding and tolerance between Jews and Arabs, reduce stereotypes, foster positive intergroup attitudes and advance other goals in the spirit of the contact hypothesis (Allport, 1954). This model emphasizes personal similarities ('we are all human beings') and cultural and language commonalities and supports notions of togetherness and cooperation (Maoz, 2004). This model is cynically called by its critics 'the hummus and falafel model' because of its promotion of folkloristic, seemingly superficial, aspects that unite Jews and Arabs.

The coexistence model focuses on interpersonal interaction and on personal identities and does not tend to relate to issues such as the conflict between Israeli Jews and Palestinians, dilemmas of national identity and claims concerning discrimination of the Palestinian citizens of Israel (Maoz, 2000a, 2000b). As such, this model can be seen as supporting the status quo of the existing structural relations between Jews and Palestinian Arabs in Israel rather than aiming at social or political change. To echo Dovidio *et al.* (Chapter 12), it is a model that tends to 'meet the immediate needs of members of advantaged and disadvantaged groups for being liked and respected but may not translate to sustained efforts to challenge the status quo to create structural social change'.

Strengths and dilemmas

The strength of the coexistence model lies in its emphasis on widely shared and agreed-upon commonalities such as 'we are all human beings'. Thus, it avoids painful disagreements and can foster mutual respect and sympathy. The focus on commonalities renders the coexistence model especially suitable for young children, who may not yet be cognitively and emotionally equipped to deal with the painful complexity of conflict (Stephan, 2001). Indeed, this model has been found in research to be particularly successful in interventions with young children – kindergarten and elementary school students, for example (Maoz, 2001). Furthermore, the consensual and apolitical nature of the coexistence model attracts participants who would normally object to an intergroup encounter, as well as participants who hold nationalistic or militant political opinions.

However, the limitations of the coexistence model are also clear. Many Jews and Palestinians arrive to the encounter with a strong expectation that they will discuss the relationships between the sides. Encounters that avoid doing so can be seen by such participants, at best, as disappointing, irrelevant and neglectful of their needs and interests (Maoz, 2000a, 2000b). At worse such encounters can be viewed as immoral; that is, as intentionally perpetuating existing power relations by focusing on changing individual-level prejudice while ignoring the collective and institutionalized bases of discrimination (see Dixon *et al.*, 2005; Maoz, 2000b; Reicher, 1986, 2007).

The joint projects model

Closely related to the coexistence model is the joint projects model, which derives its academic rationale from the classic social-psychological study by Muzafer Sherif (1966). Sherif's research demonstrated that working together towards a common, superordinate goal reduces intergroup hostilities, increases liking and cooperation and fosters a common identity transcending the separate identity of each group (see also Dovidio *et al.*, Chapter 12 of this volume).

Similar to the coexistence model, the joint projects model also became prominent in the mid-1980s, and since then has remained a popular way of organizing Arab–Israeli encounters. Examples of joint projects are numerous and include joint music events, joint theatre projects, Jewish–Arab choirs, Jewish–Arab art projects, scientific projects, joint study groups, environmental projects, mixed soccer teams, Jews and Arabs building curricula together and more.

In most cases, the joint projects model, like the coexistence model, emphasizes commonalities and does not tend to directly deal with separate national identities, political conflict and claims regarding discrimination towards the Palestinian citizens of Israel. Thus, like the coexistence model, the joint projects model can be defined as a model that leaves the status quo intact and does not aim for a structural change in the relations between the Jewish majority and the Palestinian Arab minority in Israel (Wright and Lubensky, 2009).

Strengths and limitations

The joint projects model is often seen as an ideal model for improving intergroup relations, as it includes a concrete, visible process of working together that results in a joint product – potentially reflecting (also to outside audiences) the success of intergroup cooperation. Moreover, shared interests and cooperation are often regarded as especially effective tools for reducing intergroup hostilities and transcending separate group identities (Aronson and Patnoe, 1997). Indeed, studies of joint Jewish–Arab soccer teams show that this model was highly effective in improving intergroup attitudes (see Salomon, 2006).

However, the joint projects model also has limitations. First, as described above, encounters focused on a joint project do not directly deal, in most cases, with issues related to the conflict. For participants interested in discussing the relations between Jews and Arabs engaging (for example) in a joint art project, this can be experienced as disappointing and as highly irrelevant to their actual needs and preferences.

Second, the joint project does not always elicit the same degree of involvement in its Jewish and Arab participants. For example, writing together curricular materials on marriage traditions of Jews and Arabs may elicit high interest in Jewish teachers, but may seem to their Palestinian Arab counterparts as irrelevant as it does not directly deal with national identities and associated patterns of conflict. As a result, Jewish teachers may become highly involved in the work while Palestinian Arab teachers show less commitment (Maoz, 2000b). Such a process can, paradoxically, serve to strengthen existing stereotypes of Jews as over-dominant and controlling and of Arabs as lazy and passive (Maoz, 2004). Unfortunately, even topics that may initially seem ideal for joint projects may elicit low interest or even aversion of one of the participating groups. Maoz (2000b) describes such a case that evolved between Jewish and Arab teachers participating in a project aimed at building joint curricular materials. Another illustrative example is brought in Connolly's (2000) ethnographic study of a Northern Irish cross-community initiative. This initiative aimed but failed to encourage, through joint disco dancing, cooperative interaction of protestant and catholic youngsters, as participants' subjective (emotionally ambivalent) perspective on this activity was not taken into account. Finally, the failure of a joint project to produce cooperative intergroup interactions, and, even more so, the failure of the two groups to create together a product, can be experienced by participants as well as by outside viewers as more concrete, significant and outwardly visible than a failure of a regular dialogue project (in which participants are not expected to produce a concrete joint product).

Such criticisms of the coexistence and the related joint projects models have led to the emergence of the more politically focused confrontational model.

The confrontational model

In contrast to the coexistence and the joint projects models of planned encounters between Israeli Jews and Palestinians, the confrontational or group identity model emphasizes the conflict and power relations between groups. The goal of this model is to modify the construction of identity of members of the minority and majority groups, and encourage greater

awareness among Jewish participants regarding the asymmetrical relations between Jews and Palestinian Arabs in Israel, and of their role as a
dominant or oppressive group (Halabi and Sonnenschein, 2004;
Sonnenschein et al., 1998). This model also seeks to empower the members of the Palestinian Arab minority by having them experience direct
confrontation with the Jews, which includes discussion of national identities, national and civil aspirations and discrimination (Halabi and
Sonnenschein, 2004; Maoz, 2004; Sonnenschein et al., 1998).

The confrontational/group identity model is a clear product of the
needs and dynamics in the field. It was first presented and applied by
Palestinian Arab facilitators and participants in the early 1990s, who were
not satisfied with the dominant coexistence model and felt it did not
address their needs and concerns as a national minority group. These
were joined by some Jewish colleagues who agreed with them and supported their claims (Maoz, 2000a). Theoretically, the confrontational
model derives from the social identity theory (Tajfel and Turner, 1986)
and thus emphasizes intergroup (rather than interpersonal) interaction as
a tool for transforming intergroup relations (see also Hewstone, 1996
and Miller, 2002 for an elaborate discussion of the effectiveness of
intergroup versus interpersonal interaction in transforming intergroup
attitudes). The confrontational model's perspective regarding social
change largely reflects major criticism of the contact hypothesis.
Reicher (1986, Chapter 1 of this volume) argues that the contact hypothesis misrepresents the deeper causes of conflict and inequality and is thus
unable to contribute substantively to their solution. He thus suggests a
shift from a model of change focused on the reduction of personal
prejudice to a model of change focused on directly challenging the status
quo (see also Dixon et al., 2005 and several other chapters in the present
volume). The confrontational model of encounters between Israeli Jews
and Palestinians can be viewed as realizing, to a large extent, the
approach advocated by Reicher. It clearly and explicitly strives for social
and political change, aiming at transforming the asymmetric structural
relations between the Jewish majority and the Palestinian Arab minority
in Israel.

Strengths, dilemmas and limitations

The clearest strength of the confrontational model is in its direct and
explicit discussion of issues such as the relations between Jews and
Palestinian Arabs in Israel, asymmetry, discrimination and of dilemmas
related to expression of Palestinian national identities and to the definition
of Israel as a Jewish democratic state (Ron et al., 2009). Although difficult

and even painful, there are many Palestinian and Jewish encounter facilitators and participants who do not see the dialogue between them as complete or even as relevant to their needs and interests unless it explicitly deals with these issues (Maoz, 2000a). Discussion can help reach deeper awareness and understanding of the situation of conflict, the dilemmas it involves and the implications of living in a situation of asymmetrical conflict for both groups and for the Israeli society at large (Maoz *et al.*, 2002; Ron *et al.*, 2009).

However, the direct confrontation can also distress and alienate Jewish participants. It can thus create negative attitudes and distrust towards Arabs and towards the practice of encounters between Israeli Jews and Palestinians (Maoz *et al.*, 2007). Moreover, the boundaries between confrontation and verbal violence are often not clearly demarcated. Thus, confrontation models can be more susceptible to destructive intergroup communication patterns that include degradation and delegitimization of members of the other group as well as verbal violence (Maoz *et al.*, 2007). Criticism of the confrontational model and of its potential drawbacks led to the emergence of the narrative model of encounters between Israeli Jews and Palestinians.

The narrative-story-telling model

Towards the end of the 1990s, another model arose that combines both the coexistence and the confrontational aspects of the relations between Israeli Jews and Palestinians. This model – most prominently identified with the late Israeli psychologist Dan Bar-On – uses a narrative approach in which participants from both groups engage in 'story-telling' of their lives in the conflict, sharing their personal and collective narratives, experiences and suffering in the conflict (Bar-On, 2000, 2002, 2006, 2008; Bar-On and Kassem, 2004).

The narrative-story-telling model combines interpersonal interaction with interaction through group identities and the forming of the personal ties with discussions of the conflict and of power relations (Maoz, 2004). It is based on the assumption that, in order to reach reconciliation, groups in intractable conflicts must work through their unresolved pain and anger through story-telling. Encountering the experience and suffering of the other through story-telling is seen as enabling groups involved in conflict to rehumanize and construct a more complex image of the other, while creating intergroup trust and compassion (Bar-On, 2006, 2008; Maoz and Bar-On, 2002). Although the narrative-story-telling model does not explicitly aim at social-structural change, it does prominently address – through the life stories told and through the discussions following the story-telling – the asymmetric power between Israeli Jews and Palestinians and the difficulties and dilemmas this situation breeds for both groups (Bar-On and Kassem, 2004).

Strengths and limitations

The strength of the narrative-story-telling model as a tool for conflict transformation stems from the power of personal stories in creating immediate empathy towards outgroup members (Bar-On, 2002, 2006). The exposure to multiple stories about lives in the conflict has been found to also increase the understanding of the complexities of one's own group and of the other group's personal and collective trajectory in the conflict (Bar-On, 2002, 2006; Bar-On and Kassem, 2004). Furthermore, the narrative-story-telling model answers some of the limitations and combines the advantages of both the coexistence and the confrontational models that preceded it. Similar to the coexistence model, the narrative-story-telling model relies on creating personal ties and empathy to each other as human beings. However, in contrast to the coexistence model and similar to the confrontational model, the narrative-story-telling model does not ignore the conflict and power asymmetries between Israeli Jews and Palestinians. Nevertheless, and contrary to the confrontational model, the discussion of these issues through personal stories enables increased intergroup acceptance and understanding and avoids dead-end arguments about who is more moral and more humane.

In spite of its clear strengths, the narrative-story-telling model is not free from dilemmas and limitations. Bar-On (2006) discusses the challenge of creating the 'good enough story' – the story that encourages intergroup empathy and does not alienate or hurt the other participants. He raises the following questions: How do we identify a 'good enough' (Ross, 2000) story? How do we (and should we) encourage the telling of such stories and discourage the telling of stories that can escalate intergroup hostilities and hurt or degrade outgroup members? Closely related, does the authenticity of the stories told matter (Bar-On, 2006)? Should the story be authentic? Factually true? How do we know if it is indeed true? Do we stop or openly refute a story that we judge as being an inaccurate representation of historical facts?

The dilemmas associated with the story-telling methodology serve to remind both researchers and professionals in the field of conflict transformation that using story-telling (or any other method) does not automatically ensure success (Ross, 2000). Especially when employed between groups in intractable conflict, attention should be paid to the possible pitfalls and limitations – and to ways to avoid them.

Discussion and conclusions

The four models of planned encounters between Israeli Jews and Palestinians discussed in this chapter are based, to varying degrees, on established social-psychological theories of intergroup relations. My analysis suggests that applying these models in the harsh reality of protracted asymmetrical conflict results in creative adaptations and adjustments, as well as with limitations and dilemmas that arise from the unique encounter of social-psychological theory with the reality of conflict and social inequality.

A major question regarding contact interventions in the context of a protracted asymmetrical conflict – such as the conflict between Israeli Jews and Palestinians – is the extent to which these interventions are actually intended at inducing social-structural change that will lead to more egalitarian relations between the involved groups. In part, this question can be addressed through turning our attention to the structure and nature of the encounter process itself. To what extent do particular interventions demonstrate in their structure and in the intergroup interaction they facilitate the principles of equality and social justice that they advocate for (Maoz, 2005)?

Research on equality and social justice in intergroup interactions in planned encounters between Israeli Jews and Palestinians shows that the coexistence and joint projects models tend to preserve and perpetuate Jewish dominance and control while encouraging Arab submissiveness and passivity (Maoz, 2000a, 2000b, 2004). Furthermore, an organizational structural analysis also indicated that the majority of organizations that use coexistence encounter models tend to retain Jewish dominance in their hierarchy and distribution of resources (Maoz, 2001).

In this sense, coexistence models can be viewed as perpetuating the existing status quo of Jewish dominance and is thus counterproductive to inducing social change through transforming the existing asymmetric relations between Israeli Jews and Palestinians. In contrast, confrontational and narrative encounter models have been found to display high equality and social justice in the interaction between Jews and Arabs within the encounter (Maoz, 2005). Especially in confrontational models, an equal and socially just distribution of conversational resources between Jews and Arabs was found to exist between encounter participants and facilitators. Even more importantly, organizations conducting confrontational encounter activities were found to be highly egalitarian and socially just in terms of their hierarchy and distribution of organizational resources between Jews and Arabs (Maoz, 2001). Confrontational encounter interventions that model in their structure and in the interactions within them a more egalitarian social arrangement are thus more likely to lead to social change.

However, the likelihood of the encounter's success in bringing about social change also notably depends on the extent to which the encounter produces constructive or destructive intergroup interactions. The narrative encounter model was found to increase trust and create empathy between Israeli Jews and Palestinians as well as increase their understanding of the complexity of the conflict situation (Bar-On, 2000, 2006; Bar-On and Kassem, 2004; Maoz and Bar-On, 2002). The effect of the confrontational model in this respect is less consistent. In some cases it was found to increase Jewish–Arab empathy and help participants reach a more complex perspective on the conflict (Maoz et al., 2002; Steinberg and Bar-On, 2002). However, in other instances, direct confrontations between Israeli Jews and Palestinians led to destructive interaction and to verbal violence (Maoz et al., 2007). A tentative comparison of several case studies indicates that, alongside other factors, the effectiveness of the encounter model in transforming intergroup relations may importantly depend on the target population it addresses. Thus, the risk for destructive interaction and verbal violence in confrontational models is increased when encounters include participants that initially hold extreme opinions against the other group. While this may be true to some extent for all the encounter models, the confrontational model, that encourages direct confrontation and expression of opinions about the conflict, seems to be especially vulnerable to the escalation of verbal violence (Maoz et al., 2007).

In sum, although existing research can give some indication of the conditions determining the extent to which the different encounter models are likely to bring about social change, much more systematic research is needed in order to have a clearer picture of what succeeds where and with whom.

Meanwhile, the identification of major social-psychological models of intergroup encounters can theoretically and practically contribute to our understanding of the role of structured communication between groups in conflict in achieving peace and reconciliation.

First, the classification into coexistence, joint projects, confrontational and narrative models of intergroup encounters can be applied to other contexts and forms of contact-based interventions around the world (Niens and Cairns, 2005; Saunders, 1999). This classification can be used by researchers, organizers and facilitators of contact-based interventions, conducted in settings of protracted, asymmetrical conflict, as a tool for understanding the nature and dynamics of the intergroup communication within the encounter and for appraising the possible effectiveness of different intervention models in inducing social change. Second, the classification into four models can also be used to analyse discrete episodes (whether planned or everyday spontaneous interactions) of communication between members of groups in asymmetric conflict. In many cases such interactions can be easily classified as predominantly emphasizing the 'coexistence' aspect ('let's forget our group identities and concentrate on personal similarities'), as 'joint projects' oriented ('let's focus on working together and leave aside other things'), as 'confrontational' ('let's directly argue about the conflict') or as 'story-telling' ones. Such classification can help understand the dynamics of the interaction and the goals of its participants, and even predict constructive and destructive patterns of communication that are likely to occur in each of these types of intergroup communication.

Extensive research has focused on explicating the conditions of optimal contact and on assessing the effectiveness of such contact in improving intergroup relations (Dixon, 2005, 2007; Pettigrew, 1998; Pettigrew and Tropp, 2006). But can contact interventions also be effective in situations of protracted asymmetrical ethnopolitical conflict (Salomon, 2004)? Can they improve intergroup relations and foster peace and reconciliation?

The present study has attempted to address these questions by moving 'beyond the utopianism of the classic contact theory' (Dixon and Durrheim, 2003) and critically observing the evolution of intergroup contact interventions embedded in the messy, deeply divided and often violent arena of the protracted asymmetrical Israeli–Palestinian conflict. The analysis brought here was importantly inspired by a recent school of thought that studies processes and effects of contact in non-optimal conditions of deeply divided societies (Dixon and Durrheim, 2003; Dixon *et al.*, 2005, 2007). It also joins a growing number of studies presenting a critical approach to planned encounters between Israeli Jews and Palestinians (Abu-Nimer, 1999, 2004; Bekerman, 2002, 2009, in press; Halabi and Sonnenschein, 2004; Helman, 2002; Salomon, 2004; Suleiman, 2004).

Building on these important traditions of research, our study takes a first step towards identifying and studying social-psychological models and mechanisms of intergroup contact that may be effective in bringing about social change – leading to reconciliation and to improvement of intergroup relations in the non-optimal conditions of protracted asymmetrical conflict.

References

Abu-Nimer, M. (1999). *Dialogue, Conflict Resolution and Change: Arab–Jewish Encounters in Israel*. Albany: State University of New York Press.
  (2004). Education for coexistence and Arab–Jewish encounters in Israel: potential and challenges. *Journal of Social Issues*, **60**(2), 405–22.

Al-Haj, M. (2002). Multiculturalism in deeply divided societies: the Israeli case. *International Journal of Intercultural Relations*, **26**, 169–85.

(2005). National ethos, multicultural education, and the new history textbooks in Israel. *Curriculum Inquiry*, **35**(1), 47–71.

Allport, G. W. 1954. *The Nature of Prejudice*. Reading, MA: Addison-Wesley.

Amir, Y. 1969. Contact hypothesis in ethnic relations. *Psychological Bulletin*, **71**, 319–42.

Aronson, E. and Patnoe, S. (1997). *The Jigsaw Classroom* (2nd edn). New York: Longman.

Bar-On, D. (ed.) (2000). *Bridging the Gap*. Hamburg, Germany: Koerber.

(2002). Conciliation through storytelling: beyond victimhood. In G. Salomon and B. Nevo (eds.), *Peace Education: the Concept, Principles and Practices around the World* (pp.109–16). Mahwah, NJ: Lawrence Erlbaum Associates.

(2006). *Tell Your Life Story: Creating Dialogue Among Jews and Germans, Israelis and Palestinians*. New York: Central European University Press.

(2008). *The Others Within Us: Constructing Jewish–Israeli Identity*. New York: Cambridge University Press.

Bar-On, D. and Kassem, F. (2004). Story telling as a way to work through intractable conflicts: the German–Jewish experience and its relevance to the Palestinian–Israeli context. *Journal of Social Issues*, **60**, 289–306.

Bar-Tal, D. (2002). The elusive nature of peace education. In G. Salomon and B. Nevo (eds.), *Peace Education: the Concept, Principles and Practices around the World* (pp.27–36). Mahwah, NJ: Lawrence Erlbaum Associates.

(2004). Nature, rationale, and effectiveness of education for coexistence. *Journal of Social Issues*, **60**(2), 253–71.

Bekerman, Z. (2002). The discourse of nation and culture: its impact on Palestinian–Jewish encounters in Israel. *Peace and Conflict: Journal of Peace Psychology*, **8**, 259–76.

(2009). Education programs for improving intergroup relations between Palestinians and Jews in Israel. In J. Banks (ed.), *The Routledge International Companion to Multicultural Education*. New York: Routledge.

(in press). Identity work in Palestinian–Jewish intergroup encounters: a cultural rhetorical analysis. *Journal of Multicultural Discourse*.

Connolly, P. (2000). What now for the contact hypothesis? Towards a new research agenda. *Race, Ethnicity and Education*, **3**, 169–93.

Dixon, J. A. and Durrheim, K. (2003). Contact and the ecology of racial division: some varieties of informal segregation. *British Journal of Social Psychology*, **42**, 1–24.

Dixon, J. A., Durrheim, K. and Tredoux, C. (2005). Beyond the optimal strategy: a 'reality check' for the contact hypothesis. *American Psychologist*, **60**, 697–711.

(2007). Contact and attitudes towards the principle and practice of racial equality. *Psychological Science*, **18**, 867–72.

Glaser, B. and Strauss, A. L. (1967). *The Discovery of Grounded Theory: Strategies for Qualitative Research*. Chicago, IL: Aldine.

Halabi, R. and Sonnenschein, N. (2004). The Jewish–Palestinian encounter in a time of crisis. *Journal of Social Issues*, **60**(2), 375–87.

Helman, S. (2002). Monologic results of dialogue: Jewish–Palestinian encounter groups as sites of essentialization. *Identities: Global Studies of Culture and Power*, **9**, 327–54.

Hewstone, M. (1996). Contact and categorization: social psychological interventions to change intergroup relations. In C. N. Macrae, C. Stangor and M. Hewstone (eds.), *Stereotypes and Stereotyping* (pp. 323–68). New York: Guilford.

Maoz, I. (2000a). Power relations in inter-group encounters: a case study of Jewish–Arab encounters in Israel. *International Journal of Intercultural Relations*, **24**, 259–77.

(2000b). Multiple conflicts and competing agendas: a framework for conceptualizing structured encounters between groups in conflict: the case of a coexistence project of Jews and Palestinians in Israel. *Peace and Conflict: Journal of Peace Psychology*, **6**, 135–56.

(2001). Conceptual mapping and evaluation of Jewish–Arab coexistence activities in Israel (1999–2000). Summary evaluation report – submitted to the Abraham Fund. Jerusalem, Israel.

(2004). Coexistence is in the eye of the beholder: evaluating intergroup encounter interventions between Jews and Arabs in Israel. *Journal of Social Issues*, **60**, 437–52.

(2005). Evaluating the quality of communication between groups in dispute: equality in contact interventions between Jews and Arabs in Israel. *Negotiation Journal* (Jan), 131–46.

(2006). Moving between conflict and coexistence: encounters between Jews and Arabs in Israel. In E. Podeh and A. Kaufman (eds.), *From War to Peace: the Israeli–Palestinian Peace Process* (pp.319–41). Hove, UK: Academic Press.

(2009). Educating for peace through planned encounters between Arabs and Jews in Israel: a reappraisal of effectiveness. In G. Salomon and E. Cairns (eds.), *Handbook of Peace Education*. New Jersey: Psychology Press.

(2011). Contact in protracted asymmetrical conflict: twenty years of planned encounters between Israeli Jews and Palestinians. *Journal of Peace Research*, **48**, 115–25.

Maoz, I. and Bar-On, D. (2002). The link from working through the Holocaust to current ethnic conflicts: describing and evaluating the TRT group workshop in Hamburg. *Group*, **26**, 29–48.

Maoz, I., Bar-On, D. and Yikya, S. (2007). 'They understand only force': a critical examination of the erruption of verbal violence in a Jewish–Palestinian dialogue. *Peace and Conflict Studies*, **14**(2), 27–48.

Maoz, I., Steinberg, S., Bar-On, D. and Fakhereldeen, M. (2002). The dialogue between the 'self' and the 'other': a process analysis of Palestinian–Jewish encounters in Israel. *Human Relations*, **55**, 931–62.

Miller, N. (2002). Personalization and the promise of contact theory. *Journal of Social Issues*, **58**, 387–410.

Niens, U. and Cairns, E. (2005). Conflict, contact, and education in Northern Ireland. *Theory into Practice*, **44**, 337–44.

Pettigrew, T. F. (1998). Inter-group contact theory. *Annual Review of Psychology*, **49**, 65–85.

Pettigrew, T. F. and Tropp, L. R. (2000). Does intergroup contact reduce prejudice? Recent meta-analytic findings. In S. Oskamp (ed.), *Reducing Prejudice and Discrimination: Social Psychological Perspectives* (pp.93–114). Mahwah, NJ: Lawrence Erlbaum Associates.

(2006). A meta-analytic test of intergroup contact theory. *Journal of Personality and Social Psychology*, **90**(5), 751–83.

Reicher, S. (1986). Contact, action and racialization: some British evidence. In M. Hewstone and R. Brown (eds.), *Contact and Conflict in Intergroup Encounters* (pp.152–68). Oxford, UK: Blackwell.

(2007). Rethinking the paradigm of prejudice. *South African Journal of Psychology*, **37**(4), 820–34.

Ron, Y., Maoz, I. and Bekerman, Z. (2009). 'Jewish-democratic' or 'of all its citizens'? The effect of Jewish–Arab dialogue programs on Jewish-Israeli ideological perspectives. Unpublished manuscript.

Ross, M. (2000). 'Good-enough' isn't so bad: thinking about success and failure in ethnic conflict management. *Journal of Peace Psychology*, **6**, 27–47.

Salomon, G. (2002). The nature of peace education: not all programs are created equal. In G. Salomon and B. Nevo (eds.), *Peace Education: the Concept, Principles and Practices around the World* (pp.3–14). Mahwah, NJ: Lawrence Erlbaum Associates.

(2004). Does peace education make a difference in the context of an intractable conflict? *Peace and Conflict: Journal of Peace Psychology*, **10**(3), 257–74.

(2006). Does peace education *really* make a difference? *Peace and Conflict: Journal of Peace Psychology*, **12**(1), 37–48.

Saunders, E. (1999). *A Public Peace Process: Sustained Dialogue to Transform Racial and Ethnic Conflict*. New York: St Martin's Press.

Sherif, M. (1966). *In Common Predicament: Social Psychology of Intergroup Conflict and Cooperation*. Boston, MA: Houghton-Mifflin.

Sonnenschein, N., Halabi, R. and Friedman, A. (1998). Legitimization of national identity and the change in power relationships in workshops dealing with the Israeli/Palestinian conflict. In E. Weiner (ed.), *The Handbook of Interethnic Coexistence* (pp.600–14). An Abraham Fund Publication. New York: Continuum.

Steinberg, S. and Bar-On, D. (2002). An analysis of the group process in encounters between Jews and Palestinians: using a typology for discourse classification. *International Journal of Intercultural Relations*, **26**(2), 199–214.

Stephan, W. G. and Stephan, C. W. (2001). *Improving Intergroup Relations*. Thousand Oaks, CA: Sage.

Strauss, A. and Corbin, J. (1998). *Basics of Qualitative Research: Techniques and Procedures for Developing Grounded Theory*. Thousand Oaks, CA: Sage.

Suleiman, R. (2004). The planned encounter between Israeli Jews and Palestinians: a social-psychological perspective. *Journal of Social Issues*, **60**, 323–37.

Tajfel, H. and Turner, J. C. (1986). The social identity theory of intergroup behavior. In S. Worchel and W. G. Austin (eds.), *Psychology of Intergroup Relations* (pp.7–24). Chicago, IL: Nelson-Hall.

Wright, S. and Lubensky, M. (2009). The struggle for social equality: collective action versus prejudice reduction. In S. Demoulin and J. Dovidio (eds.), *Intergroup Misunderstandings: Impact of Divergent Social Realities*. New York: Psychology Press.

14   From prejudice to collective action

Clifford Stott, John Drury and Stephen Recher

Standing in front of one of the largest civil rights crowds ever to assemble in the United States of America, Martin Luther King delivered his now famous 'I have a dream' speech. He spoke directly of the possibility of social change but also of the context of brutal persecution.

> I am not unmindful that some of you have come here out of great trials and tribulations. Some of you have come fresh from narrow jail cells. And some of you have come from areas where your quest – quest for freedom – left you battered by the storms of persecution and staggered by the winds of police brutality. You have been the veterans of creative suffering. Continue to work with the faith that unearned suffering is redemptive. Go back to Mississippi, go back to Alabama, go back to South Carolina, go back to Georgia, go back to Louisiana, go back to the slums and ghettos of our northern cities, knowing that somehow this situation can and will be changed. (King, 1963)

King's speech occurred at a time when the civil rights movement in the US had arguably reached a high point of empowerment. But at the same time blacks and whites still had among other things separate schools and separate designated areas in restaurants and on public transport, and were even often denied access to the vote because of poor levels of literacy. The election of Barack Obama to the US presidency *perhaps* reflects how far the US has progressed from those days of racial oppression (see also Gaines, Chapter 5, this volume).

Even this anecdotal glance at American social history reminds us that the 'prejudicial' political and social reality of the US in the 1960s did not give way simply because large numbers of previously 'prejudiced' whites simply overcame their 'irrational' bigotry. In the case of the civil rights movement of the US the 'Montgomery bus boycott' in Alabama in 1956, the 'Greensboro sit-ins' in North Carolina in 1960, the 'March on Washington for jobs and freedom' in 1963 and the 'Selma to Montgomery marches' in Alabama in 1965 were all collective actions that were central precursors to the anti-discriminatory legislation of the mid-1960s – legislation that paved the way for today's more 'progressive' situation. But King's words remind us that the historically advantaged white community did not accept such progressive social transformation meekly. Social change was an achievement precisely because it overcame reactionary attempts to prevent it.

It is our contention, then, that one of the main issues of the prejudice problematic is the lack of recognition of the centrality of crowds, collective action and intergroup dynamics in social change. The starting point for the present chapter is therefore the observation by Wright and Baray in Chapter 11 that we can understand and classify two types of theoretical approach to 'the problem of intergroup inequality'. The first is the dominant approach in social psychology – which Wright and Baray term the 'prejudice reduction' model – that focuses on changing the attitudes of one (usually dominant) group towards another (usually subordinate) group. A second approach to the same problem is to look instead at how disadvantaged group members respond to their subordinate social position. Wright and Baray describe this as the 'collective action' approach, for it privileges understanding the activity and agency of subordinated groups that struggle to overcome the prejudice and discrimination that they are suffering.

The real-world model for this distinction is perhaps the situation in the US, described above. While some concerned liberals in the establishment sought to change the prejudiced views of (other) whites through strategies such as desegregation and contact, those who were the subject of the prejudice – the black working class – resisted first through the civil rights movements and later through riots and other forms of militancy. In this chapter, we therefore aim to further demonstrate the usefulness of Wright and Baray's 'collective action' perspective.

However, we shall first build upon their position by suggesting that the application of the principles of their model is in fact broader than they initially suggest. We agree that in general both negative and positive group-level perceptions can be transformed through changes in the structure of intergroup relations, which in turn occurs through collective action by subordinated groups. In developing this theme, however, we argue that the collective action of subordinate groups inevitably takes place in a context where dominant groups act and *react* to such collective action. It is our contention that such reactions occur and are given legitimacy on the basis of both prejudicial representations of the subordinate group and the interpretations and discourses that surround the subordinate group's collective actions.

In this chapter we will show how the collective action of subordinate groups – and the resultant changes in negative or positive group-level perceptions – can only be adequately understood when theory takes into account dynamic interactions between powerful and subordinated groups – interactions which do or do not serve to restructure the material reality of behavioural relations between those groups.

Through a close analysis of the dynamics of crowd events we shall show evidence that, on the one hand, where 'dominant' group action is perceived as repressing the 'subordinate' groups, two sorts of changes to group-level perceptions are observable. First, the dominant group becomes defined negatively *as* a group, even when previously its members were judged positively or were not judged in terms of a group at all. Second, within the subordinated group as a whole there is dramatic reduction in negative attitudes towards those who, while perceived as 'acting *with* us', are not seen as 'one *of* us'. These social actors become re-evaluated both more positively and more inclusively, as a group. On the other hand, we will also discuss evidence of processes where the dominant group facilitates the subordinate group's actions that coincide with clear shifts within subordinated groups towards validation and appreciation of that dominant group, when previously they were judged negatively.

Before we discuss these issues, it is necessary to clarify the terms of our argument. We take the view that the concept of 'prejudice' is not just ambiguous as a concept but is a political as well as a psychological category. It is a matter of *judgement* whether the views held by protesters that 'the police are partisans for an illegitimate government' is an unwarranted overgeneralization or an adaptive appraisal of their real social relations (Oakes *et al.*, 1994). Moreover, none of the examples of social category relations we will be describing in this chapter are the traditional kinds of 'prejudice' that dominate the psychological literature, such as white hostility towards blacks, which we all object to and are seeking to overcome. But our examples are less clear cut because they focus upon political protesters, environmental direct activists and even football supporters, who we studied in contexts of changing relations with each other and with the police. But we focus upon them, as they are 'real world' examples of intergroup hostility and conflict. As such they cast empirical light on the role played by collective action and group-level dynamics in 'prejudice reduction' and social change as well as related psychological processes such as stereotype change, social influence and efficacy.

The chapter begins with an overview of a protest event where we will show how the perspectives and actions of a dominant group defined and then redefined the perceptions and feelings which the subordinate group expressed towards the outgroup and other ingroup members. We will show, first, that where the dominant group saw the subordinated group as a threat it subsequently *treated* them in oppositional terms. Consequently, there was a corresponding increase in the denigration of and hostility towards that dominant group among the subordinated group. Moreover, within the subordinated group there was a corresponding decrease in hostile group attitudes towards more 'radical' members of the subordinated category. Second, we will present a study of reducing levels of intergroup hostility and negative intergroup attitudes among English football (soccer) fans. Here we will demonstrate that where the dominant group treats subordinated groups as less oppositional (i.e. as 'respectable citizens') and facilitates the subordinate group's aims, then we see shifts towards validation and appreciation of the dominant group and the marginalization of those individuals within the subordinated group who seek conflict and hostility. We will conclude by exploring the implications of these analyses for understanding the *dynamics* of intergroup prejudice and conflict.

The dynamics of increasing hostile intergroup attitudes and conflict

Across a variety of crowd events, including a student protest (Reicher, 1996), a riot during demonstrations against a form of local taxation (Drury and Reicher, 1999; Stott and Drury, 2000) and cases of football crowd 'disorder' (Stott and Reicher, 1998a; Stott *et al.*, 2001, 2007), our analyses have identified a common pattern of intergroup interaction and psychological change that we argue underpins the emergence and escalation of intergroup hostility during crowd events. We characterize this pattern as follows.

First, the crowd (of protestors, football fans or whatever) typically begin in a relatively heterogeneous state. In the protest events, for example, the majority identified themselves as 'moderates' who simply wanted to express their view to the authorities, while a minority were more 'radical' and saw the authorities as antagonistic. Second, in contrast, crowd members were perceived as homogeneously dangerous by the authorities (notably the police) and treated as such – that is, they were denied the ability to express themselves as they wished (be this demonstrating their opposition to the government or simply enjoying themselves as football fans). More specifically, this action of denial by the police outgroup was experienced as not only illegitimate (e.g. a negation of 'rights') but also indiscriminate (an attack on 'everyone', on 'the whole crowd' *as* a crowd). Third, this police (outgroup) action therefore then radicalized the more 'moderate' crowd members, in two ways. First, it turned them against the police and legitimized conflict (as a reassertion of rights). Second, it brought the 'moderates' psychologically closer to the 'radical' minority in the crowd who they had shunned prior to interaction with the police.

We will illustrate this process through reference to some ethnographic research carried out at an anti-roads (environmental) protest event (Drury and Reicher, 2000, 2005; Drury *et al.*, 2003). The building of the 'M11 link road' was part of the UK national roads programme of the 1990s. Part of the construction work took place in the leafy and relatively affluent east London suburb of Wanstead. Since the road was seen as part of a national programme a number of 'protestors' came to the local area from all over the country because they saw this protest as part of a wider national campaign.

From the beginning, while there was widespread opposition to the road locally, there was a clear division between the outside protestors and people from Wanstead, particularly in terms of the means through which their protest was expressed. For example, while 'locals' wrote letters of complaint about the road to the newspapers, the protestors attempted to stop construction through direct actions, mainly in the form of climbing into trees on the route of the road, or onto the construction machinery.

Since Wanstead was a relatively affluent suburb, being a resident was affirmed and identified through a 'respectable', middle class physical appearance. Hence, some of the protestors who came to Wanstead because of the anti-road campaign were seen in negative terms and were rejected because their appearance offended these middle class values and this sense of pride in the respectability of the area. For example:

I've got to be honest, in the early days I really did wonder just what we were getting into. This was September, October. The appearance of some of these people in a town like Wanstead, it's a very strange sight. I don't actually feel surprised or ashamed at my early reaction. I think it's the reaction of a great many people in this town now. They do take against people straggling round the town in dreadlocks and very very tatty boots and very very tatty anoraks and all the other bits and pieces of the lifestyle which to most of these people is a total anathema. (Drury *et al.*, 2003, p. 196)

But, in early November 1993, the contractors erected eight-feet-high wooden fencing round a section of 'George Green', an area of land within Wanstead defined by locals as 'public space'. A few days later, a crowd, which outnumbered security guards and police, pushed down most of this fencing. Campaign participants then occupied the land, at the centre of which was a large and very old chestnut tree. The chestnut tree was subsequently evicted on 7 December, in a day-long event at which more than 200 campaign participants were present at any one time. During the eviction the crowd itself was relatively heterogeneous. Around half were 'local' people from Wanstead; the rest were 'protestors' from elsewhere. There was a wide range of age groups involved, including both children and pensioners, with most perhaps aged in their twenties.

The eviction began at 5.30 in the morning, when hundreds of police arrived with bailiffs. The police's first task was to move people physically from the base of the tree and then to keep them away from it by forming a cordon. As such they pushed through the crowd and then, having captured the space around the tree, forced the crowd away. A handful of campaign participants that were actually in the tree then had to be removed by bailiffs using hydraulic platforms and cutting equipment. It was these intergroup interactions between the police and bailiffs on one side against those within the protests on the other that transformed relations and hence perceptions within and between the different groups involved.

(1) Police action alienates a peaceful majority

In the first place, prior to the police intervention, all the Wanstead participants we interviewed stressed their 'local' identity in their explanation for their presence under the tree: they as 'locals' saw it as a 'right' to be on the public space of George Green. Most of these 'locals' accepted a division of labour between those within the crowd, explicitly or otherwise. In their accounts of the event they describe how there was a 'local' role that was in contrast to that of the more radical 'protestors':

I mean my instinct is just to stay as near the tree as possible with as many locals as possible on the outside with perhaps the ... the main protesters sort of in the middle, so they've got to get through us first. (Drury et al., 2003, p. 200)

The nature of their involvement – of joining in with and yet remaining apart from 'other' participants – suggests an experiential division within the crowd that matched this behavioural division of labour. However, those within the crowd understood the form of the police action as indiscriminately 'heavy handed'. This in turn contradicted the sense of self of the 'locals' who saw themselves as a 'peaceful majority' in the crowd. They were not the 'radicals' chained to the tree (like the direct activists), and they were certainly not using violence, or indeed doing anything other than to warrant being politely asked to move or, at most, being dragged away:

I've never been to anything like this so I just expect people to sit down. I mean I'm all for non-violence, I don't want to fight just to stay put and only be moved if you're dragged away, and if that involves – well, I mean the thing is to just try and stay put and try and – try not to provoke anything. (Drury and Reicher, 2000, p. 587)

Police officers were accused of meting out harsh treatment even when it wasn't needed in order to secure the compliance of all protestors. These references to violence tended to refer to the police in general terms. It was the *category* which was violent rather than particular individual police officers. Specific incidents, such as an elderly man who had his glasses broken, became 'iconic' in that they were mentioned many times by different protestors. Such incidents exemplified the emerging sense of illegitimacy in the intergroup relationships, since they stressed both the extremity of police action and the vulnerability of the victim.

Moreover, when this 'peaceful majority' of 'locals' referred to legitimate, peaceful action, they were referring not only to themselves as individuals, but also to the majority of the crowd. Yet these 'locals' equally stressed how everyone in the crowd was being treated as members of an illegitimate category.

They treated us like criminals, and we had a right to be there, and we weren't doing any harm, we were just there. (Drury *et al.*, 2003, p. 200)

Thus the objection to police violence was not simply due to the physical consequences but also because of what it seemed to indicate about the identity of campaigners. The police were seen as using '*the same tactics as they would against football hooligans*' (Drury and Reicher, 2000, p. 591). Some explicitly contrasted their own self-conception with the conception that police action seemed to imply:

They were treated as if they just weren't human, and that's horrific – that's wrong, the police aren't there to do that to any of us. We all deserve protection by the police and they were there – they were the destroying body, terrible thing. (Drury and Reicher, 2000, p. 591)

From the police perspective, however, the distinction between the 'peaceful majority' and the more militant direct activists wasn't a clear one at all. Based on both past experience (when the fences were torn down a month earlier), and on their ideological perspective (Hoggett and Stott, 2010; Stott and Reicher, 1998b) they were of the view that the physical crowd was one psychological crowd – that by simply being present, so-called 'peaceful' locals could descend into violence and destructive behaviour. In effect the police held a 'prejudiced' view of those within the crowd that rationalized their treatment of all people in the crowd as dangerous. According to one Police Commander involved in policing one of the events:

You had an emerging horde of people that had left behind their social responsibilities and just gone ahead and damaged property. And the mixture of crowd was school-kids, ordinary Mr and Mrs Wanstead and protesters. (Drury and Reicher, 2000, p. 588)

(2) Ingroup inclusion and reducing of 'prejudice' towards previously shunned radicals

If 'everyone' felt in danger from the violence of the police, then the crowd as a whole – not only 'protestors' but also 'locals' – shared a common relationship to them. Simultaneous with the perceived indiscriminate attack by the police, feelings of solidarity became enhanced within the crowd; that is, there was a greater coming together psychologically:

the bonding you have when there's a big pile of you packed together and the police are pulling you out, that's, you know, complete strangers and you're grabbing them and you're holding them and everything, not the kind of thing people would normally never dream of doing to somebody you don't know. And there was a real kind of good feeling amongst protesters towards each other. (Drury *et al.*, 2003, p. 201)

According to at least some campaign participants, in the face of the police action, the feeling of enhanced solidarity within the crowd translated into a breakdown of the previous division of labour and 'prejudiced' views by 'locals' towards 'protestors':

When the police came everyone like sat down around the tree and like linked arms and everything, and you could see local middle-aged women thinking 'Shall I? Shan't I?' You know, 'Ooh it's a bit muddy', and they just sat down anyway and like joined in and you know got muddy with the rest of us. It was really empowering. (Drury *et al.*, 2003, p. 201)

Thus, in response to the conflictual relations with the police, 'locals' changed their prior 'prejudiced' views of, felt closer to and even coacted with 'protestors' who were previously defined as 'other'. Psychologically, to be positioned as 'oppositional' and as 'the same' as the 'radical' protestors by the social reality of police actions meant that those 'radical' elements now became viewed in a new, less 'prejudiced' light. In fact, whereas previously the contrast had been between 'us' as 'locals' and 'the protestors', now it was between all those who took the 'necessary action', no matter where they were from, and those who supported the building of the road – or who passively stood by and let the 'illegitimate' road construction go ahead.

Evidence of this enhanced and changing solidarity within a crowd event might represent just a transitory context-dependent variation in self-perception and 'prejudiced' attitudes. However, in the weeks following the eviction, interviewees explicitly mentioned greater feelings of 'togetherness' among all those involved in the campaign. To be the same as those once defined as other was a profound revelation, and the basis of the new unity was said to be common opposition to the authorities (police and road contractors):

Interviewer: How do you feel about everybody involved now?

CP2: This is stupid but I was born I was literally a baby during the war. But I heard these stories of the Blitz bringing us together, and I have found this to be true. In the streets of Wanstead, people that you've never ever noticed before suddenly find they have a common cause, they know you, they know what you stand for, they come up and we are we're on an entirely new community feeling here, as if we've suddenly discovered our sense of community, because obviously there is a common enemy, there is a common cause, much as there was in the war. (Drury *et al.*, 2003, p. 201)

This change went hand in hand with an acceptance of the direct activists' definition of the struggle; it wasn't local, but global:

CP6: The emphasis has grown more on the whole roads programme rather than just specifically this particular road here. (Drury *et al.*, 2003, p. 204)

(3) Increased 'prejudice' towards the police

For those who already saw the police as 'agents of state', the experience of the eviction changed nothing. For others, however, it was a life-changing experience, not only for those who now counted as one of 'us' but also for those who now became redefined as 'other'. In the first place, then, there was a rejection of other Wanstead residents who did not take action:

The residents that won't come over here to stand up to be voiced, to be known to that we want a green and pleasant land, as far as I'm concerned they are zombies, the living dead. (Drury *et al.*, 2003, p. 197)

Second, and strikingly, was the rejection of the police more generally. Specifically, understandings of the police among local Wanstead campaigners were transformed from 'protector of my rights' to an antagonistic 'outgroup':

You know, I mean that was an experience in itself, wasn't it? I always thought that they [the police] were for the people. But in fact they're not for the people in a sense. They keep saying they were doing a job for us, but they weren't, they weren't with us, were they? Definitely weren't with us. . . . In a sense, it was like a revolution it, you know what I mean, because you knew then what you were fighting against. (Drury *et al.*, 2003, p. 202)

Their experience of the George Green eviction had consequences not only for the way they saw the police but in their trust in them as an institution:

They are armed in France, they are very aggressive, and I always assumed that in England things were different, that the police were sort of – I don't know, just the Dixon of Dock Green image, but I always assumed they were mild and nice and would help you find the way. But now I've reached the stage where I really don't trust any of them, I really do not. (Drury and Reicher, 2000, p. 591)

Moreover, as one local put it, even if individual officers might behave in friendly ways, '*I simply don't trust them as a body*' (Drury and Reicher, 2000, p. 592). Such loss of trust was linked to a more profound reconceptualization of the police. They were no longer trusted because they were no longer seen as neutral. Instead of being above sectional interest in society, they came to be seen as being a partisan political force:

I stood on the edges at Wapping as a newspaper worker when I was working, I never became involved, I saw it, I heard the stories, I truthfully didn't want to believe it. Now that I've seen the police in action, now that I've seen the police when they are determined to forget the Dixon of Dock Green image, I just don't believe what I've seen. It's profoundly altered my view of the police service as a service. Basically I believe that they're a political army on the streets as opposed to a political army in khaki. (Drury and Reicher, 2000, p. 592)

Intergroup dynamics and psychological change

What this study exemplifies, then, is how changes in group-level *perceptions* can originate within and through collective *action* in its intergroup context. Specifically, for the 'local' protestors, the origins of the (1) reduction in negative attitudes, or at least differentiation, towards the direct activists, and (2) emergence and increases in negative attitudes towards the police as a social category, are each explicable theoretically in terms of a set of concepts, conditions and dynamics that comprise the elaborated social identity model (ESIM) of crowd behaviour.

First, then, the ESIM involves a *reconceptualization* of 'context' and 'social identity' and, crucially, of the relationship between them. In general, theorists in the social identity tradition have tended to treat context (more accurately, 'comparative context', which is to say the organization of social reality in categorical terms) as an objective determinant of social identity. However, while this may be true if context is only considered as prior and separate to identity, it is hard to conceptualize how identity can then change through action in context. For the ESIM, then, context and identity are understood not as separate orders of reality but interdependent moments in a single historical process. In other words, the ESIM adopts a *process* model of identity.

Consequently, social identity is understood as the way in which people position themselves relative to others. This identity in turn provides the perspective from which forms of action come to be seen as meaningful and legitimate. Context is conceptualized as those forces external to actors that enable or constrain their identity-based action. Given that crowds are intergroup events, it follows that the understandings of one group drive their actions that then subsequently constrain (or facilitate) the actions of the other.

Put in slightly more theoretical terms, the identity-based actions of one group constitute the social context for another over time and vice versa. For the M11 protestors, the social contexts were the actions of the police – who formed cordons, initiated 'heavy-handed' evictions and so on. But such actions were at the same time the expression of police understanding of their relationship to the protestors – as a threatening, dangerous and hostile crowd.

Second, the ESIM suggests that the *conditions* necessary for the emergence and development of intergroup conflict during crowd events are two-fold: (1) there is an asymmetry of categorical representations between crowd participants and outgroups, such as the police. For example, during the eviction protest at George Green, crowd participants that defined themselves as 'citizens in a democracy' had expectation of a neutral relationship with the police. In contrast, they were constituted as a danger by the police and treated accordingly, thus placed within in an antagonistic relationship; (2) there is also an asymmetry of power. It was not just that the police viewed the crowd on George Green in 'prejudicial' terms; they had the personnel, the organization and the resources – in other words the *power* – to translate their views into social action and thus to transform the social context within which the crowd defined themselves. Whatever their intentions, crowd members subsequently found themselves in a common relationship of antagonism to the police along with the more radical 'protestors'.

Third, then, there is a *dynamic* whereby police assumptions concerning the homogeneity of the crowd and police practices which impose a 'common fate' on all crowd members leads to a self-fulfilling prophecy on a collective scale (Stott and Reicher, 1998b). That is, the initially heterogeneous crowd actually becomes as psychologically homogeneous as it was initially only *perceived* to have been by the police. Moreover, to the extent that police action is seen as not only indiscriminate but also illegitimate (e.g. denying the right to protest and using offensive tactics to disperse the crowd), then the entire crowd unites around a sense of opposition to the police and the authorities whose interests they are protecting. This will be reflected in behavioural changes – notably, conflict with the police. It will also be reflected in psychological changes. That is, those who initially saw themselves as 'moderates' change their understanding of their relationship with the authorities and hence their own identity. Being treated as radicals, they come to see themselves as radical. In addition, the emergence of a common radical self-categorization within the crowd leads to feelings of consensus and to expectations of mutual support that empowers crowd members to express that radicalism and to take on the police (Drury and Reicher, 1999).

Putting all three elements together, the ESIM can be summarized as follows: people's sense of their social position (*social identity*) changes to the extent that, in acting on their identity (*participating in a crowd event*), they are repositioned as a consequence of the understandings and reactions of an outgroup (*treated as oppositional by the police*). This repositioning leads both to a new identity and new forms of inter and intragroup action (*intergroup hostility, variations in 'prejudice' and conflict*).

Consequently, when viewed in these terms rather than negative group-level perceptions (i.e. prejudice) being irrational or a misjudgement, our analysis suggests that such feelings are 'rational' or at least a meaningful justification for hostility against another group. They are a group-level understanding that makes sense of real relations of power between groups from the perspective of the actor. What would be irrational, perhaps, would be for the crowd participant to try to predict the behaviour of the phalanx of police officers in riot gear charging towards them on the basis of individual personalities. Group membership and the antagonism of the broader intergroup relationship is by far the best predictor for what will happen next.

The dynamics of reducing conflict and prejudice during crowd events

Thus far our analysis of crowd events suggests that at a more general level the psychology underpinning intergroup hostility may not be just an outcome of intrapsychic processes of cognition. Rather, that such cognition reflects the adaptive apprehension of the material realities of the intergroup context created by the action of another (at times more powerful) group. Where these intergroup relations are experienced as illegitimate we see corresponding increases in 'prejudice' towards that outgroup and decreases in prejudice towards others. In this section we will explore a corresponding process of reducing intergroup hostilities but this time in a social context where the dominant group (once again the police) rather than being 'prejudiced' towards the subordinate group's actions actually facilitates them. We will show how in these contexts what can be observed are shifts within subordinated groups (in this case English soccer fans) away from hostility and negative group-level attitudes.

Perhaps more than any other group of fans at international level, England fans have traditionally been synonymous with violence, racism and prejudice (e.g. Burford, 1990). But, over recent years, there has been a radical decline in the levels of conflict involving English fans travelling to international competitions. This transformation in intergroup hostility was most marked around the UEFA Football (Soccer) European

Championships in Portugal in 2004 (Euro2004). During this tournament there were no major incidents of disorder in cities hosting matches, despite the presence in Portugal during the tournament of an estimated 150,000 English nationals. So what underpinned this transformation where a group renowned for violence, hostility and prejudice found itself in relative harmony with other groups? To address this question we draw upon a body of detailed research that explored the underlying social and psychological processes governing the behaviour of crowds during the tournament (see Stott and Pearson, 2007; Stott et al., 2007, 2008).

(1) Police action as facilitative

England fans travelled to the tournament with an understanding that two quite different forms of social relations with the police were possible. On the one hand, there was a historically dominant experience of inappropriate, indiscriminate and heavy-handed policing. Before travelling to Portugal, England fans openly described how they expected the police in Portugal to be like those experienced elsewhere and to attack them simply for engaging in 'harmless' behaviours.

I fully expect the Portuguese Police to be very edgy and just the breakout of a song by 200 English fans in a pub could see batons being thrown. (Stott et al., 2007, p. 86)

On the other, there was recognition that a more positive and less confrontational style of policing was possible. Each approach was understood by fans to have very different consequences for their behaviour.

I think the main issue is how the police are going to treat England supporters. The low [profile] is my preference as I feel that this leads to less conflict between police and fans. The heavy-handed approach seems to have people on the edge and leads to confrontation between fans and police. (Stott et al., 2007, p. 86)

But the Portuguese public security police (PSP), rather than confronting fans, actually treated them with respect and facilitated their enjoyment. Contrary to the more pessimistic expectations and 'prejudicial' attitudes expressed about the police before the tournament, fans subsequently characterized their relations with them during the tournament as friendly and accommodating.

I have only good things to say about the way we were policed ... There was no in-your-face threatening police action; they were very helpful, easily approachable, probably my best experience of police control at an England match abroad. (Stott et al., 2007, p. 87)

This social context of intergroup *legitimacy* corresponded with evidence of a social identity among England fans defined not in terms of hostility towards other groups but in terms of nonconfrontational football fandom. Thus, far from being 'prejudiced' towards fans from other nations in this context, England fans embraced them as fellow 'partygoers' out to enjoy this 'carnival of football'.

The majority of all nations there were all law-abiding fans who were taking a holiday whilst watching their nation. Met some great Germans, Swedes and Dutch and they knew their football and knew how to enjoy themselves, just like our group. (Stott *et al.*, 2007, p. 88)

(2) The rejection of 'hooligans' from the 'ingroup'

Given this form of identity, it was those fans seen to be acting in a hostile way that were differentiated from the social group:

[Int: Do you see yourself as similar or different to those fans arrested during incidents?] Different. I am a supporter of England – they are not. (Stott *et al.*, 2007, p. 88)

This differentiation between 'ordinary fans' and 'hooligans' corresponded with situations in which those trying to initiate conflict were marginalized and unable to influence others towards intergroup conflict. But it was not simply that the majority of England fans tried to differentiate themselves psychologically from confrontation. At times some even actively prevented it by intervening, sometimes with force and sometimes in collaboration with the police, against those more 'radical' fans that were understood to be seeking to disrupt the intergroup harmony.

For example, on spotting a group of Croatian 'hooligans' seeking to attack a crowd of England fans in central Lisbon, an England fan approached the police in an attempt to get them to move the Croatian fans away. When subsequently interviewed, his self-motivation was expressed in terms of seeking to actively protect the nonconfrontational nature of the norms dominating and defining the ingroup, even in the face of open threats of violence from another group.

C: Why did you go and speak to the police?

EF: If something kicks off they [England fans] will all be in. This is fantastic [points towards the crowd of celebrating England fans], this is England. But if something kicks off they'll all be in and we'll get the blame and it's fucking wrong.

C: So did you go and explain that to them?

EF: I don't care what you say it's in the heart [bangs his hand on his chest] we are all fucking hooligans [gesticulates towards the Rossio and his group of friends in the bar where he had been sitting] and if somebody has a go at your country, we've been bred for the last two thousand years to fight, we're all going to have a go back. I saw them lads come around and it was fucking obvious that they [the Croatians] were going to have a go. I mean all credit at least they [the PSP] are doing something about it now but why has it taken them so long? So I got up and did something about it, to get the police to move them Croatians before the England boys sussed out what was going on because if they did it would have gone off. (Stott *et al.*, 2007, p. 88)

(3) Reduction of 'prejudice' to the police

Our analysis suggests that this sense of 'self-regulation' or 'norm enforcement' was important not just because it was a major determinant of an almost total absence of collective conflict during the tournament (Stott *et al.*, 2007, 2008). It is also important because it corresponds with evidence of a widespread transformation in intergroup attitudes between England fans and police. Prior to the tournament, a measure of England fans' ingroup identification showed strong negative correlation with a measure of perceived similarity to the police in Portugal. However, having experienced legitimacy in their intergroup relationships with the police, this correlation was significantly and positively transformed, now characterized by a strong positive correlation (Stott *et al.*, 2008). In other words, prior to the tournament many England fans held 'prejudiced' attitudes towards the police and saw themselves in an antagonistic relationship to them. However, subsequent to the tournament these 'prejudiced' attitudes had been completely reversed.

Conclusions

The starting point for the present chapter was the observation by Wright and Baray in Chapter 11 that we can understand and classify two types of approach to 'the problem of intergroup inequality'. On the one hand there is the 'prejudice reduction' and on the other 'the collective action' models of social change. We have sought in this chapter to support and develop Wright and Baray's collective action approach. We have done so by demonstrating how changes in the nature of intergroup attitudes and hostility can be interlinked with changes in social relations brought about through the dynamics of collective action and intergroup relations.

Of course the use of examples of 'football hooliganism' and 'environmental protest' to make arguments about the dynamics of prejudice will be open to question. But we use them because they provide examples of actual conflict and intergroup hostility and are therefore phenomena with which our theories should articulate. Indeed, we are not alone in trying to understand wider phenomena through these cases. Richard Danzig, Chairman of the national security think-tank, the Center of New American Security, and senior advisor to Barack Obama, was quoted as describing Burford's (1990) journalistic account of English 'hooligans' as 'one of the best books I've read on terrorism in recent years'. He is said to have argued how this study of 'hooligans' teaches us all fundamental lessons about the nature of terrorism more generally (Shipman, 2008). Given such links are apparently made in the corridors of power, it would be somewhat superfluous for us to simply ignore them in the context of our theorizing.

Regardless of one's political position with respect to the policing of environmental activists and football fans, what we have discussed here is further evidence which shows that alteration in the levels of 'prejudice' both within and between groups can and does occur through the collective action of subordinate group members. However, what our studies of crowd events also demonstrate is that group-level perceptions of others are rooted in broader representations of group relations and that these perceptions change when, through collective action, the nature, the experience and hence the representation of group relations are changed. Our studies do support the contention that this can occur through the explicit mobilization of subordinate group members. But we have also shown that the actions of dominant groups also impact upon social reality and therefore the perceptions and feelings that subordinate group members have towards both the dominant group and themselves.

Where dominant group action is perceived as repressing the subordinate groups, two sorts of changes in group-level perception are observable. First, the dominant group becomes defined more negatively *as* a group, where previously its members were judged positively or were not judged in group terms at all. Second, within the subordinated group as a whole, there is a dramatic reduction in negative attitudes towards those 'acting *with* us' but who were not previously 'one of us'. In other words, those previously differentiated become re-evaluated both more positively and more inclusively as a group, and previously existing 'prejudices' disappear. In contrast, where dominant group action is seen as facilitating subordinated groups, different forms of psychological change are evident. On the one hand there is a perception of legitimacy in intergroup relations along with emergent bonds of identification and reductions in 'prejudice' between powerful and subordinated groups. On the other, those seeking to promote intergroup hostility or 'prejudice' are marginalized and unable to influence the broader community.

What this suggests is that an adequate theoretical understanding of the psychology of intergroup hostility should not ignore the role of the dynamics of intergroup interaction. While such dynamics form a self-evident component of the history of the struggle against prejudice undertaken by the civil rights movement in the US, the salience of these issues in our theorizing is less obvious. What our theoretical approach suggests is that the ability to promote negative intergroup attitudes and influence others towards intergroup conflict goes hand in hand with the material and dynamic realities of the social context. The dominance of the assertions of those promoting 'prejudice' among communities are in turn governed, at least in part, by the intergroup relationships that groups create through their own social action. What is more, where dominant group action represses the subordinate group, we see clear shifts towards shared denigration and hostility, whereas when the dominant group facilitates the subordinate group, then we see clear shifts towards validation and appreciation. It is our contention that an understanding of how to reduce prejudice must therefore go hand in hand with an understanding of how to confront and change the material and social realities of the relationships between groups.

References

Burford, B. (1990/1992). *Among the Thugs*. London: Secker and Warburg.

Drury, J. and Reicher, S. (1999). The intergroup dynamics of collective empowerment: substantiating the social identity model. *Group Processes and Intergroup Relations*, **2**, 381–402.

(2000). Collective action and psychological change: the emergence of new social identities. *British Journal of Social Psychology*, **39**, 579–604.

(2005). Explaining enduring empowerment: a comparative study of collective action and psychological outcomes. *European Journal of Social Psychology*, **35**, 35–58.

Drury, J., Reicher, S. and Stott, C. (2003). Transforming the boundaries of collective identity: from the 'local' anti-road campaign to 'global' resistance? *Social Movement Studies*, **2**, 191–212.

Hoggett, J. and Stott, C. (2010). The role of crowd theory in determining the use of force in public order. *Policing and Society*, **20**, 223–36.

Oakes, P. J., Haslam, S. A. and Turner, J. C. (1994). *Stereotyping and Social Reality*. Oxford, UK: Blackwell.

Reicher, S. D. (1996). 'The Battle of Westminster': developing the social identity model of crowd behaviour in order to explain the initiation and development of collective conflict. *European Journal of Social Psychology*, **26**, 115–34.

Shipman, T. (2008). Barack Obama aide: why Winnie the Pooh should shape US foreign policy. *DailyTelegraph*, available on: www.telegraph.co.uk/news/ newstopics/uselection2008/barackobama/2139573/Barack-Obama-aide-Why-Winnie-the-Pooh-should-shape-US-foreign-policy.html (retrieved 17 June 2010).

Stott, C. and Drury, J. (2000). Crowds, context and identity: dynamic categorization processes in the 'poll tax riot'. *Human Relations*, **53**, 247–73.

Stott, C. and Pearson, G. (2007). *Football 'Hooliganism', Policing and the War on the 'English Disease'*. London: Pennant Books.

Stott, C. and Reicher, S. D. (1998a). How conflict escalates: the inter-group dynamics of collective football crowd 'violence'. *Sociology*, **32**, 353–77.

(1998b). Crowd action as inter-group process: introducing the police perspective. *European Journal of Social Psychology*, **26**, 509–29.

Stott, C., Adang, O., Livingstone, A. and Schreiber, M. (2007). Variability in the collective behaviour of England fans at Euro2004: 'hooliganism', public order policing and social change. *European Journal of Social Psychology*, **37**, 75–100.

(2008). Tackling football hooliganism: a quantitative study of public order, policing and crowd psychology. *Psychology Public Policy and Law*, **14**(2), 115–41.

Stott, C., Hutchison, P. and Drury, J. (2001). 'Hooligans' abroad? Inter-group dynamics, social identity and participation in collective 'disorder' at the 1998 World Cup finals. *British Journal of Social Psychology*, **40**, 359–84.

Conclusions and future directions: the nature, significance and inherent limitations of the concept of prejudice in social psychology

John Dixon and Mark Levine

Susan Fiske (2002) recently took stock of the progress made by social psychologists in tackling what she evocatively labelled the 'problem of the century'. She noted that although 'much remains to be learned', 'much is known' already (p. 128). Reading her paper, one is struck by how the image of the bigot in social psychology has shifted over the long history of prejudice research. Along with the blatant, simple, hot, direct biases of 'ill-intentioned extremists', psychologists nowadays study the more subtle, complex, cool, implicit biases of 'aversive racists'. One is struck, too, by the methodological ingenuity of recent work in the field, which is increasingly exploiting techniques drawn from cognitive psychology and neuroscience. Above all, one is struck by the enduring commitment among prejudice researchers to the ideal of balancing advocacy and scholarship, to *changing* as well as understanding society. The political spirit that accompanied Samelson's (1978) 'abrupt reversal' is alive and well.

Our aim in this book has not been to devalue the many contributions made by the social psychology of prejudice. Rather, we have sought to evaluate some foundational assumptions of prejudice research, notably its individualistic orientation, its emphasis on the role of irrational cognition and emotional antipathy in intergroup relations, and its commitment to a prejudice reduction model of social change. By necessity, our coverage has been selective, and we not had space to discuss a number of other important challenges to the prejudice problematic; for example, challenges arising from developments in the field of evolutionary psychology (e.g. Neuberg and Cottrell, 2006).

The book's overall argument is important not only because the prejudice problematic represents social psychology's main framework for understanding problems of conflict and discrimination, but also because it shapes so powerfully how social psychologists approach the entire business of understanding relations within and between groups, providing a (often unacknowledged) network of epistemological assumptions, theoretical concepts, methodological tools and political values. It shapes, too, how we frame processes of social change, delimiting the wider project of improving relations between divided communities. What might we see if we did not look at intergroup relations through a lens coloured so strongly by the prejudice problematic? How might we rethink the problem of social change? Our contributors have attempted to explore these kinds of questions.

In this concluding chapter, we draw out some general themes and implications from the foregoing discussion, without pretending to be exhaustive in our coverage. In the first section, building on and sometimes extending earlier chapters, we discuss three deep-seated limitations of the prejudice problematic. In the second section, we revisit the (vexed) question of social change, exploring the problem of reconciling prejudice reduction with alternative models of social change.

Challenges to the prejudice problematic

The limits of irrationalism

Proponents of the idea that prejudiced cognitions are fundamentally inaccurate and irrational tend to work within the bounds of a correspondence model of truth. That is, they presuppose the existence of an independent and external social world that the individual mind may represent with varying degrees of accuracy. According to this view, prejudice arises when individuals' mental representations of others are clouded by negative emotions, based on erroneous preconceptions, or infected by one of the litany of intergroup biases that social psychologists have catalogued so painstakingly (e.g. see Lilienfeld *et al.*, 2009). As a result, their view of the social world becomes distorted, their images of others failing to 'correspond' with their 'true' characteristics. Establishing such a lack of correspondence is far from straightforward. Individuals' attitudes towards others can appear discriminatory and yet express a rational assessment of the evidence of social reality, a distinction that Allport (1954) probed in his famous parable of the anthropologist and the hotelier. What seems to be required are objective, agreed upon, criteria for determining the accuracy of social judgements in everyday contexts, a yardstick against which a lack of correspondence can be precisely gauged.

Outside of the field of prejudice research, the complexities involved in establishing and applying such criteria have been extensively debated, particularly with regards to judgements of personality (e.g. Funder, 1987, 1995; Jussim, 2005). Within the field of prejudice research, such discussion has been somewhat submerged. In practice, prejudice researchers have resolved questions of correspondence by becoming the (often unacknowledged) 'standard setters' (Kruglanski, 1989) of truth criteria. In some studies, the inaccuracy of social perceptions has been presumed on vaguely specified and a priori grounds; for example, much work on negative stereotyping works on the *supposition* that it distorts and simplifies social reality, largely without providing strong supporting evidence (see also Jussim *et al.*, 2009). In other studies, the criteria for establishing judgemental inaccuracy have been built into the architecture of research design, allowing researchers to identify participants' deviations from accurate thinking. To use a famous example: in Allport and Postman's (1946) study, racial bias was evidenced by the finding that participants reported a black protagonist holding a cutthroat razor when the stimulus picture shown to them clearly depicted the razor in the hands of a white protagonist. From their Olympian vantage, the researchers knew – in a way that participants did not and could not know – that such memories were *distortions* of the social reality that was verifiably manufactured within the study's design.

The dramatic nature of such simple experimental demonstrations may hide as much as it reveals about ordinary social judgements, however. In many everyday contexts, the criteria through which the accuracy of social perceptions is appraised are more complex, contestable and, above all, *relative to the background assumptions of the group members making the judgement*. Furthermore, and despite what they might wish, prejudice researchers do not generally occupy some sort of privileged vantage from which to trump the reasoning of ordinary people and become the ultimate arbiters of 'accuracy'. In our view, this is not only because we lack empirical evidence about the targets' 'true nature', but also because, even if such evidence was available, its interpretation would be mediated by our own shared assumptions, values, categories and ways of 'making sense'. As Sherif and Sherif (1979, pp. 16–17) once noted, social judgements are 'not ordinarily arrived at inductively through "rational" evaluation of direct experience in social life. Everything we know about culture, and language in particular, informs us that our reference groups have ready-made categories for us which color even our direct experiences and trial-and-error encounters with the social world around us ... We are still plagued by the arbitrary historical dichotomy between "rational" and "irrational" thinking, and too frequently the "irrational" is simply a label for thinking which leads to conclusions we do not like.'

Sherif's statement draws us into deep philosophical waters, raising complex questions about the nature of the relationship between mind and social reality that we cannot hope to resolve in this brief discussion. As is well known, his own work on so-called 'realistic' conflict between groups proposed an *instrumental* account of intergroup perceptions, demonstrating how such perceptions express the deeper structure of intergroup relations and are effectively a rational, collectively evolved, response to the conflicts and conjunctions of interests embedded within this structure (for extensions of this theoretical tradition see the work of Bobo, 1999; Esses *et al.*, 1996). To be sure, a simple theory of realistic conflict leaves many unanswered questions, e.g. are intergroup conflicts of interests 'real' or merely 'perceived', and why do some objectively deprived groups acquiesce in their subordination and others resist? Notwithstanding these complexities, however, most variants of realistic conflict theory (RCT) challenge the idea that 'prejudice' constitutes an individual-level misperception of the social world. They suggest that, at the very least, such perceptions may have a *pragmatic rationality* (cf. Swann, 1984) in servicing group interests. They suggest, too, that there is a 'psycho-logic' (Sherif, 1967) to prejudice, which derives from shared understandings of the nature of social reality, as well as from the broader patterns of allegiance and division that flow from such understandings. In the rest of this section, we outline two more recent challenges to the concept of prejudice as individual misperception.

Self-categorization, social identity and the 'veridicality'
of intergroup perceptions   As Chapter 2 elaborates, the first challenge is rooted in self-categorization theory (SCT). In essence, SCT builds on Sherif's (1967) legacy in order to rescue the concept of intergroup perception from the clutches of the prejudice problematic. Oakes *et al.* (1994) argue, for example, that most social psychological research on stereotyping – important exceptions notwithstanding (e.g. Vinacke, 1957) – has presupposed that it is a process that inflexibly distorts and falsifies social reality, albeit while serving other cognitive functions for the individual. By contrast, SCT treats stereotypes as flexible representations that typically *correspond with* the objective features of social contexts. Of course, in any given situation, the nature of social reality is highly complex, and its interpretation is always mediated by participants' shared beliefs about the relationship between themselves and others. Just as contextual features 'cue' (or render psychologically salient) certain kinds of social categories and comparisons, so too our *social identities* lead us to interpret social reality from a *particular vantage point* and to seek social consensus and validation from fellow ingroup members. For self-categorization theorists, then, stereotyping is conceived as psychologically valid from a *specific shared perspective* that, in turn, is shaped both by the dynamics of social identification and by the wider structure of social reality.

The so-called 'veridicality' of social stereotyping is revealed by its responsiveness to social change. Far from expressing simplistic or fixed representations of others, the content of stereotypes about self and other is exquisitely attuned to the shifting realities of intergroup relations at a macro-level, a process that Oakes *et al.* (1994) illustrate via an astute re-reading of the early literature, including research inspired by Katz and Braly's (1933) classic work (e.g. Meenes, 1943). Within the immediacy of day-to-day situations, too, stereotypes have a psychological truth in that they systematically 'fit' with the available information, an idea supported by experimental work in the self-categorization tradition (e.g. Haslam *et al.*, 1995). A qualification is required here. It is important not to confuse the claim that stereotypes are *psychologically veridical* with the claim that they are *socially acceptable or beneficial*. The point of the SCT argument is not to condone the application of pejorative stereotypes or to disregard their harmful consequences. Rather, they want to expose the inherent limits of research that conflates stereotyping with individual misjudgement and thus to open up an alternative perspective on the problem of changing intergroup relations.

Reynolds *et al.* (Chapter 2) argue that these limits are as much meta-theoretical as theoretical in character. In particular, self-categorization theorists challenge three ontological assumptions that underpin the majority of the psychological literature. The first assumption holds that stereotyping is primarily a problem of individual perception. To the contrary, self-categorization theorists treat stereotypic beliefs as socially produced, circulated and shared constructs (Tajfel, 1981) that, revealingly, are often not seen as 'prejudiced' by ingroup members themselves. The second assumption holds that individuals are somehow more real than groups. For Reynolds and colleagues, to the contrary, groups exist in the world and have tangible, higher order, properties, functions and relations. *A fortiori*, to deny the psychological validity of representing group-level characteristics is to perpetuate a spurious form of individualism. The third, and closely related, assumption holds that viewing people in terms of their individual characteristics is inherently more valid than viewing them as representatives of social groups. If one accepts the ontological reality of the social group, then a more nuanced approach is required. In some contexts, group-based representations will provide the most valid 'fit', enabling perceivers to make best sense of available information; in other contexts, representations at an individual level will be more psychologically valid.

This 'appropriate standards' (see also McCarty, 1999) critique points to two wider implications of the prejudice problematic. The first concerns the role of prejudice research in perpetuating the general assumption that it is only when we think and act as individuals, and view others in terms of their individuality, that human beings can be considered fully rational. In a recent polemic, Spears (2010) has rallied against this trend, providing several telling examples of the 'reasonableness' of group-based cognition and reinterpreting research on phenomena such as group polarization and minimal group discrimination. Like Oakes and colleagues, Spears insists that the supposed irrationality of group-based judgements often reflects a misapplication of baseline standards; that is, the judgement of group-level perceptions and actions using individual-level criteria. 'Group outcomes that look biased and irrational at first blush,' he suggests, 'may turn out to be quite rational and less biased when judged from a more appropriate group perspective. Reality and rationality may look and feel different at the group level than they do at the individual level. By the same token, this group reality may feed back into processes assumed to reflect quite basic cognitive information processing biases' (p. 15).

The second implication concerns how we frame the problem of social change. If negative beliefs about others are not primarily a matter of individual-level misperceptions but are instead grounded in the deeper structure of intergroup relations, identities and associated forms of collective cognition, then the effectiveness of standard prejudice reduction techniques is likely to be limited at best. Rather than targeting individuals for re-education in order to 'correct' their erroneous beliefs, we should be developing interventions that can transform this deeper social structure and the relationships it sustains. For many self-categorization theorists, this means adopting a model of change that is focused on the dynamics of collective action rather than prejudice reduction, a theme echoed in several of our book's chapters (e.g. see Chapters 1, 2, 6, 11, 12 and 14).

Thinking ill of others with sufficient warrant   A second challenge to the assumption that 'prejudice' reflects individual irrationality and misjudgement is grounded in the philosophy of social constructionism. This perspective has been particularly influential in British social psychology over the past few decades and is represented most explicitly in Chapters 7 to 10 of the present volume. Breaking with what we have called a correspondence model of truth, research in this tradition focuses on the discursive and interactional practices through which social communities actively create and reproduce the meaning of social reality, including the reality of others (e.g. see also Durrheim and Dixon, 2004; Edwards, 2003; Speer and Potter, 2000). In order to illustrate its implications for prejudice research, we shall briefly discuss the work of Condor and colleagues (e.g. Condor and Figgou, Chapter 10) and Reicher (e.g. Chapter 1).

Condor and colleagues point out that prejudice is not merely a topic that concerns psychologists and other social scientists: it is also a topic that concerns social actors in everyday situations. They argue that research on such lay understandings of prejudice is surprisingly sparse. Psychologists have tended to treat ordinary people as the 'unreflexive formulators' or 'bearers' (Figgou and Condor, 2006, p. 219) of prejudice rather than as agents capable of reflexively constructing what counts and does not count as prejudice in a given situation. In order to address this gap, their research focuses on 'prejudiced talk' in everyday situations; that is, on 'verbal behaviour which respondents themselves orient to as containing actually or potentially derogatory accounts of other ethnic, national or racial groups' (Condor, 2006, p. 3). Four general themes of their research are worth highlighting. First, Condor and colleagues argue that ordinary people are able to mobilize varying conceptions of prejudice – grounded in a range of culturally and historically embedded understandings – in order to make sense of their own and others' behaviours (e.g. understandings of prejudice as 'categorical accounting', 'intolerance of difference', 'antipathy towards lower status groups', and so on). Second, they argue that the process of defining prejudice must be construed as a *collaborative accomplishment*; that is, as something that community members do together as they *jointly formulate* the meaning of their relationship to others in everyday situations (see also Durrheim, Chapter 9). Third, they argue that people expend an enormous amount of discursive labour in 'dodging the identity of prejudice' (Wetherell and Potter, 1992). Not only do they orient to their personal reputations but they also seek to manage the reputations of others, including the social groups to which they belong, assuming joint responsibility for suppressing and mitigating (accusations of) prejudice (Condor *et al.*, 2006). Fourth, and crucially, they argue that some activities that social scientists might label 'prejudiced' are constructed as rational and legitimate by group members themselves. In their study of Greeks' representations of Albanians, for example, Figgou and Condor (2006) found that participants frequently placed acts of hostility towards others outside the frame of 'prejudice', attributing them instead to more reasonable concerns such as fear and risk management.

Of course, some social psychologists might dismiss participants' accounts of intergroup relations as mere impression management or view them as giving only hazy insights into the psychological process of which participants are not fully conscious. The constructionist perspective bypasses such issues by treating everyday processes of social construction as important in their own right (and not merely as a more or less accurate guide to what is happening in people's heads). Whether or not one accepts its deeper implications for psychology's philosophy of science (e.g. see Harre and Gillet, 1994), we believe that this perspective opens up some key issues for prejudice research. Perhaps most important, it moves to centre stage the collaborative, sense-making practices through which individuals and communities themselves may actively portray the mistreatment of others as normal, accountable and legitimate; that is, how they may come to think 'ill' of others *with* sufficient warrant.

In Chapter 1, Reicher develops this theme by suggesting that prejudice researchers who seek to determine whether or not checklists of intergroup beliefs and stereotypes match the actual features of members of target groups miss the point. He argues that *descriptions* of social reality are equally *explanations* of reality and, by implication, an attempt to control the political future. When British colonialists declared black South African pastoralists to be 'lazy', for example, they were not merely making a factual observation: they were attempting to justify depriving them of their land and to force them to work underground in the mines (Harsch, 1979). In other words, prejudiced beliefs are about *creating* as much as *representing* social reality. The key question, then, is not 'are such representations of others right or wrong?' but 'are they effective in maintaining systems of inequality?' (and, indeed, the forms of ethnic or racial classification on which they are built; cf. Pehrson and Leach, Chapter 6). In the next section, interrogating a second foundational assumption of the prejudice problematic, we argue that this ideological process need not operate via the attribution of uniformly negative qualities to others. Nor, indeed, is it necessarily accompanied by expressions of unadulterated hostility. To the contrary, prejudice may operate via positive stereotypes, warm feelings and even conditional love.

The limits of affective negativity

The 'velvet glove' of benign discrimination   Sherif's summer camp studies are arguably the most famous social psychological studies ever conducted on prejudice (Sherif *et al.*, 1961). Their fame derives in part from the genuine animosity they manufactured between the rival groups of boys. The food fights, name calling, burning of insignia and stockpiling of weaponry have recalled all too starkly the emotional and physical violence of real world conflict for generations of social psychologists. In a fascinating thought experiment, however, Mary Jackman (1994) asks us to consider how events might have unfolded in the summer camp studies had the following conditions prevailed: (1) relations were protracted indefinitely in time; (2) one group of boys achieved stable dominance over the other in terms of the commandeering of valued resources; and (3) that this dominance depended on their securing a continuous transfer of benefits from the subordinate group. Such conditions, of course, mirror real relations of class, race and gender more faithfully than the brief, equal status, zero-sum competition engineered by Sherif. Jackman argues that they also yield a very different pattern of social and psychological responses than that evidenced by the summer camp studies.

The point of her thought experiment is not to discredit Sherif's contribution. Instead, Jackman wants to highlight the contextual specificity of the summer camp findings and to challenge the assumption that unbridled antipathy typifies relations in historically unequal societies. Rather than hostility, she argues, real relations of domination and subordination are marked by emotional complexity and ambivalence, with positive responses such as affection and admiration being mingled with negative responses such as contempt and resentment. Sherif's work constitutes the exception rather than the rule. According to Jackman (1994, 2005), it also captures a more general tendency for social psychologists to over-emphasize the role of antipathy within intergroup relations.

Jackman's (1994) landmark book, *The Velvet Glove*, addresses this problem, exposing the insidious role of positive intergroup emotions in the reproduction of systems of inequality. Under conditions of long-term, stable inequality, she contends, it is simply not functional or feasible for members of dominant groups to maintain uniformly hostile attitudes towards subordinates. Given that dominants are dependent on subordinates' cooperation in order to sustain a smooth transfer of benefits (e.g. in the form of labour and services), the ideal social system is one of paternalism. Within paternalistic systems, role differentiation allows dominants to define the ideal characteristics of subordinates in ways that sustain the status quo, and then to reward those who display these characteristics with affirmation, admiration and even love. Such systems sugarcoat the harsh realities of inequality by framing social relations in more palatable terms for both dominant and subordinate group members. For dominants, exploitation is transformed into paternalistic regard and protectionism. For subordinates, the bonds of connection fostered by paternalistic institutions encourage identification with the very roles on which their subordination is founded. It also encourages positive feelings towards the dominant group and decreases support for collective action to challenge the status quo.

Gender relations provide the clearest illustration of the role of paternalistic influences on intergroup attitudes, exposing the inherent limits of a concept of prejudice based solely around antipathy. Such relations were largely ignored in early psychological research in the field, when the foundations of the prejudice problematic were laid, and they were barely mentioned in Allport's (1954) classic text. Yet few commentators would nowadays dispute that gender inequality and associated forms of discrimination remain pervasive. To provide but a few examples: women are subjected by men to domestic and sexual violence in many societies, they remain underrepresented in political institutions, they earn less than similarly qualified men and they shoulder the majority of housework and childcare. Men are often complicit beneficiaries of these forms of gender inequality. At the same time, evidence suggests that many men express warm emotional attitudes towards women. Indeed, they tend to like them more than they like other men, a phenomenon that is sometimes labelled, not a little ironically, the 'women are wonderful effect' (Eagly and Mladinic, 1989, 1993). If men behave in ways that maintain gender inequality and discriminate against women, then it is not because they feel some sort of generic hostility towards them. The traditional concept of prejudice as 'antipathy' does not seem to fit well.

Ambivalent sexism   This paradox has been investigated by a growing number of social psychologists, notably by psychologists working within the theoretical framework of ambivalent sexism developed by Peter Glick and Susan Fiske. According to Glick and Fiske (Chapter 3), sexist attitudes come in two forms. *Hostile sexism* (HS) refers to attitudes of overt 'hostility towards women who challenge male power' (Glick *et al.*, 2004, p. 715), and this concept is broadly consistent with an approach that treats prejudice as antipathy. *Benevolent sexism* (BS), by contrast, refers to attitudes that seem supportive towards women, treating them as 'wonderful fragile creatures who ought to be protected and provided for by men' (Glick *et al.*, 2004, p. 715), but also as creatures who lack agency and independence. HS and BS are manifest in all cultures and, according to Glick, Fiske and others, their ubiquity expresses a fundamental ambivalence in attitudes towards women (Glick and Fiske, 2001). On the one hand, as a subordinate group, women must be kept in their 'proper place', which encourages the development of hostile attitudes that derogate those who threaten (the legitimacy of) male advantage. On the other hand, men are highly dependent on women for, among other benefits, the transfer of emotional support, childcare and sexual gratification. This dependency triggers a more 'benevolent' attitude system in which women who 'know their place' are rewarded by admiration, sacrifice and protectiveness and thereby encouraged to conform to traditional gender roles. In everyday situations, the expression of these hostile or benevolent attitudes is highly flexible, varying, for example, according to whether female targets are perceived as undermining ('career woman') or supporting ('homemaker') the gender hierarchy.

Ambivalent sexism theory is relevant to our argument because it provides the strongest psychological challenge to the idea that intergroup prejudice – and associated forms of discrimination – operates primarily via attitudinal hostility. The point of the theory is not simply to explain how men express and reconcile the polarized nature of their attitudes towards women, but also to explore the broader ideological role of HS and BS in maintaining gender inequality. Two issues are worth flagging here. First, BS is associated with a range of discriminatory beliefs, attributions and behaviours (e.g. see Abrams *et al.*, 2003; Chapleau *et al.*, 2007; Rye and Meaney, 2010). Yet because of its veneer of affectionate regard for (certain types of) women, it is less readily perceived as sexist than HS (Barreto and Ellemers, 2005) and is thus a highly defensible ideology in societies where gender equality is a social ideal. Second, as well as shaping men's gender attitudes, BS plays a powerful role in structuring women's attitudes towards other women. Sibley, Overall and Duckitt's (2007) longitudinal research indicates, for instance, that women who score high on BS are more likely to express hostile attitudes towards their own gender in the future. They are also more likely to judge women who transgress traditional gender roles harshly and to support female behaviour that affirms these roles, such as the use of beauty products (Forbes *et al.*, 2006).

As this brief review illustrates, emerging research on ambivalent sexism has gone some way to answering Jackman's (2005, p. 89) call for social psychologists to 'dethrone hostility' as the affective hallmark of discriminatory relations. To what extent, however, can work on attitudes in the field of gender relations be generalized to other kinds of intergroup relations?

Doubtless, gender relations are in several senses a 'special case', entailing unusually intense forms of familial, sexual and reproductive interdependency. Even so, Glick and Fiske (Chapter 3) insist that the ambivalent attitudes that mark such relations are repeated within other forms of intergroup hierarchy. Jackman (1994, 2005) likewise argues that systems of domination based around relations of race and class typically involve a complex blend of hostile and paternalistic elements. In her analysis of national survey data on race attitudes in the US, for example, Jackman (1994) found that many white Americans who expressed inclusive feelings towards African Americans also expressed conservative or reactionary political attitudes towards policies designed to create racial equality in the domains of housing, employment and education. Positive intergroup emotions, in other words, happily coexisted with rejection of race-targeted interventions. Of course, such findings do not refute the claim that emotional hostility plays a key role in maintaining racial inequality in many contexts. However, they do suggest that flagrant antipathy is not the whole story of racial and ethnic discrimination, and that warm feelings do not necessarily engender concrete support for political transformation.

The darker side of inclusion   Developing the latter theme, psychologists studying other 'positive' intergroup processes have recently begun to wonder if their impacts on social change are as unequivocally beneficial as is commonly assumed. Emerging work on common identification provides a case in point. Proposed originally by Samuel Gaertner and Jack Dovidio, the so-called common identity model holds that inducing members of different social groups (e.g. blacks and whites) to view one another as members of a shared ingroup (e.g. Americans) tends to improve their intergroup attitudes, reducing intergroup bias and increasing positive responses such as liking and empathy (see Gaertner and Dovidio, 2000, 2009). Research on this model is now extensive and overwhelmingly supportive, and common identification is widely viewed as one of the most promising psychological interventions to improve intergroup relations. In the elaboration of their own model presented in Chapter 12, however, Dovidio and colleagues have discussed the so-called 'darker side of we', exploring some of the often unacknowledged consequences of social inclusion. To begin with, they concede that the ideological terms of inclusion are often a site of intergroup struggle and domination. Members of historically advantaged groups typically favour assimilative forms of inclusion (a 'one-group' representation of common identity) that leave intact the existing status hierarchy, whereas members of disadvantaged groups prefer a dual identity model, which tends to better protect their group interests. Perhaps more crucial, when disadvantaged group members are led to think in terms of their common identification with an historically advantaged outgroup, they also tend to de-emphasize ongoing relations of power, injustice and inequality, adopting what is arguably an overly 'optimistic' view of intergroup relations. As we detail in the next section, this kind of evidence has instigated a searching re-evaluation of the model of social change that underpins prejudice research.

The limits of a prejudice reduction model of social change

Two routes to social change in historically unequal societies   If irrational hostility towards the disadvantaged is defined as the problem, then the cognitive and emotional rehabilitation of the advantaged becomes the solution. We need, the argument goes, to get such people to like others more and to abandon their faulty stereotypes. In due course, incidences of discrimination will decline, creating a more equitable society in which the potential for intergroup conflict wanes. The prejudice problematic, in short, comes with a ready-made antidote, which is a model of social change grounded in the psychology of prejudice reduction.

Over the course of the history of social psychology, this model has been periodically criticized. Commentators have flagged, among other flaws, the dangers of providing psychological solutions to problems that are structural, institutional or ideological (e.g. see Henriques *et al.*, 1984; Pehrson and Leach, Chapter 6). They have also worried about the implication, embedded in several conceptualizations of prejudice, that social change is inevitably curtailed by certain universal and intractable features of human psychology (e.g. Hopkins *et al.*, 1997). Nevertheless, prejudice reduction remains by far social psychology's most intensively researched and passionately advocated perspective on how to improve intergroup relations.

It is not, however, the only perspective. Another model of social change that has engaged many psychologists focuses on the role of collective action in achieving social justice. Its guiding assumption is that social change is predicated upon mass mobilization, a process that typically brings representatives of historically disadvantaged groups (the main beneficiaries of change) into conflict with representatives of historically advantaged groups (who seldom give up their privileges without a struggle). Researchers working in this area have sought to understand the psychological mechanisms that lead the disadvantaged to recognize, reject and jointly challenge social inequality. Moreover, instead of taking prejudice reduction as their outcome measure, they have tracked changes in perceptions of intergroup injustice and discrimination, together with associated behavioural reactions such as readiness to engage in collective protest (for overviews see Dion, 2002; Klandermans, 1997; van Zomeren *et al.*, 2008).

Although these two traditions of research have developed largely in isolation, in our experience most psychologists intuitively presume that they focus on psychological processes that are complementary to the broader struggle to achieve a better society. Prejudice researchers concentrate on changing the hearts and minds of the advantaged, and collective action researchers study how, when and why the disadvantaged take political action. The two models seem to fit together as different parts of the puzzle of social change. Recent research indicates, however, that their interrelationship may be more complicated.

According to Wright and Baray (Chapter 11), these two models of social change involve psychological processes that work in opposing directions. On the one hand, prejudice reduction diminishes our tendency to view the world in 'us' versus 'them' terms, encouraging us to view others either as individuals (e.g. Brewer and Miller, 1984), as part of a common ingroup (e.g. Gaertner and Dovidio, 2009) or at least as people who share 'crossed' category memberships (e.g. Crisp and Hewstone,

1999). Such interventions foster positive emotional responses towards others, such as empathy and trust, while decreasing negative responses such as anxiety and anger (e.g. Esses and Dovidio, 2002; Pettigrew and Tropp, 2008; Stephan and Finlay, 1999). The overarching objective of this model of social change is to diminish the likelihood of intergroup conflict in historically divided societies. On the other hand, collective action interventions are based on the assumption that group identification is a powerful motor of social change (Klandermans, 1997). Within this model of change, an 'us' versus 'them' mentality is generally construed as functional and strategic: it encourages members of disadvantaged groups to form coalitions and to act together in the common interest. Collective action also generally requires the emergence of 'negative' intergroup emotions and perceptions, including collective anger and a sense of relative deprivation (e.g. Grant and Brown, 1995; van Zomeren *et al.*, 2004), which impel group members to recognize injustice and become motivated to challenge the status quo. The goal of this model of change is not to reduce but to instigate intergroup conflict in order to challenge institutional inequalities in historically divided societies. Conflict is viewed as the fire that fuels social change rather than a threat to extinguish at the point of conflagration.

Paradoxical effects of intergroup contact   Recognition of the potentially contradictory relationship between these two models of social change has inspired research on the 'ironic' effects of prejudice reduction on the psychology of the disadvantaged. This research has focused on the impact of interventions to promote intergroup contact, extending work on the contact hypothesis (Allport, 1954). The contact hypothesis is the most important tradition of research on prejudice reduction (e.g. Pettigrew and Tropp, 2006). Its basic premise is simple. Interaction between members of different groups reduces intergroup prejudice, particularly when it occurs under favourable conditions (e.g. equality of status, cooperative interdependence). Evidence supporting this idea is extensive and, many believe, conclusive. Pettigrew and Tropp's (2006) widely cited meta-analysis found that contact decreased prejudice in over 94 per cent of 515 studies reviewed. A follow-up analysis (Pettigrew and Tropp, 2008) suggested that this effect was largely explained by reductions in intergroup anxiety and increases in intergroup empathy, as well as by improvements in participants' knowledge about members of other groups.

Like most traditions of research on prejudice, research on the contact hypothesis has focused mainly on the reactions of members of historically advantaged groups (e.g. whites in South Africa). In some recent studies, however, the impacts of positive intergroup contact on the psychology of the historically disadvantaged has been prioritized (e.g. blacks in South Africa). As well as employing standard prejudice indices as outcome measures, researchers have used measures of broader political attitudes, with some provocative results (see Dixon *et al.*, 2007, 2010; Saguy *et al.*, 2009; Tausch *et al.*, 2009; Wright and Lubensky, 2008).

Dixon, Durrheim and colleagues (2007, 2010) conducted two national surveys of racial attitudes in South Africa. Their first survey explored the relationship between interracial contact and South Africans' willingness to support race-targeted policies being implemented by the African National Congress (ANC) government to redress the legacy of apartheid, including policies of land redistribution and affirmative action. They identified a revealing divergence in the results for white and black respondents. For whites, positive contact with blacks was *positively* correlated with support for government policies of redress; for blacks, positive contact with whites was *negatively* correlated with support for such policies. In other words, contact was associated with increases in whites' and decreases in blacks' support for social change. In their second survey, Dixon *et al.* (2010) investigated the relationship between interracial contact and black South Africans' perceptions of racial discrimination in the post-apartheid era. They found that respondents who reported having more positive contact experiences with whites also perceived the racial discrimination faced by their group to be less severe. As Figure C.1 indicates, this effect was mediated both by perceived personal discrimination and by blacks' racial attitudes. That is, the negative relationship between contact and judgements of collective discrimination was partly explained by reductions in respondents' sense of being personally targeted for racial discrimination and also by increases in their positive emotions towards whites. Research conducted in Israel by Saguy *et al.* (2009, study 2) and in India by Tausch *et al.* (2009) has confirmed these 'ironic' effects of intergroup contact. In both studies, positive contact was associated with less support for social change among members of disadvantaged groups (Arab Israelis and Muslims respectively).

Viewed as a whole, the evidence produced by this line of research indicates that contact may well improve the intergroup attitudes of the historically disadvantaged, but may also, paradoxically, reduce the extent to which they acknowledge their group experiences of injustice and support actions designed to challenge such injustice. From a prejudice reduction perspective we have a success; from a collective action perspective a failure. Further, this work shows that the very processes that underpin prejudice reduction help to explain the 'ironic' impacts of intergroup contact on political attitudes. Perhaps most significant, several studies

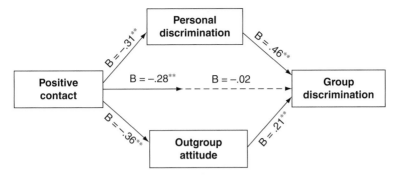

Indirect path through attitudes, Sobel z = −2.6, p < .01.
Indirect path through personal discrimination, Sobel z = −6.3, p < .01.

Notes:
* p < .05; ** p < .01.

Figure C.1: Path analytic model for indirect effects of contact quality on perceptions of group discrimination (taken from Dixon *et al.*, 2010)

suggest that it is precisely *because* contact improves intergroup attitudes (prejudice reduction) that it also decreases perceptions of injustice, support for race-targeted policies and readiness to engage in collective action. When the disadvantaged come to like the advantaged, when they assume they are trustworthy and good human beings, when their personal experiences suggest that the collective discrimination might not be so bad after all, then they become more likely to abandon the project of collective action to change inequitable societies.

Prejudice reduction and social change revisited: some suggested parameters and future directions

The question of change is the one that has troubled us most while editing this volume. An enduring strength of work on prejudice, as we noted in the book's introduction, is that it shifted the target of social science research on intergroup relations. The study of immutable differences between groups became recast as the study of (potentially mutable) dominant group bigotry. In the wake of this profound scientific, and also moral and political, reversal, the applied social psychology of prejudice reduction was born. Few areas of research have better exemplified Kurt Lewin's maxim that social psychologists should be willing to get the proverbial 'seats of their pants' dirty.

The message presented in several of our book's chapters, however, has complicated this optimistic history of the contribution of prejudice reduction interventions. Perhaps the most important question we have left hanging, then, is: what are the prospects for reconciling a prejudice reduction model of social change, designed to help people get along better, with a collective action model of change, designed to mobilize struggles to achieve social justice?

There are a number of possible positions in this debate that must still be had by the psychological community. One pole of the debate might be anchored by arguments that the two forms of social change are simply incommensurable and that the drive for prejudice reduction has for too long obscured, if not obstructed, more pressing questions about core distributive justice (i.e. justice based on equality of distribution resources such as wealth, jobs and health). The other pole of the debate might be anchored by arguments that the two forms of social change are complementary and mutually reinforcing (i.e. that liking one another will ultimately lead to social justice in a deeper sense). Between these two extremes, we suspect, the debate will unfold. We hope it will be informed by contributions from both traditions of psychological research on social change, as well as from work unfolding in cognate disciplines.

We shall conclude the book simply by recommending some possible parameters within which this debate might unfold, which concern the importance of acknowledging: (1) the relational nature of intergroup attitudes and perceptions; (2) the political as well as the emotional and cognitive effects of prejudice reduction; (3) the importance of considering social context when evaluating models of change; and (4) the complex relationship between intergroup harmony and conflict in the transformation of historically unequal societies.

(1) Relationality

Shelton's (2000) influential analysis of the race prejudice literature brought to social psychologists' attention several consequences of focusing exclusively on the reactions of historically advantaged groups and treating historically disadvantaged groups as 'passive' targets of discrimination. One consequence is that the fundamentally *relational* nature of intergroup attitudes has often been overlooked. Shelton's own research has demonstrated, for example, that interracial attitudes emerge in and through the dynamics of interaction, with the actions of members of one group (e.g. blacks) forming the context in which the reactions of the other (e.g. whites) take shape and find expression, and vice versa (see Shelton and Richeson, 2006). Investigating one group's attitudes in isolation, she argues convincingly, inevitably impoverishes our understanding.

Several contributors to this book suggest that this principle of relationality is equally important when evaluating the success of interventions to promote social change. Such interventions generally shape the lived experiences of members of *both* historically advantaged and disadvantaged groups (e.g. by fostering more frequent intergroup contact). Moreover, they shape not only their respective attitudes and behaviours, but also upon the overall nature of their relationship (e.g. by identification in which 'us' and 'them' become 'we'). Yet for much of the history of prejudice research and collective action research the relational consequences of particular forms of intervention have been radically underspecified. Prejudice researchers have tended to isolate the responses of the advantaged, collective action researchers the responses of the disadvantaged.

Our first recommendation, then, is that the relational implications of intervention be brought to the foreground of research on interventions to promote social change, just as Shelton's work has brought them to the foreground of work on interracial attitudes in a more general sense. We also recommend that researchers move beyond a simple 'dominant' versus 'subordinate' group model and attempt to explore other, more complex, forms of relationality. For example, we still know comparatively little about the role of prejudice reduction interventions in shaping horizontal relations between minority groups, and this strikes us as a context in which the social psychologies of prejudice reduction and collective action might well work in harmony. That is, by diminishing so-called 'horizontal hostility' (White and Langer, 1999), prejudice reduction might also increase members' willingness to build coalitions to challenge the forms of inequality they experience in common. By the same token, we hypothesize that interventions designed to improve a subordinate group's attitudes towards a dominant group (e.g. by creating new forms of inclusion or conferring concessionary benefits) may have the unacknowledged consequence of increasing its members' prejudice towards other subordinate groups. This pattern is all too familiar within post-colonial societies in Africa and the near East, for example, where the 'divide and rule' strategies altered both horizontal and vertical relationships between groups in complex ways. In short, in an increasingly *multi*cultural, *multi*ethnic world, social psychologists need to track the impact of interventions on the overall positional matrix of intergroup perceptions, attitudes and behaviours. The 'one group at a time' approach is clearly inadequate.

(2) Expanding our conception of a successful intervention 'outcome'
Researchers have employed varying indices when evaluating the success of prejudice reduction, which have become more subtle and sophisticated over time. Indices of blatant and controlled intergroup attitudes have been complemented by indices of indirect and automatic attitudes. Self-report indices have been complemented by behavioural and physiological indices. Scales measuring generic antipathy have been complemented by scales measuring specific intergroup emotions and associated 'action tendencies'. By and large, however, the overall conception of a 'successful' intervention outcome has remained within the boundaries of the prejudice problematic. Research on prejudice reduction continues to track shifts in negative emotions and stereotypes (or close proxies).

This emphasis on the cognitive and emotional rehabilitation of the bigoted individual has arguably led to an underutilization of other relevant outcome indicators. Notably, as Wright and Lubensky (2008, p. 18) remark, 'when efforts to reduce prejudice focus exclusively on getting dominant group members to think nicer thoughts and feel positive emotions about the disadvantaged group, they may not necessarily increase support for broader structural and institutional changes'. Consider, for example, evidence on whites' attitudes to policies designed to promote racial equality in societies such as the US and South Africa. Several researchers have reported that such resistance intensifies when such policies comes to threaten directly whites' material advantages (see Bobo and Kluegel, 1993; Dixon *et al.*, 2007; Schuman *et al.*, 1997; Sears *et al.*, 1997). Thus, whites endorse the *principle* of racial equality more readily than they endorse concrete attempts to *implement* racial equality, maintaining a so-called principle-implementation gap (Dixon *et al.*, 2007). Further, they endorse *race compensatory policies* (e.g. job skills training) more readily than *racial preferential policies* (e.g. affirmative action), arguably because the latter do not merely increase blacks' potential ability to compete with whites for resources and opportunities, but also involve a reallocation of such resources and opportunities (Tuch and Hughes, 1996). White policy attitudes seem to express, in other words, what we earlier described as an 'instrumental' rationality.

According to Jackman and Crane (1986), this attitudinal pattern is unlikely to be altered by traditional forms of prejudice reduction, which put the eradication of erroneous beliefs and 'parochial negativism' at the heart of the problem of social change. In their analysis of national survey data gathered in America, they found that interracial contact led whites to express greater emotional acceptance of blacks, but had limited effects on their support for concrete policies designed to redress injustice in the domains of employment, housing and schooling. On the basis of such evidence, one could infer that prejudice reduction has little beneficial impact on the policy orientations of the advantaged. We believe that this conclusion is hasty. More recent research has suggested that positive interracial contact may sometimes increase support for race-targeted policies among members of advantaged groups. Dixon *et al.* (2007), for instance, found that contact was positively associated with whites' support for policies designed to promote racial transformation in post-apartheid South Africa, albeit that this relationship was stronger for race compensatory policies (e.g. job skills training) than for race preferential policies (e.g. affirmative action in the workplace). Future research should clarify how, when and why prejudice reduction shapes the policy orientations of advantaged and disadvantaged groups across different social and historical contexts.

Our general point is that prejudice research might benefit from a more expansive definition of the ideal outcomes of intervention, incorporating measures that tap shifts in political judgements and commitments as well as standard measures of attitudes and stereotypes. In particular, we need to know more about the relationship between prejudice reduction and support for interventions that challenge the *institutional core* of disadvantage in historically unequal societies, altering the distribution of wealth, opportunity and political power. Over the history of prejudice research, the goal of getting individuals to like one another more has arguably drawn attention away from these equally, if not more, important outcomes.

(3) Contextualizing change Dixon *et al.* (2010) have recently argued that the value of models of social change cannot be assessed meaningfully in generic or 'either-or' terms. Rather, they must be evaluated in terms of their consequences within particular historical, economic and political circumstances. This may sound like a rather obvious point for *social* psychologists to make; after all, the discipline is frequently defined as the study of human behaviour *in context*. However, in our experience, social psychologists are all too often tempted to offer general solutions to specific problems, overlooking what Cherry (1995) calls the 'stubborn particulars' of social processes. For this reason, we believe that attempts to weigh the relative virtues of collective action and prejudice reduction models of social change must be grounded in an analysis of the specific contexts in which intergroup relations are embedded.

The first author of this chapter, for example, grew up in South Africa and Northern Ireland. Both societies have a long history of division and intergroup violence, and both are currently in a process of social and political transition. The kinds of social problems they face are in many ways quite different, however, and so, in our view, are the kinds of 'solutions' that they may require. Although South Africa has made considerable progress towards racial equality in the post-apartheid era – largely through the collective will and action of its black citizens – it remains a society characterized by gross inequalities of wealth and opportunity. Indeed, with a Gini coefficient of just under 58, South Africa is one of the world's most unequal societies, and many of its citizens suffer the consequences in terms of high crime, unemployment, poverty, food insecurity, high infant mortality and lack of access to basic medical care, housing and education. In such a society, collective action to achieve structural and political change remains of paramount importance. As such, as Reicher (2007) warns, if attempts to reduce prejudice serve to 'dissipate such action, then [they] may do more to impede that to facilitate progress' (p. 831).

The situation in Northern Ireland is very different. Although 'the troubles' were of course rooted in a longer history of deprivation and discrimination, Northern Irish citizens do not suffer anything like the same absolute or relative levels of poverty as South Africans. Moreover, and crucially, the 'sectarian' divide in terms of the disbribution of wealth and opportunity in Northern Ireland is not comparable with the 'racial' divide in South Africa. For this reason, we suspect that the forms of social change that the two societies require might ultimately prove to be rather different. At least in the shorter term, the 'improvement' of sectarian relations in Northern Ireland is likely to depend more heavily on interventions designed to promote intercommunity tolerance, empathy and forgiveness (see e.g. Hewstone *et al.*, 2006) than on interventions to promote collective action to challenge material inequality.

The point of this brief and wholly inadequate discussion is not to prescribe how social psychologists working in these (or other) societies should approach the question of social change. We simply wish to emphasize that the evaluation of models of social change cannot be done in the abstract. Rather, it must be grounded in an analysis of the particularities of the contexts to which they are being applied. In our view, the hegemony of prejudice reduction models of change has meant that social psychologists rarely attempt to think through their limitations or consider alternatives. Indeed, the idea that psychologists should be promoting getting people to like one another more is so powerful that alternatives are sometimes difficult to imagine.

(4) Complexities of harmony and conflict   The promotion of intergroup harmony has always been a cardinal objective of research on prejudice, and understandably so. Research on prejudice gathered impetus as

a way of explaining the mass violence of the Second World War, and subsequent bloodshed throughout the twentieth and early twenty-first centuries have done little to allay social scientists' concerns about 'the toll in death, suffering and displacement caused by large-scale conflicts caused by groups defined by ethnicity, nationality, religion or other social identities' (Eidelson and Eidelson, 2003, p. 183). In the face of such events, the promotion of harmonious relations has become an unquestioned moral imperative for many prejudice researchers. However, intergroup harmony also has a negative face. To borrow Jost et al.'s (2004) terminology, it carries insidious, if often unacknowledged, 'system-justifying' consequences. Seemingly tolerant and inclusive intergroup attitudes not only coexist with gross injustices, but also serve as a mechanism *through which* such injustices are reproduced. As we have seen, convergent lines of evidence can be marshalled to support this claim, including evidence on the effects of ambivalent sexism (Glick and Fiske, Chapter 3), common identification (Dovidio et al., Chapter 12) and intergroup contact (Wright and Baray, Chapter 11).

If the unquestioned acceptance of intergroup harmony as an 'absolute good' is simplistic, then so too is the unquestioned rejection of intergroup conflict as an 'absolute bad'. Unlike harmony, whose meaning is often taken for granted by social scientists, conflict has been intensely scrutinized as a social problem to be explained. In seeking to understand its psychological causes, researchers have relied heavily on the prejudice problematic, conceiving intergroup tensions as the outcrop of fundamentally irrational, and emotionally charged, forms of social cognition. As Keltner and Robinson (1996, p. 101) remark, 'There is perhaps no more dangerous force in social relations than the human mind. People's capacity to categorize, interpret and "go beyond the information" readily lead to stereotyping and dehumanization that escalate and entrench group conflict.'

Whatever its other contributions, this perspective on social change has also entrenched the assumption that conflict is inherently pathological, disconnected from human rationality and without social value. It has obscured the possibility that, at least in some circumstances, conflict is 'a normal and perfectly healthy aspect of the political process that is social life' (Oakes, 2001, p. 16). Certainly, conflict in the form of collective resistance by members of disadvantaged groups is a mechanism – several of our book's contributors would argue the primary mechanism – for achieving equality in historically unequal societies. Its psychological correlates of anger, strong ingroup identification and a sense of injustice do not integrate easily with a prejudice reduction model of social change, but they are often necessary to achieve progress in a political and structural sense.

The latter point raises several challenging, and perhaps uncomfortable, questions for prejudice researchers. As well as reducing negative stereotypes and emotions, should we be seeking to promote 'positive' conflict; that is, conflict that confronts not only the direct violence of overt discrimination, but also the indirect violence of structural inequality? How might such interventions be squared with the broader project of reducing prejudice and creating a more tolerant society? What form might they take? The latter chapters of this book have all broached such questions in various ways.

Our general argument here is similar to that made by Georg Sorensen (1992) in his discussion of the field of international peace studies. Sorensen criticized researchers' tendency to extol the core value of 'peace' while leaving its fundamental contradictions unexamined. More specifically, he railed against a utopian perspective in which inconvenient questions are ignored – questions, for example, about the apparent ineffectiveness of exclusively non-violent solutions to problems of structural oppression in some societies and, conversely, about the apparent effectiveness of short-term 'developmental violence' in establishing longer-term peace in others. We believe a comparable problem inflicts much psychological research on prejudice reduction. Social harmony has become an unquestioned ideal to be promoted, social conflict an absolute evil to be vanquished. Breaking with this approach, we advocate greater openness among prejudice researchers to interrogating the complex relationship between conflict and harmony as it unfolds within processes of social change within historically unequal societies.

References

Abrams, D., Viki, G. T., Masser, B. and Bohner, G. (2003). Perceptions of stranger and acquaintance rape: the role of benevolent and hostile sexism in victim blame and rape proclivity. *Journal of Personality and Social Psychology*, **84**, 111–25.

Allport, G. W. (1954). *The Nature of Prejudice*. Garden City, NY: Doubleday.

Allport, G. W. and Postman, L. (1946). An analysis of rumor. *Public Opinion Quarterly*, **10**, 501–18.

Barreto, M. and Ellemers, N. (2005). The burden of benevolent sexism: how it contributes to the maintenance of gender inequalities. *European Journal of Social Psychology*, **35**, 633–42.

Bobo, L. (1999). Prejudice as group position: microfoundations of a sociological approach to racism and race relations. *Journal of Social Issues*, **55**, 445–72.

Bobo, L. and Kluegel, J. R. (1993). Opposition to race-targeting: self-interest, stratification ideology or racial attitudes? *American Sociological Review*, **58**, 443–64.

Brewer, M. B. and Miller, N. (1984). Beyond the contact hypothesis: theoretical perspectives on desegregation. In N. Miller and M. B. Brewer (eds.), *Groups in Contact: a Psychology of Desegregation*. New York: Academic Press.

Chapleau, K. M., Oswald, D. L. and Russell, B. L. (2007). How ambivalent sexism towards women and men supports rape myth acceptance. *Sex Roles*, **57**, 131–6.

Cherry, F. (1995). *The Stubborn Particulars of Social Psychology: Essays on the Research Process*. London: Routledge.

Condor, S. (2006). Public prejudice as collaborative accomplishment: towards a dialogic social psychology of racism. *Journal of Community and Applied Social Psychology*, **6**, 1–18.

Condor, S., Figgou, L., Abell, J., Gibson, S. and Stevenson, C. (2006). 'They're not racist . . .' Prejudice denial, mitigation and suppression in dialogue. *British Journal of Social Psychology*, **44**, 441–62.

Crisp, R. J. and Hewstone, M. (1999). Differential evaluation of crossed category groups: patterns, processes, and reducing intergroup bias. *Group Processes and Intergroup Relations*, **2**, 307–33.

Dion, K. L. (2002). The social psychology of perceived prejudice and discrimination. *Canadian Psychology*, **43**, 1–10.

Dixon, J., Durrheim, K. and Tredoux, C. (2007). Intergroup contact and attitudes towards the principle and practice of racial equality. *Psychological Science*, **18**, 867–72.

Dixon, J., Durrheim, K., Tredoux, C., Tropp, L. R., Clack, B. and Eaton, E. (2010). A paradox of integration? Interracial contact, prejudice reduction and blacks' perceptions of racial discrimination. *Journal of Social Issues*, **66**, 401–16.

Durrheim, K. and Dixon, J. (2004). Attitudes in the fiber of everyday life: the discourse of racial evaluation and the lived experience of desegregation. *American Psychologist*, **59**, 626–36.

Eagly, A. H. and Mladinic, A. (1989). Gender stereotypes and attitudes toward women and men. *Personality and Social Psychology Bulletin*, **15**, 543–58.

(1993). Are people prejudiced against women? Some answers from research on attitudes, gender stereotypes and judgments of competence. In W. Stroebe and M. Hewstone (eds.), *European Review of Social Psychology* (Vol. 5, pp. 1–35). New York: Wiley.

Edwards, D. (2003). Analyzing racial discourse: the discursive psychology of mind–world relationships. In H. van den Berg, M. Wetherell and H. Houtkoop-Steenstra (eds.), *Analyzing Race Talk: Multidisciplinary Approaches to the Interview*. Cambridge, UK: Cambridge University Press.

Eidelson, R. J. and Eidelson, R. I. (2003). Dangerous ideas: five beliefs that impel groups towards conflict. *American Psychologist*, **58**, 182–92.

Esses, V. M. and Dovidio, J. F. (2002). The role of emotions in determining willingness to engage in intergroup contact. *Personality and Social Psychology Bulletin*, **28**, 1,202–14.

Esses, V. M., Dovidio, J. F., Danso, H. A. and Jackson, L. M. (1996). Historical and modern perspectives on group competition. In C. S. Crandall and M. Schaller (eds.), *Social Psychology of Prejudice: Historical and Contemporary Issues*. Seattle, WA: Lewinian Press.

Figgou, L. and Condor, S. (2006). Irrational categorization, natural intolerance and reasonable discrimination: lay representations of prejudice and racism. *British Journal of Social Psychology*, **44**, 1–29.

Fiske, S. T. (2002). What we know about bias and intergroup conflict, the problem of the century. *Current Directions in Psychological Science*, **11**, 123–8.

Forbes, G. B., Jung, J. and Haas, K. B. (2006). Benevolent sexism and cosmetic use: a replication with three college samples and one adult sample. *Journal of Social Psychology*, **145**, 635–40.

Funder, D. C. (1987). Errors and mistakes: evaluating the accuracy of social judgment. *Psychological Bulletin*, **101**, 75–90.

(1995). On the accuracy of personality judgment: a realistic approach. *Psychological Review*, **102**, 652–70.

Gaertner, S. L. and Dovidio, J. F. (2000). *Reducing Intergroup Bias: the Common Ingroup Identity Model*. Philadelphia, PA: Psychology Press.

(2009). A common ingroup identity: a categorization-based approach for reducing intergroup bias. In T. Nelson (ed.), *Handbook of Prejudice* (pp.489–506). Philadelphia, PA: Taylor and Francis.

Glick, P. and Fiske, S. T. (2001). Ambivalent sexism. In M. P. Zanna (ed.), *Advances in Experimental Social Psychology* (Vol. 33). Thousand Oaks, CA: Academic Press.

Glick, P., Lameiras, M., Fiske, S. T., Eckes, T., Masser, B., Volpato, C. *et al.* (2004). Bad but bold: ambivalent attitudes toward men predict gender inequality in 16 nations. *Journal of Personality and Social Psychology*, **86**, 713–28.

Grant, P. R. and Brown, R. (1995). From ethnocentricism to collective protest – responses to relative deprivation and threats to social identity. *Social Psychology Quarterly*, **58**, 195–212.

Harre, R. and Gillet, G. (1994). *The Discursive Mind*. London: Sage.

Harsch, E. (1979). *South Africa: White Rule, Black Revolt*. New York: Monad.

Haslam, S. A., Oakes, P. J., Turner, J. C. and McGarty, C. (1995). Social categorization and group homogeneity: changes in the perceived applicability of stereotype content as a function of comparative context and trait favourableness. *British Journal of Social Psychology*, **34**, 139–60.

Henriques, J., Hollway, W., Urwin, C., Venn, C. and Walkerdine, V. (1984). *Changing the Subject*. London: Methuen.

Hewstone, M., Cairns, M., Voci, A., Hamberger, J. and Niens, U. (2006). Intergroup contact, forgiveness, and experience of 'the troubles' in Northern Ireland. *Journal of Social Issues*, **62**, 99–120.

Hopkins, N., Reicher, S. and Levine, M. (1997). On the parallels between social cognition theory and the new racism. *British Journal of Social Psychology*, **36**, 305–29.

Jackman, M. R. (1994). *The Velvet Glove: Paternalism and Conflict in Gender, Class, and Race Relations*. Berkeley, CA: University of California Press.

(2005). Rejection or inclusion of outgroups. In J. F. Dovidio, P. Glick and L. A. Rudman (eds.), *On the Nature of Prejudice: 50 Years after Allport* (Ch. 6). Oxford, UK: Wiley-Blackwell.

Jackman, M. R. and Crane, M. (1986). 'Some of my best friends are black . . .': interracial friendship and whites' racial attitudes. *Public Opinion Quarterly*, **50**, 459–86.

Jost, J. T., Banaji, M. R. and Nosek, B. A. (2004). A decade of system justification theory: accumulated evidence of conscious and unconscious bolstering of the status quo. *Political Psychology*, **25**, 881–919.

Jussim, L. (2005). Accuracy in social perception: criticisms, controversies, criteria, components, and cognitive processes. *Advances in Experimental Social Psychology*, **37**, 1–93.

Jussim, L., Cain, T. R., Crawford, J. T., Barber, K. and Cohen, F. (2009). The unbearable accuracy of stereotyping. In T. D. Nelson (ed.), *Handbook of Prejudice, Stereotyping and Discrimination*. New York: Psychology Press.

Katz, D. and Braly, K. (1933). Racial stereotypes in 100 college students. *Journal of Abnormal and Social Psychology*, **28**, 280–90.

Keltner, D. and Robinson, R. J. (1996). Extremism, power, and the imagined basis of social conflict. *Current Directions in Psychological Science*, **5**, 101–5.

Klandermans, B. (1997). *The Social Psychology of Protest*. Oxford, UK: Blackwell.

Kruglanski, A. (1989). The problem of being 'right': the problem of accuracy in social perception and cognition. *Psychological Bulletin*, **106**, 395–409.

Lilienfeld, S. O., Ammirati, R. and Landfield, K. (2009). Giving debiasing away: can psychological research on correcting cognitive errors promote human welfare? *Perspectives on Psychological Science*, **4**, 390–8.

McCarty, C. (1999). *Categorization in Social Psychology*. London: Sage.

Meenes, M. (1943). A comparison of racial stereotypes of 1935 and 1942. *Journal of Social Psychology*, **17**, 327–36.

Neuberg, S. L. and Cottrell, C. A. (2006). Evolutionary bases of prejudices. In M. Schaller, J. A. Simpson and D. T. Kenrick (eds.), *Evolution and Social Psychology*. New York: Psychology Press.

Oakes, P. (2001). The root of all evil? Unearthing the categorization process. In R. Brown and S. Gaertner (eds.), *Blackwell Handbook of Social Psychology* (Ch. 1). Oxford, UK: Blackwell.

Oakes, P. J., Haslam, S. A. and Turner, J. C. (1994). *Stereotyping and Social Reality*. Oxford, UK: Blackwell.

Pettigrew, T. F. and Tropp, L. R. (2006). A meta-analytic test of intergroup contact theory. *Journal of Personality and Social Psychology*, **90**, 751–83.

   (2008). How does intergroup contact reduce prejudice? Meta-analytic tests of three mediators. *European Journal of Social Psychology*, **38**, 922–34.

Reicher, S. (2007). Rethinking the paradigm of prejudice. *South African Journal of Psychology*, **37**, 820–34.

Rye, B. J. and Meaney, G. J. (2010). Self-defense, sexism, and etiological beliefs: predictors of attitudes toward gay and lesbian adoption. *Journal of GLBT Family Studies*, **6**, 1–24.

Saguy, T., Tausch, N., Dovidio, J. and Pratto, F. (2009). The irony of harmony: intergroup contact can produce false expectations for equality. *Psychological Science*, **20**, 14–121.

Samelson, F. (1978). From 'race psychology' to 'studies in prejudice': some observations on the thematic reversal in social psychology. *Journal of the History of the Behavioral Sciences*, **14**, 265–78.

Schuman, H., Steeh, C., Bobo, L. and Krysan, M. (1997). *Racial Attitudes in America: Trends and Interpretations* (revised edn). Cambridge, MA: Harvard University Press.

Sears, D. O., van Laar, C., Carrillo, M. and Kosterman, R. (1997). Is it really racism? The origins of white Americans' opposition to race targeted policies. *Public Opinion Quarterly*, **61**, 16–53.

Shelton, J. N. (2000). A reconceptualization of how we study issues of racial prejudice. *Personality and Social Psychology Review*, **4**, 374–90.

Shelton, J. N. and Richeson, J. A. (2006). Interracial interactions: a relational approach. In M. P. Zanna (ed.), *Advances in Experimental Social Psychology*. New York: Academic Press.

Sherif, M. (1967). *Group Conflict and Cooperation: their Social Psychology*. London: Routledge and Kegan Paul.

Sherif, M. and Sherif, C. W. (1979). Research on intergroup relations. In W. G. Austin and S. Worchel (eds.), *The Social Psychology of Intergroup Relations*. CA: Brooks/Cole.

Sherif, M., Harvey, O. J., White, B. J., Hood, W. R. and Sherif, C. (1961). *Intergroup Conflict and Cooperation: the Robber's Cave Experiment*. Norman, OK: University Book Exchange.

Sibley, C. G., Overall, N. C. and Duckitt, J. (2007). When women become more hostilely sexist toward their gender: the system-justifying effect of benevolent sexism. *Sex Roles*, **57**, 743–54.

Sorensen, G. (1992). Utopianism in peace research: the Gandhian heritage. *Journal of Peace Research*, **29**, 135–44.

Spears, R. (2010). Group rationale, collective sense: beyond intergroup bias. *British Journal of Social Psychology*, **49**, 1–20.

Speer, S. A. and Potter, J. (2000). The management of heterosexist talk: conversational resources and prejudiced claims. *Discourse and Society*, **11**, 543–72.

Stephan, W. G. and Finlay, K. (1999). The role of empathy in improving intergroup relations. *Journal of Social Issues*, **4**, 729–43.

Swann, W. B. (1984). The quest for accuracy in person perception: a matter of pragmatics. *Psychological Review*, **91**, 457–77.

Tajfel, H. (1981). *Human Groups and Social Categories*. Cambridge, UK: Cambridge University Press.

Tausch, N., Saguy, T. and Singh, P. (2009). Contact between Muslims and Hindus: benefits and limitations. Unpublished manuscript.

Tuch, S. A. and Hughes, M. (1996). Whites' racial policy attitudes. *Social Science Quarterly*, 77, 723–41.

van Zomeren, M., Postmes, T. and Spears, R. (2008). Toward an integrative social identity model of collective action: a quantitative research synthesis of three socio-psychological perspectives. *Psychological Bulletin*, **134**, 504–35.

van Zomeren, M., Spears, R., Fischer, A. and Leach, C. W. (2004). Put your money where your mouth is! Explaining collective action tendencies through group-based anger and group efficacy. *Journal of Personality and Social Psychology*, **87**, 649–64.

Viki, G. T. and Abrams, D. (2002). But she was unfaithful: benevolent sexism and reactions to rape victims who violate traditional gender role expectations. *Sex Roles*, **47**(5–6), 289–93.

Vinacke, W. E. (1957). Stereotypes as social concepts. *Journal of Social Psychology*, **46**, 229–43.

Wetherell, M. and Potter, J. (1992). *Mapping the Language of Racism: Discourse and the Legitimation of Exploitation*. London: Sage.

White, J. B. and Langer, E. J. (1999). Horizontal hostility: relations between similar minority groups. *Journal of Social Issues*, **55**, 537–59.

Wright, S. C. and Lubensky, M. (2008). The struggle for social equality: collective action vs. prejudice reduction. In S. Demoulin, J. P. Leyens and J. F. Dovidio (eds.), *Intergroup Misunderstandings: Impact of Divergent Social Realities*. New York: Psychology Press.

Index

Adorno, T. 2, 5, 9, 20, 52, 66, 120, 142, 143, 150, 154, 155, 159, 178

Aggression, 9, 11, 51, 52, 64, 66, 88, 141, 180, 267

Allport, 1, 2, 4, 5, 6, 7, 8, 9, 15, 20, 21, 29, 30, 33, 34, 36, 38, 45, 46, 48, 49, 53, 54, 63, 66, 71, 72, 86, 105, 115, 116, 117, 120, 121, 135, 149, 158, 159, 160, 161, 163, 164, 166, 178, 196, 200, 205, 213, 217, 219, 229, 231, 240, 244, 248, 251, 264, 271, 273, 274, 283, 305, 306, 312, 317, 326, 328

Ambivalent sexism, vii, viii, 14, 71, 75, 80, 87, 313, 314

Anti-racism, v, 15, 120, 168, 172, 175, 177

Authoritarian personality. *See* Authoritarianism

Authoritarianism, 6, 52, 54, 64

Aversive racism, 6, 128, 135, 137, 181, 218, 219

Benevolent sexism, v, 13, 14, 70, 71, 72, 74, 75, 76, 77, 78, 79, 80, 81, 82, 83, 86, 87, 101, 102, 326, 330

Blumer, H. 7, 20, 133, 251, 264

Categorization
Category salience, 230
Recategorization, 66, 249, 251, 266

Cognitive rigidity, 8

Collaborative cognition, vi, 16, 17, 200, 203, 204, 205, 206, 213, 215

Collective action model of change, 17, 18, 228–42, 315–19

Crowd dynamics, 289–302

Common identity, 249, 250, 251, 255, 256, 257, 258, 260, 262, 263, 275, 315

Contact hypothesis. 249 *See* Intergroup contact

Dehumanization
Human uniqueness, 91, 92, 102
Objectification, 93, 97, 98, 102, 103

Discourse and prejudice, 134–5, 150–3, 160–1, 189–95, 309–11

Discrimination
Ethnic, 314
Racial, 2, 4, 27, 150, 151, 152, 153, 170, 191, 192, 196, 257, 267, 318, 327

Dollard, J., 2, 9, 21, 51, 52, 64, 66

Du Bois, W. E. B., v, 14, 105, 106, 107, 108, 109, 110, 111, 112, 113, 114, 115, 116, 117, 118, 119

Dual identity, 18, 249, 251, 252, 253, 254, 256, 257, 259, 260, 263, 265, 315

Empathy, 11, 23, 165, 184, 279, 281, 315, 317, 324, 330

Essentialism, 103, 124

Fiske, S., v, ix, 6, 9, 13, 21, 34, 36, 54, 66, 70, 71, 74, 75, 76, 79, 81, 84, 86, 87, 89, 98, 99, 101, 102, 103, 105, 106, 107, 116, 117, 119, 135, 201, 202, 217, 250, 264, 265, 267, 304, 313, 325, 328

Freud, S., 10, 21, 107, 109, 117

Frustration–aggression, 10

Gender inequality, v, viii, 13, 14, 70, 71, 72, 79, 80, 85, 312, 313, 314, 328. *See also* Ambivalent sexism, Benevolent sexism *and* Hostile sexism

Hostile sexism, vii, 76, 80, 81, 313

Ideology, 13, 20, 34, 70, 72, 73, 75, 78, 83, 92, 115, 130, 131, 132, 134, 135, 140, 142, 143, 144, 145, 149, 154, 158, 176, 218, 246, 253, 266, 273, 314, 326

Implicit association test, 182, 197

Implicit attitudes, 181, 186, 197

Implicit prejudice, 179, 183, 187, 188,
    196, 198
    Critique of, 182–4
Individualism, 6, 7, 121, 124, 129, 203, 204,
    216, 221, 308
Infrahumanization, 91. *See also*
    Dehumanization
Intergroup contact, 5, 11, 17, 18, 20, 22, 46,
    63, 67, 167, 225, 230, 240, 244, 245,
    248, 249, 254, 258, 261, 262, 264, 266,
    270, 271, 272, 282, 285, 317, 318, 321,
    325, 327, 329
    Planned encounters, 271, 273–82
Intergroup threat, 102, 129, 135. *See also*
    Stereotype threat
    and competition, 60, 86, 102, 129, 138,
    165, 227, 312, 327
Intolerance of ambiguity, 8, 52, 54

Jackman, M. R., 72, 73, 79, 83, 87, 226,
    245, 311, 312, 314, 322, 328, 329

Modern racism, 121, 122, 124, 125, 126,
    141, 142, 150, 192

Prejudice
    and irrationality, 8–9, 33–5, 147–8,
    163–5, 305–11
    Benevolent, 72. *See also* Benevolent
    sexism
    Collaborative, 205–6
    Denial of, 140–2, 150–3, 172
    Distributed inhibition of, 214
    Envious, 83
    Old and new, 122–4. *See also* Implicit
    prejudice, Modern racism *and*
    Symbolic racism
Prejudice reduction model of change, 12,
    17, 40, 228–42, 315–26

Racial identity, 15, 105, 106, 107, 109, 110,
    111, 113, 114, 115, 116, 118, 259
Racialization, 15, 130, 132, 174, 178, 285
Realistic conflict, 307
Reconciliation, vi, 18, 112, 167, 269, 270,
    272, 278, 281, 282, 283
Rhetoric, 101, 149, 154, 156, 166, 171, 174,
    196, 202, 219

Scapegoat, 9
Sears, D. O., 6, 21, 45, 51, 66, 121, 124,
    127, 128, 133, 136, 137, 138, 140, 155,
    192, 199, 215, 220, 322, 330
Self-categorization theory, 56, 57, 68, 69,
    221, 267
Sexism. *See* Ambivalent sexism, Benevolent
    sexism *and* Hostile sexism
Sherif, 6, 13, 23, 49, 50, 56, 60, 63, 68, 129,
    138, 225, 275, 285, 306, 307, 311,
    312, 330
Social dominance, 6, 69, 129
Social Identity Theory, 217, 249, 285
Stereotype threat, 15, 106, 107, 113, 114,
    115, 184. *See also* Stereotypes
Stereotypes, 6, 11, 13, 16, 21, 36, 52, 53, 54,
    56, 59, 60, 62, 67, 77, 83, 84, 85, 86,
    87, 88, 96, 99, 100, 103, 119, 129, 134,
    142, 144, 145, 152, 160, 172, 179, 180,
    183, 186, 188, 189, 190, 191, 192, 194,
    196, 198, 204, 213, 216, 217, 218, 219,
    227, 231, 232, 239, 240, 257, 265, 266,
    271, 274, 276, 307, 308, 311, 315, 322,
    323, 326, 327, 329
Stigma, 77, 117, 203
Symbolic racism, 21, 136, 156, 199

Tajfel, H., 9, 10, 23, 31, 34, 47, 49, 56,
    59, 61, 63, 68, 71, 74, 88, 103, 111,
    115, 119, 129, 138, 185, 195, 197,
    199, 206, 217, 220, 227, 231, 246,
    248, 249, 250, 251, 267, 277, 285,
    308, 330
The prejudice problematic, vi, 3, 6, 11, 12,
    15, 16, 17, 19, 20, 51, 90, 128, 158,
    159, 160, 161, 163, 165, 166, 167, 168,
    171, 172, 173, 176, 177, 185, 186, 195,
    200, 202, 206, 287, 304, 305, 307, 308,
    311, 312, 322, 325
Threat, 32, 33, 37, 39, 46, 83, 84, 85, 86, 96,
    119, 128, 133, 138, 198, 245, 288,
    317. *See also* Stereotype threat
Turner, J. C., v, x, 2, 13, 45, 46, 47, 48, 49,
    50, 55, 56, 57, 58, 59, 60, 62, 63, 64,
    66, 67, 68, 69, 118, 203, 218, 220, 221,
    225, 227, 231, 243, 246, 248, 249, 250,
    251, 267, 277, 285, 288, 302, 307, 328,
    329